A TOUR GUIDE TO MISSOURI'S CIVIL WAR

Friend and Foe Alike

A TOUR GUIDE TO MISSOURI'S CIVIL WAR

Friend and Foe Alike

by GREGORY WOLK

"I had been comparing the memoirs with Caesar's Commentaries...I was able to say in all sincerity that the same high merits distinguished both books—clarity of statement, directness, simplicity, manifest truthfulness, fairness and justice toward friend and foe alike..."

Mark Twain, on the *Personal Memoirs of Ulysses S. Grant*

MONOGRAPH PUBLISHING

PUBLISHED BY
MONOGRAPH PUBLISHING, LLC
1 Putt Lane
Eureka, Missouri 63025
636-938-1100

LIBRARY OF CONGRESS NUMBER CATALOGING-IN-PUBLICATION DATE: ON FILE

ISBN: 978-0-9799482-6-8

PRINTED IN THE UNITED STATES OF AMERICA BY MULTI-AD
10 09 08 07 6 5 4 3 2

COVER DESIGN BY K. SONDEREGGER
MADE YOU LOOK
http://madeyoulook.net/index.php?section=1

BOOK DESIGN BY ELLIE JONES
MATHISJONES COMMUNICATIONS, LLC.,
1 Putt Lane, Eureka, Missouri 63025
636-938-1100

COVER ART: THE GUERRILLAS, BY ANDY THOMAS
MAZE CREEK STUDIOS
Carthage, Missouri
www.andythomas.com

To Deb, my partner for life

From New York to Missouri, and with me on all of the roads I have traveled

Foreword

by Stuart Symington, Jr.

Most Americans tend to think of the American Civil War as a matter of battles and dates. It began on April 12, 1861 with Confederate cannon shelling Fort Sumter, and it ended with the surrender of Lee's army at Appomattox on April 9, 1865.

Not so, in the case of Missouri. As Gregory Wolk reminds us in this definitive Tour Guide to Missouri's Civil War, President Franklin Pierce signed the Kansas-Nebraska Act on May 30, 1854, thereby precipitating enduring border warfare between Missouri border ruffians and Kansas jayhawkers over the slavery question. Moreover, Missouri's Civil War arguably did not end until April 3, 1882 when Bob Ford shot Jesse James, Civil War Confederate guerrilla and post-Civil War bank robber, who has achieved mythic status as a putative southern Robin Hood.

The fact is that Missouri suffered a unique combination of border and guerrilla warfare, along with the third highest number of conventional engagements of any state in the Union, exceeded only by Virginia and Tennessee.

What sets this tour guide apart, and puts it in a class with Baedeker and Michelin, are its meticulous driving instructions and the thoroughness of the attention, including numerous illustrations, it gives to some 235 historic sites with Civil War associations, located throughout the length and breadth of Missouri.

The sites listed in the tour guide understandably paint a broad picture of familiar themes. We read about westward expansion, states rights and secession, slavery and economic issues, the abolition movement, the development of railroad and telegraph technology, the role of German and Irish immigrants in the Union military, the involvement of Native Americans in the conflict, military equipment, strategy and tactics, martial law, and military justice.

However, anyone who reads this book, or better yet, drives one or more of the five tour loops it covers, will understand, perhaps for the first time, the way that the Civil War affected the daily lives of men, women and children throughout Missouri, in more ways, for a longer period of time, and more profoundly then it affected the people of any other state in the union. Massachusetts residents, by and large, read letters from the front. Georgia did not howl until Sherman got there. But Missourians suffered, day-in and day-out, before, during and after the 1861-1865 period we know as the American Civil War.

The true worth of this tour guide may transcend its association with Civil War tourism, battles and dates. Sadly, lingering resentments, fueled by memories of bitterness and brutality, still tend to color our view of the Civil War in Missouri. But we can hope that by telling the Civil War stories of so many people, this tour guide may encourage us to hear their voices, to honor the brave and to pity the suffering. This in turn could help us to observe the 150th anniversary of our Civil War in a fitting way by substituting, once and for all, reconciliation for resentment.

Table of Contents

A TOUR GUIDE TO MISSOURI'S CIVIL WAR
Friend and Foe Alike

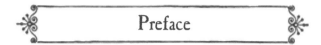

Preface

For those unfamiliar with Missouri's rich Civil War history, a startling statistic: More battles or engagements were fought in Missouri than in any state except Virginia and Tennessee. This Guide will introduce cultural travelers, and the general reader, to scores of Civil War heritage sites that still exist in Missouri today. The Guide is divided into five driving tours, each covering a distinct region of the state and referred to as "Tour Loops." The Tour Loops begin at page 13. This preface is intended to orient the reader and traveler generally to the times and places that make up Missouri's Civil War.

Consider Missouri's position in 1861, politically as well as geographically, and it is easy to see why the greatest conflict in

American history came to Missouri early and stayed late. The Missouri Compromise of 1820 permitted slavery to exist in this new state, far north of the old Mason-Dixon Line. Southerners flocked to Missouri and slave-holders populated a great portion of the central and northern regions of the state. This is the so-called "Boonslick" region, which straddles the Missouri River from nearly one end of Missouri to the other, and in some places touches the state of Iowa. So a national debate and a poor fix meant that the slave culture took root in places north of the 40th parallel - north of places like Pittsburgh, Columbus and Indianapolis. Slavery existed in Missouri in places two hundred fifty

Daniel Boone, from a painting by Chester Harding

WHAT'S A BOONSLICK?

In 1799, Daniel and Rebecca Boone moved from Kentucky and established a home in St. Charles County, Missouri. Their grown sons, Nathan and Daniel Morgan Boone, emigrated with them. Two sources of salt were discovered to the west, north of the Missouri River - "salt licks," which referred to the practice of wild game to lick salt deposits appearing at the ground surface. One of these sources was acquired by the Boone brothers, and hence was known as "Boone's Lick." The road which connected St. Charles to these sources became the Boonslick Road. Later, the entire region that straddled the Missouri River became known as the Boonslick. Now, it is known as Missouri's "Little Dixie."

miles north of the southern most tip of free Illinois.

War came to Missouri long before it arrived in the rest of the United States, because of the fight over the political future of Kansas. The Missouri Compromise dictated that slavery would not exist in the land that would become Kansas. Kansas, when it was still considered part of the Great American Desert, was to be reserved for time immemorial as a homeland for Native Americans who were being displaced from the east. And so while on Missouri's east and north borders there was "yankee" territory, its western border was a kind of wasteland, where the border followed a line of longitude that divided an area abundant in precipitation (Missouri) from one that is so rain-starved it supports deciduous forests only in stream bottoms (Kansas). This western border of the United States – pretty much the western border of the English-speaking world - was static for thirty years, at about the 95th Meridian of west longitude.

Missouri's southern border was the Missouri Compromise line (36° 30' of latitude). Then came the war with Mexico and the California gold rush, and the line of compromise could clearly be seen for what it was. The slave-holders could never maintain a balance of power in Congress as the country marched west, to the Pacific, in order to incorporate its new possessions. The rules changed. Native Americans would not have Kansas, and whether it was free or slave would depend on what the European population decided. This was Congress' next great compromise, known as the Kansas-Nebraska Act of 1854. Unwittingly, Congress had supplied the spark that would ignite a national Civil War.

Few fully realize the brutal character of the war along the Missouri-Kansas border in 1854 - 1860. Boston abolition proponents formed the New England Emigrant Aid Company and provided financial support for would-be voters who would move to Kansas from the North. Southern-leaning and slaveholding families in western Missouri sent envoys to stake claim in Kansas, to create another voting bloc. Violence and murder were practiced by both sides, and no one out there seemed to subscribe to the middle view, which was to prohibit slavery in the territories while it continued to exist in the South.

America's frontier moved inexorably to the west for generations before 1860. Cheap western land was a cure-all for everything, from inflated land prices in some parts of the east, to southern farms that seemed to "play out" after a generation or two. So, the sons and daughters of the people from Virginia and the Carolinas, and from Kentucky and Tennessee, who came with slaves to the rich valley of the Missouri had a natural expectation that land to the west would be available to them. This is not to apologize for those who brought slavery to the Boonslick. In hindsight, there was an inevitability of strife built into Congress' Missouri Compromise. By the 1850s, circumstances combined to turn the western border into a tinderbox, where John Brown of Ohio would rehearse his raid on Harper's Ferry and where an army of Missourians honed their military skills – learned in the Mexican War – throughout the decade.

A second important demographic was at work in Missouri in mid-century. The year gold was discovered in California, old Europe was rocked by revolution.

A great wave of immigration came from central Europe in the years after 1848, and many of these people followed an earlier pattern of migration that had populated a significant part of eastern Missouri. The Forty-eighter's, as they were known, were mostly German, and more of an urban and radicalized group than the rural Germans who had come to Missouri before.

John Brown

Then, too, the Irish famine occurred in 1845-48. By 1861 St. Louis had the largest proportion of persons of foreign birth of any city in the United States - Irish, Germans, Poles, Hungarians, Czechs. The St. Louis melting pot was teeming with industry and commerce. These people, and eastern industrialists who employed them, were natural enemies of an agrarian gentry that held power in the Boonslick.

For the most part, this Guide describes the battle sites and military campaigns that occurred in Missouri during the years 1861-1865. The relative absence of reference to the African American combat experience reflects the fact that African American units did little fighting within Missouri's borders. But in 1862, the first battle of an African American regiment in the Civil War occurred along that smoldering western border between Missouri and Kansas. Familiar history to the contrary, the first battle did not involve a Massachusetts regiment, and it was not in South Carolina. The Battle of Island Mound, Missouri, October 29, 1862, was fought by men of the First Kansas Colored Regiment against a party of Southern partisan cavalry. Missouri is entitled to claim the First Kansas as its own. Before 1862, Kansas' population of free African American males of military age was almost nil; the recruits who filled the ranks of the First Kansas were escaped or liberated Missouri slaves. The site of Island Mound is west of Butler, Missouri; directions to it may be found in this Guide in Connecting Route D. Work is underway to establish the site as a Missouri State Park.

Beginning in 1863, Missourians filled the

Pvt. Reuben Bibb, 65th U.S.C.T.

ranks of African American regiments in Iowa and Arkansas, and four regiments that bore the standard of Missouri. As with the other border states, however, slavery continued to exist in Missouri throughout the Civil War. The Emancipation Proclamation freed slaves only in states that were in rebellion. But as the Civil War went on, more and more men left bondage to join the army. Near the war's end a bizarre experiment paid Missouri slaveowners the $300 bounty that people who were already free received for themselves.

The Civil War officially got underway on April 12, 1861 when Confederate cannon fired on Fort Sumter in Charleston harbor. On April 20, 1861, secessionist forces seized the federal arsenal in Liberty, Missouri, northeast of present day Kansas City. Then, in St. Louis on May 10, 1861, in the so-called "Camp Jackson Affair," armed and organized infantry confronted each other for the first time. This watershed in Missouri history occurred when a detail of regulars and federalized militia sent to break up a camp of Missouri militia fired into a crowd of protestors. The confrontation left dozens dead or injured, most of them civilians. In the wake of Camp Jackson, Civil War campaigning in the west began in earnest.

There follows a brief history and chronology of the principal conventional military campaigns featured in this Guide. Missouri, famously, also has a history of unconventional war, which is covered in the Tour Loops. This brief chronology of the conventional campaigns is supplemented by detailed campaign summaries at the beginning of each Loop.

3

Sterling Price

The First Phase

The first phase of the Civil War in Missouri was war in the traditional sense - infantry fighting with shoulder arms. For all practical purposes, this phase ended in April 1862, just about one year after it began. It ended when the Confederacy suffered twin defeats at the southern edges of Missouri, at Pea Ridge, Arkansas, on March 7-8, 1862, and at Island No. 10, southeast of New Madrid, Missouri, on April 4-7, 1862.

Phase one began in 1861 with a campaign to control the Missouri Valley. Brig. Gen. Nathaniel Lyon boarded U.S. Regulars and specially enrolled German regiments on river steamers and pushed off from St. Louis for the state capital, Jefferson City. There, the Union force drove Missouri's elected government out of the capital. Simultaneously, Lyon directed a force to the southwest part of the state, to secure Springfield. Lyon's force moved west out of Jefferson City, attacking a hastily assembled pro-southern force in one of the Civil War's first engagements, on June 17, 1861, east of Boonville.

Lyon's movement forced pro-southern militia forces in the center of the state, which had recently been organized into the Missouri State Guard, to flee south. Lyon's force in Springfield, under Col. Franz Sigel, moved west and north to attempt to block the State Guard until Lyon's regiments could overtake them. Sigel fought the State Guard in a particularly bloody battle at Carthage on July 5, 1861. Sigel's command was overwhelmed, but he saved his army in a textbook retreat. The pro-southern forces escaped to Cowskin Prairie in the very southwest corner of the state, there to train and equip through the month of July. Lyon reached Springfield on July 13, 1861, and the combined Lyon/Sigel force fortified the town.

The Missouri State Guard, now commanded by former Missouri Governor Sterling "Pap" Price, consolidated with regular Confederate units operating in Arkansas in late July. The combined force moved northeast and clashed with Lyon on August 10, 1861, at Wilson's Creek, outside Springfield, in a fierce battle, the western equivalent of Bull Run. The Southern forces were victorious, killing Lyon and driving the federals back in the direction of St. Louis. Southern troops occupied Springfield until mid-October.

Price moved back to the Missouri River and the Boonslick in a campaign that began in late August and ended with the siege and capture of Lexington, Missouri, on September 20, 1861. Price's action electrified the South, but he did not have forces strong enough to remain and occupy Lexington. By the time Lexington fell to Price, the federal commander in St. Louis, Gen. John C. Fremont, after numerous delays, had set in motion a large, cumbersome force that moved west along the Pacific Railroad. Price retreated to Springfield before Fremont could block the route to his base.

Fremont turned his army to the south, and entered Springfield on October 25, 1861. Price abandoned Springfield without offering a fight, except for a brief stand on the western edge of town. This was the occasion of a magnificent charge by Fremont's cavalry, known as "Zagonyi's Charge," which pitted the Southern defenders against a Union force composed largely of European expatriates – brandishing sabers and clad in velvet jackets.

However, over the winter of 1861-1862, Southwest Missouri remained in Southern hands, and the Southern soldiers of the Missouri State Guard, in camp near Osceola in St. Clair County, began to enroll in the regular Confederate service. By January, 1862, the northern army in Missouri had a new commander, West Pointer turned Iowa politician, Samuel Ryan Curtis. From headquarters in Lebanon, Missouri, Curtis pulled together 15,000 troops. They stepped off from

Wartime view of Springfield, Missouri

Lebanon on February 10, 1862, bound for Springfield to the southwest. Springfield fell to Curtis' troops, bloodlessly, on February 13. This was the fifth time Springfield changed hands in the War.

Curtis moved quickly down what is still called the Wire Road, driving Sterling Price before him in a series of small engagements.

Price, as he had before Wilson's Creek, joined up with regular Confederate troops in Arkansas, and together they moved north to cut off Curtis. Price succeeded in reaching Curtis' rear on March 7, 1862 at Elkhorn Tavern, Arkansas and launched a vicious attack that very nearly broke the Union force. Curtis held his position, however, and won a victory on March 8. The battle at Pea Ridge is regarded by most experts as the Union's most decisive victory west of the Mississippi River. The battlefield of Pea Ridge, commemorated by a beautiful National Battlefield park, lies just 2 1/2 miles south of the Missouri border, on a line between Springfield, Missouri and Bentonville, Arkansas.

While Lyon was maneuvering to capture Springfield, the Union also began a campaign to control the Mississippi River along Missouri's eastern border. This story starts in Quincy, Illinois, in the middle of July, 1861, and from there follows the early Civil War career of U. S. Grant. Grant's meteoric rise later in the conflict was presaged by his advancement in 1861, as he moved from northeast to southeast Missouri, and from an obscure colonelcy to the command of the District of Southeast Missouri. He fought his first real battle at Belmont, Missouri, on November 7, 1861, where he showed some of the pugnacity that was to become his hallmark. Grant's headquarters moved from Palmyra, Florida and

Mexico, in North Missouri, to Ironton and Cape Girardeau in the southeast, between July 14 and September 1, 1861.

Grant's superior officer during his brief stay in North Missouri was John Pope, an Illinoisan and friend of the Lincoln Administration. Pope would take command of the forces in southeast Missouri in February, 1862, just after Grant's success at Fort Donelson on the Cumberland River, and he marshaled these forces for a drive into Missouri's "bootheel." Pope's first objective was the town of New Madrid, Missouri, which he captured on March 14, 1862 after a day-long bombardment. The important Confederate stronghold at Island No. 10, 10 miles south, southeast of New Madrid, surrendered on April 7, 1862.

Grant's superior officer during his brief stay in North Missouri was John Pope, an Illinoisan and friend of the Lincoln Administration

A footnote to the successful Union campaign to control the Mississippi is described in Tour Loop One of this chapter. In October, 1861, Meriwether Jefferson Thompson took a cavalry force north through Union lines in a daring effort to destroy Union communications and lines of supply. Although this little known campaign failed to delay the Union drive down the Mississippi, it deserves study, and provides an excellent introduction to Missouri's "Swamp Fox."

The Second Phase

Lone Jack, Missouri

The Union army's early successes at Pea Ridge and Island No. 10 set the stage for three years of unconventional war in Missouri, because a great mass of people in the central, west-central and north-east regions of the state (the Boonslick) maintained their sympathies for the Southern cause. The Missouri anomaly was made more distinctive because the Boonslick was separated from the geographic South by the Ozark mountains, an area that remained (as did many other mountainous regions) mostly Union in sympathy. In Civil War times in Missouri, south was north and vice versa.

Once the South's organized armies had been driven out of Missouri, the first consequence was a broad campaign to bring Missouri recruits down from the Boonslick into Arkansas. The officers and men of the old Missouri State Guard were incorporated into the Confederate service. Then prominent men carrying new Confederate commissions went north into the Boonslick to recruit. The recruiters included Joseph Orville Shelby of Waverly in Lafayette County, and John T. Hughes and Upton Hays of Jackson County. This Guide features the far-ranging operations of Confederate Colonel Joseph Porter, in a conventional campaign with unconventional consequences. Porter's exploits, occurring in his home territory of Northeast Missouri from April, 1862 until he headed south in October of that year, forms the basis for much of Tour Loop Two.

A concerted effort to get the recruits south began in August, 1862. Porter fought far north in Kirksville on August 8, 1862, which signaled the beginning of the movement south. Notable battles occurred outside of Kansas City that month,

in Independence and Lone Jack, as the recruits from western Missouri started on their way. The recruiting season ended in Newtonia, in Newton County in southwest Missouri at the end of September, 1862, where these troops consolidated and fought off the pursuing federals.

Just south of Newtonia, three new regiments of Confederate cavalry were consolidated into a brigade, which was soon dubbed the "Iron Brigade," and placed under the command of JO Shelby. The Confederates, joined near Newtonia by Native American and Texas regiments, moved into Northwest Arkansas. Bitter engagements occurred in Arkansas during the winter, at Cane Hill in November and on December 7, 1862 at Prairie Grove. Union troops commanded by Brigadier General Francis Herron of Iowa were camped on Wilson's Creek a little south of Springfield, Missouri. They marched over 100 miles in three days, arriving just in time to hold the Confederates in position at Prairie Grove until another Union force arrived and defeated them.

The Missouri Confederate recruits were hardened veterans when they emerged from their Arkansas campaign. The stage was set for 1863.

Joseph O. Shelby

The conventional war in Missouri in 1863 was marked by three great Confederate cavalry operations that started in Arkansas. The 1863 Confederate raids were remarkable feats of planning, execution and endurance.

On December 31,1862, Confederates led by Gen. John Sappington Marmaduke began a mounted operation from a base deep in Arkansas that would bring the war to Springfield, Missouri, once again. The strategically located town changed hands five times in 1861 and 1862, but this time the Confederate objective was neither to control territory nor to recruit troops. The plan was to relieve pressure on Confederate forces in the wake of the Prairie Grove defeat, and to break the vital Union supply line which stretched over 100 miles from a railhead at Rolla, to Springfield. This was a traditional cavalry raid. It resulted in a sharp fight near the center of town on January 8, 1863, known as the Battle of Springfield; Union blockhouses withstood Marmaduke's attack, but he burned the Union supply depot.

On September 21, 1863 JO Shelby began a trek with 750 horsemen of his Iron Brigade.

Marmaduke was on the move again by April 19, 1863, from a base at Batesville, in eastern Arkansas. His objective was to hit fortified points at Patterson and Bloomfield in southeast Missouri, and to burn Grant's supply base in Cape Girardeau. Marmaduke's force exceeded 5,000 men, and represented the largest cavalry raid mounted by Confederates to that point in the war. The raid ended in a battle on the hills that encircle Cape Girardeau, in which Marmaduke was repulsed.

On September 22, 1863 JO Shelby began a trek with 750 horsemen of his Iron Brigade. On October 2, he entered the state of Missouri near Pineville, in the southwest corner of the state, and combined with another cavalry force there. Striking north by northeast, Shelby's force passed through Neosho,

Missouri Confederates in Texas

Greenfield, Humansville, Warsaw and Tipton, finally taking Boonville on October 11, 1863. Moving northwest from Boonville, and by now chased by federal troops converging from both east and west, Shelby was trapped near the Saline County town of Marshall, but managed to escape with his force nearly intact. He then moved west to briefly occupy his hometown of Waverly. Once Shelby had returned to Arkansas, the raid had covered at least 1300 miles from start to finish.

As Southern fortunes in the west continued to fade in 1863, the flow of manpower from Missouri reversed itself. Men left the service of the Confederate armies to return home to protect homes and families in the pro-Southern parts of Missouri. West and central Missouri came under the reign of partisans and guerrillas, and 1863 was punctuated not only by the conventional cavalry operations noted here, but also by Quantrill's deadly attack in August on Lawrence, Kansas. Quantrill's story is told in Tour Loop Four.

7

The Final Phase

There is one event that occupies a position of pre-eminence in the history of Missouri's Civil War, and that event is Price's 1864 Expedition. On September 19, 1864, Price crossed into Missouri from Northeast Arkansas with some 12,000 mounted troops. He intended to capture St. Louis and turn west to Kansas City, taking up recruits on the way. From the standpoint of the Union-leaning population, and the federal authorities in a state that, in September, 1864, was far from the center of military operations, the sudden appearance of Price's command was startling. The memory of Price's Expedition lives on in communities all over Missouri.

Since we consider Confederate combatants to be Americans (remembering that Mr. Lincoln never acknowledged them to be anything else), it can be said that Price's Expedition was probably the largest mounted operation in all of American military history. It is very hard to pin down the numbers engaged on the Confederate side,

Rolla City Cemetary

particularly considering that Price added to his complement of troops once he entered Missouri. It has been written that Price entered Southeast Missouri from Arkansas with 12,000 men; some estimates put the number closer to 13,000. Accepting these estimates as true, only Wilson's 1865 Raid in Alabama (estimated strength 12,000 to 13,500) ranks around or near it in size. Price's operation covered more than 1,500 miles. In distance traveled, nothing can compare to it.

By September 1, 1864, Grant had pinned down Lee's army at Petersburg, Virginia. Farther west, Sherman was poised to enter the city of Atlanta, having cut off John Bell Hood's last rail connection to the south. By this time, Confederate troops in the Trans-Mississippi were stationed at Camden, Arkansas. Camden lies in the very bowels of Arkansas, merely 40 miles from the Louisiana line.

The Expedition of 1864 has a special place in this Guide because most every Tour Loop - all except for Tour Loop Two - touches upon the Expedition to one degree or another. The expedition was that massive. It began (as did Shelby's 1863 Raid) in the southern reaches of Arkansas. It entered Missouri in the southeast, then reached the outskirts of St. Louis, traversed the breadth of the state along the Missouri River corridor, culminated in what now is the center of Kansas City, veered into Kansas at Mine Creek, and faded away along Missouri's western border before re-entering Arkansas near the end of October, 1864. It produced battles - and modern tourist venues - in nearly every nook and cranny of the state south of the Missouri River.

Price's Expedition also saw the culmination of the unconventional War in Missouri, as well-drilled and firmly established guerrilla bands co-operated with Price. The whole summer and fall of 1864 became a bloodletting in Missouri's Boonslick. Bloody Bill Anderson's brand of warfare came to the forefront. There has never been anything like it on this continent.

The Missouri partisans wintered in Texas in 1864, as they usually did. Some of them returned to their home territories in May, 1865. The War in the East was over, and most of the Missouri men who returned soon laid down their arms. The huge majority of the Southern men who came back, regular troops and irregulars as well, settled back into their normal lives. By the 1880s, much of the nation was forgetting the pain and suffering that accompanied the years 1861-1865, and the era of remembrance – an inevitable glorification of what was not glorious in any way – had begun. The elections of 1876 brought an end to Reconstruction, and now only our African-American citizens were made to suffer. Thanks to the pen of Missouri's Mark Twain, the booming post-War times already had a name that befitted them. The Gilded Age, it was.

This Guide always refers to Missouri's Civil War. Several reasons argue for the use of the possessive case. It avoids a familiar argument of generations past. You may believe that the war in Virginia and Pennsylvania, and in Georgia and Mississippi, was the War Between the States, or you may call it the

The James' home, St. Joseph

War of the Rebellion or the War for Southern Independence, but what we had in Missouri was our very own civil war. It was a war of civilians against civilians, of citizen militia against Southern irregulars, of neighbors against neighbors, and some times all of them against each other. And just as it began before there was a War in the rest of the country, Missouri's Civil War went on, and on, and on. We mark its end by the crack of a pistol shot in April 1882, in the parlor of a rented house in St. Joseph.

The very moment that the war officially came

to an end in Missouri, outside of Lexington in May of 1865, one of the Missouri men who arrived from Texas (a boy then) was shot through the chest by a federal patrol. He barely survived, and then went into hiding. He emerged to launch an incredible career of crime and mayhem. He did not commit all of the crimes of which he was accused, but he committed many crimes, murder included. His life defined an age in the western United States. He was Jesse James. He survived in the wild for nearly two decades, not without the active support of a Southern-sympathizing population which made his continued freedom the symbol for all its woes, real or imagined.

On April 3, 1882, in the rented house in St. Joseph, Jesse James was killed in what amounted to a state-sponsored assassination. Like many men who symbolize a cause and who die young, James has never been forgotten. Unlike any other phenomenon in Missouri history, his reputation circumnavigates the globe. He remains to some Missourians a symbol of resistance. As we come together to commemorate Missouri's Civil War in the years ahead, let him serve as a reminder that there is some rebel in all of us.

Union Camp, Rolla, MIssouri

USING THIS GUIDE

Loops, Parts & Routes

The five driving tours in this Guide cover the following Missouri regions: St. Louis and the Southeast, North Central, South Central, the Kansas City Region, and Southwest Missouri. Each of the these tours is in the form of a "Loop," so dedicated travelers can select a starting and ending point and visit 30 or more Civil War heritage sites within any selected region. Each Loop requires at least two days to complete.

The Guide also includes seven "connecting routes," which commence at page 243. These routes serve a variety of purposes, notably to shorten the length and time of travel for a tour loop (e.g., Connecting Route E), or to highlight an important campaign or series of sites not within a Tour Loop proper (Connecting Route A). Others permit travelers to maximize their Missouri Civil War experience while moving from one Loop to another.

Each Loop has four or five tour segments. Each segment (Parts I, II, etc.) takes the traveler in the direction of a cardinal point on the compass. Whenever possible the Loop segments, and the connecting routes as well, follow historic roads that were the roads upon which military campaigns were waged. Fifteen campaigns are featured in the Guide. As you plan your trip, or when you bring your Guide home, read the introductions at the beginning of each Loop to gain an overview of the campaigns. As you go, the Guide keeps you abreast of the action, which some times moved in the direction opposite to yours. Fortunately, in most cases the key parts of featured campaigns are contained within a single Loop. The exception, as noted in the Preface, is Price's 1864 Expedition. Read the whole history of this campaign by consulting the introductions to Loops One, Three, Four and Five.

Tourists who are not yet serious students of the Civil War should not feel daunted. Tour planning help is available – and criticism is welcomed – if you visit the website www.friendandfoe.org. Many sources are available, at bookstores, libraries and on-line,

which will help you zero in on particular Missouri regions, campaigns or battles, once you decide where you want to go.

Naturally, this Guide assists without requiring the traveler to stick to a Tour Loop. Drive a part of a Loop when you visit any major Missouri city. If you are driving through Missouri, leave the Interstate and enjoy a featured campaign route. Seasoned travelers of all stripes know how to plan a "road trip." Make your next one a Civil War adventure.

To give an example, here is the track of Marmaduke's Division of Sterling Price's Army of Missouri, during Price's 1864 campaign:

Tour Loop One, Part III Northbound from Bloomfield to Fredericktown;

Connecting Route A northbound, rejoining Loop One at Stop 43;

Part III Northbound to Washington;

Connecting Route C westbound from Washington to Hermann;

Local roads west to Jefferson City;

Connecting Route F westbound to Loop Three, Stop 112, at Syracuse;

Tour Loop Three, Part III Northbound to Boonville;

Tour Loop Three, Part I Westbound to Lexington;

Connecting Route G Westbound to Independence, joining Loop Four at Stop 144;

Tour Loop Four, Part III Westbound.

Before you go, realize that the maps in this guide are not a substitute for good highway maps and advance planning. Be sure to plan your route in advance, and have a navigator in the shotgun seat.

Drive carefully.

Glossary of Terms

Southern and *Southerner* are terms used to describe white people who immigrated to Missouri (or whose ancestors did) from places like Virginia, North Carolina, Tennessee and Kentucky. The terms generally refer in this Guide to civilians and citizen-soldiers who sided with the cause of the Confederate states. In most cases it is not appropriate to refer to this cultural group as "Confederate" or as secessionist. Some Southerners owned slaves, but many (slaveholders or not) were unionists. Many of Missouri's Southerners lived in the northeast and western sections of the state.

Bushwhacker can apply to Northerners, but the term most often refers to Southerners who fought alone or in small bands without sanction of any government. This Guide uses the terms "guerrilla" or "Southern guerrillas" when referring to this group.

Missouri State Guard was a militia-like army organized by the Missouri legislature in 1861. This is sometimes abbreviated "MSG." It was the largest military force operating under a state's authority that ever fought in opposition to the federal government. Many of the battles that are detailed in this Guide – all of them that occurred in 1861 – had Missourians fighting under the banner of the MSG. It is not appropriate to refer to the Missouri army of 1861 as "Confederate."

Partisan Cavalry and *Partisan Rangers* refer to Southerners who fought in Missouri with the sanction of the Confederate government. These men always fought on horseback. It is difficult to identify what units were and were not sanctioned, partly because the Confederate government distanced itself from these men as the war progressed. It is generally acknowledged, for example, that William Quantrill was a *Partisan Ranger* (although he was not a *Southerner*) and that William Anderson by this definition was not a *Partisan Ranger*, although he was a *Southerner*). Anderson was a *guerrilla*.

Confederate is a term used to describe men who fought in the service of the Confederate States Army. Missouri *Southerners*, including most veterans of the MSG, fought in Missouri as *Confederates* after 1861. Some Missourians were *Confederates* from the earliest days of the war, but they enrolled and fought elsewhere, for the most part.

Northern and *Northerner* is a generic term for Missouri people who were not Southern. In the context of the mid-nineteenth century, it is more accurate to describe these people as easterners, if they were white. This description applies to immigrants from New York and Ohio, but also Hamburg and Budapest. In the parlance of this Guide, African-Americans are considered *Northerners*, even though they would be *Southerners* if not for their race.

Unionist describes Missouri civilians who disfavored secession.

Union usually refers to combatants who were officially enrolled in volunteer or regular regiments of the U. S. Army. The term is sometimes used in this Guide generically, to refer to *Northern* soldiers who fought in organized units that were not regularly enrolled in federal service, or who fought only under state authority (see *EMM, below*).

The *Enrolled Missouri Militia or EMM* was organized in 1862 by the by the *unionist* provisional (unelected) government of Missouri. The *EMM* acted as a militia or home guard. By the terms of their enlistment, soldiers of the *EMM* could not be deployed outside of the boundaries of Missouri. These troops were generally drawn from the *Northern* population, but some were *Southerners* (see Tour Loop Four).

Missouri State Militia Cavalry regiments were also organized under the authority of the provisional government of the state, under terms similar to those governing the *EMM*, However, the federal government equipped and paid these troops. Some regiments of MSM Cavalry developed into tough and competent fighting units; other regiments operated on or over the fringe of respectability. They were *Northern* equivalents of the *Partisan Rangers* on the *Confederate* side.

Jayhawkers were Kansas guerrilla fighters who took their nickname from a mythical bird (a cross between a blue jay and hawk). The term predated the Civil War and at first applied to Kansans generally. Units of cavalry that were sanctioned by the U. S. government early in the war turned to plundering and murder in western Missouri. Eventually, the federal government distanced itself from these units, and disbanded them, but the verb *jayhawking* entered the language as a synonym for stealing. *Red Legs* refers to a similar class of Kansas guerrillas, who wore leggings of red leather, but were never sanctioned by anyone.

TOUR LOOP ONE

Southeast Missouri has a rich Civil War history. Along the Mississippi River, historically the southeast region of the state was tied to St. Louis commerce, but then as now, the culture of the region looks primarily to the South

This Loop takes a southward course from St. Louis down the great River to New Madrid. It offers southbound Interstate 55 travelers an in-depth view of Civil War history for the price of a detour or two. The Tour turns back north at New Madrid, and from there, tracks two Southern campaigns, one in 1861 and the other in 1864, each nearly reaching the St. Louis suburbs.

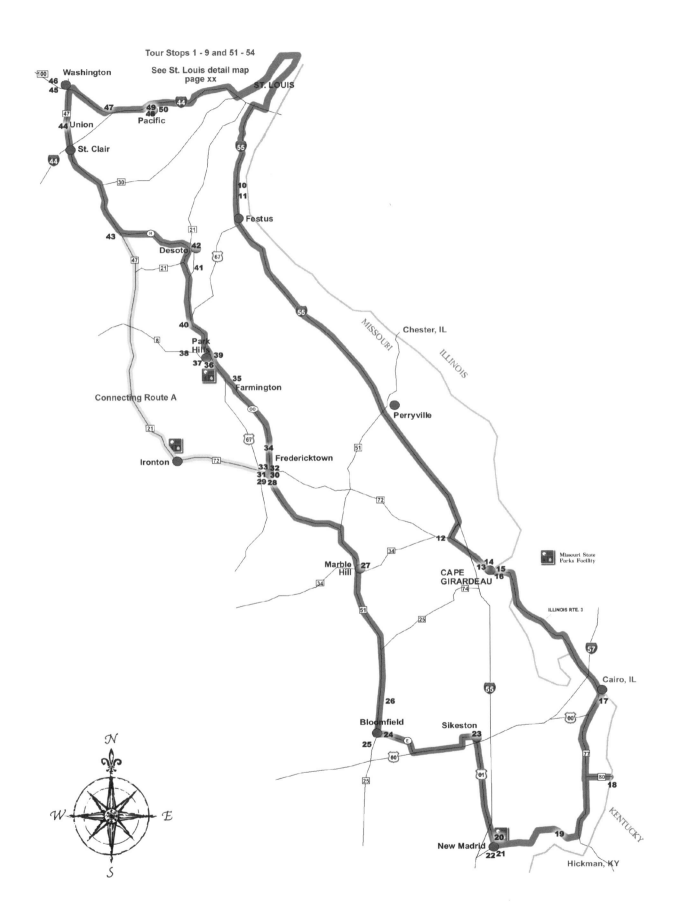

Tour Stops 1 - 9 and 51 - 54
See St. Louis detail map
page xx

Washington
Pacific
Union
St. Clair
Desoto
Park Hills
Farmington
Connecting Route A
Ironton
Fredericktown
Marble Hill
Perryville
Chester, IL
MISSOURI
ILLINOIS
CAPE GIRARDEAU
Bloomfield
Sikeston
Cairo, IL
ILLINOIS RTE. 3
KENTUCKY
New Madrid
Hickman, KY

Missouri State
Parks Facility

ST. LOUIS

N
W   E
S

14

A TOUR OF ST. LOUIS AND SOUTHEAST MISSOURI

City and Swamps

T he predominant military theme of this Tour Loop is the Union's campaign to control the valley of the Mississippi. The predominant personality is Ulysses S. Grant, architect of the Union victory on July 4, 1863 at Vicksburg, Mississippi, where culminated that campaign. Grant shares billing in this Loop with other interesting characters. More of Grant's story is told in Tour Loop Two.

Ironton, Missouri, is the seat of Iron county, situated inland about 70 miles west of Cape Girardeau. It is best known as the site of a horrific battle in 1864, but it is also the place where the Vicksburg campaign has its tap-root. Ironton is a feature on Connecting Route A, depicted at page 244 of this Guide. You must go to Ironton, to the Ste. Marie du Lac Catholic Church two blocks south of the courthouse. It is here, precisely at a spring on the church grounds and approximately on August 10, 1861, that Grant's drive down the great river began.

Ste. Marie du Lac, Ironton

This guide is not a history book. It does not shy away from the part of history that descends from the memories of fallible men. We will warn you when the sources are suspect, but we cannot – will not – ignore the stories that vividly connect our present to the signposts of our past. Having this in mind, it is fit that our journey should begin at the Ironton spring, and with the story written by John Wesley Emerson, mostly about John Wesley Emerson.

Grant was assigned to Ironton in August, 1861 to command a small force that guarded the precarious end of a railroad. Grant camped on the property of lawyer Emerson (this we know is

true). Thirty-five years later, Emerson wrote that Grant asked that a map be brought to him. Emerson brought him a map, and for days Grant worked feverishly in his tent. Then he showed Emerson the "X"s he had drawn running up the Cumberland and Tennessee Rivers. It was an outline of the campaign that would make Grant famous. Then Grant pointed to a spring that bubbled up near his tent, and he told Emerson in so many words that he would follow the waters of that spring to the Gulf of Mexico.

Emerson's spring still flows on the church grounds in Ironton. If it is not the actual headwater of the Vicksburg campaign, then it must stand unchallenged as the mythical one. The part of the American myth typified by the life of U. S. Grant is all about persistence. Already by the 1880s, Emerson, who counted himself a friend of Grant's, was doing his part to perpetuate Grant's mythical quality. Grant, as a fellow officer described him in 1864, had a look about him "as if he had determined to drive his head through a brick wall." Grant was the man always persistent in the face of failure. Is Emerson's story true? Bruce Catton, in his landmark study in 1960, *Grant Moves South*, has much to say about Emerson's tale, but Catton does not debunk it. Perhaps Catton felt that the story is too important for debunking.

Coincidentally, Emerson Electric Company of St. Louis – in 2009 it was number 94 on Fortune's list of 500 – is named for John Wesley Emerson. He invested in the start-up company in 1890.

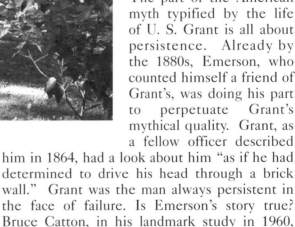

Grant's River Campaign

Grant left Ironton on August 17, dispatched to an unwanted assignment in Jefferson City. He had already sent part of his small garrison south to probe for a Confederate army under Gen. William Hardee of Georgia that threatened Ironton. By the end of August, 1861, though, Grant had returned to Cape Girardeau in command of all troops in Southeast Missouri. Meanwhile, the troops at Ironton came under the command of Union Gen. Benjamin Prentiss. On August 30 Prentiss was ordered to bring six regiments of infantry from Ironton to join Grant in Cape Girardeau. Prentiss' command included the 2nd and 7th Iowa regiments, which were with Prentiss seven months later in the Hornets Nest at Shiloh.

Grant was consolidating his available forces. Soon, he was ready to move south by way of the Mississippi River. Grant's first move was to Cairo, Illinois, where he established headquarters on September 4, 1861. He soon established a fortified outpost on the Missouri side of the Mississippi, opposite Cairo, at Bird's Point.

During the first week of September, Confederate forces entered Kentucky, violating that state's declared neutrality, and established a massive defensive work at Columbus, Kentucky. Grant immediately countered the move by entering the state, and he captured Paducah on September 6, 1861. He then began probing south and southwest from Cairo. On October 2, Grant captured the town of Charleston, Missouri, on the Cairo & Fulton Railroad, and he gradually pushed out a "bulge" surrounding Cairo. Confederate forces still held points in Missouri north of Cairo, though, on the Mississippi and inland from there.

While Grant maintained his headquarters at Cairo, in mid-October, 1861 the Missouri State Guard moved north through Missouri's interior in a counterstroke designed to retard Grant's movement south. The State Guard force was commanded by M. Jeff Thompson, a Virginian lately the mayor of St. Joseph, Missouri. It culminated in the Battle of Fredericktown on October 21, 1861, in which a Union force sent by Grant dealt a defeat to Thompson. This was Thompson's Big River Campaign, which is described below.

In early November, Grant was ordered to create a diversion on both sides of the Mississippi to deter the Confederates from send-

Camp Blood, Pilot Knob, MO, September 1861 (Harper's Weekly)

ing reinforcements to Sterling Price's State Guard army in southwest Missouri. Before undertaking this mission, Grant learned that Jeff Thompson had re-concentrated his command at Bloomfield, Missouri. Grant ordered columns of troops from Bird's Point, Commerce and Cape Girardeau to move inland to Sikeston and Bloomfield. By November 8, 1861, they had driven off Thompson's State Guard and occupied Bloomfield.

Meanwhile, on the 6th, Grant set out for Belmont from Bird's Point with 3100 troops of four Illinois and one Iowa regiments, on steamers escorted by the gun ships Lexington and Tyler. Early on November 7, Grant found that Confederate troops were in fact crossing into Missouri. In lieu of specific orders he converted his mission of diversion into a full scale engagement. Grant attacked a Confederate fort on the Missouri side opposite Belmont, and was repulsed. He withdrew to Bird's Point. The Battle of Belmont was Grant's first Civil War battle in command in the field.

GRANTS MISSOURI YEARS

Ulysses S. Grant's Missouri connections began at West Point in 1842, when Fred Dent of St. Louis became his roommate. After West Point, Grant's first post was at Jefferson Barracks near St. Louis; soon he was introduced to Fred's sister, 18 year old Julia Dent. After a long engagement, they married in 1848. When his first stint in the regular Army ended, Grant lived on the Dent estate, farming two parcels, for most of his St. Louis years, 1854-1860. The Dent home, "Whitehaven," was owned by Grant and his wife for a time during his presidency. Restored in the 1990s, it is now the Ulysses S. Grant National Historic Site, administered by the National Park Service.

In the wake of business failures, Grant moved to Galena, Illinois in 1860 to work as a clerk in his father's harness shop. When war came, Grant nearly had to beg for a commission. His first assignment was as a recruiter. He just happened to be in St. Louis on May 10, 1861 to witness the Camp Jackson incident. He then was appointed to command the 21st Illinois Volunteer Infantry.

Grant entered northeast Missouri at the head of the 21st Illinois in the second week of July, 1861. His mission: To defend the Hannibal & St. Joseph Railroad, then the western-most link in the nation's rail network. His activities until August were concentrated on Missouri's railroads, as he and the 21st Illinois moved south, stopping at Mexico on the North Missouri Railroad and then at the terminus of the Iron Mountain Railroad, at Ironton, 80 miles south of St. Louis. At Mexico, in Audrain County, Grant learned that he had been appointed a brigadier general. It is said that he was in Ironton 48 hours after receiving orders to move to the scene of action, and it was in Ironton that he received his brigadier's commission. He was forever after General Grant.

Grant was transferred to Jefferson City, Missouri in mid-August, 1861, but used political connections in Galena to get back into action in Southeast Missouri. His fighting career began soon after he took command in Cape Girardeau, August 1, 1861. His first battle, at Belmont, Missouri on November 7, 1861, had as its objective the Confederate gibraltar at Columbus, Kentucky. This effort failed, but in his fashion he followed failure with an "end-around." Columbus was abandoned when Grant captured Fort Donelson, east in the Tennessee-Cumberland valley. His victory at Donelson catapulted Grant to national prominence.

Thompson's Big River Campaign

At some point in history, probably in the 1830s, miners discovered a mountain north of present day Ironton that was, literally, a solid chunk of iron ore. It became known, simply enough, as "Iron Mountain." Other significant iron deposits discovered in the vicinity included the mountain known as Pilot Knob, a few miles north of Ironton.

When the railroad boom reached the west in the 1850s, St. Louis industrialists identified the iron district as a prime target for a line, to bring ore to St. Louis. Construction of the St. Louis Iron Mountain Railroad began in St. Louis in 1853. By 1858 the line had reached Pilot Knob. A large iron furnace was built there. Thus, the Ironton area became a point of great strategic importance during the Civil War. But Ironton relied for its supplies upon a thin line that wound its way through the rugged country south of St. Louis.

One of the most vulnerable points on the St. Louis Iron Mountain was located in the extreme northwest corner of St. Francois (pronounced Francis) County. Here, the railroad had to cross the most significant stream on its route, the Big River. Just north of the modern town of Blackwell, a triple-span bridge carried the railroad over the Big River. This bridge was Thompson's objective.

When Grant brought Prentiss southeast from Ironton, he left his defensive line between Cape Girardeau and Ironton undermanned, and Thompson seized the opportunity to disrupt the railroad and punch a hole in the Union line.. He was also in search of that most valuable materiel of war - lead. Thompson's Big River Raid took him into the heart of Missouri's famous Lead Belt. From early in the eighteenth century, until long after the Civil War, the Lead Belt area contained the largest known deposit of the metal ever discovered.

Thompson took about 500 cavalrymen, including some Mississippians, from a point just north of Bloomfield through Bollinger, Madison and St. Francois Counties to reach the Big River Bridge, 100 miles distant. Arriving there on October 15, ahead of schedule, Thompson surprised two companies of a raw Illinois regiment and burned the bridge to the ground. He then returned south, approximating his approach route.

Thompson's route of march is nearly intact today, and the guided route (Tour Stops 26 to 41)

follows the track of Thompson's cavalry as near as possible.

Thompson commanded the First Division of the Missouri State Guard, with the rank of brigadier general. In addition to cavalry, he had infantry near Bloomfield, too. Colonel Adin Lowe of Doniphan, Missouri, followed with the infantry after Thompson moved north. The two joined forces near Fredericktown, as Thompson and his cavalry were returning from Big River. Just now, Union troops from Ironton and Cape Girardeau under orders of Ulysses Grant were converging on Fredericktown to close the gap in Grant's lines west of Cape Girardeau. Thompson and Lowe moved south a few miles, but then turned back north and fought at Fredericktown on October 21, 1861. Thompson lost his battle, but returned to Confederate lines at New Madrid with a hoard of lead - 18,000 pounds of the stuff - that he had captured in the mines just north of Fredericktown.

Pope's Island No. 10 Campaign

Not long after Belmont, Grant changed his short-term focus from the Mississippi to the Cumberland and Tennessee Rivers. On February 16, 1862, he bagged the Confederate garrison at Fort Donelson, Tennessee, and became a national celebrity. Grant's successes in the valleys of the Tennessee and Cumberland forced the Confederates to abandon Columbus, their stronghold on the Mississippi. The Confederates moved their line, and the armaments from Columbus, 50 miles downriver to an island in the Mississippi below New Madrid, Missouri. This was Island No. 10. Here they created a formidable bastion, although one not having the advantages of the heights located at Columbus. From March 5, 1862 to April 9, 1862, this was the western anchor of the Confederate line of defense through Tennessee.

On February 18, 1862, General John Pope, previously commanding Union forces in northeast Missouri, was assigned to command the new Army of the Mississippi. He was given the task of renewing the Union drive down the Mississippi. Pope assembled an army of 10,000 men at Commerce, Missouri, a steamboat landing ten miles south of Cape Girardeau. In early March, 1862, Pope moved on Sikeston and took the town and the Cairo & Fulton Railroad from Jeff Thompson. Pope's army swelled to 18,000 on the march. Pope marched overland, south

Virginian by birth, and with a name to prove it, Meriwether Jefferson Thompson emigrated to Missouri in 1847 and settled in St. Joseph. He was a businessman and railroad promoter. After becoming active in politics he became St. Joseph's mayor by 1860. It was Thompson who on April 3, 1860 handed the mail to the first rider, in ceremonies that inaugurated the Pony Express.

Thompson joined the Missouri State Guard at its inception in 1861. By the end of that year he commanded the First Division of the MSG and had reached legendary status as the "Swamp Fox," operating an independent command in southeast Missouri. Thompson took part in Marmaduke's 1863 Raid on Cape Girardeau, then in August, 1863 was captured in Pocahontas, Arkansas. He spent time in St. Louis' Gratiot Street prison, and Johnson Island and Fort Delaware prisons, before his exchange in 1864. Jeff Thompson was one of the great "characters" of all Missouri history. He was famous for the grandiloquence of his military pronouncements, and was known as a poet and a thespian while confined at Fort Delaware. A relatively pleasant experience there contrasted with those of his release. Thompson was one of 50 officers sent to Charleston, South Carolina because Union authorities thought that the Confederates were holding Union prisoners as human shields, and the Fort Delaware prisoners were sent there to share their fate. The prisoners were exchanged instead, on August 2, 1864.

Thompson made his way back to Missouri and joined Price's 1864 Expedition. When David Shanks was killed outside of Jefferson City, Thompson took command of Shelby's Iron Brigade, which Thompson commanded with distinction until the end of the War. Oddly, Thompson was never commissioned a Confederate officer, and was still a General of the Missouri State Guard when he surrendered one of the last and largest remaining bodies of Confederate troops, in Jacksonport, Arkansas on May 11, 1865.

Thompson was a fighter and (as an amateur soldier) an innovator. As he said upon taking command of the First Division, "I am a rip-squealer, and my name is FIGHT!"

Thompson resided in New Orleans after the War, and died in 1876 after returning to St. Joseph in ill health. He was only 50 years old. He is buried in Mt. Moriah Cemetery in St. Joseph.

from Sikeston, on a rugged causeway built through the swamps - El Camino Real (Kingshighway) from the days of the Spanish occupation and U.S. Highway 61 today - and he laid siege to New Madrid.

Pope waited north of town until he was able to bring heavy siege guns into play, and while his engineers were struggling to build a canal to bypass Island No. 10. The Southern garrison abandoned New Madrid on March 14, 1862 after a brief bombardment, leaving Pope in possession of the town.

Pope invested the area south of New Madrid, where Island No. 10 was situated, but to get his troops in position for attack the U.S. Navy had to run the gauntlet of the Confederate batteries on the island. On April 4, 1862 the St. Louis-built U.S.S. Carondelet led the way, and within several days Island No. 10 was in federal hands.

U.S.S. Carondelet at Island No. 10

Marmaduke's 1863 Cape Girardeau Raid

John Sappington Marmaduke was a son of a wealthy and famous family from Saline County, Missouri, who attended Harvard and Yale before entering the U.S. Military Academy at West Point. He was an officer in the 2nd U.S. Cavalry, in New Mexico, when the War broke out. He would become a Confederate cavalry officer of some renown, and a post-war governor of Missouri. In April, 1863, Grant was moving inexorably towards Vicksburg on the Mississippi, and Marmaduke was in northern Arkansas, at Batesville, where he assembled 5,000 cavalrymen. Dire circumstances called for a raid north, to draw Union attention and resources.

Marmaduke probably intended to strike at Ironton, but his strategy (as for a similar raid in southwest Missouri in January, 1863) was to keep the Union defenders in Missouri guessing as to his ultimate destination. He divided his force into two wings, heading them north by widely divergent routes. The wings would consolidate at Jackson, Missouri, the county seat of Cape Girardeau County. The Union forces in southeast Missouri, commanded by Gen. John McNeil, were able to escape from the interior and consolidate as well, which they did within strong fortifications that ringed the town of Cape Girardeau, on the Mississippi River. Marmaduke determined to make an attack on Cape Girardeau, and he did on April 26, 1863. His forces were repulsed, and he retreated back to Jackson.

McNeil received reinforcements by way of a Union cavalry detachment that came from the west and collided with Marmaduke's command as they were camped in the vicinity of Jackson the night of April 26. The Confederates organized a hasty retreat and escaped down Crowley's Ridge, fighting rear-guard actions until they reached the St. Francis River at Chalk Bluff, Arkansas (near Campbell, Missouri) on May 2. A battle there held off the Federals long enough for Marmaduke to elude the pursuit.

Price's 1864 Expedition
Action in the Southeast

The real object of Price's Expedition has long been debated. The military object was St. Louis, by order of Confederate General Kirby Smith. But the national elections were looming when Price entered Missouri in September, 1864, and the anti-Lincoln forces were in trouble, notably because of Sherman's success at Atlanta. Most certainly, the presence of a large force of Confederate troops moving north in Missouri would have some impact on the northern electorate's growing perception that the War was nearly won. However, Price brought along Missouri's Governor-in-exile, Thomas C. Reynolds, and according to most scholars, a prime feature of Price's plan was to take Jefferson City and install Reynolds as Governor. Such a development might have had a serious impact upon the presidential election set for the first Tuesday of November, 1864.

Price pulled his forces together at Pocahontas, Arkansas on September 13, 1864. Three divisions, commanded respectively by JO Shelby, John S. Marmaduke and James Fagan of Arkansas, proceeded north by separate and parallel routes, keeping a distance from each other in order to maintain sources of forage and supplies. All three wings entered Missouri on September 19. Shelby, on the left, entered the state south of Doniphan, and passed through that town on the way to Fort Benton at Patterson, Missouri, which he captured on September 22. Fagan's route in the center took him through Greenville, and Marmaduke, on the right, headed through Poplar Bluff and Bloomfield. The objective in this phase of the Expedition was Fredericktown, where the three wings united on September 25. Little action or opposition occurred south of Fredericktown, as the Confederates had achieved a level of surprise.

Maj. Gen. William S. Rosecrans (of Chickamauga fame) was the Union commander in St. Louis. Once apprised of the threat coming from the south, Rosecrans moved to protect St. Louis. The defenses of St. Louis were seriously undermanned this late in the War and this far from the principal battle fronts. Fortunately for Rosecrans, he found A.J. Smith's 16th Army

GENERAL STERLING PRICE, 'OLD PAP'

Sterling Price is Missouri's own "marble man." He was born in 1809 in the Virginia County of Prince Edward, which adjoins Appomattox County, and he was educated there. As a young man, he with his parents emigrated to Missouri. Price established a home and plantation in Keytesville, north of the Missouri River in Chariton County, and he entered politics.

Price served one term in the U.S. Congress in 1844-1846, just before the Mexican War. When Missourians were called up, Price obtained a commission as Colonel and led a contingent of troops to New Mexico where he occupied Santa Fe. He led a cavalry raid into the Mexican state of Chihuahua that was the last campaign of the Mexican War. He returned to Missouri a bona fide war hero. He was elected Governor of the state in 1852, and served one term, from 1853-1857.

Although a slave owner, Price was a so-called conditional unionist, and he fought hard to keep Missouri in the Union. He was a delegate to the Missouri Constitutional Convention in 1861, established to address the question of secession, and was elected chairman of the convention. In March, 1861, despite the fact that all but 17 of the delegates were born in slaveholding states, the convention voted 98-1 to reject secession. As war clouds gathered in the next two months, Price appears to have been sincere in seeking compromise, but events soon overtook these efforts.

Sterling Price was the only natural choice to command the Missouri State Guard when it was established in 1861, and he accepted the appointment. He would lead the MSG through the remainder of 1861, winning notable victories at Wilson's Creek and Lexington. After the Battle of Pea Ridge, in March 1862, Price (now a Major General in the Confederate Army) and his soldiers were transferred east of the Mississippi. They distinguished themselves at Iuka and Corinth, Mississippi, and other places.

Price returned to the West in the Spring of 1863, and thereafter fought in and from Arkansas. He organized and led an incursion into Missouri in September and October, 1864, known as Price's Expedition, which ended in disaster and defeat and represented the last organized Confederate campaign west of the Mississippi. He was one of the Confederate officers who went to Mexico for a time after the War, but he returned to Missouri, to St. Louis, and died there in 1867. He is buried in Bellefontaine Cemetery.

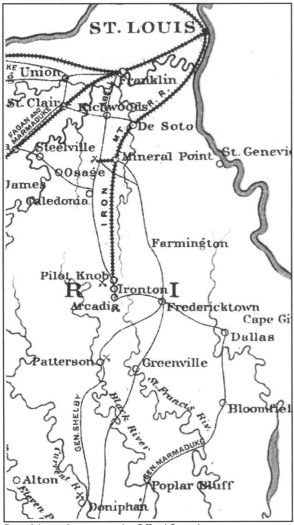

From Atlas to Accompany the Official Records

launched an all out assault. The Confederates were decimated as they executed repeated frontal assaults. Price's troops went into camp, and at 2:30 a.m. on the morning of September 28 the Union defenders (1400 of them) managed to escape the fort undetected and unharmed.

Many historians consider Pilot Knob to be the battle that saved St. Louis, since Price lost 2 or 3 days on this diversion. This is not the case. A. J. Smith's 16th Corps - composed of 8,000 or 9,000 veteran infantry - was already in position to block Price's advance. Indeed, some of the soldiers defending Ft. Davidson were from the 16th Corps, dispatched there from St. Louis. Price decided at Fredericktown, no doubt, to abandon his first objective and concentrate on his second, the state capital of Jefferson City.

The federals fleeing Pilot Knob, commanded by Gen. Thomas Ewing, were unable to move north to safety because Shelby's Division was moving south from Potosi on the same road in order to rejoin Price. Ewing moved west in a driving rainstorm, through some of the roughest country in the Ozarks, and reached the Southwest Branch Railroad at Leasburg on September 30. A battle was fought at Leasburg, after Shelby's frustrated troopers finally caught up with Ewing, but reinforcements arrived by rail and the Pilot Knob garrison was safe. It was

Immanuel Lutheran Church, Pilot Knob

Corps in transit at Memphis, and General Sherman consented to divert it to St. Louis. Then too, Maj. Gen. Alfred Pleasonton of the U. S. Cavalry, who had bested J.E.B. Stuart at Brandy Station and commanded the Union cavalry at Gettysburg,, had been assigned to the Department of Missouri in April, 1864. He would command the cavalry that chased Price across Missouri.

After Fredericktown, Price again sent his divisions in separate directions. With the bulk of the army, he moved west 15 miles in order to attack a fort at Pilot Knob, Missouri, just north of Ironton. From Fredericktown, Price sent Shelby north, through Farmington and Potosi, to sever the St. Louis Iron Mountain Railroad, which Shelby did most efficiently. After some fighting in Ironton on September 26, the Union units in the area retreated into Fort Davidson, the federal earthwork in Pilot Knob, and on the 27th Price

a miraculous escape, made more dramatic because of Thomas Ewing's presence. Ewing – brother-in-law of William T. Sherman - was by 1864 the most hated Union man in Missouri. His story is found in Tour Loop Four.

Shelby's Division, and part of Marmaduke's which had joined in the chase, tore up a section of the Souhwest Branch, going as far south as Cuba, Missouri, then moved northeast along the present-day route of Interstate 44 to join the remainder of Price's force at the town of Union. Most of Price's army, however, moved north from Pilot Knob on the route of highways 21 and 47, to Union. The Confederates did get close to St. Louis, to a rail junction at Pacific on the western border of St. Louis County, but the expedition in eastern Missouri had now become an exercise in railroad-busting. Price's men did a good job of this. Then they moved west in the direction of Jefferson City.

CRAZY LIKE A...

In the early days of the Civil War and throughout much of the rest of his life, Sherman was strongly tied to Missouri. The ties bound him so that his earthly remains lie in St. Louis' Calvary Cemetery.

An Ohioan who once felt an affinity for the South, Sherman ran a Louisiana military school (later LSU) until Louisiana voted to secede. He then accepted a position as president of a St. Louis streetcar company, and he was living there on May 10, 1861. Sherman, with his son, was at the Missouri Militia's Camp Jackson that day when shots rang out and they had to "hit the dirt" along an embankment on Olive Street. Sherman, a West Pointer, received a military commission soon afterwards, and went east where he fought at the Battle of First Bull Run (Manassas) in July 1861. Next assigned to Kentucky, in October, 1861 Sherman found himself embroiled in controversy when comments he made to the Secretary of War were reported to the press. As a result, in November of that year Sherman was assigned to a low profile position in Missouri, but was recalled within a matter of days. This is when Sherman was thought to have suffered a nervous breakdown. He went on leave, home to Ohio, and when he came back he served as commandant of Benton Barracks in St. Louis until February, 1862. Then he joined U. S. Grant in time to see action at Shiloh.

When he assumed command of the U.S. army of the western frontier just after the Civil War, Sherman made his headquarters in St. Louis. He lived in a house presented to him by a group of admirers. From this house, in 1884, a stone's throw from the site of Camp Jackson, Sherman composed his second most memorable quote, the one that ended "...if elected I will not serve."

Sherman died in New York in 1891.

Part 1 - Southbound

Tour Stop 1

BELLEFONTAINE CEMETERY is far and away the most significant historic cemetery in the Midwest. There are nearly 90,000 burials here, which include such luminaries as explorer William Clark and brewing magnate Adolphus Busch, and hundreds of others. You have been circling Bellefontaine since you exited I-70, and so as you may have imagined you cannot do this site justice on this trip. Plan to come back to St. Louis and reserve a day to tour Bellefontaine and its neighbor, Calvary Cemetery, just to the north. Calvary is the resting place of Dred Scott and William Tecumseh Sherman.

St. Louis' phenomenal growth in the years after the Civil War attracted "the best and the brightest" from all over the west and the south, and not surprisingly many of the men who prospered in those years were high-ranking veterans of the Civil War. When these men passed on, many were laid to rest in St. Louis' premiere cemeteries, Bellefontaine and Calvary. As a result, taking the two cemeteries together, there are more generals of both armies buried here than in any other place. There are cemeteries with more Union generals, and cemeteries with more Confederate generals, but no place where so many of both armies lie side by side. We'll take you to the graves of three men at Bellefontaine who figured prominently in the war for control of the Mississippi.

From the entrance gate, proceed east on the road you are on, past the first intersection. Continue on the road which seems to be the straightest route available (Willow Ave.). This road turns into Lawn Avenue at about the point you see a large monument with the name "Peper." Go a bit further on Lawn, until you reach a "T", where you will see signs for both Lawn and Autumn Avenue. At this point, you turn left. You can see a large pink granite mausoleum in a gothic design in front of you from here. That is your destination. Take the second right (Woodbine Ave.) and park in front of the large mausoleum (Adolphus Busch). On foot, cross Woodbine at the Busch mausoleum, keeping to the right of the Walker plot and the Lindell monument. To your right front you will see a large grouping of modest monuments of identical design. In this grouping is the grave of MAJ. GEN. JOHN POPE. Pope was the hero of the Union victory at Island No. 10, and was then promoted to become the goat at the Union disaster of Second Bull Run (Manassas) in Virginia.

To reach Tour Stop 1

From downtown St. Louis, take I-70 north 4.9 miles to the exit at Broadway. Bear left off the exit ramp and continue north on Broadway for approximately 1 mile, and turn left at S. Calvary Avenue. After 3/4 mile you reach W. Florissant Avenue, and you turn left here. Go south for 3 miles to the entrance to Bellefontaine Cemetery on your left.

1

James B. Eads
1820 - 1887

America's best known self-taught engineer was born in Lawrenceburg, Indiana, on the Ohio River. He is best known for engineering the splendid bridge in St. Louis that bears his name today. The Eads Bridge, when completed in 1874, contained the longest load bearing arch ever constructed. It was the first major bridge to use steel in its construction.

Eads arrived in St. Louis in 1833. While still a young man, he went into business as an underwater salvage contactor. He made a fortune raising sunken riverboat cargos, and in the process pioneered the use of the diving bell. At the outbreak of the Civil War, Eads obtained a contract to construct seven ironclad river steamers, known as the "City Class" gunboats. The first of these to be launched, the *U. S. S. St. Louis*, was the first ironclad warship constructed in the western hemisphere. It beat its east coast counterparts *Virginia* and *Monitor* by several months.

When you leave in your car, make the first right turn immediately after the Busch mausoleum, proceed down the hill to the first right turn you can make, turn right and then turn immediately left at the next intersection, Woodland Avenue. Proceed along Woodland for .1 mile to the next intersection, then park in the vicinity of the Milburn monument. Walk up the hill on the opposite side of Woodland, to the pine tree. Here, is a large raised monument resembling a sarcophagus. This is the grave of JAMES BUCHANAN EADS.

The last gravesite you will see today provides an interesting counterpoint to the Eads story. Continue straight ahead on Woodland Avenue, past the next intersection (Glade). After you pass the Cozzens monument on your right, pull over and look for a small, square stone in black granite and the name Emerson. Off to the right is a smaller stone, in poor condition, with a rounded top. Here lies PRIMUS EMERSON, also an early St. Louis industrialist. Emerson was the founder and proprietor of the Carondelet shipyard where Eads built his City Class gunboats. A Southern sympathizer, he leased the yard to Eads and went south when war came. In Memphis, Emerson designed and built the famous Confederate ram *C.S.S. Arkansas*.

Proceed ahead on Woodland Avenue as it circles around to the right. You should soon be able to see to your left the cemetery gate where you entered. Turn left, back to Willow Avenue and proceed to exit the cemetery.

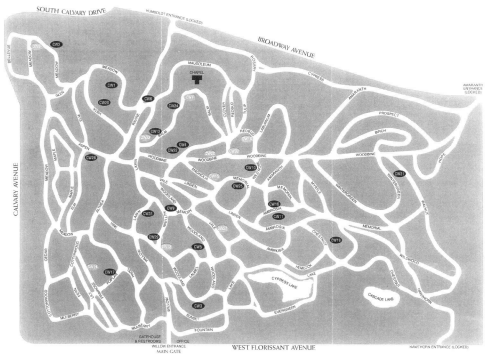

Tour Stop 2

Like its neighbor, CALVARY CEMETERY has too much Civil War to see on this trip. Today, you will see only Calvary's two most famous residents.

Drive forward on the road you entered, bearing left at the first fork. By this time, you should see an American flag on a flagpole in your front. This is your objective. You will make one right turn, proceeding past the second road that enters from the right. To your left, the group of monuments at the foot of the flagpole is the Sherman plot, and the grave of GEN. WILLIAM TECUMSEH SHERMAN. Sherman's grave is flanked by those of his wife, Ellen Ewing Sherman, his son Willie, and another son and daughter. Willie's stone reminds us that he died in 1863 at age 9, after he contracted yellow fever while in camp with his father in Mississippi. Sherman had many ties to St. Louis, but ultimately he was laid to rest in St. Louis because first Willie, then Ellen in 1888, were buried here.

As you stand facing the Sherman plot, you can imagine Confederate Gen. Joseph E. Johnston standing approximately here, hatless in the rain, when he served as one of Sherman's pallbearers in 1891. He died about a month later, aged 84, from complications of a severe cold he contracted as a result.

Back in your car, drive straight ahead on the road you followed to reach Sherman's grave. Follow this road for approximately .3 miles, to the third intersection. Turn right on the road that appears to angle up the hill, proceed for .1 mile and park when you see the Lacey-Thole monument on your left. On the other side of the road, right where you are, a modern granite stone marks the grave of DRED SCOTT. Next to Dred Scott's stone is a marker dedicated to his wife and co-plaintiff HARRIET SCOTT, although (it has recently been confirmed) Harriet is not buried here. Modern historians have begun to realize that Harriet Scott's will and persistence were the prime factors in producing the couples' famous case.

Find your way back to the cemetery gate, the way you came in. Upon exiting, there is a sharp left available to you which turns directly on to Calvary Drive. It is best to scoot through here.

To reach Tour Stop 2:

Exit the cemetery, turn right, and return to the point where Calvary Avenue meets West Florissant. The entrance to Calvary Cemetery is just to the north of this intersection, on your right. Turn into the cemetery entrance.

Dred Scott
1799 - 1858

Born a slave in Virginia, Scott first lived in Missouri in about 1830, when the Peter Blow family brought him with them to St. Louis. Blow sold Scott to Dr. John Emerson, an Army surgeon. Scott began his trek to freedom when Emerson took him to Rock Island, Illinois, in 1833. Several years later, Scott married Harriett Robinson at Fort Snelling, Minnesota Territory.

In 1846, Scott and his wife filed separate petitions in St. Louis Circuit Court, seeking their freedom according to a Missouri law which had long acknowledged that slaves taken to free territory were entitled to their freedom. They lost their first trial in 1847; but the court granted a new trial. After some maneuvering in the appeals courts, the case again went to trial in 1850. The Scotts won. However, the Missouri Supreme Court, speaking through a 2-1 majority, reversed years of precedent in holding that the Scotts were not free as a result of years residing in free territory.

The case which produced the infamous 1857 decision of the United States Supreme Court was commenced in federal court in St. Louis in 1854, and sought to use federal law to override the Missouri Supreme Court decision.

The Scotts were freed through the intervention of the Blow family, two months after the U.S. Supreme Court decision. Dred Scott passed away about a year later.

To reach Tour Stop 3:

Exit the cemetery, turn left on to Calvary Drive, and retrace your route back to Interstate 70. There is a well-marked route that crosses the interstate and directs you eastbound. Once on I-70 southbound, drive 3.5 miles to the Broadway exit. Drive south on Broadway until you are at the center point of the Gateway Arch (on your left), and you will see Tour Stop 3 on your left.

To reach Tour Stop 4:

From Stop 3 you will proceed south on Broadway for 2.5 miles, until you arrive opposite the Anheuser-Busch Brewery complex. The road you have been on has changed from Broadway to Seventh Street, and is now Broadway again. Continue to Arsenal Street, in the shadow of the brewery, and turn left here. In one block, turn right on Second Street, and park in front of the impressive gates to the federal mapping agency that is towards the river.

Tour Stop 3

Tour Stop 3 is St. Louis' OLD COURTHOUSE. The city's most prominent landmark building is now a part of the Jefferson National Expansion Memorial, as is the Arch and the Museum of Westward Expansion beneath the Arch. The Old Courthouse houses exhibits devoted to St. Louis history, and restored courtrooms. It is most famous as the site of the original trial in the Dred and Harriet Scott freedom case. The east steps of the courthouse was the site of slave auctions before the war, and is thought to be the place where an impoverished U.S. Grant freed his only slave in 1859.

Tour Stop 4

You stand in the middle of the site that in 1861 was THE ST. LOUIS ARSENAL. As you look up the hill to the west, in what is now Lyon Park, you will see a monument erected in memory of the first Union general killed in the Civil War, Nathaniel Lyon. The federal government gave the park to the City on condition that a monument to the not-too-popular Lyon be constructed, and this monument was completed in 1874.

Looking east, toward the river, you see the limestone buildings, some of which predate the Civil War, when the St. Louis Arsenal was the largest repository of arms and ammunition in the western United States. Aside from Lyon Park, the Arsenal grounds have remained federal property to this day. The great stone wall which extends across the northern boundary of the property was part of the facility that existed during the war. At that time, the river bounded the Arsenal walls on the east, and a sally port opened on the river. On the night of April 25, 1861, Lyon's garrison used this sally port to remove some 20,000 muskets and other war materiel to the safety of Illinois, by way of the steamer *City of Alton*.

In May, 1861, the Missouri Militia was camped in western St. Louis, on the present-day site of St. Louis University, and fear mounted that the militia had designs to capture the Arsenal. Lyon fortified the Arsenal, and the heights up the hill in front of you, and the feared attack never came.

On May 10, Lyon marched from here with 7,000 troops,

composed mostly of irregular units drawn from the German-American population of St. Louis, to the militia's Camp Jackson and took into custody the state militia lawfully assembled there. This was the spark that ignited the Civil War in Missouri.

When Lyon marched on Camp Jackson, Ulysses Grant was visiting the Arsenal on a recruiting mission for Illinois' governor, and was here to see Lyon off.

Tour Stop 5

This house is the JOHN S. BOWEN HOME. The home is in private ownership, so please be content to see the house from here.

You are now in a St. Louis neighborhood that was once the independent town of Carondelet. John Stevens Bowen (an architect by profession) designed and built this house in 1859 and lived here until he reported to Memphis in May, 1861, there to organize and train a regiment that would be part of the famous First Missouri Brigade (Confederate). He never came home again.

Bowen is thought to have been acquainted with U.S. Grant during Grant's St. Louis years, and this is no doubt true. The fraternity of West Point graduates in St. Louis was a small one. Bowen seems to have taken on the role of conciliator between his former West Point mates, too. He was the Colonel of the 2nd Regiment of the Missouri Volunteer Militia at Camp Jackson. He unsuccessfully interceded with Nathaniel Lyon in an attempt to avert the Camp Jackson affair in 1861. Later, in front of Vicksburg, it was Bowen who contacted Ulysses Grant to make arrangements for his superior, Gen. John Pemberton, to meet with Grant to surrender Vicksburg.

Before Vicksburg, Bowen and his First Missouri Brigade nearly stopped Grant cold at the Battle of Champion Hill, Mississippi.

To Reach Tour Stop 5:

Return to Broadway by way of Arsenal Street, and turn left (south). When you pass under the highway (interstate 55), look for Cherokee Street and the signs directing you to southbound I-55. Enter I-55 here, and then proceed south for 3.5 miles to the exit for Loughborough Avenue. Turn left upon exiting, and proceed east for 5 blocks to Michigan Street. Turn left here, and drive to the end of the block. Pull over if you can in front of the library at the corner of Kraus Street. Tour Stop 5 is the house on the corner which is opposite to you on the diagonal.

Maj. Gen. John S. Bowen
1829 – 1863

Bowen was a native of Georgia, who attended the University of Georgia before entering the U. S. Military Academy. Graduating in the West Point class of 1853, Bowen served in the U. S. Cavalry on the frontier before returning to Georgia to begin a career as an architect. While stationed at Jefferson Barracks in 1855, Bowen met and married Mary Kennerly of a prominent St. Louis Southern family. Indeed, Mary's aunt was the second wife of the explorer William Clark.

The Bowens moved to St. Louis in 1857, and there John became active in the Missouri State Militia. At Camp Jackson as Chief of Staff to General David Frost, commanding the militia, Bowen was captured and paroled. He then fled south to begin a brilliant but abbreviated career as a Confederate warrior.

Bowen contracted dysentery during the siege of Vicksburg, symptoms first appearing on July 4, 1863. He died on July 13, 1863 near Raymond, Mississippi with Mary at his side.

To Reach Stops 6 – 8

Turn right on Kraus Street, and go down the hill 3 blocks to the intersection of Broadway. Turn right on Broadway and drive south 2.7 miles to a point where Broadway turns sharply to the left, where you will see a brown sign for Jefferson Barracks Park. Turn left here in order to stay on Broadway. Soon, you will pass through World War II-era guard posts at the gate of the park, and within .2 mile you come to a street called North Street. Turn left, looping around the historic buildings in this area and find the parking lot for the Visitors Center for Jefferson Barracks Historical Park, which will be on your left just after you enter North Street. When you leave the Visitors Center, return to the place you turned left on North, then go left on this road (Grant Road). Proceed south for .6 mile, being careful to bear right at the intersection at the bottom of a hill. As you ascend this hill, near its crest, on your left is a road called Scenic Circle Drive, and a gate made of cannon barrels. Turn left here for Tour Stop 7. When you leave here, continue driving south on Grant Road, until it intersects with Hancock Road, then turn right on Hancock. Proceed west on Hancock for .6 mile, to the intersection of Gregg Rd. At this point, as a sign indicates, you will see a building under renovation that is to be the Missouri Civil War Museum. Stop 8 is on your left.

Tour Stop 6

JEFFERSON BARRACKS HISTORICAL PARK was established in 1950 when much of the historic military base was decommissioned, and the property donated to St. Louis County. Part of the original property, at the parade ground, is still an important Missouri National Guard post.

Jefferson Barracks was established in 1826, and was active as a U.S. Army training base through World War II. For many years, including the years of the Civil War, Jefferson Barracks was one of the most important army installations on the western frontier. So much so, that more officers who would rise to the rank of general in the Union and Confederate armies would serve here before the War than at any other post. These include Generals Grant, Buckner, Hancock, Ewell, Pickett, Sherman, Johnston, Sheridan, Hood and Stuart. Future Confederate President Jefferson Davis was stationed here in 1829 while a young lieutenant, just out of West Point.

Stop by the Visitors Center, where you can obtain a map of the entire park; there is also a good inventory of books on military history and the history of Jefferson Barracks.

Tour Stop 7

This is Jefferson Barracks' GRANT HOUSE OVERLOOK. The gate and fence are constructed of Civil War surplus cannon and gun barrels, and the park houses the original iron gates which once protected the U.S. Arsenal. The site has no particular affinity to General Grant, except a nearby picnic pavilion is named for him. There is ever-so-faint evidence around the parking lot of entrenchments that once protected this spot.

Tour Stop 8

Stop 8 is the historic Jefferson Barracks' PARADE GROUND. The American flag has flown over this piece of ground for more than 180 years. The hulking barracks buildings on the south side of the field were build in the 1890s, and efforts are underway to turn one of these buildings into a museum, and develop other cultural sites befitting the great history that is here.

Tour Stop 9

This Veterans Administration facility, JEFFERSON BARRACKS NATIONAL CEMETERY, contains what was known as the "Old Post Cemetery," where soldiers and dependents who died at the post in the years before the Civil War were laid to rest. The cemetery was one of the early sites designated as a National Cemetery, in 1866. However, this one is somewhat unique. Many of the national cemeteries were established to re-inter casualties that had been buried near battlefields. Jefferson Barracks was the site of the largest military hospital complex in the west, drawing wounded Union and Confederate soldiers from all of the major campaigns on the Mississippi. The Civil War sections of the cemetery consist in large part of graves of the wounded who died at the hospital.

As in the case of Bellefontaine and Calvary, there are too many important graves and monuments here to take in on this trip. For more information, see the Veterans Administration site at www.cem.va.gov/pdf/jeffbarr.pdf, or better yet, buy Bill Winter's, *The Civil War in St. Louis, a Guided Tour*, at any major bookstore in St. Louis.

We will take you to a point near the Old Post Cemetery, and suggest you stroll the grounds from there.

From the gates of the cemetery, proceed to and half way around the circle in front of you, to Longstreet Drive. Go east on Longstreet as far as you can go in a straight line (1/2 mile from the entrance gate) until you reach a small circle around a monument. This is the Minnesota Monument, erected in 1921 to honor 164 Minnesotans - at least one from each of Infantry Regiments 1 - 10 - who are buried at Jefferson Barracks.

9

To reach Tour Stop 9:

Tour Stop 9 is the Jefferson Barracks National Cemetery, a massive facility which lies just to south of the parade ground. From the point on the west side of the parade ground, continue south on Gregg Road to the point were it ends near the barracks buildings, then turn right on Sherman Rd. Turn left on Randolph Rd., then left and right, and soon you will find yourself on Sheridan Road. Proceed south until you reach the gates of the cemetery, on your left. Pull in.

Pull over on one of the streets which radiate from here. The streets are very narrow, and be careful where and how you park. The sections of the cemetery towards the River, on both sides of Longstreet from here to the next crossroad in the distance, contain Civil War burials, as do most of the sections you passed on Longstreet to get here. As you face the River, the Confederate sections are at your right rear. The Old Post Cemetery is at your left front, beyond the next crossroad.

When it is time to leave, go to South Street, which is one block south of the Minnesota monument. Head west in the direction of the cemetery gate. You will dip down a hill, and as you start up the next hill watch for an area on your right that does not have graves. Then, 6 rows further west there is a similar blank area. Stop here and find grave number 4608, the grave of ASA V. LADD.

THE ASA LADD STORY

On October 29, 1864, six Confederate prisoners were executed in St. Louis by firing squad. All six are buried here together. This act was the sad and shocking end to the campaign known as Price's Expedition.

Dear Wife and Children:
I take my pen with trembling hand to inform you that I will be shot between 2 and 4 o'clock this evening. I have but a few hours to remain in this unfriendly world. There is six of us sentenced to die because of the six Union soldiers that were shot by Reeve's men. My dear wife, don't grieve for me. I want you to meet me in Heaven. I want you to teach the children piety, so that they may meet me at the right hand of God. . . . If you don't get this letter before St. Francis River gets up, you had better stay there until you can make a crop, and you can go in the dry season. It is now past 4 a.m. I must bring my letter to a close, leaving you in the hands of God. I send you my best love and respects in the hour of death. Kiss all the children for me. You need have no uneasiness about my future state, for my faith is well founded...

Good-by Amy, Acey Ladd

Tour Stop 10

To Reach Tour Stop 10:

The TOWN OF KIMMSWICK was founded in 1859, just before the Civil War. There are great shops and restaurants here, which makes it a good place to take a break, but the only Civil War history is buried in the river bank at an inaccessible place south of town.

In December, 1864, just to the south of Kimmswick, a federal warship the *USS Monarch* sunk after it became trapped in the ice on the River. Every so often, when the Mississippi is very, very low, the ribs of the *USS Monarch's* hull appear on the surface of the Missouri bank. Unfortunately, the site is not accessible. The *Monarch* was one of the "Ellet Rams," a flotilla of small ironclads, commissioned and manned by the U. S. Army and placed under the command of Col. Charles Ellet. On June 6, 1862, Ellet's flotilla joined in the attack upon Southern gunboats defending Memphis, Tennessee, in one of the great naval battles of the Civil War. The *Monarch*, with its "M" between the stacks, is shown in the engraving below, while in action at the Battle of Memphis. It is behind the vessel in the foreground (the *C.S.S. General Beauregard*), ramming the *Beauregard* as the battle reached its climax.

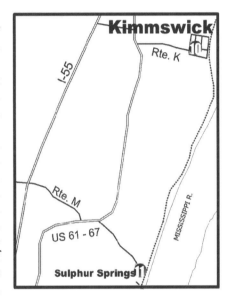

When you reach Sheridan Road, turn left. In 1/2 mile, you will reach Telegraph Road, where you turn left. Go south to Interstate 255, and enter the highway westbound. Proceed west on 255 for approximately two miles, then exit southbound on Interstate 55. You will stay on I-55 for 11.7 miles, to exit 186, the Imperial exit. Exit here, and turn left on Main Street. Proceed east for .4 mile to Highway 61-67, and turn right. At the first left, Highway K, turn left and drive into the town of Kimmswick.

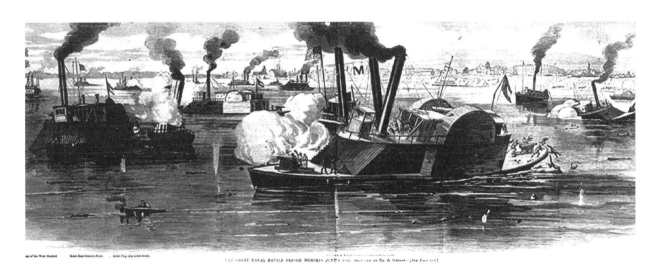

To reach Tour Stop 11:

Retrace your route back to Highway 61-67, and turn south (left). Proceed south for 1.7 miles to Sulphur Springs Road, turn left. Drive to the end of this road, to a small settlement on the River, Tour Stop 11, which is the town of Sulphur Springs.

Tour Stop 11

Tour Stop 11 is what remains of SULPHUR SPRINGS DEPOT, a river landing which was a bustling port and Union supply base during the Civil War. The importance of this site was dictated by the River, and by the railroad which runs along the river. This was the Iron Mountain Railroad, which hugged the Mississippi from St. Louis to a point just below here, where it turned inland and extended as far as Pilot Knob. The existence of the railroad made Pilot Knob the most strategic spot in southeast Missouri during the first year of the War; Sulphur Springs was the principal landing point for troops and supplies headed for Pilot Knob.

A large earthwork was constructed up on the hill to the north, representing St. Louis' southernmost line of defense on the river. Also, situated here during the Civil War was Camp Curtis. After the Battle of Fredericktown, from November, 1861, to January, 1862, Camp Curtis was home to the 8th Wisconsin and its eagle mascot "Old Abe."

To reach Tour Stop 12:

Return to Highway 61-67 and turn left. You will quickly come to the intersection of Route M, where you turn right. In about 1/2 mile, Route M reaches Interstate 55.

Tour Stop 12

This stop is the GRAVE OF COL. WILLIAM. L. JEFFERS. Jeffers commanded the 8th Missouri Cavalry (Confederate). Early in the War, he became famous in this area as the "Captain of the Swamps." His connection with Jackson pre-dated the War. He was a prominent citizen here, and hence was buried in Jackson upon his death in 1903. Jackson was captured and occupied by Confederate raiders in 1863 and 1864, and a skirmish occurred just south of town in 1862, but there are today no other signs in Jackson of its role in the Civil War.

Tour Stop 13

A marker here commemorates the April 26, 1863 BATTLE OF CAPE GIRARDEAU. You are at the approximate center of the advance position of the Confederate line, which extended north to south for a distance of two miles. The Union defensive line ran along the heights to the east, where the defenders (principally the 1st Nebraska and 32nd Iowa infantry regiments) were posted. This was mostly an artillery fight; after threatening the well-fortified heights for a time, Marmaduke withdrew to Jackson with heavy losses.

Cape Girardeau has an excellent Civil War driving tour, which features a number of sites associated with the battle. Stop at the visitors center at Broadway and Fountain Street for a map of the tour.

Tour Stop 14

Somewhere in the area of Themis and Spanish Street is the GRANT-PRENTISS MEETING SITE. There is no marker or monument. This, however, is as fine a site as there is to contemplate the character of the man Grant.

Grant took command of all federal armies in Southeast Missouri upon his arrival in Cape Girardeau on August 30, 1861. He had been relieved of command at Ironton two weeks before, and replaced there by Gen. Benjamin Prentiss. In the intervening period, Grant had been to St. Louis, and supposedly pulled some strings in Washington to regain command of the forward elements of his former command.

On September 2, 1861, Grant saddled up at his headquarters down Themis Street, one block east. He was riding up to Jackson

To reach Tour Stop 13:

As you leave Jackson Cemetery, go east on Monroe Street for one block. Turn right on S. Hope Street, which is U.S. Highway 61. One block south, turn left and follow 61 for 8.5 miles to its intersection with Broadway in Cape Girardeau. Turn left. Drive east on Broadway for .4 miles to Cordelia Avenue, and turn right. Take the next left (Thilenius Street) and then pull over as you approach the next intersection, which is Caruthers Street. Tour Stop 13 is on the grounds of the Central Middle School at the southeast corner of this intersection.

To reach Tour Stop 14:

Continue east on Broadway until you reach Spanish Street within two blocks of the river. Find a place to park. You then want to walk south on Spanish Street for one block to the corner of Themis. You should be standing in front of the historic Common Pleas Courthouse.

Maj. John Wesley Powell
1835-1902

Powell was born in New York State and moved with his family to Illinois in 1851. He attended Illinois College in Jacksonville, and later Oberlin College, where he studied botany and natural sciences. As war approached, he involved himself in a program of self-study, to learn military engineering. In 1861, he joined the 20th Illinois Volunteer Infantry.

The 20th Illinois was stationed in Cape Girardeau, Missouri, in July 1861. Powell, then a sergeant, designed and oversaw the construction of the ring of forts which protected the union garrison, evidence of which still exist. At Cape Girardeau, he organized Battery F, 2nd Illinois Light Artillery (composed mostly of Missouri recruits), and was promoted to Captain. While in command of the battery at Shiloh, Powell received a wound which resulted in the amputation of his right arm. He returned to service to fight at Vicksburg and Meridien, and rose to the rank of Major.

Powell achieved his greatest fame for the expedition he led in 1869, down the Colorado River through the Grand Canyon. He is also considered the father of the U.S. Geological Survey, and served as its director for 23 years. Following his death in 1902, he was buried at Arlington National Cemetery.

To reach Tour Stop 15:

Walk down Themis toward the river, until you reach Water Street. On your right find the Port Cape Girardeau Restaurant.

to meet Prentiss, where he expected Prentiss would halt his command. As Grant moved north along Water Street, he noticed a column of Union cavalry moving south along Spanish. He doubled back to where you are now, where he came upon Prentiss, who had proceeded to Cape Girardeau despite orders. A dispute, which had first surfaced in Ironton, was in progress as to who was the senior brigadier. Prentiss argued the point when the two met here. Grant did not argue. He issued peremptory orders to Prentiss to countermarch his regiments back to Jackson. Prentiss offered his resignation, which Grant refused. Prentiss placed himself under arrest and went to St. Louis. Still, he took his command back to Jackson. Grant remembered Prentiss kindly in his Memoirs. Seven months after the men met here, nearly to the day, Prentiss saved Grant's army in the Hornet's Nest at Shiloh.

Tour Stop 15

GRANT'S HEADQUARTERS in Cape Girardeau is Tour Stop 15. Walk down Themis toward the river, until you reach Water Street. On your right find the Port Cape Girardeau Restaurant. Grant commandeered this 1830's building, which became his headquarters in southeast Missouri.

However, Grant commanded at Cape Girardeau for only a few days. He moved his headquarters to Cairo, Illinois on September 4, 1861. By September 7, Grant had taken Paducah, Kentucky. Grant's Civil War career was in high gear.

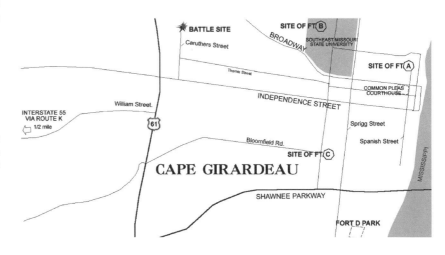

Tour Stop 16

This is Cape Girardeau's FORT D. It is the only one still existing of four Civil War forts (A, B, C and D) that once defended the city. On orders of Gen. John C. Fremont, construction of these defensive works got underway in July, 1861, at a time when Cape Girardeau was the front line of Union-controlled territory in the Trans-Mississippi. The construction of Fort D was the first such project of a young sergeant and self-taught engineer from Jacksonville, Illinois, John Wesley Powell.

To reach Tour Stop 16:

From the Port Cape building, drive south on Water Street four blocks, to William Street (Rte. 34). Turn right here. Proceed four blocks west, to the intersection of South Sprigg Street, and turn left (south) here. Drive 1.1 miles south on Sprigg, until you reach Locust Street. Turn left here. In a block and a half, you will come to a park which is Tour Stop 16.

ILLINOIS INTERLUDE

To reach the next Tour Stop you will drive across the Mississippi River on the new Emerson Bridge and spend some time driving in Illinois. You should realize that Southern Illinois is notorious for strict enforcement of posted speed limits. Cairo has some wonderful Civil War history, so the trip is worth it. Consult a map, and drive south on Illinois Route 3 from Cape Girardeau until you reach an attraction south of Cairo, right at the confluence of the Mississippi and Ohio Rivers (Fort Defiance). Driving instructions resume at the entrance of Fort Defiance.

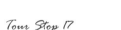

You are at the site of a pre-war rail center and the town of BIRD'S POINT, Grant's beachhead in Missouri while he commanded at Cairo. This was the eastern terminus of the Cairo & Fulton Railroad. Its tracks extended about to the spot where you are standing, and a town grew up as a result. Flooding and levee-building have destroyed all remnants of the town, and fortifications built on Grant's orders.

It is important to understand the rail transportation network in and around Cairo in 1861. In 1856, the Illinois Central Railroad completed its main line from northern Illinois to a terminus at Cairo. During the same time, the Mobile & Ohio was building a road from Mobile, Alabama northward. Ultimately, these lines would join to create the Illinois Gulf Central, but in 1861 railroad

Directions to Tour Stop 17 are noted on the following page.

To reach Tour Stop 17:

Upon leaving the parking lot of Fort Defiance in Cairo, drive south for 1.9 miles, across the Mississippi Bridge to an unmarked road on your right. This is the first right you can take once you are on the Missouri side of the bridge.

As soon as you turn into the unmarked road, look to your right and pull into the gravel drive that rises over the levee at this point. Stop right here and walk to the top of the levee to see the next tour stop.

To reach Tour Stop 18:

Continue your trip by returning first to U.S. Highways 60 and 62, and turn right. Proceed southwest for 5.2 miles to the town of Wilson City. At this point turn south on Missouri Route 77. Stay on 77 for 10.6 miles, until the road intersects with Missouri Rte. 80. Turn left here. Head east for 5.9 miles and look for a Missouri State Parks marker at the point of an intersection. This is Tour Stop 18.

builders were not up to the challenge of bridging the Ohio River. So, the Mobile & Ohio terminated on the banks of the Mississippi at the town of Columbus, Kentucky, about 15 miles south of Cairo. Passengers and freight were ferried between these points.

In view of the railroads converging on the east side of the River, Missouri promoters incorporated the Cairo & Fulton Railroad in 1853. By 1860, they had completed 30 miles of the line, extending west from its eastern terminus at Bird's Point. At the same time, plans were underway to build a branch line from Charleston, Missouri (about 11 miles west of here) to a point opposite Columbus. Construction of this branch line began just as war broke out. In this way, rail commerce from Missouri's interior could move north by way of the connection at Cairo, or south through Columbus.

Tour Stop 18

Tour Stop 18 is the BATTLE OF BELMONT site. You will locate the state marker by continuing on Route 80 nearly to the point where you reach the river. The marker gives an excellent description of the battle. Due to the wooded nature of the area, it is hard to conceptualize the entire scene and the momentous nature of the events that unfolded here on November 7, 1861. Here, General Ulysses Grant commanded troops in battle for the first time in his Civil War career.

Belmont was a small settlement in 1861, but due to the proximity of the terminus of the Mobile & Ohio, across the River, plans were underway to make it a center of commerce - the branch line of the railroad connecting to Charleston. You will notice remnants of the abandoned railroad grade around the area. The branch line was completed after the War. In November, 1861, workmen had just begun to grade the road, at a point 1/2 mile west of where you are standing, and the railroad grade is the one and only landmark remaining from the time of the battle. Kentucky has a state park across the River, that preserves the Confederate entrenchments at Columbus, but it takes a drive of 50 miles, back up to Cairo and down through Kentucky, to get there.

Part II - Westbound

Tour Stop 19

This bayou is probably a remnant of BISSELL'S CANAL. You have now entered the locale of the campaign for Island Number 10. The map that follows will give you an idea of the physical features in the area, particularly the great bends of the Mississippi at this point. This was the reason for Bissell's Canal, as will be explained.

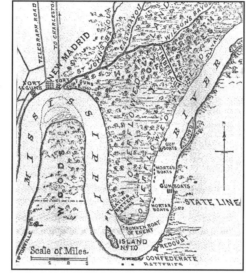

By March, 1862, the powerful fleet of Eads ironclads built at Carondelet and at Mound City, Illinois, were on line, but neither the gun ships, nor troop transports, could reach Pope at New Madrid unless they could pass the batteries at Island No. 10. About March 20, Pope's men discovered that a tributary of St. John's Bayou, known as Wilson's Bayou, nearly reached the River east of the town. Pope directed that a canal be dug through the swamps to connect the River and Bayou. In 19 days, the men of the Engineer Regiment of the West, under the command of Col. Josiah Bissell, completed this canal, having to invent a means of cutting large cypress trees below the water line. The canal was not deep enough to accommodate the gunboats, but Pope was able to use it to get his transports to New Madrid without passing Island No. 10. A week later, after the *USS Carondelet* ran the batteries at Island No. 10, Pope had what he needed to force a surrender of the island bastion.

The Federals tried the technique employed by Bissell at New Madrid several times during the war, notably in front of Vicksburg and at Yazoo Pass. The first try, Bissell's, was the only one to achieve even a limited success.

Cutting Bissell's Canal, from "Battles and Leaders of the Civil War."

To reach Tour Stop 19

Return via Route 80 to Route 77, and turn left (south). Proceed south for exactly 12 miles, to the intersection of Rte. 102. Turn right here. Head west on 102 to the point where it ends, in 2.1 miles. Here, turn left (Rte. A) and proceed .6 mile to another "T". Turn right here on County Road 520, which follows the levee on the land side. After a few miles this road becomes Route WW.

There is an intersection 8.5 miles from the point you turned off Route 102 where WW turns off to the right. Continue west on WW for about 1.1 mile where the road crosses a small stream, known in these parts as a bayou. Stop on the bridge.

BRIDGE OF SIGHS

Josiah Bissell arrived in St. Louis in 1857, leaving a cloud behind him in his native Rochester, New York. Bissell's father was a contractor for the Erie Canal, and engineering was a natural choice of occupation for the young Bissell. In those days, as in the case of many professions, no particular training was required to set up shop as an engineer. Josiah Bissell did not have the benefit of formal training in the field. Nevertheless, in 1854 Bissell undertook to span the Genesee River in Rochester with a suspension bridge. Because of Bissell's worries about his design, the bridge came to be known locally as the "bridge of sighs." His design competed with a pioneering project of John Roebling at Niagara. In April, 1857, after a heavy snow, Bissell's bridge collapsed into the Genesee gorge.

Tour Stop 20

To reach Tour Stop 20:

Proceed west on Rte. WW for approximately 9 miles, where you reach an intersection within the city of New Madrid. WW turns to the right at this point, but you need to stay on the road in front of you, which here turns into Vandenvender Ave. Stay on this street for 5 or 6 blocks until you reach Main Street. Turn Right. Go north for 4 blocks to Dawson Rd., and turn right. In one block, turn right into the parking area. The Visitors Center is across the street and is Tour Stop 20.

This is a Missouri State Parks facility, the HUNTER-DAWSON HOUSE State Historic Site. Built in 1859 by a prominent New Madrid merchant, who died just before the house was completed, the house provides a fascinating glimpse into "Southern" Missouri in the Civil War era. The house is believed to have served as John Pope's headquarters during the siege of New Madrid, discussed below.

Tour Stop 21

To reach Tour Stop 21:

Return to Main Street, turn south (left) and drive into downtown New Madrid. When you reach the levee, on the river at the foot of Main Street, you will see Tour Stop 21 on your left.

The NEW MADRID HISTORICAL MUSEUM has an excellent collection of Civil War exhibits and artifacts, and it may be the only place where the Island No. 10 campaign is a featured theme. The precursor to that campaign, the siege and occupation of New Madrid itself, is also represented in the museum exhibits.

Tour Stop 22

This is the site of FORT THOMPSON. This earthwork was completed by Confederate occupiers of New Madrid in February, 1862, and named for M. Jeff Thompson. Fort Thompson became the key point for the defense of New Madrid when Pope moved south from Sikeston at the start of his Island No. 10 campaign.

Pope's forces arrived on the northern edge of town on March 3, 1862, having confronted terrible weather but little opposition on the march from Sikeston. The Confederate defenders included troops from Tennessee, Arkansas, Louisiana and Alabama, supported by gunboats moored on both sides of town. These troops were drawn mostly from Columbus, Kentucky, as that strong point was being disassembled after being isolated by Grant's victory at Ft. Donelson.

Pope's forces entrenched about ½ mile north of town, and laid siege for two weeks. The Confederate gunboats presented a formidable obstacle; because of the river's height during that season, the gunboats floated above the Mississippi's natural levee, and thus commanded the whole town. Pope estimated that the gunboats had twenty or more heavy guns trained on him, along with fourteen more from within Fort Thompson. Pope requested heavy siege cannon to deal with the situation; they arrived late on March 12, 1862 (taking the same tortuous route through Sikeston and down the old Camino Real). The next evening, having placed the guns in position, Pope began a general bombardment that did considerable damage to the Confederate gunboats. That evening, finding their position untenable, the Confederates evacuated New Madrid and fled safely south by way of the river.

The Confederate forces that evacuated New Madrid were commanded by Confederate Gen. Alexander P. Stewart. He graduated with Pope in the West Point class of 1842, and indeed was Pope's roommate for the last two years of their academy careers.

New Madrid became Pope's staging area for his move on Island No. 10, as detailed in the campaign summary for this loop.

New Madrid waterfront, 1862

To reach Tour Stop 22:

Return to Main Street and drive south to the top of the levee. Here, there is a State Parks marker that describes the Island No. 10 campaign. Drive west on the road atop the levee for about a 1/2 mile, where you can exit the levee at Capitol Boulevard. Turn right here. Drive north one block to Mott Street, and turn right. Stop in another block (just past Lewis Street) and look to your right. It is thought that Fort Thompson was in this general vicinity.

Lt. Gen. Alexander P. Stewart
1821 - 1908

Alexander Stewart was born in Tennessee. After attending and graduating from West Point, Stewart became a professor of mathematics, serving at Cumberland and Nashville Universities from 1845 until 1861. In that year, at the outset of the Civil War, he joined the Tennessee militia as a major of artillery. A rather unlikely background for the man who attained the highest rank of any Tennessean who served in the Confederate Army.

Stewart solidified a reputation as a fighting general in 1863 and 1864, while serving in the Confederate Army of Tennessee in places such as Chickamauga, Atlanta, Franklin and Nashville. After the War, Stewart was an insurance executive in St. Louis for a time. He accepted a professorship at the University of Mississippi at Oxford, and eventually became the University's President. In his later years, General Stewart lived from time to time in St. Louis with a son, which is the reason he was buried in St. Louis' Bellefontaine Cemetery when he passed away in 1908.

Drive east on Mott Street for one more block. Turn left on Old Kings Highway, go north for .9 mile to Route U (Dawson Road), and turn left. In .2 mile, turn right on U. S. Highway 61, and head north to the I-55 exit, 2.5 miles. Continue past I-55, and drive straight north for 15.9 miles, to the intersection of U. S. 61 and Kingshighway in Sikeston. Turn left on Kingshighway. Drive north 1 mile to Malone Street, in the heart of Sikeston, then turn left. The next Tour Stop is in two blocks on your right.

Stop 23 is the SIKESTON DEPOT MUSEUM. This art and history museum is housed in the historic Sikeston depot of the Missouri Pacific Railroad, built in 1916. An exhibit covers the Civil War in this area.

Outside of St. Louis and Kansas City, in Missouri only Sikeston sits at the junction of two or more Interstate highways. As a result, Sikeston is prospering again. The town was founded in 1860, when the Cairo & Fulton Railroad reached this far from Bird's Point. It sits on a barely discernible geologic feature known as the Sikeston Ridge, upon which the Spanish had laid out a segment of El Camino Real in the 1700s. When the C&F Railroad reached this road, it was natural that a town would spring up. As elsewhere in Missouri, railroad building halted during the Civil War, so Sikeston remained the western terminus of the Cairo & Fulton for the duration.

Ridge or no ridge, flat is the predominant feature of the landscape around here. This is Missouri's "Bootheel," a massive alluvial area that looks and feels like the Deep South. In the 1860s, massive swamps spread in almost every direction. Here is where Missouri's Swamp Fox, Jeff Thompson, earned his reputation. This Tour Loop is turning north, and for most of its northward course Thompson is a predominant figure.

In early November, 1861, Thompson's Confederate command occupied Sikeston. Grant's army ran Thompson off when he began to move towards Bloomfield, Missouri. Col. W.H.L. Wallace of Illinois drove west along the Cairo & Fulton from Grant's forward position at Charleston. His force took Sikeston, previously a major Confederate base, on November 6, 1861, then continued on to Bloomfield.

By February, 1862, Thompson had reoccupied Sikeston. He appeared with 80 horsemen just south of town - probably about where you turned on to Kingshighway - as Pope's army consolidated here on February 28, 1862. A small skirmish occurred there and Thompson retreated south. This was Sikeston's only Civil War battle. Pope repaired the railroad, and Sikeston became his base of supply for the Island No. 10 campaign.

Our Tour heads west from Sikeston, to Bloomfield, before turning north.

Tour Stop 24

The first Stop on this tour segment is the STODDARD COUNTY CIVIL WAR CEMETERY. This is a magnificent memorial dedicated to Stoddard County Southern soldiers, and some civilians, who lost their lives in the Civil War. While the cemetery does contain some graves of Civil War veterans, the memorial itself is a grouping of government-issued veteran's stones that tell where the honored soldier died, and in some cases where he is buried. The memorial presents a striking lesson in history and geography, reflecting many of the places in Missouri where our Civil War was fought, and where the men and boys of this rural county died far from home. Sadly, many died in prisons in and around St. Louis.

The site of the memorial is a spot that, according to local legend, had been the burial place of unknown Southern casualties during the War. As a result, regular burials never occurred here. This was also the site of a defensive work constructed in 1861 while Bloomfield was still controlled by Southern forces, to guard the eastern approach to the town. The main road from the east once ascended this hill.

Before you leave the cemetery, walk west from the memorial and look for a veteran's grave marker that has an oval photo attached to it, the GRAVE OF "IRISH BILL" KINGSLEY. Kingsley was a Confederate cavalryman who died in Stoddard County in 1906, aged 123. As a young man, he was a British sailor and he fought in the battle of Trafalgar in 1805.

Tour Stop 25

Tour Stop 25 is the STARS & STRIPES MUSEUM in Bloomfield. This excellent military history museum is devoted to the "Soldier's Newspaper," the Stars & Stripes. The museum, founded in 1991, has recently undergone an expansion.

The museum has only a tenuous relation to Jeff Thompson: Union troops chasing the Swamp Fox out of Bloomfield made history here, on November 9, 1861. You will recall that this was two days after Grant attacked Belmont.

To Reach Tour Stop 24:

To get to Bloomfield, proceed west on Malone Avenue, through town, and continue west on West Malone, which is Business Route 60. There is an intersection just before you reach Morehouse, with signs directing you to U.S. Highway 60. Once you reach U.S. 60, turn right and proceed west on U.S. 60 for 5.2 miles to the intersection of Route N. Turn right (north) on N, and drive north approximately 2 miles to State Route E, where you turn left. Take Rte. E 6.5 miles to the outskirts of Bloomfield. You will see a brown sign on the road announcing your arrival at Tour Stop 24, and you turn left into the cemetery soon after you see the sign. Drive to the right rear of the cemetery.

To reach Tour Stop 25:

Return to Hiway E at the entrance to the cemetery, and turn left. In .4 mile, at the bottom of the hill, you will arrive at Missouri Route 25, where you turn left. Go south 1.2 miles to the top of a hill, where you will see a helicopter and tank sitting close to the road on your right. Continue past this point, and turn right at the top of the hill, which is also the entrance to a Missouri veterans cemetery.

As previously noted, Grant from his headquarters in Cairo sent three columns of infantry to neutralize Bloomfield. The middle column was commanded by Col. Richard Oglesby of Illinois. This column, consisting of the 8th, 18th and 29th Illinois regiments, left Commerce, Missouri, on the Mississippi on November 5. Oglesby's regiments, which arrived in Bloomfield on the 8th, had in their enlisted ranks a number of newspaper men, printers, publishers and editors. The newspapermen found the offices of the Bloomfield Herald abandoned by its pro-Southern owner, who had fled with Thompson. The next morning, the federals occupying Bloomfield awoke in their camp to find they had a new camp paper, which its publishers had dubbed Stars & Stripes.

The museum has an original copy of the paper's November 9, 1861 edition, and exhibits devoted to the history of this great publication, through the world wars, Viet Nam and up to the present.

CROWLEY'S RIDGE

As you drove west from Sikeston, in this landscape that is otherwise low and flat, a hill rose up to meet you. Crowley's Ridge is a geologic feature that is the only one of its kind in North America. At one time, many millions of years ago, the Mississippi flowed on the west side of this line of hills, and the Ohio River flowed on the east. This feature was left intact while the rivers laid down alluvial plains on either side. When the Mississippi changed course to join the Ohio further north, backwaters remained and created the huge swamps that typified this area in the 1860s. Because the ridge rose above the swamps, it was a highway for military traffic throughout the Civil War.

Crowley's Ridge begins just south of Cape Girardeau, and it extends south for a total of 220 miles, joining the Mississippi at Helena, Arkansas. It is broken by streams in only a few places. Situated at the very end of this ridge, if you follow it to Helena, is the grave of Confederate icon Major General Patrick Cleburne.

The ridge is pronounced "Kro-lee."

Part III - Northbound

Tour Stop 26

This is the approximate site of CAMP SPRING HILL, which was Thompson's recruiting base and headquarters in the early days of the War. When the Missouri State Guard was organized in May, 1861, Thompson was appointed commander of the First Military District, which encompassed generally all of southeast Missouri.

Thompson's cavalry, called "dragoons" (a term applied to mounted infantry carrying carbines), stepped off from Camp Spring Hill on October 12, 1861, headed north. His force, about 500 strong, included some Mississippi troopers. Thompson's second in command, Col. Adin B. Lowe, stayed behind with the infantry, while it continued to equip. He was later to move on Fredericktown with his force of 2500 men.

To reach Tour Stop 26:

From the museum entrance, return to Highway 25, and turn left (north). From the junction of Highway E, continue north for 10.5 miles, to the intersection of Missouri Route 91. Turn right on 91, then head east for 2.7 miles, to the intersection of County Road 317. Stop at the entrance of this gravel road for Tour Stop 26.

Tour Stop 27

This is the BOLLINGER COUNTY MUSEUM OF NATURAL HISTORY. There is a major deposit of dinosaur fossils here in Bollinger County, and the museum was established to display them. It has a viewing room, where visitors can watch as museum workers process and preserve the bones. The museum also a small collection of Civil War artifacts.

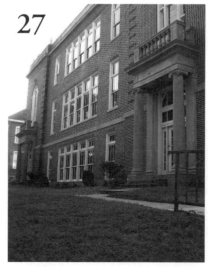

Marble Hill was known as Dallas at the time of the Civil War. Its importance derived from its location on the old Nacogdoches trail to Texas, which is now State Highway 34. Highway 34 continues east to Jackson.

A Union brigade commanded by Col. J. B. Plummer came west on Highway 34 from Cape Girardeau, and camped here on October 20, 1861. They would move the next morning on Fredericktown, by your route of travel.

To reach Tour Stop 27:

Retrace your route back to Highway 25. Turn right (north). In about 5.5 miles, you will arrive at the town of Advance, where Route 25 turns to the east. Do not remain on Route 25, but turn left at the intersection where the Rhodes gas station is located. Three blocks to the left, you will turn right on Oak Street, following the signs for State Route 91. Drive north 15.5 miles to Main Street in the town of Lutesville (this road becomes State Route 51 part way to Lutesville, but this is imperceptible to northbound travelers). 15.5 miles since you turned on Oak Street, turn right on Main (which continues to be Route 51), and drive 1/2 mile to an intersection of State Route 34. Continue straight ahead here. The first road on your left, east of this intersection, is Mayfield Drive. Turn left and drive to the top of the hill.

To reach Tour Stop 28:

Return to the main crossroads in Marble Hill (Highways 51 and 34) and turn right (north) on State Highway 51. Proceed north on Highway 51 for 10.1 miles, then turn left on State Route OO. Take OO west for 1.5 miles, the turn right on County Road 846. Drive west and north on this road for 1.6 miles, and then left. This road continues to be CR 846. Drive west for about 3.5 miles into the village of Marquand. Turn left on Route A (Morley Street). Route A turns sharply right at an intersection just west of Marquand.

Continue north on Route A from this point for a distance of 7.2 miles to an intersection, County Road 229, and turn right here. Go north for 1.3 miles, then bear left on to County Road 203. Take 203 for about 4 miles, to S. Mine la Motte Street in Fredericktown. Turn left on Mine la Motte, drive toward town for .3 miles and turn left on John Holt Drive. Proceed west for .2 mile to the entrance to Christian Cemetery. Turn left into the cemetery and drive to the area of the flagpole. Turn right after this road has bent to the left at the pole, taking note of the gravel drive that enters just after you have turned right. Tour Stop 28 is anywhere at the fence line at the very south end of the cemetery where you can get a view through the trees.

This valley is the site of the BATTLE OF FREDERICK-TOWN, on October 21, 1861.

At this time, Grant maintained his headquarters at Cairo. Jeff Thompson's dragoons had completed their raid far to the north, to the Big River bridge. Thompson, on his return trip, drove off a small federal garrison at Fredericktown on October 17, 1861. On that day, Thompson's infantry joined him after a long march from Camp Spring Hill. Thompson's brief occupation of Fredericktown created a gap in Grant's defense line, and so Grant sent troops from Ironton to the west, and from Cape Girardeau to the east, to close the gap. Learning of these Union movements, Thompson evacuated Fredericktown, moving 10 miles to the south. Because he did not want to end his raid without a battle, Thompson then marched back north and posted his artillery and troops on the hill to your south, ready to trap the federals now in Fredericktown.

On October 21, Adin Lowe, with about 1100 men of Thompson's infantry, advanced into the valley in front of you, and took cover behind a rail fence. Apparently they planned to fire on the federals' flank as they marched in pursuit of Thompson, but Plummer's men fanned out along this ridge when they discovered that Thompson was nearby. This ridge was wooded then, and your view through the trees is not unlike the view of the men of Company F of the 17th Illinois Infantry, which formed in line somewhere near this spot. The 17th had the task of feeling out the State Guard's defenses, and it marched down into the valley unaware of the presence of Lowe's force.

The State Guard poured fire into the ranks of the 17th, and it is said that the first man wounded was a private in Company F, James C. Earp.

Lowe's position was now disclosed, and the left side of the Union line, posted here and to your left, pummeled his troops with rifle and cannon fire. Lowe remained in the valley, as the entire Union line advanced on him. Now it was time for the State Guard to run for their lives, and they did, but not before Colonel Lowe took a bullet in the head that killed him instantly.

This site was also likely the campground for some 12,000 to 13,000 Confederate troops that consolidated here before moving on Pilot Knob during Price's 1864 Expedition.

Tour Stop 29

Tour Stop 29 is on the GREENVILLE ROAD, now Business Route 67. This is the approximate location of battery B of the 1st Illinois Light Artillery. This was the center of the Union line in the battle of Fredericktown. The discharge of one of the guns placed here opened the battle. As you face the valley, on your right Plummer had posted his 20th Illinois, and regiments he had "borrowed" from Col. William P. Carlin's brigade, the 21st and 33rd Illinois, and on the right flank, the 1st Indiana Cavalry. More about Carlin below. After Lowe's forces retreated on the left, the action shifted to the right, and after a battle of 2 1/2 hours the Indiana cavalry attacked across the valley and broke Thompson's grip on the hills across the way. The battle came to an end as Thompson retreated south on the Greenville Road, at a point about .6 mile south of here. Thompson put a cannon and some infantry in the middle of the road. The Indiana cavalry smashed into it. Major John Gavitt was killed in the charge.

Tour Stop 30

Tour Stop 30 is CARLIN'S HEADQUARTERS. This building, now a private home, was occupied by Col. William Carlin of Illinois during most of the Battle of Fredericktown.

Carlin led a brigade of infantry that was stationed at Ironton, and Grant ordered him to move on Fredericktown. Carlin arrived from the west about 8:00 a.m. on the morning of October 21. Finding that Thompson had evacuated the place, Carlin went to bed in this house. He was sick, according to his official report. Meanwhile, the 3,000 troops he brought with him roamed about town.

To reach Tour Stop 29:

Return to the gravel road near the flagpole, and turn left. Drive west on this road about 150 years and stop at the edge of Business Route 67.

James Cooksey Earp
1841 - 1926

The oldest of the Earp brothers was born in Kentucky in 1841, before the family moved to Monmouth, Illinois. In 1861, he enlisted in the 17th Illinois Infantry, and soon found himself in Missouri.

He was shot through the right shoulder at the October 21, 1861 Battle of Fredericktown, losing much of the use of his arm. Earp was discharged from the army. His wound disabled him for the rest of his life. James was a gambler, and saloon owner in Tombstone when his brothers made their mark on history. One can only presume that he was not at the OK Corral because of the wound he received in Fredericktown. James died in Los Angeles in 1926 and is buried in the family plot in San Bernadino.

To reach Tour Stop 30:

Turn right on Business Route 67. Drive north into town, for .8 mile, stopping in front of a two story brick structure at the southeast corner of Main and College Streets.

Plummer's brigade, probably 3500 strong, was ordered to the relief of Carlin, and made good time westward from Cape Girardeau. Carlin approached from the south so as to cut off Thompson's retreat, but - and here begins the sort of comic/tragic story that often typified early Civil War battles - Plummer sent a courier towards Carlin to advise him of his whereabouts. Thompson captured the courier, and knew that the two columns (together outnumbering him 2 to 1) were converging on his position at Fredericktown. This is why he evacuated the town after first occupying it. Thompson planned to attack one of the columns before they could form a junction. Had he launched his attack at 8:00 a.m. the battle might have turned out quite differently. But he didn't.

Plummer arrived at Fredericktown early in the morning of October 21. He conferred with Carlin, just long enough for Carlin to claim that he outranked Plummer and therefore commanded the entire force. Carlin relented however, and Plummer immediately commenced a movement south. Thinking he was pursuing a fleeing Thompson, Carlin detached several of his regiments to accompany Plummer, as has been noted. Nevertheless, he retained the 38th Illinois and 8th Wisconsin regiments in town, as a "reserve." While this decision kept perhaps 1500 Union troops out of the ensuing battle, as described at Tour Stop 32 Carlin had unwittingly set the stage for history to be made.

"I would rather get that eagle than capture a whole brigade or a dozen battle flags."

Major General Sterling Price

"OLD ABE"

In World War I, the Army established an infantry division it named the 101st Division. Then after the war, the division was reconstituted as a unit of the Wisconsin national guard and headquartered in Milwaukee. The unit adopted an eagle-on-shield motif as its symbol, in recognition of the Eighth Wisconsin Regiment and its famous bird (See Tour Stop 32). When the division was called up for active duty in World War II, it retained its numeric designation. The men of the 101st were also to be groomed to take part in the developing field of airborne operations. The success of their endeavor, on the fields of Normandy and in every American conflict since, is legendary. By accident, it seems, the division's heritage and its symbol suited its new role perfectly.

The "Screaming Eagles" trace their nickname to that day in Fredericktown, long ago.

Tour Stop 31

The BATTLE OF FREDERICKTOWN CIVIL WAR MUSE-UM opened its doors in 2008, and is the "must see" stop for travelers visiting this small historic city.

Tour Stop 32

This is Fredericktown's WAR EAGLE MONUMENT. Before construction of the current courthouse in 1899, a more modest structure stood here.

The 8th Wisconsin Volunteer Infantry was recruited and enrolled in Eau Claire, Wisconsin in September, 1861, then rushed into service soon after their arrival at Benton Barracks, St. Louis, on October 14. Perhaps because of their inexperience, the 8th formed part of Carlin's reserve, assigned to guard the army's baggage while most of their comrades marched into battle. The 8th brought with them their "pet," a young bald eagle the troops named "Old Abe." They outfitted him with a perch, and assigned a bearer to carry him in parades. Close to the action in Fredericktown, Abe's handler tethered him to the roof of the old courthouse to keep him out of harm's way. When the sounds of battle reached here, Old Abe seemed energized by the action and let loose a barrage of screeches. After this, the 8th Wisconsin developed into a splendid fighting unit, and carried Old Abe into battle. He fought in at least 37 battles, was wounded twice, and after the War returned to Wisconsin a full-fledged hero. Old Abe lived for years in a special room built for him in the basement of the Wisconsin Capitol, but he died after a fire in the building in 1881. The Capitol later burned down, and Old Abe's stuffed carcass burned up in the fire. To this day, however, a bronze replica of the famous bird oversees the workings of the Wisconsin legislature.

To reach Tour Stop 31:

Drive north into the next block, and park the car. The next two Stops are within walking distance. Tour Stop 31 is an old home on your left, at 156 South Main Street.

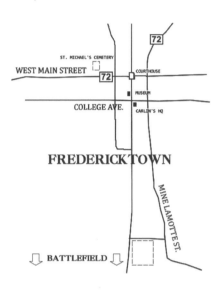

To reach Tour Stop 32:

Walk north to the imposing courthouse. Tour Stop 32 is at the southeast corner of the courthouse.

To reach Tour Stop 33:

Loop around the courthouse and proceed west on West Main, proceeding 2 blocks to St. Michael's Church, on your right. Park in the lot and walk to the cemetery at the rear of the church building. The next site is in the far right corner of the cemetery.

Tour Stop 33

A large grave monument here marks the GRAVE OF COL. ADIN LOWE. A prominent settler of Doniphan in Ripley County, to the south, Lowe had only a brief time to prove that he had the makings of a soldier, which he did, down in the valley below Fredericktown.

Lowe's story has a postscript: As Price began his 1864 Expedition, a detachment of the hated and brutal 3rd Missouri Militia Cavalry

was completing a mission to destroy the town of Doniphan. They spared only one house, which was the house of Adin Lowe. Whether this omission was out of respect for the widow of the Southern hero of Fredericktown we will never know. Then, a guerrilla force operating in advance of Price's troops came upon the burning town, and mistaking that one surviving house as the home of a unionist, burned it to the ground. *C'est la guerre.*

The guerrillas in Doniphan were led by Sam Hildebrand of St. Francois County, about whom you will learn later.

To reach Tour Stop 34:

Go one block east of the courthouse on E. Main, and turn left on Lincoln Street (State Route 72). Proceed .8 mile to a "T", and go left on Route 00, leaving highway 72 at this point. Head north on 00 for 3.7 miles, where there is a roadside park on your left. This is Tour Stop 34.

Tour Stop 34

Tour Stop 34 has a monument, but not a Civil War monument. This is the site of MINE LA MOTTE, named for the man who discovered it in 1715, the French governor of Louisiana, Antoine de La Mothe Cadillac. As the monument notes, this is the oldest lead mine west of the Mississippi River. When it was visited by soldiers contending during our Civil War, the mine had already been in operation for over 140 years, and a substantial industrial complex had grown up nearby.

During the time Thompson's infantry occupied Fredericktown, October 18 - 20, 1861, the Southern troops came here, destroyed the works, and hauled off 18,000 pounds of lead, which Thompson delivered into the Confederate lines at New Madrid. The place suffered further damage in September, 1864, when Shelby's men came up this road on the way north to Farmington.

Tour Stop 35

To reach Tour Stop 35:

Your next stop is the courthouse, located on the site of the former ST. FRANCOIS COUNTY COURTHOUSE in use at the time of Price's Expedition in September 1864.

JO Shelby visited Farmington as part of his northward movement to support Price's attack on Pilot Knob. Shelby's men launched an unsuccessful attack on the old courthouse on September 26, 1864. They withdrew in the face of stiff resistance by a small detachment of the 47th Missouri Volunteer Infantry. Two days later, rebel horsemen appeared in force and the Union detachment in the courthouse surrendered after a brief fight.

You have now entered the realm of southeast Missouri's most famous bushwhacker, Sam Hildebrand. While the next several Tour stops divert attention to a sampling of Hildebrand lore, keep in mind that you continue to closely track the route of Thompson's 1861 raid. The Hildebrand story begins at about the same time that Thompson arrived in St. Francois County.

Hildebrand's enduring legacy in this area derives in large part from outlaw exploits after the Civil War that turned him into a "dime novel" subject. His story in many ways parallels that of Jesse James - down to the mythical faked assassination and survival in Texas to ripe old age. On the contrary, the evidence shows he died violently in 1872 at age 36 at the hands of an Illinois deputy sheriff. As Jesse James owes much to Southern revisionist literature of post-War Missouri, so too Hildebrand's legacy has profited by a book, *The Autobiography of Samuel S. Hildebrand*, sometimes referred to as his "Confessions." Hildebrand supposedly dictated the book in 1869 to Dr. Abram Keith of Big River Mills, Missouri, as he lay wounded in Dr. Keith's fruit cellar. A masterpiece of this genre, the Autobiography has recently been republished, edited and annotated by journalist and historian Kirby Ross. For the first time, the facts of Sam Hildebrand's life during the Civil War can be separated from the fiction.

On his paternal side, Hildebrand descended from a Pennsylvania Dutch family that immigrated to Missouri in the early 1800s. Sam was born in 1836 at his family home several miles north of present day Bonne Terre. Despite his "Dutch" heritage, and despite contrary protestations recorded in the Autobiography, it appears that Hildebrand and his family sided early with the Southern cause. Like many such families, the Hildebrands suffered terribly at the hands of pro-Union neighbors and militia. But no one dealt retribution more fiercely than Sam Hildebrand.

Continue north on Route OO for another 3.1 miles to Old Fredericktown Road, which is on your left. Turn left here. In 2 miles, you will enter on a more substantial road, Route DD, and follow this for 1/2 mile. DD then turns sharply right, but you continue straight ahead to stay on Old Fredericktown Road. You will stay on this road for another 8.4 miles (being careful to bear left at a cross road in about 5 miles), arriving in Farmington at Route H. Turn right here, and proceed north for about 13 blocks to Liberty Street. Turn left, drive two blocks to the courthouse.

He lived in northern Arkansas during the latter part of the Civil War, and with a small band of guerillas repeatedly visited his old haunts in St. Francois County, including Farmington. A memorable visit occurred on June 26, 1864, when the band "went into Farmington to see the sights and to get a bottle of good old 'tangle-foot'," and then kidnapped and murdered three men.

Tour Stop 36

Tour Stop 36 is the MISSOURI MINES STATE HISTORIC SITE. This state facility opened in 1980 on property donated by the St. Joseph Lead Company after the company shut down its operations in the "Old Lead Belt" and moved them 35 miles west of here.

36

The site contains an excellent museum housed in the works of St. Joe's Federal Mine in the heart of the Old Lead Belt. The museum introduces the visitor to the history of lead mining in this region of Missouri. As you continue on the tour to the north, you will visit the original site of the St. Joe Lead mine and headquarters, the town of Bonne Terre. This hugely successful company, now known as the Doe Run Company, nearly died at birth in 1864, the year it was founded, when a series of calamities including Price's Expedition descended on Bonne Terre. St. Joe survived to become, at one point during the twentieth century, the leading lead producer in an area where 80% of the United States' lead ore was mined.

To reach Tour Stop 36:

Turn north on Washington Street, which borders the Courthouse on the east. Drive six blocks to Karsch Blvd. (Highway 32), and turn left. In about a mile and a half, this road merges into northbound U.S. Highway 67. Take the highway north 3.7 miles to the Business Route 67 exit in Park Hills, then turn left. You will still be on Highway 32 westbound at this point.

You will notice a large industrial complex on your left as you drive along Business Route 67. Exit and follow the brown signs to Tour Stop 36.

To Reach Tour Stop 37:

After you exit the State Historic Site, drive west on Highway 32 for .8 miles to Elvins Boulevard East, and here turn right. After you cross the tracks, you are immediately on Front Street in the town of Elvins. Turn right on this Street and drive about four blocks to the intersection of Mill Street. This street is unmarked, but there is a large sign for the Lead Belt Material Company. Turn left. Tour Stop 37 is a cemetery on your left.

Tour Stop 37

HILDEBRAND'S GRAVE is here in the Hampton Cemetery. To locate Hildebrand's stone, walk to the two trees shown in the photograph at left, and look to the left of the trees. Sam's grave is marked by a small, flat stone you will find in this area.

Tour Stop 38

a cemetery on your left.

The large stone house to the north is the BERRYMAN HOUSE. Dick Berryman owned or occupied the house during the Civil War years. Berryman, a boyhood friend of Sam Hildebrand, became a Major in the regular Confederate service. He may or may not have accompanied Sam on some of his forays into Missouri, but for sure he was here in September, 1864. Berryman and Hildebrand went ahead to prepare the way for Price's Expedition. According to Hildebrand they had recruited some 300 men, who were to join the Confederate host when Price reached this part of the state. The house itself is an architectural jewel, dating from 1832 and now well maintained by the present private owners.

This is what happened in this neighborhood in October, 1864, during Price's Expedition:

The Big River rises in Iron County and snakes its way through St. Francois County to join the Meramec River near St. Louis. At some point along the river north and east of here - centered southeast of present-day Bonne Terre - early American settlers founded a town, now gone, they called Big River Mills. This was a pro-Southern town where Hildebrand commonly found shelter among friends. Some of the Hildebrand/Berryman recruits may have camped near the Berryman house, as Hildebrand reports a small skirmish here. But the bulk of them congregated in Big River Mills proper. On October 5, 1864, Maj. Samuel Montgomery, commanding a detachment of the veteran 6th Missouri Union Cavalry, received word that a force of Southerners was at Big River Mills, grinding flour.

38

On October 6, Montgomery set out from Victoria on the Iron Mountain Railroad with 200 troopers. Heading southwest, he learned that Hildebrand and Berryman had 300 men at Big River Mills, and he determined to attack them. He did on October 7, 1864, and claimed to have killed 21 men there.

Sam Hildebrand
1836 - 1872

Son of one of the early settlers of St Francois county, Hildebrand had his baptism of fire in 1861, when federal sympathizers captured and lynched his brother Frank. Later, federal troops shot and killed his 13 year old brother, Henry, and burned the family home. Hildebrand traveled south and was allegedly commissioned a "major" by Jeff Thompson.

Hildebrand became a notorious killer during and after the War, and the story of his life is legendary in southeast Missouri. Throughout the War, he carried old "Kill-Devil," his musket, and when it was recovered after his death, it allegedly had 80 notches carved in its stock. In 1872, Hildebrand was shot dead in a gunfight in the town of Pinckneyville, Illinois. His body was returned to St. Francois County and buried in Hampton Cemebary in Elvins, just southwest of Park Hills.

To reach Tour Stop 38:

Leave Hampton Cemetery, Front Street and turn left. Drive north for approximately 1.1 mile, then turn left on Route Z (W. Main Street). Drive a mile to the northwest, where Main Street joins State Highway 8, and turn left here. Drive west for 1.4 miles to the town of Gumbo, and turn left at the road here where you see the Gumbo Assembly of God Church. You will go south a block on this road, then turn left on the old route 8. The next Stop is very visible on the left in less than .2 mile.

To Reach Tour Stop 39

Continue east on old route 8, which will rejoin the new highway. Turn right here and then retrace your trip back to the place where Main Street met Highway 8. Continue straight on when you reach this intersection, and in another .6 miles you will reach Business Route 67 (Highway 8 also continues to the left). Turn left. In approximately 2.1 miles you will reach U.S. Highway 67. Go straight, under the highway, and drive east for .8 mile. There is a cemetery on your right, and the Stop is up towards the back of this cemetery.

To reach Tour Stop 40:

Return to U.S. Highway 67, and take the ramp on to the highway north-bound. Go north 3.6 miles to the State Highway 47 exit at Bonne Terre. Go left on 47 and drive into the center of town, .7 mile, to the point where Route 47 turns sharply left (at Allen Street). You will find Tour Stop 40 directly in front of you at this point.

Tour Stop 39

You have located the THOMAS HAILE GRAVE, which bears his date of death: October 7, 1864. The evidence suggests that part of Montgomery's force crossed Flat River at the place then known as the Herod ford (where the bridge you crossed is now located), and that several Confederates were killed at the crossing. The Haile family home stood down the Flat River valley, near where it joins the Big River about a ¼ mile to the north. The main part of Big River Mills was north of the Big River at this point, but the Haile property on the south side was considered part of the town.

Thomas Haile was 73 years old, a former judge, and a veteran of the War of 1812. He was standing on his porch when the Union cavalry arrived, and he suffered the fate of more than one Confederate sympathizer. The federals shot him dead. He was suspected of providing aid and comfort to Sam Hildebrand, and no doubt he was guilty of this offense. In August, 1864, Union militia had killed his son, Irvin Haile, for the same crime.

Tour Stop 40

Tour Stop 40, THE BONNE TERRE MINE, is a modern tourist attraction. This is the site of the original St. Joseph Lead Company mine. Over the course of a century the mine reached massive proportions, running under the whole town to a depth of 350 feet. When the mine was abandoned in the early 1960s, its lower reaches filled with crystal-clear water, and the site is now a mecca for scuba divers. It is billed as the world's largest underground lake. Walking and boat tours are available to non-divers, and provide a glimpse of the early days of mining operations.

During Price's 1864 Expedition, a band of guerrillas cooperating with Price seized the St. Joe Mine in Bonne Terre, as Price's forces moved north. According to a report received by St. Joseph Lead's Board of Directors in 1865, the incursion kept the mine in Bonne Terre out of operation for two months. It is not clear when this occurred, or whether it is true that the Confederates operated the mine for a time in 1864.

In Hildebrand's autobiography, he claims to have been in Bonne Terre on October 7, 1864 and that he met up there with Montgomery's cavalry, en route to Big River Mills. Hildebrand pretended to be a Union sympathizer and trotted along with the Union troopers for a while to cover his identity. Or so he says.

Tour Stop 41

You are near the site of the BIG RIVER BRIDGE. You can make out the modern bridge to the east, through the trees, but you cannot get closer to the old Big River Bridge, the objective of Thompson's Big River campaign in 1861.

On October 15, 1861, Thompson's dragoons reached this spot from the south. He was two days ahead of the schedule he had set for himself. The bridge was defended by 3 companies of the 33rd Illinois Volunteer Infantry, the so-called "Teacher's Regiment" or "Brains Regiment." The regiment was organized by teachers and students of the Illinois Normal School (now Illinois State University at Bloomington). A number of students and graduates of Knox College in Galesburg also enrolled, hence the nicknames. This was their first post in the war zone, and it would be their first taste of combat.

Thompson sent part of his force (a portion of his Second Regiment Dragoons) clear around the bridge, approaching from the east side of the Big River, and circling around from the north, probably on the high ground along Klondike Road. Thompson's forces attacked a stone fortress which stood at the top of the bluff to your left. The 33rd Illinois soon surrendered. Sgt. George Foster of the 33rd was killed in action, the first man of this regiment lost to combat wounds in the War. Thompson lost 2 killed and several wounded. He burned the bridge to the ground.

To reach Tour Stop 41:

Return to Route 47, and turn left. In about two blocks, turn right on Division Street, which is also County Road E. Set your odometer here. Drive north on Rte. E (bearing left north of town) for a total of 10.2 miles to Klondike Road, which intersects E at this point from the left. Turn left on Klondike. Proceed northwest for 3.4 miles, where this road intersects with Knorpp Road. Turn left, and proceed about 1.3 miles, to the small town of Vineland. Continue straight ahead when you reach the old store building, and turn left at Wilson Hollow Road, which is about .2 miles further on this road. Drive south for 1.4 miles, where you will reach a dead end. Look for a granite monument off to your left.

To reach Tour Stop 42:

Retrace your route back up Wilson Hollow Road. Bear left at two intersections in Vineland, then in .2 miles you will arrive at State Highway 21. Turn right on Highway 21, and drive north for 3.2 miles, to Vineland School Road. Turn right. This road dead ends in a mile and a half, at Main Street in Desoto. Turn left on Main Street, then travel north for about .8 mile to a street that affords a crossing of the railroad tracks. Tour Stop 42 is the large frame building that is immediately in your front.

This building was once THE DESOTO HOUSE. The most historic building in Desoto is now known as the Arlington House Bed & Breakfast. Built in 1860 as a hotel, the structure has witnessed nearly the entire history of the town. It is said that U.S. Grant visited here in 1861, but all we know for sure is that he passed through Desoto several times on his way to and from his post at Ironton, down the line of the Iron Mountain Railroad. More certain is the claim that Jefferson Davis became a guest at the Desoto House in September, 1875. The Confederate ex-President spoke at an agricultural fair here on September 8 of that year, during a speaking tour of the western states.

Desoto's Civil War history began just about the time the Civil War began. General Lyon, in command in St. Louis, was disturbed by secessionist activities here and in Potosi (about 20 miles to the southwest) Lyon sent a small force to these places. They arrested a few people, and in Desoto, hauled down a secessionist flag. This was on May 16, 1861. No casualties were reported, but this small campaign preceded all of the land engagements in the eastern United States.

Federal troops occupied Desoto throughout the War, except for one day late in September, 1864. During Price's Expedition, Desoto served as the principal federal advance position for the defense of St. Louis. The Battle of Pilot Knob unfolded on September 26, 1864, along the railroad to the south. A division of veteran federals under General A. J. Smith awaited developments here with orders to interpose itself between the Confederate column and St. Louis. However, Smith withdrew to a point closer to St. Louis on September 28. As 5,000 federals prepared to leave Desoto they assembled in front of the hotel to witness the hanging of a Confederate prisoner from Pilot Knob. The prisoner had slashed several members of his guard while being transported here.

The next day, a small force of Confederates entered the abandoned town. They torched the Desoto House, but they extinguished the flames (so the story goes) when a young lady named Mary Jelkyl pleaded to save it. The Confederates did destroy a railroad bridge north of town, and soon left to join Price's main column, moving north and west.

City & Swamps

Tour Stop 43

This valley was the RICHWOODS CAMP of Price's Army. Two of Price's divisions – probably 7,000 men in all – fought at Pilot Knob on September 26 and 27, 1864 and then moved north. These divisions camped at Richwoods on the night of September 30, 1864, and as you might imagine they filled the entire area within your view.

By October 1, 1864, Price lost any opportunity he may have had to capture St. Louis. Price probably decided to abandon this objective even before the Battle of Pilot Knob, because he had learned that the Union had brought A.J. Smith's Army Corps into position south of St. Louis, blocking his direct route.

From Richwoods, Price detached a brigade that moved on Pacific, Missouri. On October 1, this brigade skirmished with a Union detachment, the only Civil War engagement to occur in St. Louis County. This engagement is discussed at Stops 49 and 50.

Toussaint Charbonneau, guide for Lewis & Clark and husband of Sacagawea, is buried in the cemetery of St. Stephen's.

Tour Stop 44

This is the location of THE SKIRMISH AT VITT'S MILL on October 1, 1864. The mill building survives, as does the gray house, purportedly used as a hospital for Union casualties. Marmaduke's and Shelby's divisions of Sterling Price's army approached Union from the south, having departed the morning of October 1 from their camp at Richwoods. A few hundred Union militia received the alarm and rushed to Union, where they fortified the small hill on which Vitt's Mill stands.

The brigade of Gen. John B. Clark, Jr. of Marmaduke's Division, led the Confederate advance. Clark dismounted most of his command about a mile south of town, but sent two regiments of mounted infantry acting as cavalry to attack the flanks of the Union position.

To Reach Tour Stop 43

Depart the hotel, cross the tracks and turn left on Main Street. Drive south about 3 blocks to Miller Street (Rte. N). Turn right. Proceed west on Rte. N, bearing right on Margaret Street, until you reach, Missouri Highway 21 in about 1.4 miles. Cross Highway 21, and this road becomes Route H. Drive west on Rte. H for 14.5 miles to Missouri Highway 47, and cross 47 and drive through the town of Richwoods. You will arrive at St. Stephens Church about a mile and 1/2 after crossing Highway 47. Pull in to the Church, and park in the rear near the cemetery.

To reach Tour Stop 44:

Return to Highway 47 and turn left. Drive north for 18.6 miles to St. Clair, where State Highway 47 bears to the right and becomes Commercial Avenue. Go north on 47 through town, bearing left in about .9 mile. You will reach I-44 in another 1/2 mile. Cross the Interstate and continue north on Highway 47 for 5.7 miles, where Highway 47 intersects with State Route 100, at Union. Turn left here, and then take the second right, which is the continuation of Highway 47.

(Continued on next page)

Turn left at the first opportunity, which is East Main Street. Drive west two blocks on Main to Maple Street and turn right. One block to the north, turn right on E. State Street. Tour Stop 44 is the brick mill building that sits at the east end of State Street. As you approach the building, note the gray brick home on your left. Pull over in the vicinity of the mill building.

To reach Tour Stop 45:

Continue on State Street, which connects with Main Street (your route of entry). Return to Highway 47 on Main, and turn left. In .1 mile, turn right on Old Country Farm Road, and be prepared to make an immediate left on "Rock Road." Pause here, as this is the old road to St. Louis and the point where Lawther severed the road. Vitt's Mill is visible through the trees to the west.

Drive north on Rock Road, past the railroad overpass, and in 1/2 mile bear right on to Route V. Continue north on Route V for 1.9 miles, and turn left at Clearview Road. This is the intersection of the old St. Louis Road, and the South Point Road (now Clearview); Cabell's troops passed this point on October 2, 1864, heading west to Union after the battle at Pacific.

Bear right in .2 mile, and then continue north on this road for a total of 4.4 miles (the road changes names) when you will arrive at the intersection of State Highway 100. Continue straight ahead (crossing Highway 100) for another .4 mile on South Point Road, to East 5th Street, and turn right. Go east on 5th Street for .2 mile and turn left on Crystal Lane. Tour Stop 45 is any place along here where you can stop with a view of the railroad bridge.

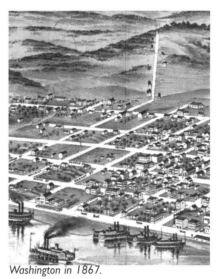

Washington in 1867.

The Confederate 10th Missouri Cavalry, commanded by Col. Robert Lawther, attacked the Union left (your left as you face the mill) and cut the St. Louis Road. Lawther's attack produced a precipitous retreat by the Union defenders. Confederate reports claim over 100 Union casualties, including 70 captured. The Confederates suffered no casualties in the fight.

Previously, on April 20, 1861, fifty Franklin County men assembled at Vitt's Mill and volunteered for service in the Union army Nathaniel Lyon was assembling in St. Louis. David Murphy, a school teacher in Union, brought these men together and became their captain. Murphy's company would be the first from outside of St. Louis to come to the aid of the beleaguered Lyon. More of this story at Tour Stop 47.

Tour Stop 45

This is the site of the town of SOUTH POINT. Now incorporated into the city of Washington, South Point was an independent community in 1864. Just south of here, about where South Point Road crossed Highway 100, Lawther's 10th Missouri camped for the night after its arrival from Union in the early morning hours of October 2, 1864. The remainder of Marmaduke's forces took a route from Union that is to the west, and Lawther joined him south of Washington to prepare for an attack. Lawther's Confederates did enter South Point on October 2, fired the depot that was here, and destroyed a railroad bridge on the site of the bridge in your front.

45

A small contingent of Union home guards defended Washington. They took to the boats rather than face Marmaduke's advancing troops. At the time, the Missouri River's course was just north of the railroad bridge, and the boats carrying the Union evacuees passed here just after dawn on October 2. Lawther's cavalry fired on the boats as they came into view, wounding one Union soldier.

Tour Stop 46

Tour Stop 46 is the JOHN B. BUSCH HOME AND BREWERY. The original part of this home was built in the 1850s by John B. Busch, one of 22 children sired by Ulrich Busch of Mainz, Germany. You passed the buildings that survive from Busch's Washington Brewery, which he founded in 1854 or 1855, down the hill next to the creek to the north.

After entering the town of Washington on October 2, Marmaduke spent only a day here. His thirsty troops found their way to the Washington Brewery and consumed as much of Busch's brew as they could. They dumped the rest into the creek. Meanwhile, the Confederates briefly occupied the Busch home. Mrs. Busch fed their officers while the men searched for the Busch treasure they believed was hidden in the home.

Busch was a lieutenant in Company L of the 54th Regiment, E.M.M. He was serving with his unit when the Confederates visited his home. In Missouri, "Busch" means beer, and vice versa, and of course you are wondering if there is a connection here. Indeed there is. John B. Busch was the older brother of Adolphus Busch of St. Louis. His descendants claim that beechwood was first used in brewing beer at John Busch's Washington Brewery.

To reach Tour Stop 46:

Return to the point where you left South Point Road. Turn right here, which is the continuation of East 5th Street. Your route to reach the next tour stop, along 5th Street, generally follows a line of entrenchments that was hastily dug by Washington's defenders as Price's army approached. Drive west on 5th Street for 2.3 miles to Jefferson Street (following Market). Turn left. In .4 mile, when you emerge from the little valley, turn right at the VFW hall on your right.

46

Part IV - Eastbound

To reach Tour Stop 47:

Tour Stop 47

Drive south on Jefferson Street for .8 mile to State Highway 100, and turn left. Stay on 100 for 11 miles, then turn left on Highway 100 just before you reach the Interstate. Drive east for 2.0 miles, crossing over I-44 once, then arriving at another I-44 exit. Turn left at the point you reach this exit, but drive across the Interstate without entering it yet. You are still following the signs for Highway 100 eastbound. After you visit Tour Stop 47, you will return to this point and enter I-44 eastbound, but first you continue to the town of Gray Summit, to a point which is 1/2 mile east on Highway 100. Stop in front of the old two story brick structure that sits at the 1/2 mile point. The point of interest here is directly in front of you, to the right of what looks like a road bridge on the route you are traveling.

This is what remains of "THE CUT" on the old Pacific Railroad. The brick building is an antebellum hotel, once called the Stites Hotel, located here because Gray Summit was an important point on the railroad. When the Pacific Railroad was originally laid out, engineers had to get from the valley of the Meramec (to the east) into the valley of the Missouri River, and found this place best suited for this purpose. When the tracks reached here, the engineers dug a cut in order to level the terrain on which the tracks ran. After the Civil War, the railroad dug a tunnel under this ridge, and abandoned the tracks over this summit.

The old right of way is discernible down the road that intersects from the right, just across the cut, and (along with the Stites Hotel) allows you to conjure up the scene on the afternoon of October 1, 1864, when Gray Summit was a bustling rail center. Price's Expedition was in full flower.

As discussed at Tour Stop 43, although Price was no longer targeting St. Louis, he still wanted to get as close to the city as he could, and so he sent Cabell's Arkansas brigade from Richwoods to Pacific. Cabell came through Gray Summit on his return trip, tearing up the tracks here and burning most of the town. Cabell then moved to Union to rejoin Price.

We are about to conclude the story of Price's 1864 Expedition in this part of the state. As you enter St. Louis, we draw your attention to the very early days of the Civil War. David Murphy of Vitt's Mill, and the long-gone tracks in Gray Summit, provide the vehicle to transport you back to that time.

The men David Murphy enrolled in Union (Tour Stop 44) were primarily of German stock, as were many of the urban volunteers then assembling in St. Louis under Nathaniel Lyon and Frank Blair to support the federal cause. On April 23, 1861, eleven days after the firing on Ft. Sumter, Murphy took his men to Washington to board a train for St. Louis. Southern sympathizers too saw the coming storm, and a group of men, bent on lending their aid to Southern partisan groups organizing in St. Louis, arrived at the Washington depot on the same day to board the same train. It seems that Murphy's plans became public, because other Southerners gathered at the depot here in Gray Summit in an unsuccessful effort to haul Murphy and his company off the train.

The train steamed east from Washington. The Union and Southern recruits had words, needless to say, but all boarded and took places in separate cars. The conductor informed Murphy of the confrontation brewing at Gray Summit. East of South Point, Murphy joined the engineer in the cab and ordered him to run straight through Gray Summit. The train came through here, barreling from your left to your right through the cut with Capt. Murphy holding a pistol at the head of a reluctant engineer.

The Franklin County contingent became Company L of a three month regiment, the First Missouri Volunteers (Union). They participated in the affair at Camp Jackson on May 10, and the expedition to DeSoto on May 16 (See Stops 42 and 54).

Tour Stop 48

Today, two railroads converge on PACIFIC, but at the time of the Civil War a single line of the Pacific Railroad ran from St. Louis to this point, where the "Southwest Branch" of the line split off and headed to Rolla. The main line continued west, through Gray Summit and on to Jefferson City and beyond. To your east is the point of the junction at the time of the Civil War, and the two lines of track you crossed reflect the two branches of the Pacific Railroad. As a result of this junction, Pacific (originally called Franklin) was a critical military resource from the beginning days of the Civil War.

Union troops first occupied Pacific in force in October, 1861, when a new Iowa regiment (the 9th Infantry) built a camp here, named for its lieutenant colonel, Francis Herron. The 26th Missouri Volunteer Regiment soon joined the Iowans patrolling the railroad. These units spent a dismal winter in Pacific, until they both shipped out in February, 1862. The 9th Iowa headed down the Southwest Branch, joined the campaign for Pea Ridge, and ultimately would gain fame as one of the hardest fighting units in the western theatre of operations. The 26th Missouri, meanwhile, joined Pope in the assault on New Madrid and Island No. 10, and later fought at Vicksburg and in Sherman's March through Georgia.

The Union established a military hospital in Pacific, probably where the Railroad Plaza is now. It was intended to receive casualties from Fremont's October, 1861, Southwest Campaign, and it did. Early in the War though, its patients came mostly from the ranks of the Iowa and Missouri troops stationed here. Ravaged by rampant measles

To reach Tour Stop 48:

Return to Interstate 44 by the route you entered town, then enter I-44 eastbound. Drive east 3.2 miles to Exit 257. Turn left on to Osage Street upon exiting the highway, then drive east for one mile to First Street in Pacific. Turn left here. Drive south for 3 blocks, to Station Plaza which is just south of the second set of tracks, and park near the Great Pacific Coffee Company, facing north if you can.

Brig. Gen. Wm. Lewis Cabell
1827-1911

William Lewis Cabell was born in Virginia in 1827. AFter graduating from West Point in 1850, Cabell served in the 7th U.S. Infantry in Indian Territory and took part in the Mormon campaign in 1858. He resigned his commission in 1861 to enter the Confederate service. He was at the First Battle of Manassas in the role of Chief Quartermaster of Beauregard's army.

Cabell went west in early 1862, first as a quartermaster, but then became a line officer. He led Texas and Arkansas troops in battles in Mississippi and Arkansas, ultimately heading a division of cavalry. He was captured during Price's Expedition, at the Battle of Mine Creek in October, 1864.

Cabell died in Dallas, Texas in 1911, having made his home there after the war. He served four terms as Mayor of Dallas, and also was U. S. Marshall for the Northern District of Texas.

To reach Tour Stop 49:

Drive north on First Street and cross Osage Street. One block north, turn left on Walnut Street and drive to the top of the bluff, to Blackburn Park.

and dysentery, Camp Herron became known as "Hell's Half Acre." By Christmas week, 1861, the Iowa and Missouri boys here were dying at the rate of one or two a day.

John Charles Fremont commanded Union forces in Missouri for a hundred days in 1861. He has received little credit for his military administration in Missouri. Two developments in the field of military medicine, however, occurred here, for which Fremont merits the lion's share of credit. He established a network of hospitals, used private resources to fund and operate them, and outfitted railroad cars to serve as mobile hospitals. The use of hospital cars began in October, 1861. They transported wounded soldiers from the front to hospitals in Jefferson City, Pacific and St. Louis. This was the first time in history that a railroad was used for this purpose.

Also in October, 1861, the Sisters of the Holy Cross of South Bend, Indiana, responded to Fremont's call for volunteers, and came to Pacific to serve as nurses at the hospital. Here, at Cairo, Illinois, and at several other locations, the Sisters from South Bend first ventured into nursing, a profession for which they are renowned today.

Tour Stop 49

Here, HUGHEY'S ARKANSAS BATTERY of Cabell's brigade posted its guns during the October 1, 1864 Battle of Pacific. Tour Stop 50 gives a more complete description of the battle, which is also mentioned in Tour Stop 43.

Brig. Gen. William L. Cabell, who later became a four-term mayor of Dallas, Texas, was an Arkansan when the Civil War broke out. Price detached Cabell's brigade, of Gen. Fagan's division, to take out infrastructure on the Pacific and Southwest Branch railroads with 8 regiments of cavalry, 1500 to 2000 men strong. Cabell performed his mission admirably. Most notably, they destroyed a substantial bridge at Moselle between St. Clair and Pacific that took the federals a month to repair. Cabell was ordered to proceed two miles east of Pacific and destroy a railroad bridge there.

49

Cabell had three or four artillery pieces, and the magnificent view you have from Blackburn Park is the same view enjoyed by the cannoneers of Capt. W. H. Hughey's battery. Look off to the east, where the road and railroad wind round the bend in front of another bluff, and you can imagine why the battery was here and the effect it had upon a Union infantry brigade when it rounded that bend.

Cabell entered the town at dawn on October 1st, from the south. His troops drove off a small militia garrison and began the work of tearing up the

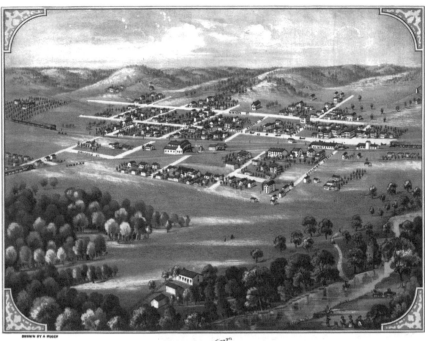

PACIFIC FRANKLIN

tracks and burning the depot. They looted and burned some of the stores in town. The Confederates had done their work by the time a Union force began an attack two miles east of town.

Tour Stop 50

The BATTLE OF PACIFIC began at this point. Here at 9:00 a.m on October 1, 1864, four veteran Union regiments disembarked from a train that brought them here from St. Louis in search of Cabell. The federal units included the 49th and 117th Illinois, the 178th New York and the 52nd Indiana, designated the 3rd Brigade of the Right Wing of the Sixteenth Army Corps. This brigade, commanded by Col. Edward H. Wolfe of Indiana, was part of the force commanded by General A. J. Smith that was in Desoto on September 28. We can pinpoint where the battle began because the battle reports show that Cabell destroyed a bridge on the railroad two miles east of Pacific, and the bridge in front of you is our only candidate. Presumably, the Union troops came by rail as far as possible - to the point of the destroyed bridge.

After disembarking from the cars at this point, the 52nd Indiana formed a line of battle on both sides of the tracks, and the 49th

To reach Tour Stop 50:

Return to Osage Street, which is Business Route 44 and historic Route 66, and turn left. Go east 2.2 miles to Dozier Crossing Road, and turn right. Cross both sets of railroad tracks and stop at Franklin Road. You need to turn around here, and stop where you have a view of Franklin Road and the bridge west of here by which the railroad crosses a small stream.

50

A young Ulysses S. Grant

Illinois and the 178th New York went into line behind the 52nd. It appears the 117th Illinois remained here in reserve. Wolfe deployed skirmishers who immediately engaged Confederate skirmishers The entire Union line began a forward movement. As the federals advanced, some soldiers of the 49th Illinois joined the skirmish line. The Union force proceeded in this fashion along the Franklin road (now Bus. Rte. 44) until rounding the bend in the road that you viewed from Blackburn Park.

When Wolfe's force came within view of the town, it confronted a force of Confederates drawn up in line of battle just to the east of the town. Hughey's artillery then began to shell the advancing line. The federals continued their advance, and entered Pacific without encountering much additional resistance. The resistance offered was no doubt intended to support a Confederate withdrawal already underway.

The battle at Franklin, (now Pacific), was really only a skirmish, to be sure. Federal reports show less than 10 casualties on the Union side, with none killed in action. The federal reports claim several dead on the Confederate side. Nevertheless, this was the only Civil War engagement to occur in St. Louis County.

There is an interesting postscript however to the action at Pacific. Two and a half months later A. J. Smith was with General Thomas at the Battle of Nashville. His Third Brigade - Wolfe's brigade - was the first to penetrate the Confederate defenses on Shy's Hill. The battle of Nashville finally broke the back of the Confederate Army of Tennessee.

Tour Stop 51

To reach Tour Stop 51:

Return to Business Route 44 and turn right. Head east on this road for about three miles, and there you will enter I-44 eastbound. Drive east for 14 miles, then take the ramp for I-270 southbound. Leave the Interstate in two miles, at Gravois Road (Highway 30), and turn left.

Look to your left once you get 3.0 miles east on Gravois, and you will see a log structure facing the road that is part of Anheuser-Busch's "Grant's Farm." The cabin was built by Ulysses Grant when he lived near here before the Civil War. The entrance to this tourist venue is off Grant Road, past the entrance to Tour Stop 51.

Continue to the bottom of the hill here, 3.2 miles since you left I-270, and turn left on Grant Road. The entrance to Stop 51 is well signed, on your right.

Tour Stop 51 is the U.S. GRANT NATIONAL HISTORIC SITE. The house preserved here is located in the suburban country estate of Grant's father-in-law, Frederick Dent, known as "White Haven." Like many West Point graduates, Grant was stationed at Jefferson Barracks in St. Louis right after he graduated in 1843, as this was the most important army post on the frontier. Also, like many others, he courted and won a Southern girl from St. Louis. He met Julia Dent at White Haven at the suggestion of Julia's brother Fred, Grant's roommate at West Point. Grant's first visit here was in the company of future Confederate General James Longstreet, a West Point acquaintance who was also a cousin of Fred Dent. Grant married Julia in 1848 at the Dent's city home. James Longstreet was a groomsman.

When Grant resigned from the Army in 1854 he came to live in St. Louis. He scratched out a living on 80 acres a little north of here, which he called "Hardscrabble Farm," and was successful in nothing except marriage before he moved to Illinois in 1860.

The visitor will find everything one expects at a National Park Service cultural site and more. The information center and museum, along with the knowledgeable staff, provide visitors a vivid picture of Grant's life and times.

Tour Stop 52

This is the GRAVE OF MAJ. ADOLPH PROSKAUER, who commanded the 12th Alabama Regiment, CSA, at the Battle of Gettysburg. Proskauer was born in Germany and lived most of his life in Mobile, Alabama. He had a distinguished Civil War career and was wounded at least four times, including at Gettysburg and Chancellorsville. He moved to St. Louis in the 1880s to engage in the cotton trade, and died in 1900. He was one of the founders of Jewish Hospital of St. Louis. A nephew, Joseph M. Proskauer, was a famous lawyer and judge in New York who gave his name to Proskauer & Rose, today one of New York's largest law firms.

The New Mt. Sinai Cemetery was established here about 1870, and is to St. Louis Jews what Bellefontaine is to Protestants and Calvary is to Catholics. Hundreds of prominent St. Louisans are laid to rest here, including playwright and novelist Fannie Hurst.

To reach Tour Stop 52:

Return to Gravois Road, and turn left. Drive east on Gravois for 2.4 miles, where the New Mt. Sinai Cemetery is on your right. Enter the cemetery and bear to the right, then take a quick left so you are driving south between the mausoleum and the reception building. Drive to the next intersection. You will be facing a stone with name Cook. Turn right. Tour Stop 52 is just 25 yards or so to your right.

To reach Tour Stop 53:

Exit the cemetery and turn right on Gravois. Drive down the hill a distance of .8 mile, and turn right on Germania Street just across the bridge. Drive east for one block, and turn left on Stolle Street. Three blocks ahead, there is an old cemetery on your left. Stop when you reach the cemetery. There is a fence here that separates the road from the cemetery, and to walk the cemetery you can drive ahead to the point where the road turns left.

To reach Tour Stop 54:

Continue ahead on Stohl Street until the road turns left and it passes through the cemetery. This road intersects with Gravois Road just ahead. Turn right on Gravois. Drive north on Gravois for 1/2 mile, and turn left on Kingshighway. Drive north on Kingshighway about 3 miles, where you will turn right on Vandeventer Avenue. In 3.3 miles, Vandeventer crosses Lindell Boulevard. Turn right on Lindell. Go east on Lindell for 1 mile, and turn right at a small street called Cardinal Avenue, which is the next turn after Compton Avenue.

Tour Stop 53

The GRAVE OF CONSTANTIN BLANDOWSKI is in the distance at the south end of the Greenwood Gardens Cemetery. Blandowski was born in Silesia, a part of Prussia that is now Poland, in 1828. He took part in the revolution that rocked the Austro Hungarian Empire, which ended unsuccessfully in 1849. He fled to the United States in 1850 and came to St. Louis via New York. In 1861, he was making his living in St. Louis as a fencing instructor. At the onset of the Civil War, Blandowski was commissioned as a Captain and company commander in Sigel's 3rd Regiment of U.S. volunteers. Blandowski was mortally wounded on May 10, 1861. He died on May 26. He was first buried on May 27, 1861. Blandowski was not buried here originally, but was re-interred here years later when a cemetery closer to town was abandoned. Blandowski was arguably the first Union officer killed in the American Civil War, but poor Constantin lingered until after his east coast counterpart, Col. Elmer Ellsworth, was shot dead in an Alexandria, Virginia hotel on May 24.

Blandowski's wounding occurred at Camp Jackson in St. Louis, which is your next Tour Stop.

Tour Stop 54

The site of CAMP JACKSON was east of the point where you crossed Grand Avenue. Where you are now could be the point where an incident turned into a disaster.

In Missouri, it is easy to get into an argument about this event. The Southern point of view asserts that State Militia (800 or 900 volunteers strong) were goin usual business, conducting a camp of drill and instru Northern view holds that the militia had taken delive ment of federal property - cannon seized from the U. Baton Rouge, Louisiana - and had designs on the A

66

Louis. Perhaps the one thing that can be said for sure is that if regular army Capt. Nathaniel Lyon had not been in St. Louis at the time, whatever happened next might have settled the debate. Lyon, however, took the most aggressive stance imaginable. On May 10, 1861 he marched about 7,000 troops to this area to take the militia into federal custody. Surrounded on all sides, the commander of the state troops had no choice but to surrender.

The Federals lined up on Olive Street under guard, intending to march their prisoners back promptly to the Arsenal. But, chance intervened. A horse kicked Lyon and he lay unconscious or incapacitated for an hour. The column of prisoners on Olive Street moved in fits and starts, or not at all, for most of this time, while a crowd of onlookers grew ever larger. We have a number of accounts of what next ensued, of course colored by who is giving the account. One first-hand account tells us that Captain Blandowski was mounted, in command of Company F of the 3rd Missouri Volunteer Regiment (more descriptively, *Die Schwarze Garde*), when he was hit with a clod of dirt thrown from the crowd. This was followed by some exclamation, perhaps in German, but in any case Blandowski's men interpreted it as an order to "Fire!". The nervous troops did fire, gunfire was returned by the crowd, and the net result was 28 civilians dead, two dead from Company F, and many wounded. Among the casualties were women and children.

A smaller and similar incident occurred in Baltimore in April, but that incident did not involve opposing military forces. Taking that small and questionable distinction into account, near this spot on May 10, 1861 there occurred the first casualties of the American Civil War.

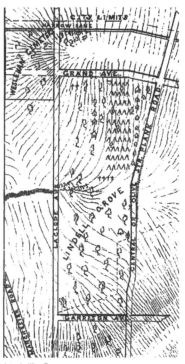

Lindell's Grove

Blandowski's memorial stone stands in Jefferson Barracks National Cemetary.

TO STAY ON THIS LOOP

Olive Boulevard, where Stop 54 is located, becomes Lindell Boulevard as you drive west. To begin the Loop at Tour Stop 1, drive west on Olive and Lindell for 2.3 miles to Kingshighway. Turn right (north) on Kingshighway. In 3 miles, this road crosses Interstate 70, and then in .6 miles Kingshighway ends at Bellefontaine Cemetery. The entrance to the cemetery is immediately on your right, on West Florissant Avenue.

To rejoin the Tour Loop in downtown St. Louis, drive directly east on Olive Boulevard.

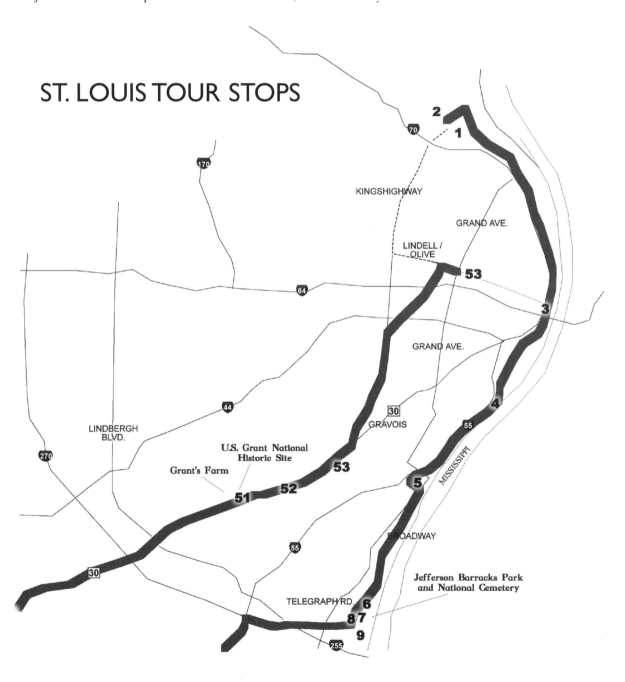

ST. LOUIS TOUR STOPS

TOUR LOOP TWO

Missouri has kept its Civil War history largely under wraps, and nowhere in the state does this history lie out of sight so much as it does in Northeast Missouri. Considering the proximity of this region to Iowa and Illinois, it is a wonder that this area is not a magnet for Civil War tourism. This Loop features a number of battlefields, and a chronology of U.S. Grant's first days as a Civil War soldier, but predominantly the theme is the brother-on-brother war that is the hallmark of Missouri's experience in the late phases of the war. This is not a tour for the squeamish, but on the other hand, it is time to realize that you don't have to drive to Tennessee to be fully immersed in the Civil War.

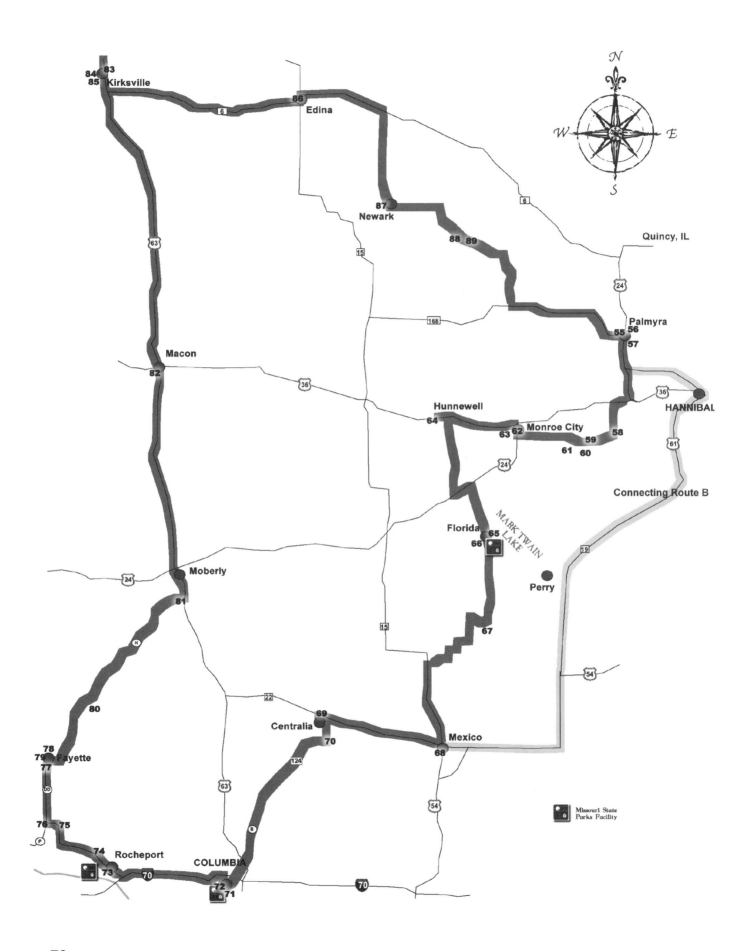

Kirksville

84 83
85

6   Edina   86

63

87
Newark

88 89

15

Quincy, IL

24

Palmyra
55 56
57

Macon
82

36

Hunnewell   Monroe City   58

64   63 62   59
61 60

24

15   Florida 65
66

MARK TWAIN LAKE

Perry

Connecting Route B

19

24

Moberly
81

24

H

54

80

78
79 Fayette
77

DD

76 75

P

74
73 Rocheport   70

Mexico
68

22   Centralia 69
70

124

63

B

COLUMBIA

70

72
71

70

54

Missouri State
Parks Facility

A TOUR OF NORTH CENTRAL MISSOURI

Sick of Killing

M issourians are sensitive to the suggestion that Missouri was once a breeding ground for criminals, and of course Jesse James was no Robin Hood. The legends that built up around the lives of the James brothers, the Youngers and others, have much to do with post-Civil War Missouri politics. The legends were a product of a concerted effort by Southerners who resented the influx of northern/eastern business and financial interests - banks and railroads - into their home territory. This was Missouri's version of reconstruction.

As a matter of fact, Missouri's age of the outlaw reflects this reality: federal authorities never did end the Civil War that raged in Missouri's Boonslick region. For the most part, central and western Missouri were pacified, but a small body of men schooled in the tactics of the guerrilla - some few who did not die in 1864 - carried on. As the tours in this Guide will reveal, these men were by and large driven by events to adopt the vicious brand of warfare which became their hallmark during and after the Civil War.

The Brush Creek Church

They are not glorified in these pages. On the other hand, there is a history behind the terror of 1864, history ignored by the victors and not often discussed in the literature of the mainstream. This story - how it began and how it reached its climax - unfolded in Northeast Missouri.

Much of Tour Loop Four is devoted to the guerrilla war in Missouri, specifically with reference to the Civil War exploits of the James brothers. The character that dominates this Tour Loop Two is the infamous William T.

Anderson. The James brothers rode with "Bloody Bill" in the late summer and early fall of 1864, when Anderson in the space of two months made his mark on history. Anderson's reign epitomizes the end-stage of a brutal and tragic process. But the story begins near the town of Palmyra, close by Hannibal in Marion County. It begins just as Missouri's conventional war was ending, down deep in the swamps near New Madrid. The story ends on September 27, 1864, in a field near Centralia, Missouri, as the crow flies 20 miles due northeast from Columbia.

In 1862, General Price's immediate reaction to the Confederate losses at Pea Ridge and Island No. 10 was to dispatch recruiting agents into the Boonslick, to tap into the pool of Southern men and boys left behind. Quite a few newly-minted Confederate officers went north to recruit in their home territories in the spring of 1862. This was to make for a hot time in the summer, here and in western Missouri, when the recruits were ready to move south.

The recruiter with the most distant and dangerous mission lived in Lewis County, Missouri, about 25 miles southwest of Keokuk, Iowa. His name was Joseph Chrisman Porter, and we date phase two of Missouri's Civil War to the day in April, 1862 that he arrived home.

First in time, but pretty much outside of the theme of this Tour Loop, is the story of U. S. Grant's first tentative steps as a Civil War field commander, spread across the landscape of north Missouri.

Campaigns in this Tour

Grant's River Campaign

The Civil War in North Missouri began on July 13, 1861, when an Illinois regiment that was not quite ready for action got trapped in a place called Monroe Station. Another Illinois regiment, the 21st Illinois, was camped on the Illinois River some distance east of Quincy, Illinois, and it was dispatched to the rescue. Colonel Ulysses Grant, at the head of the 21st regiment, had marched his men overland from their boot camp in Springfield, Illinois, despite the availability of a railroad, to toughen them. With news of the emergency at Monroe Station, Grant put his men on the train to Quincy, and they crossed into Missouri that same day, fanning out to guard the Hannibal & St. Joseph Railroad in the vicinity of Palmyra.

The action in Monroe Station had ended by the time the 21st Illinois was deployed to the west. The 21st Illinois was sent instead to guard a river crossing of the Hannibal & St. Joseph Railroad near the Shelby County town of Hunnewell. Grant remained there for a week or so, but soon after he first arrived near Hunnewell he took his men on their first campaign in the war zone. On July 14, he set out for Florida, Missouri, where Missouri State Guard General

Thomas Harris had established a camp. After a march of 15 miles, Grant came upon Florida to find that Harris had abandoned his camp. The incident inspired a famous passage in Grant's *Memoirs*:

"It occurred to me at once that Harris had been as much afraid of me as I had been of him. This was a view of the question I had never taken before; but it was one I never forgot afterwards. From that event to the close of the war, I never experienced trepidation upon confronting an enemy, though I always felt more or less anxiety. I never forgot that he had as much reason to fear my forces as I had his. The lesson was valuable."

Florida, a town in Monroe County that has all but disappeared, in 1835 was the birthplace of Samuel L. Clemens. In 1861, Clemens may have been in that camp that Harris hastily abandoned. There is only one source for this proposition, and it is the notorious story-teller Mark Twain. A verifiable connection between the two men, that bloomed late in Grant's life, is expanded upon as part of this Tour Loop (Stops 65 - 66). When we get you to the town of Florida, as you will see, we can hardly let you ignore Missouri's greatest humorist and northeast Missouri's premier tourist draw.

Grant and the 21st Illinois returned to the Salt River Bridge, but soon were transferred to Mexico, Missouri, in Audrain County on the North Missouri Railroad. They served there from July 29 to August 7, 1861. Grant had several regiments under his command in Mexico, and was charged with guarding a 40-mile section of the North

Battle at Monroe Station (Harper's Weekly)

Samuel Longhorne Clemens, better known as Mark Twain, was the son of a Virginia/Tennessee family that emigrated to North Missouri in the 1820s. Clemens was born in the town of Florida, Missouri on November 30, 1835. In 1861, he joined the Missouri State Guard and was elected a lieutenant of his company. At least so said Mark Twain in an 1896 short story "The Private History of the Campaign that Failed." Twain - who did enroll in the Second Division of the MSG commanded by Tom Harris - also claimed in The Private History that he was in Harris' camp in Florida as Colonel Grant approached from the Salt River Bridge. If he was, he left the Army immediately thereafter, because in July, 1861 he began a cross-country journey to Nevada Territory with his brother Orion. It was the trip he immortalized in "Roughing It."

Clemens became a great friend of General and President U. S. Grant after both had become famous. After Grant's death in 1885, Clemens published Grant's *Memoirs*, which was, at the time, the best-selling work of non-fiction in American history. He may have exaggerated his near encounter with the famous soldier in 1861.

Clemens' brief career as a soldier does have some corroboration, because Clemens' boyhood friend Absalom Grimes became the "Confederate Mail Runner." His book of that name, written after Clemens had passed away in 1910, was published posthumously after Grimes died in 1911. Grimes' description of the exploits of the Ralls County Rangers in many ways "out-Twains Twain" in its humorous treatment of the subject. However, Grimes' work contains a tantalizing account of the Rangers' participation in a skirmish in Monroe County we know as the battle of Hagar's Hill.

Missouri road, as far west as the town of Centralia.

Grant was next ordered to proceed to southeast Missouri, and he put his men on the train and headed to St. Louis. He reached Ironton on August 9.

Porter's North Missouri Raid

Colonel Joseph Porter's home territory was northeast Missouri, and much of northeast Missouri is considered part of the Boonslick region. Southern sympathies run deep here. One of the least known cavalry campaigns of the Civil War was Porter's campaign, which went all over northeast Missouri between April and October, 1862. People interesting in understanding this raid – or recruiting mission as we have said – can thank another man of North Missouri, Dr. Joseph A. Mudd, who "wrote the book" on the subject in 1909. Mudd's *With Porter in North Missouri*, is currently in print thanks to the Camp Pope Bookshop of Iowa.

It is not known what Porter was doing from April to June, except that he established a recruitment camp at Whaley's Mill, not far from his home in western Lewis County. In late June, Porter clashed with Union cavalry at Cherry Grove, near present-day Downing, Missouri. Downing is in Schuyler County, less than 8 miles from the Iowa border. Then he attacked a small Union garrison in Memphis, the seat of Scotland

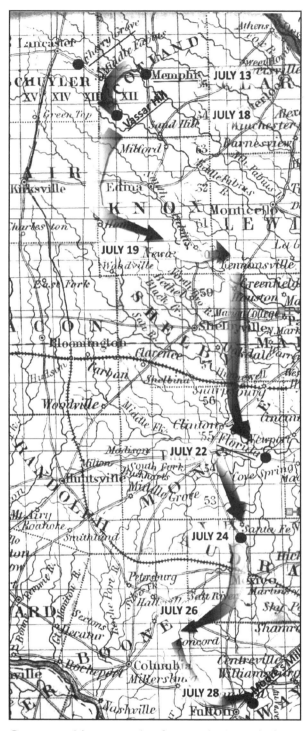

It appears Porter was ready in mid-July to take his recruits south, although only a few hundred were riding with him. He struck south from Memphis, riding 65 miles in one 24 hour period (according to Mudd). He soon attracted companies of the Third Iowa Cavalry that were stationed in Mexico, Missouri. Meanwhile, the 2nd and 11th cavalry regiments continued the chase that began at Vassar Hill. In the course of 10 days Porter fought three more battles, at Florida (7/22/62), Bott's Bluff (7/24/62) and Moore's Mill (7/28/82). Union forces converged from a number of other locales to confront Porter at Moore's Mill, just northeast of Fulton in Callaway County, and dealt him a serious loss there. If Porter was intending to get his troops south of the Missouri River, Moore's Mill changed his mind. He dispersed his men. They would meet up again far to the north, in the first week of August, 1862.

Porter was soon in the town of Newark in Knox County, attacking and beating a small Union garrison on August 1, 1862. By this time, he was bringing all of his recruits together, and he rode west in the direction of Kirksville, the Adair County seat. There he would make a stand with over 2000 troops under his command. Now, he was being chased by more than cavalry, as Union Colonel John McNeil brought infantry and artillery into action. McNeil, commanding a much smaller force than Porter, fought Porter's recruits in a battle right in the middle of Kirksville, on August 6, 1862. McNeil won

The 2nd Missouri Cavalry (Union) was also known as the "Merrill Horse." Many of the men of this top-notch unit were Michiganers.

County, taking a stack of arms there and also a prisoner who was later found dead. On July 18, 1862, elements of the 2nd Missouri Cavalry (Union) and the 11th Missouri State Militia Cavalry who were dispatched to find Porter found him indeed, at a place called Vassar Hill (the battle is sometimes called Pierce's Mill). The Union troopers suffered severe casualties; Porter, hardly any.

74

handily. Porter tried to get south with the survivors, moving southwest from Kirksville at first, but then had to disperse his men again. North Missouri remained relatively quiet for weeks after that.

Maj. James Porter
Brother of Joseph C. Porter

Coming out of hiding, Porter with just a small band rode into Palmyra, county seat of Marion County, on September 16, 1862 and held the town for a day. His men liberated Southerners held prisoner there, and destroyed records of Southern men who had been paroled in July and August.

Another Union man was missing and presumed dead once Porter left Palmyra.

Porter's Raid ended on October 16, 1862 when Porter himself crossed the Missouri River in the vicinity of Portland, Callaway County, with about 200 men. His force fought a small skirmish west of Waynesville on October 18, on the way to Arkansas.

The Centralia Raid

William T. Anderson is probably the second most famous Missouri-bred guerrilla fighter operating during Missouri's Civil War. The most famous, Jesse James, was sixteen years old when he joined Anderson's small band in the late summer of 1864. Anderson, and many other

A MAN SO NEARLY FORGOTTEN

No photograph or other image of Colonel Porter survives. No one is quite sure where he is buried. He seems to have been a natural military genius. If he had any military training, the scant historical record of his early life reveals none. In 1862, he is believed to have recruited at least 2,000 men for the Confederate service, all the while in hostile territory. In the words of his principal adversary, Union Col. John McNeil, Porter ". . . runs like a deer and doubles like a fox."

Joseph Porter was born in Kentucky Blue Grass country in 1819, and then moved with his parents to Marion County Missouri around 1830. His father moved the family home several times, eventually settling in southwest Lewis County, not far from the Knox County town of Newark. After Porter married in 1844 and started his family, he acquired a farm in the same area of Lewis County. Porter immediately answered the call of Missouri when the State Guard was organized in 1861, and he became Lt. Colonel of the Second Division, reporting to Gen. Martin E. Green. As an officer of the Missouri State Guard, Porter fought at battles at Athens, Missouri, in August 1861, then at Lexington and Pea Ridge, Arkansas. He was sent back to Lewis County in April, 1862, just after Pea Ridge, to recruit cavalry for the Confederate service. From April to October, 1862, he recruited the men who would form the First and Second Northeast Missouri Cavalry regiments, CSA.

Within several months after he went to Arkansas with the last of his Missouri recruits, Porter commanded a cavalry force of about 700 men that participated in Marmaduke's campaign for Springfield, Missouri. At the close of that campaign, on January 11, 1863, Porter was in the thick of the action during the Battle of Hartville, Missouri, where he suffered multiple wounds. He died of his wounds on February 18, 1863 at Batesville, Arkansas. The battle at Hartville was a costly one to the Confederate cause. Two cavalry commanders holding the rank of Colonel - Porter and Emmett McDonald - and Lt. Col. John Wimer, were killed in or as a result of the action at Hartville. More about Marmaduke's campaign is found in Tour Loop Five.

Missouri partisan cavalry leaders, were bringing their men into the center of the state. The word was circulated: Sterling Price was leading an army back to Missouri. When Price entered Missouri in mid-September 1864 - his famous 1864 Expedition - Southern partisan bands went on the offensive to disrupt Union communications and divert Union troops from the battle front. For perhaps the only time in the War, Missouri partisan cavalry acted on direct orders of the senior Confederate command.

On September 23, 1864, General Price with his host was converging on Fredericktown in southeast Missouri, and the partisan commands were converging in Howard County, north of the Missouri River near Boonville. The campaign that would end at Centralia began on that date when guerrilla riders attacked a wagon train moving through western Boone County, at a place called Goslin's Lane. As a harbinger of things to come, the Union cavalry escort was just slaughtered, as were the civilian teamsters, many of them African Americans. The partisans made a good haul of supplies and materiel. That night, hundreds of them camped in the fields south of Fayette, Missouri, probably the largest group of irregulars to combine in a single operation during the entire war in Missouri. Notable commanders on the scene included not only Anderson, but also George Todd and William C. Quantrill.

The combined partisan and guerrilla force rode into Fayette, Missouri on September 24, and attacked the fortified camp of the Ninth Missouri State Militia Cavalry. The attack was disjointed and ineffective, and the partisans suffered severe losses. Fayette was Anderson's idea, and Anderson was trying to take charge of the entire group. Still, they followed him, from Fayette northeast into Monroe County nearly to Paris. In Paris, a detachment of Union mounted infantry got the scent, and chased the Southern horsemen in the direction of Centralia, a whistle stop on the railroad in the northeast corner of Boone County. These forces, along with a stagecoach from Columbia and a train from St.

The Gregory Cemetery, Danville

Charles, all came together on September 27, 1864 to produce a ghastly human disaster in Centralia. This story occupies a significant part of the narrative in this Tour. It epitomizes what was unique about the Civil War in Missouri.

The Danville Raid

Sterling Price's 1864 Expedition reached its peak, insofar as the Confederate fortunes concerned, when Price occupied the town of Boonville, on the Missouri River in Cooper County. There he rested and re-equipped for several days, October 11 to 13, 1864. It was, it turned out, a brief respite, as Union forces were beginning to close in on him. On October 11, Price met on Boonville's Main Street with Bill Anderson, now reigning (2 weeks after Centralia) as the most feared of the Missouri Southern guerrillas. Price sent Anderson east, to disrupt and destroy the North Missouri Railroad.

Anderson's band crossed the Misouri River into Howard County, then traveled east, skirting Columbia on its north side. The riders, estimated to number 80, reached what was known then as the St. Charles Road, heading east. Late in the evening of October 13, 1864, these men rode into the mostly Southern town of Williamsburg, in Callaway County. Here they received some information as to the disposition of troops and defensive works in the mostly Yankee town of Danville, 8 1/2 miles to the east. Danville was the county seat of Montgomery County.

The riders came into Danville in the late afternoon of October 14,1864, and burned most of the buildings in town. Several of the townspeople were killed in the process. Henry Diggs was one of them. There were no Union soldiers to protect the town, the small garrison having been sent elsewhere, naturally, to protect the railroad.

Anderson's men - and Anderson if he was among them - continued east and reached the railroad at New Florence. The next day, October 15, they destroyed most of the town of High Hill, on the North Missouri.

In the history of armed human conflict, few men in 24 years of life have left a mark as indelible as Bloody Bill Anderson's. Reared in Huntsville, Missouri, his family moved to Kansas before the Civil War, and Anderson is believed to have enlisted in the Missouri State Guard in 1861. Little is known of his early history or his service before August, 1863.

The demon in Anderson was vengeance. A bad policy - Union authorities in western Missouri jailed relatives of Southern partisans on charges of aiding and abetting - became infinitely worse on August 13, 1863. A Kansas City building housing female prisoners collapsed. Four young women died, including Anderson's 14 year old sister, Josephine. Mary Anderson, 16, was disfigured and crippled. Anderson no doubt believed, as some still contend, that this was a case of criminal negligence or worse. Four days later, Quantrill began his murderous raid on Lawrence, Kansas, urged on by those intent on avenging Kansas City. Anderson rode with him.

In 1864, Anderson was ready to assert himself as leader of the most violent wing of the Missouri partisans. He spent the summer in central Missouri, spreading terror and making war without bounds. In September, 1864, Anderson's rampage culminated - and most would say his vengeance was fulfilled - in a small north Missouri town called Centralia.

Centralia made Bill Anderson the most hunted man in America. He lived another month. Trapped by a Union patrol in Orrick, Missouri, on October 27, 1864, he led a last charge and fell. His body was hauled to Richmond, Missouri, and his remains lie there in Pioneer Cemetery.

Part I - Westbound

Tour Stop 55

This is the old MARION COUNTY JAIL, built in 1858 and recently renovated. The building is remarkably well preserved, and is as haunting a Civil War place as you are ever likely to see. Here, on October 18, 1862, was played out a horrific drama that ranks among the most terrible events of the Civil War.

You have read about Joe Porter's great North Missouri Raid. On August 6, 1862 Porter's recruits fought a Union force commanded by Col. John McNeil at Kirksville, about 60 miles northwest of here. See Stop 83 in this Loop for a description of the Battle of Kirksville.

Porter and a small contingent of his cavalry entered Palmyra from the west on September 12, 1862. He had been in Lewis County, quiet and unaccounted for, since shortly after Kirksville. Porter had approached Palmyra from the north, then looped around to the west where he fought a small skirmish along present-day Highway 168.

While in Palmyra, Porter's men sought out and captured one Andrew Allsman, a notorious informer, and Allsman never returned home. We know today that several of Porter's men were detailed to escort him home, and they shot him instead. Enter Col. John McNeil, of Kirksville fame.

McNeil is the man responsible for maintaining order in North Missouri. For two months, since Porter raided Memphis, Missouri, on July 13, Porter has been running loose in McNeil's territory. Palmyra was then, as now, the seat of Marion County, a populous county in which Hannibal is situated, and it is 15 miles from Quincy, Illinois. No doubt embarrassed, McNeil decides - or if we believe McNeil, federal authorities decide - to take drastic action. So, on October 8, 1862 McNeil published a notice in the Palmyra Courier, stating that if Allsman was not returned in ten days, ten men who had been captured from among Porter's recruits would be executed. John McNeil was about to learn a lesson in public relations: When you decide to seek out publicity, be extra careful what you wish for.

On the ninth day after McNeil's deadline, five men incarcerated in the Marion County jail were selected for execution. Five others who were being held in

To reach Tour Stop 55:

The beginning point of this Loop is the North Missouri town of Palmyra, which is easily accessible from both Hannibal and Quincy, Illinois. From Hannibal, take U. S. Highway 61 north ten miles to Ross Street. From Quincy, U. S. Highway 24 west reaches Ross Street 25 miles after crossing the River. From your turnoff at Ross Street, drive west to Main Street, then turn right and drive north 5 blocks to the courthouse. The Tour starts at the building that is west of the courthouse, at the southwest corner of Lafayette and Dickerson.

Hannibal were also selected. The process was not by lot. Rather, McNeil decreed that sons of prominent Southern families in the area receive priority consideration.

Three of the men who awaited their fate in the Marion County jail were Willis Baker, Hiram Smith and William T. Humphrey. More of this story appears at Tour Stops 86 to 88 of this Tour Loop. Visitors arriving from the northwest will take a route from Kirksville that is largely devoted to this story.

To reach Tour Stop 56:

Go back to Ross Street the way you came, and turn left here. Cross both lanes of the highway about five blocks east (being very careful as you do), then drive east another .4 miles, to the point where the road bends slightly to the left. Look to the field to your left. It is not possible to stop here; drive further to the east to a point where you can safely turn around. You can take a better look at the site as you return. It is just west of the old mansion.

Tour Stop 56

This is the site of THE MARION COUNTY FAIRGROUNDS. It was here on the 18th of October, 1862 that the Palmyra ten were put to death.

At the jail, the ten prisoners, including five transported here from Hannibal that day, were loaded on wagons, seated on their coffins, and taken with much fanfare south on Main and east on Ross Street, to the fairgrounds. The prisoners were seated in a row on the coffins and the order was given to fire. The executions were botched, no doubt because the Union troops flinched. Seven of the 10 suffered no appreciable wounds in the volley, and were dispatched by pistol-fire at close range.

No doubt McNeil viewed the grotesque ceremony that characterized Palmyra as necessary to terrorize local residents who were in rebellion against the central government; it was an escalation of the terror of the Kirksville and Macon City killings. Naturally (viewed from a 21st Century perspective) the effort back-fired. The New York Times published a scathing account of the incident in December, 1862, followed by similar accounts in the British press. Porter's recruiting drive was immeasurably enhanced. The Palmyra massacre has left a stain still vivid 148 years later.

56

1869 view of Palmyra

Tour Stop 57

The spur track that hugs Main Street at this point was once the main line of THE HANNIBAL & ST. JOSEPH RAILROAD.

In Missouri, in 1847, some visionary men chartered a railroad company that would cross the state east to west from one end to the other, and named it the Hannibal & St. Joseph. From the wharf at Hannibal, the railroad would first loop northward to the county seat at Palmyra, then back to the south where a town called "Monroe Station" was built to receive it. From Monroe Station (now known as Monroe City) the road headed straight west to its terminus at St. Joseph, on the Missouri River. The H&SJ was completed in 1859, the first railroad to reach so far into the frontier. The broad loop you see south of Palmyra was the apex of the northward loop of the tracks, and reflected both Palmyra's influence at the time, and the commercial interests of Quincy, Illinois, which were determined to get into the action. When the Hannibal & St. Joe was built, its promoters ran a spur from Quincy to Palmyra, to extend the Chicago, Burlington & Quincy into Missouri so as to satisfy the Illinois politicians.

Another railroad, the predecessor of the great Wabash Railroad, serviced Quincy in 1860. That other railroad figures into the theme of this Loop segment as well.

The Wabash had its beginnings east of the Mississippi at a town called Meredosia, Illinois. By 1861 this line extended from Springfield to Quincy. On July 5 or 6, 1861, U. S. Grant was camped with his 21st Illinois infantry near Meredosia, having marched overland from Springfield.

The completion of the Hannibal & St. Joe inspired William H. Russell to form the Pony Express, to carry the mail from the most western reach of the nation's railroads to California. We wouldn't feel compelled to mention the Pony Express, except that William H. Russell, by happenstance, died in Palmyra in 1872 and is buried in Greenwood Cemetery on the city's north end. On March 31, 1860, a messenger from Washington arrived here from Quincy, en route to Hannibal. He carried a satchel of mail to be handed off in St. Joseph to the first Pony Express rider. He was two hours late. A special train pulled by the locomotive *Missouri* was waiting in Hannibal, and the engineer "high-balled" it to St. Joe, making the trip in less than 5 hours, saving the festivities and setting a speed record the lasted for years. The *Missouri*, which steamed up the tracks here on its epic trip, is on display at the Patee House Museum in far away St. Joseph.

To reach Tour Stop 57:

Return again to Main Street via Ross Street, then drive south on Main Street for 6 or 7 blocks. Pull over near the grain elevator. The loop of an old railroad bed is discernable here.

The Locomotive Missouri

Drive south on Main Street for 1.7 miles, where it merges with U.S. 61 and 24. Enter the highway and continue south for 1.5 miles, bearing right on to U.S. 24 when these roads split. Continue south 4.2 miles. Here, turn right (west) on U.S. 36. Go west on 36 for 1.5 miles, to Route H, which will be on your left. Turn left, then drive south for 3.5 miles, where Route H turns to the right. Slow down. At the intersection here where Route HH enters from your left, there is a gravel road to your right, called Huntington Road. Turn right here, and pull over for Tour Stop 58.

We are stopping here, on THE PARIS GRAVEL ROAD, in order to cover some general history pertinent to the next leg of your tour.

The Paris Gravel Road refers to the Paris that is the county seat of Monroe County. This is the second road that preceded the iron roads on the high ground north of the Salt River, the first being a failed plank road that ended at the town of Sidney, Missouri. Between here and the next Tour Stop, there is a beautiful stretch of the old Paris Gravel Road, still paved with gravel and still very much intact. It first descends into the valley of Big Creek, and when you emerge into the bottom land there, imagine you have been transported into the "Old South" of the 1850s.

Missouri's Salt River got its name from a river of that name that flows through Nelson County, Kentucky, near the city of Bardstown. On the tributaries of Kentucky's Salt River, beginning in 1785, some of the first European settlements in Kentucky took root. The Bardstown area, in addition to being the cradle of Catholicism west of the Appalachians, is the home of My Old Kentucky Home, of Stephen Foster fame, and "the Bourbon Capital of The World."

Kentucky Catholic transplants began arriving in Missouri's Salt River region before 1820, and they brought with them their Maryland and Kentucky culture, including the slave culture. The Salt River region had, and still has, an extraordinarily close-knit society centered on the Church. This culture spreads far and wide throughout the region, to Paris and beyond. The Paris Road, and its successor U.S. Highway 24, is Main Street for the Kentucky part of Missouri.

Maryland Catholics in Missouri

The oldest European settlement in Maryland was in St. Mary's County, on the east side of the Potomac River about 35 miles due east of Fredericksburg, Virginia. St. Mary's was the site of the 1634 landing of the Ark and the Dove, ships that transported Lord Calvert and his charge of disaffected English Catholics to the New World.

Soon after the American Revolution, 60 Maryland families, most from St. Mary's, decided they would migrate en masse to the part of Virginia that would become Kentucky. The vanguard of this group, which was known as the League of Catholic Families, arrived in central Kentucky in 1785, and were among the first settlers of the state. By the year 1800, however, agents for the Kentucky Catholics were scouting better land in the West, and by 1820 hundreds of these people had signed on for a new venture, to settle the fertile Salt River basin in northeast Missouri.

Tour Stop 59

The place on the map that was once the town of Sidney is now called SHEIL. Commerce on the Paris Road made Sidney quite a prosperous place before and during the Civil War. The stone building here was the town's general store, erected in 1860.

This is the beginning of the story of Centralia, which occupies center stage in this Tour Loop. We must digress in order to describe the 39th Missouri Volunteer Infantry. We don't know why a new regiment of infantry was formed in August, 1864 in North Missouri, although we can speculate that the guerrilla activity in July brought this about. Most of the men who would make up the 39th Missouri enrolled in August took basic training in Hannibal. Some had experience with local militia units, but no doubt many of the men were boys who were coming of age in a place thought to be a backwater in the great war, centered now in Virginia and Georgia.

A company of the 39th Missouri, Company D, came down the Paris Gravel Road on September 11, 1864, and had their first taste of "action" in the town of Sidney; horse-stealing, mostly, for four days. They were led here by the 39th's second-in-command, Maj. A.V.E. Johnston of Monroe County. You will visit his grave at Tour Stop 63 in Monroe City. As for the boys of Company D, thankfully for them they were not at the town of Centralia on the date that appears last on Johnston's gravestone, September 27, 1864.

Tour Stop 60

Tour Stop 60 is ST. PETER'S CHURCH, sometimes known as the Brush Creek Church. On the front façade of the church building is a plaque that describes the historic importance of this place. Here in 1854 was baptized a slave child who would one day

To reach Tour Stop 59:

Drive west on the Paris Gravel Road (here known as Huntington Lane) for exactly 3.6 miles. Pull over just before you reach the junction of Route DD, and you will see the ruins of a stone building in the woods on your right. This is what remains of the town of Sidney, Missouri, and it is Tour Stop 59.

To reach Tour Stop 60:

Drive to the intersection at the top of the hill. Turn left on this road, (called Sydney Road), then drive about a mile south until your reach the top of a bluff. Continue straight on this road for a few hundred yards and you will see a tree-lined drive on your right, and a sign for the Brush Creek Church.

become the world's first African-American Catholic priest. Father Augustin Tolton was born about two miles west of here, and was baptized in the log building that was the first St. Peter's on this site. The turmoil of the Civil War, as well as a strong faith nurtured by this church, is what launched Tolton's achievement.

The existing building was erected in the fateful year of 1862, and the other part of our story of the Brush Creek Church ends on August 6, 1862 - the day of the Battle of Kirksville. The story begins in the year 1634, with the landings of the Dove and the Ark, the first ships to bring Catholic settlers to Maryland. Walk to the large cross at the left rear of the cemetery, where you find broken stones laid flat on the ground including that of Monica Fenwick Hagar (1775-1858). Monica Hagar was born in St. Mary's County, Maryland, and was descended (6th generation) from Cuthbert Fenwick, a passenger on the Ark. Monica was a living embodiment of the great Catholic migration from Maryland through Kentucky to Missouri.

Augustine Tolton
1854 - 1897

"Father Gus" Tolton was born a slave in Ralls County, Missouri in 1854. Fleeing with his mother to Quincy, Illinois when his father joined the Union army, young Augustine found work in a tobacco factory in Quincy at a tender age. He and his siblings were befriended in Quincy by a priest who allowed them to attend a parochial school now known as St. Peters. His experience led ultimately to his ordination in 1886. He was the first African-American Catholic priest in history.

After serving in Quincy, Father Tolton transferred to a parish in Chicago, where he achieved a degree of fame as a preacher. He died of heat stroke during the summer of 1897, only 43 years old, and his remains were brought back to the cemetery of St. Peters Church in Quincy, where he rests today.

The stones that lie immediately below Monica's are the grave markers of two of her sons. Robert Hagar lived on a farm in neighboring Monroe County, 11 or 12 miles southwest of here, on which was located a landmark known as "Hagar's Hill." When he died in 1853, the property was willed to his son, Robert B. Hagar.

When you reach Tour Stop 62, you will learn about the battle that occurred in Monroe City on July 11, 1861, and about a small engagement 2 days before on Hagar's Hill. Robert B. "Bob" Hagar was a member of the Missouri State Guard. He rose to the rank of Captain, and was destined to be the highest ranking Southerner to die at the Battle of Kirksville. There is no stone here memorializing Captain Bob Hagar, but we know he was brought home here and laid to rest in the same year the stone church was dedicated.

The next stone in line is that of James T. Hagar - uncle to Captain Bob Hager. James and his wife Jane Lynch Hagar lived on a farm two miles west of the Church. On this property they established "Hagar's Tavern." Among their slaves was a man by the name of Peter Paul Tolton. Their neighbors, Stephen Elliott and his wife, owned a slave named Martha, and around 1850 Peter and Martha were married at the Brush Creek Church. Their second son, Augustin, was born on April 1, 1854 on the Elliott farm.

Tour Stop 61

To reach Tour Stop 61:

Return to the road at the front of the church (Gentry Road), and turn right. Drive west on for 1.9 miles. Where the road turns sharply right here, pull straight ahead on to a gravel area, and stop.

In this vicinity, probably to your right as you approached this turn, was the slave cabin that was the TOLTON BIRTHPLACE. In this general vicinity also, we think over the hill in your front, was Hagar's Tavern. The convergence of these places gives us a chance to reflect, before we leave here and re-enter the time of the iron horse and other such things wrought by an industrial revolution.

First, about "Father Gus" Tolton. After Fr. Tolton reached a certain level of fame, Quincy adopted him as its own, and the Quincy version of the story developed some of the familiar features of the escaping slave saga. On the Missouri side, people in this very Catholic area are also proud of Father Gus. According to the Missouri version, the Elliott family sent Martha and her children to safety in Illinois, and the local constable accompanied them there. After Peter Tolton left to join the army, the gossip was that the Elliotts were freeing their slaves, which caused a hue and cry in the neighborhood. Of course, one could start an argument by pointing out to Quincians that Father Tolton suffered terrible discrimination while growing up in "free" Illinois. The Catholic Church has acknowledged that Father Tolton was exposed to discrimination and ridicule from his fellow priests.

About Hagar's Tavern: A tavern was, then, something akin to a motel. James Hagar died in 1856, not long after his slave fathered Augustin Tolton. During the Civil War, the proprietress of Hagar's Tavern was James' widow, whose grave you saw at St. Peter's, "Aunt Jane" Hagar. Aunt Jane was, by all accounts, a fire-breathing, uncompromising, unrelenting pro-Southerner, and remained so for the rest of her life. During the War, her views regularly got her arrested and confined in Sidney. Hagar's Tavern was doubtless an interesting place to be in the early 1860s, even for the Union soldiers who frequented the place.

We don't judge people by their relatives, of course. Aunt Jane's brother was fellow Ralls Countian Bernard Lynch, who went on to make a name for himself in St. Louis. Sometimes he would visit Hagar's Tavern. Bernard was the proprietor of the infamous Lynch Slave Pens in St. Louis. When he was run out of town, the federals took over the place, called it the Myrtle Street Prison, and put people like Jane Hagar there for speaking their minds.

To reach Tour Stop 62:

Continue ahead on Gentry Road, which is now running north, for a mile and a half, the turn left at the "T" there. In about a mile, this west-bound road will cross Highway J. Stay on this road, which becomes Highway W, for another 4.0 miles, until you arrive on Main Street (U.S. 24) in Monroe City. Turn right (north) on Main Street. Drive north to Court Street, and turn left. Go past the gazebo in the park and pull over near the water tower.

Tour Stop 62 is the site of the former MONROE INSTITUTE, and the central feature of the Battle of Monroe Station, July 11, 1861. You have just entered Monroe County. Monroe City was established in the northeast corner of the county in 1857 and was built as a "railroad town." The Hannibal & St. Joseph Railroad reached here in 1857. The old Hannibal & St. Joe tracks, now part of the Burlington Northern system, were the second set of tracks you crossed as you came north on Main Street. That point is on a direct line from Palmyra (the west side of the Palmyra loop), 15 miles by railroad.

We need to put the date of July 11, 1861 into historic perspective. This was ten days before the first significant battle of the Civil War occurred in the eastern United States, at Bull Run or Manassas in Virginia, and six days after Missouri's first major battle, at Carthage. Federal authorities of course realized that the area here was heavily Southern, and that the Hannibal & St. Joe was of critical strategic importance if Northern interests were going to control North Missouri. This importance was already being brought home, as Southern sympathizers were out and about, burning railroad bridges whenever the chance presented itself.

The 16th Illinois Infantry, under the command of Col. Robert F. Smith, was in Palmyra in early July, 1861, and was joined there by the 3rd Iowa Infantry. Smith put 500 troops on the trains in Palmyra on July 8, and arrived to occupy Monroe Station, which he did without incident. He then marched his force south to look for State Guard General Thomas A. Harris' camp, purportedly in the Salt River valley near the town of Florida. Ten or twelve miles south of Monroe Station, Smith ran into Harris' advance elements and on July 9 fought a small engagement at Hagar's Hill, in which the Union lost 3 men to wounds. There was one casualty on the State Guard side, a mortally wounded soldier.

Hagar's Hill had more importance than the number of casualties would indicate. When Colonel Smith left Monroe Station, he did not leave anyone to guard his trains and supplies. What is more, he had advertised his movement in advance, and Southerners were coming together from all over this area to contend with him. When Smith stubbed his toe at Hagar's Hill, he apparently only then realized the precarious position he was in. After camping at Hagar's Hill on the night of July 9, Smith abandoned his offensive, and he headed back to Monroe Station on the morning of the 10th. He was greeted there by a scene that we might have anticipated: Railroad cars and the depot in flames. His base of supply, and most of his supplies, gone.

Smith went to the highest point in town, which is the place you are standing right now, and holed up in and around the substantial brick building that was then known as "the Seminary." Smith had one cannon, but very little ammunition. Southerners under Harris' command came up, until well over a thousand had surrounded Smith's position. By mid-day on the 11th, the State Guard had also brought up a cannon, a 9-pounder cast in Hannibal, and began to lob shells into the Seminary. The federals returned fire, with little effect on either side. It appears the only serious casualty at Monroe Station was a Southerner killed while discharging his gun. Three hours after the battle commenced, a trainload of Union reinforcements from Palmyra appeared to the east of town, and a few shots of grape dispersed the Southerners.

Though not mentioned in Grant's *Memoirs*, one presumes that the destruction wrought by Smith's folly made an impression on Grant. Grant came through here, on July 12 or 13, on his way to the Salt River Bridge near Hunnewell. Within a few years, Grant would become the commanding General of the armies of the United States. His victories were in no small part due to his mastery of the use of railroads to wage war.

In the realm of historic milestones, Missourians are accustomed to ceding to East Coast claims. This is a prevalent Midwestern trait, acquired over the course of generations and foisted on us by eastern so-called experts. So, the story of the Battle of Monroe Station has been lost from the historic record.

In the western world - and in this case the entire world - no war that preceded our Civil War involved railroads in any way, shape or form. This revolution in transportation, a spin-off of the larger revolution spawned by the invention of the steam engine, was bound to bring fundamental change to the way people fought wars. In the summer of '61, Col. Robert F. Smith was feeling his way around this new technology, like everyone else was.

The classic study of the railroad in the American Civil War is George Edgar Turner's *Victory Rode the Rails* (Indianapolis, The

The art of war is simple enough. Find out where your enemy is. Get at him as soon as you can. Strike him as hard as you can, and keep moving on.

Ulysses S. Grant

Bobbs-Merrill Company, 1951). Turner contends that George B. McClellan "became the first field commander to attempt the use of a railroad in combat maneuver." McClellan's attempt was carried out on July 13, 1861. What about Smith's maneuver that put his troops in Monroe Station, and the forces sent by rail to reinforce him? Minor skirmish though it was, the engagement on July 11, 1861 marked the first time that a battle was ever fought between organized military forces with the object either to destroy or to defend a railroad.

To reach Tour Stop 63:

Drive west on Court Street for four blocks, until it ends at North Oak Street. Turn left, then in a half a block turn right into the entrance to the St. Jude Cemetery. Drive ahead to the point where there is a display sign, then turn left. Drive south to Enchantment Avenue. Turn right. Drive ahead 10 or 12 rows and stop when you are parallel to the large obelisk in the section.

Tour Stop 63

This is THE GRAVE OF A.V.E. JOHNSTON, whom you met briefly in Sidney. Johnston (often spelled Johnson) was a native of Monroe County, but we know almost nothing about his family or background, or his service in the Civil War before September, 1864. We know that he enrolled in the Missouri State Guard in 1861, and we know that later the Union authorities suspected him of disloyalty to the Union cause. His story is told at Tour Stop 70. One might suspect Johnston of incompetence or rashness, but this stone stands as a testament to his loyalty.

ACCUSED

Major Johnston now states that he has an order from Genl Bartholow (a M Brig. Genl of the E. M. M. appointed by the Governor) to call in all the guns in the Country, & also those now in the Provost Marshals possession. Mayhall says that Major Johnston is disloyal -- also Col. Tinker (and I believe so too) -- and Mayhall says that he will not surrender the guns unless ordered so to do by Genl Curtis-- That Tinker & Johnston have obtained an order for all the enrolled militia of the County, who are loyal, except 60, to retire from active service, & say they intend to arm 2 Companies of conscripts -- that is disloyal men, who refused to enroll. The Pro. Mar. says he believes these Militia officers are preparing to resist the laws & orders of the U. S.--

-Letter from Provost Marshal F.A. Dick to Montgomery Blair,
January 26, 1863

Tour Stop 64

You are near THE SALT RIVER BRIDGE, which is in the woods to your south and unfortunately not accessible. The ground on which you are standing is historic as a camp site for federal troops.

The railroad bridge to the south spans the North Fork of the Salt River. Coming west from Hannibal, this bridge was the first substantial structure on the Hannibal & St. Joseph Railroad, and so it became a prime target for destruction by Southern sympathizers. At least three times during the War, the Salt River Bridge was burned. The second and third times occurred in September, 1861 and July, 1864, the latter time when Bloody Bill Anderson's band paid a visit. The first time, though, was on July 10, 1861 - the day after the Hagar's Hill fight - when Missouri State Guard troops took out the bridge.

Review the campaign summary for this Loop, and remind yourself of U. S. Grant's connection with Mark Twain. Grant's regiment arrived here in July, 1861, and was on guard duty while the bridge was reconstructed. On July 14, Grant set off from this place on his first Civil War campaign, hunting Tom Harris as Smith had done before him. You will generally follow him from here to Florida, but it is impossible now to reconstruct his route of march, or to identify the place where he rose over the hill to find that Harris was gone. Harris' camp was likely near where Highway 107 crosses Mark Twain Lake, the location submerged now in the valley below.

To reach Tour Stop 64:

Return to the cemetery entrance, then turn left (north) on N. Oak Street. Five blocks to the north, turn left on Business Route 36 (Stoddard Street). In about a half mile, this road will merge into U.S. Highway 36 (and 24). Take 36 west for 8.2 miles, past the town of Hunnewell, and as you begin to descend a hill turn left on Old Highway 36. In .2 mile, you will reach a gravel road that enters from your right, and is marked as a Missouri Conservation access point. Pull into the parking area near the Conservation Department sign.

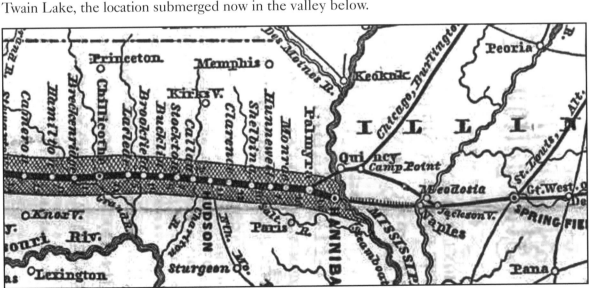

Hannibal & St. Joseph Railroad (Library of Congress)

Part II - Southbound

To Reach Tour Stop 65

Return to Old Highway 36, and turn right, and then drive 2.5 miles into the center of Hunnewell. At Center Street, which is Route V, turn right. Take this road south for 8.7 miles, until you reach U.S. Highway 24, then turn left (east). Take U.S. 24 east for approximately 2 miles, where you will see signs for Mark Twain State Park, at Missouri Highway 107. Turn right on 107.

You will take Highway 107 about 5 1/2 miles, crossing Mark Twain Lake in the process, until you see more signs for the State Park. Turn left on Route U, following the signs for the State Park. This road will dead-end in less than a mile, and Tour Stop 66 is off to your left here. Note the old Methodist Church on your right, as you will return here.

Tour Stop 65

This is the CLEMENS BIRTHPLACE MONUMENT. Samuel Langhorne Clemens was born on November 30, 1835 in a cabin located at or near this monument. At the next Tour Stop you will learn all about Missouri's most famous writer and humorist. Our visit to the town of Florida focuses on the other two main personalities we are featuring in this part of the Loop.

First, Grant. Grant reports in his memoirs that he entered Florida after his approach to Harris' camp, and it appears he stayed one or two days before returning to his camp at the Salt River Bridge. He made his headquarters at the home of Dr. James Goodier, just up Route U and catty-corner from the Methodist Church which you noted on your way here. There are ruins of the Goodier house back in the woods across from the Methodist Church. The house was still standing forty years ago.

From the church lot, imagine Grant's arrival in Florida and his encampment at and near the Goodier House. Imagine then that the ridge where the Methodist Church stands was also the approximate center of the action during the Battle of Florida on July 22, 1862. The church was built in the 1890s, to replace one that stood here in 1862.

Consult the Introduction and the campaign summary at the beginning of this Tour Loop to refresh your recollection about Porter's 1862 Raid. July 22 was very early in the chronology of the raid. The battle at Florida was the second engagement that occurred after Porter captured Memphis on July 13, 1862.

On July 22, 1862, Porter was heading south with some 300 of his new recruits, and at Florida came upon a detachment of the 3rd Iowa Cavalry. Porter forded the Salt River west of town, then circled to the south and attacked up the hill. It was a small engagement; the 3rd Iowa had no more that 50 troopers here and they were soon driven out of town. The Iowans lost 20 wounded and 2 captured, while Porter's cavalry had two killed and an unknown number wounded. One of the killed on the Southern side was a young man named Fowler, who was shot dead while a captive of the federals.

In command of the detachment of the 3rd Iowa was Col. Henry C. Caldwell, who would one day be a famous federal judge. Caldwell became the first Chief Judge of the Eighth Circuit Court of Appeals.

Tour Stop 66

The large modern building here houses the MARK TWAIN SHRINE, which is Tour Stop 66. This magnificent facility includes a museum devoted to Samuel Clemens' life, and the reconstructed cabin in which Clemens was born in 1835. The facility was constructed, and the cabin moved here, in 1958. While Mark Twain was not always kind to Missouri in his writings, we do acknowledge an immense pride in having birthed this genius, and gratitude for a tourism theme that never stops giving.

The Grant-Twain friendship to which we alluded in the introduction to this Tour was a productive one. The proceeds from Grant's *Memoirs*, which Twain published on favorable terms to the General, saved Grant's family from financial ruin. Many experts assert that Grant's *Memoirs* is the finest work of its genre ever written in the English language. Stacking assumption on top of speculation, arguably this friendship also produced the greatest American novel. The *Adventures of Huckleberry Finn* was published not long before Grant's death. Twain picked up his manuscript, which he had set aside years earlier, and he finished it in 1885. The story of Huck and Jim is a parable that chronicles Grant's conquest of the Mississippi. So says Mark Perry in *Grant and Twain: The Story of a Friendship That Changed America* (New York: Random House, 2004).

Tour Stop 67

On this field the BATTLE OF BOTTS BLUFF was fought on July 24, 1862. Porter, with approximately 400 troopers, was pursued by the Third Iowa Cavalry, which had retired from Florida and reinforced itself at its base at Paris. Here Porter turned to give battle. There was one killed on each side - the Union man was wounded then shot to death - and the two are buried side by side in the old Botts cemetery, located in the "spit" of trees on the left side of the battlefield. Someone recognized the wounded federal as the man who had killed his brother while guarding the county jail in Palmyra.

To reach Tour Stop 66:

Retrace your route back on Route U, and turn left at Shrine Road before you reach Highway 107. Follow this road for about .6 mile until it ends at the Mark Twain Memorial Shrine.

To reach Tour Stop 67:

Return to Route U, turn left, and retrace your route back to Highway 107. Turn left (south). After 2.7 miles, Highway 107 will become State Route E. Continue south on E for another 5.2 miles, and this road then becomes Route D. Continue straight ahead for another .6 miles (8.5 miles from Florida) where County Road 23 intersects from the left. Turn left on 23. In about two miles you will reach County Road 22. Turn right, and pull over at any point along this road to view the field to your left.

To reach Tour Stop 68:

Drive straight ahead and bear right at the next road. In about a mile, traveling north, you will re-connect with Route D, at the town of Santa Fe. Turn left on D and drive west for .5 mile, then turn left on Route ZZ. In 7.9 miles this road intersects Route Z, and here turn left. Route Z bears right in 1/2 mile, and then in 1.2 miles Z ends at State Route 15.

Turn left on Route 15. Drive south 9.0 miles into the heart of the town of Mexico. Continue south on Route 15, which is Western Street in Mexico, and cross the railroad tracks. Tour Stop 68 is on your right about 1/10 mile south of the tracks.

Tour Stop 68

Tour Stop 68 is the GRACELAND MUSEUM. This is the headquarters of the Audrain County Historical Society, housed in the 1857 mansion of John P. Clark. Clark was a Unionist; it is said that Ulysses Grant visited the place while stationed here.

Grant and the 21st Illinois returned to the Salt River Bridge after descending on Florida, and soon after went by rail to Mexico. This was an important stop on another railroad. The North Missouri Railroad, completed in 1858, connected St. Louis and St. Charles to the Hannibal & St. Joseph Railroad at Macon City. Grant went into camp, we think at the old county fairgrounds near the Audrain Medical Center, east of downtown. His regiment continued to drill while it patrolled the North Missouri from Centralia (west of here) to Montgomery City.

Grant was in Mexico when he learned that he had been nominated for promotion to the rank of brigadier general. By some accounts he also learned in Mexico that his appointment was confirmed. The official date of his appointment was August 7, 1861. On that day, though, Grant and his regiment were on a train barreling towards St. Louis, on the way to his next assignment, Ironton, Missouri.

A footnote, to bring the reader into a later phase of Missouri's Civil War that reached its crest in 1864 just down the road from here. In September, 1862, Union Gen. Lewis Merrill ordered three men put to death in Mexico by firing squad, expressing his desire "that it be done publicly and with due form and solemnity . . ." These were some of Porter's recruits captured during Porter's great escapade, who were accused of violating earlier paroles. What offenses were committed by Dr. William McFarland, Solomon Donaldson and John Gastemee to cause them to be paroled in the first place is unknown to us, but this incident fortunately had a relatively happy ending. The sentences of the condemned were commuted and they spent some years in prison instead. Not so for the men of Kirksville, Macon and Palmyra.

To reach Tour Stop 69:

68 If you come from central Iowa, you will join this Tour Loop at Tour Stop 83, in Kirksville. Whether you follow the tour in a clockwise direction from there to Palmyra, or counterclockwise down U. S. 63 through Macon, you will be introduced to the horror of 1862. If you arrive from some other direction, please read the descriptions at Stops 82, 85, 55 and 56 before you make a judgment about the happenings at Centralia in 1864. The line that in logic connects Mexico to Centralia, when logic follows the peculiar rules of escalating violence, is as straight as the road you travel west from here.

Tour Stop 69

A memorial here is near the old CENTRALIA DEPOT, and the September 27, 1864 event known as the Centralia massacre. We will be careful to distinguish the massacre at the depot from the Battle of Centralia, which you visit at Tour Stop 70.

You have approached Centralia from the back door. The story of how Bloody Bill Anderson reached this point is told at Tour Stops 73 to 81. His opponent at the Battle of Centralia, Maj. A. V. E. Johnston, is introduced at Tour Stops 59 and 63. Also, see the campaign summary at page 75 to orient yourself.

We will focus here on the third and fourth components in this drama, which are respectively a passenger train and a stagecoach.

Anderson roamed north and east from Fayette, and then approached Centralia from the north. His men went into camp on Young's Creek on the night of September 26, about three miles south of town. Johnston's three companies of the 39th Missouri were just now riding in the direction of Centralia from Paris, Missouri, to the northeast. At about 10:00 a.m. on the 27th, a train that had left St. Charles that morning pulled into the station in Mexico. Among its passengers were 23 or 24 Union soldiers. They were travelling home to northwest Missouri and Iowa, most of them from the 1st Iowa Cavalry and the 1st Missouri Engineer regiment. The engineers were on furlough after helping Sherman capture Atlanta, while it seems the Iowans had been furloughed or discharged down South and may have been heading home for good.

Drive south from the Graceland Museum one block, to Breckinridge Street. Turn right here, and go west about 5 blocks to Morris Street. Turn right. In 1/2 mile to the north, Morris Street ends as State Route 22 (Monroe Street). Turn left here. In 13.5 miles, you will arrive in the town of Centralia. Go to Allen Street and turn left. Take Allen Street south until you have crossed the second set of railroad tracks, then turn left immediately on Railroad Street. The next Stop is at your left, two blocks to the east.

69

SOLE SURVIVOR

Thomas Morton Goodman was a sergeant in the First Missouri Engineer regiment. A Kentuckian who moved first to Missouri and then to Page County, Iowa, Goodman was the senior Union soldier on the North Missouri train that Anderson halted at the Centralia depot. Due to his rank, Goodman was selected to serve as a hostage, because Anderson wanted a prisoner to exchange for a guerrilla captured by Union soldiers. Goodman rode around central Missouri for 10 days as Anderson's captive, then escaped while Anderson's men were crossing the Missouri River near Columbia. He wrote a book about his adventure in 1868. It is the prime source for what is known about Centralia.

In the 1870s, Goodman took his family overland to California, settling in Santa Rosa north of San Francisco. It may be an exaggeration to say that Goodman's good fortune influenced our literary history, because Goodman's oldest son, James, was 8 years old when his father nearly died. In 1897, nevertheless, James met a young man named Jack London headed for the Yukon gold fields, and they formed a partnership. James Goodman shared some of the experiences that shaped London's 1903 masterpiece, *Call of the Wild.*

Captain George Todd
1841 - 1864

George Todd was born in Quebec, Canada, and moved with his family to the Kansas City area around 1859. When war came in 1861, he was one of the first men to join up with William Quantrill's small band. By 1862 he would ride at Quantrill's right hand. His influence grew as the war wore on. In 1864 he overshadowed his former chief.

Todd was with Quantrill in Lawrence, Kansas, and with Bill Anderson at Centralia. Measured by his fearlessness and brutality, Todd deserves to be ranked with these men. After Centralia, Todd joined his partisan cavalry with Sterling Price's columns, scouting as Price moved west during his great 1864 Expedition. Todd was northeast of Independence on October 21, 1864, eyeing the federals who were approaching from the east, when a sharpshooter's bullet killed him. His men took him to the cemetery now called Woodlawn, south of Independence, and buried him that night.

To reach Tour Stop 70:

There is a marker in the City Park at Allen and Singleton Streets that includes directions to the battlefield, and to the Centralia Historical Society Museum that includes a Civil War exhibit. Your first objective is Jefferson Street (Route Y), which is ahead of you as you face east from the depot site.

Go south on Jefferson Street, for about a mile from the tracks to the southern outskirts of town, to a road called Gano Chance Road (also Route JJ). Turn left on Gano Chance Road, which makes a sharp right 1.5 miles to the east and becomes Rangeline Road. From the point of the turn, drive south for a mile and look for a gravel drive and parking area on your right.

Some of Anderson's men who consolidated on Young's Creek came into town on the morning of September 27, probably just to plunder the stores. Anderson was in charge. The train from Mexico was soon seen approaching from the east, and Anderson's men blocked the tracks. The engineer of the train knew the trouble he was in, and plunged ahead at full steam in an effort to break through. He did not break through, and the train came to a halt near the station, just across the tracks from here. Anderson's band entered the train to rob the passengers, and were surprised to find the Union soldiers on board.

Anderson lined up the Union men at track-side. Stripped of their uniforms, all but one were shot in the head. The one, Sgt. Tom Goodman of the Missouri Engineers, was held to be exchanged for one of Anderson's men who was in federal hands.

While the train was steaming west from Mexico, a stagecoach was on the road north from Columbia. A United States Congressman, James S. Rollins, was on board, bound with others in the coach for a McClellan for President rally that afternoon in Mexico. The stage was stopped by the guerrillas, and while they were in the process of searching the passengers the train from Mexico made its appearance. Rollins and the others concealed their identities long enough to avoid certain death. Then their tormentors headed to the action along the tracks.

Johnston was riding south across the prairie, and could see the smoke rising from Centralia. He had about 150 men, from Companies A, G and H of the 39th Missouri Infantry, mounted on horses and mules they had appropriated from area farmers. Anderson left the scene of the carnage at the depot, and rode back to Young's Creek where he and his 50 or 60 men joined at least 300 others. Act One was over.

Tour Stop 70

This is the CENTRALIA BATTLEFIELD. A local Boone County group, the Friends of the Centralia Battlefield, has preserved this field and welcomes the public to walk its historic ground. It is now forever in the public domain. Make no mistake: this is the scene of the classic guerrilla battle of the Civil War.

The parking area occupies a part of the campsite used by the guerrillas on the night of September 26, 1864. The camp extended along the creek to the south, and west into the valley of a small tributary. It seems that Bloody Bill Anderson was taking charge, but any authority he exercised over this large, diverse band was loose at best. There were men here who had developed fearsome reputations of their own, most notably George Todd, who certainly

"ranked" Anderson in terms of experience. But the Battle of Centralia, a classic ambush, has Anderson's stamp on it.

According to the famous quote, the Comanche was "the finest light cavalry in the world," but we submit that the men camped here should at least finish a close second. Many had four, if not six, revolvers on their persons, and most were raised as horsemen in an area known (as it still is today) for the quality of its horses. They were seasoned and hardened, motivated, ruthless and vicious.

The 39th Missouri Volunteers, on the other hand, had just been enrolled and trained, and were equipped with single-shot muzzle loading Enfield rifles, a British design that was a fine weapon when it was developed in 1853 and prized in 1861 by both armies. It was outmoded now.

When A.V.E. Johnston arrived in Centralia, the grisly scene at the depot inflamed him - and maybe it was intended to do so. Anderson sent a small band out in the direction of Centralia, just for the purpose of showing Johnston a trail of dust leading south. The townspeople warned Johnston that a large force was camped south of town, and not to follow. Johnston left a detachment from Company H to guard the town, and rode off in pursuit. He had about 120 men with him, and they arrived here about 5:00 p.m.

Cross the bridge to the battlefield. A hill rises to the west and northwest of your position. The sun would have been nearing the horizon viewable from here, when Johnston came over the hill from Centralia. Because his men were mounted, some had to hold the horses in the rear, so perhaps 85 or 90 men formed on the hill in line of battle. If they followed convention, they would have marched forward far enough to reach the "military crest" of the hill, meaning that they were

Confederate monument, Centralia

at least a man's height below the horizon from your vantage point. This is so that their figures would not be outlined by the sky.

If you were in Anderson's gang, you might have been with a small contingent that exposed itself at about the location of the Confederate monument. This group was the bait, and would have "skedaddled" into the woods when Johnston appeared on the horizon, so as to confirm his misconception that he was chasing the small band he saw riding south from town.

Of course, the Southern rangers were hidden in the woods, it is thought now in a "V" formation extending north and south at your location and west in the bed of the small stream to the left. If you were anywhere in this formation, you would have known with certainty that the hapless Johnston had swallowed the bait. Johnston's raw men lined up in their best parade-ground style, using 1861 weapons and 1861 tactics. Johnston had only the advantage of the effective range of his rifles, versus Anderson's pistols, and it was a matter of simple mathematics. How many shots could Johnston's men fire in the time it took for 350 galloping horses to cross this distance? The sources say that the men of the 39th fired only once.

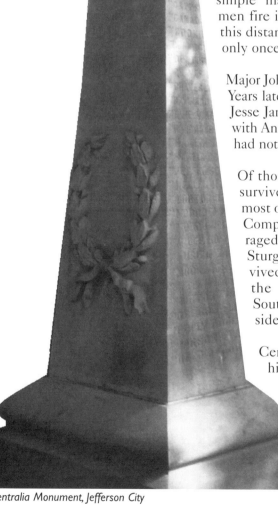

Centralia Monument, Jefferson City

Major Johnston was killed instantly by a bullet to the forehead. Years later, upon visiting this field, Frank James claimed that Jesse James fired the fatal shot. Frank and Jesse were riding with Anderson's band at this time, although Frank swore they had not been to town in the morning.

Of those men of the 39th Missouri on the firing line, two survived. The horse holders started off for Centralia, and most of them were killed en route. Most of the men from Company H who remained in Centralia while the battle raged were killed in town or as they fled west towards Sturgeon. Perhaps 15 of Johnston's men, all told, survived the day. Counting the men taken from the train, the Union death toll was more than 160; the Southerners had 3 killed. The *death* rate on the Union side was about 90%.

Certainly, many of the Union soldiers who died on this hill were killed after throwing down their arms. Given the massive superiority of Southern firepower, surely many were killed in the charge. In Missouri in 1864, reports of encounters with guerrilla forces - whichever side is doing the reporting - commonly and eerily list casualties that include no wounded or captured, so we should not be surprised.

September 27, 1864 is the most awful date in Missouri history. On the same day of the carnage at Centralia, at Pilot Knob Sterling Price's Missouri and Arkansas Confederates bashed themselves three times against the walls of Union Ft. Davidson, suffering 1000 casualties in an hour. In the East, Grant was pushing his lines west as he attempted to surround Petersburg, Virginia. Grant and Lee, as well as Price, were learning how entrenchments and modern weaponry "trumped" massed infantry. Those lessons of 1864 were forgotten, only to be re-learned in World War I, and are of academic interest today.

Today, the United States Army trains men and women on the Centralia battlefield. Counter-insurgency is the lesson plan. The style of war fought by Missourians against Missourians in 1864, then so unimaginably brutal, is sadly now commonplace in many parts of the world. We should never forget Centralia. It is here to remind us what happens to civilized people in uncivilized times.

Tour Stop 71

Columbia is the metropolis of central Missouri, a quintessential University town, and the home of the State Historical Society of Missouri. The ELLIS LIBRARY on the campus of the University of Missouri is your destination. It is on Hitt Street, one block to the west. Walk to Hitt street. The Library is a block south near a gothic tower.

College students in Missouri, as elsewhere, have no concept whatsoever of "illegal parking." One reason for this, as you know if you have a student here, is that Columbia will dutifully mail you all your son's or daughter's parking tickets unless you title the car in his or her name. When you are ready to pack the sprout off for college, put this on your checklist. You, however, should take care to park in a proper space, pay the meter, and rest assured that your quest to find the Ellis Library is worth the effort. The Art Gallery of the State Historical Society is open from 9:00 a.m. to 4:30 p.m. Mondays thru Fridays, and until 3:00 p.m. on Saturdays. Ask at the front desk for admission to the Art Gallery.

71

To reach Tour Stop 71:

Continue south on Rangeline Road to the first road that intersects from the right, Grassland School Road. Turn right, and drive west for 1.5 miles to State Route Z. Turn right (north), from which point you can return to Centralia. To continue the tour turn left at the next road, which is Union Church Road. After traveling west for 1.6 miles, turn left on Route JJ. JJ arrives at State Route 124 in 1.4 miles. Turn left on 124, and head southwest to Columbia.

When you reach the town of Hallsville, stay straight where Route 124 turns west. This road becomes Route B, and is good road from this point to Interstate 70, 12 miles south of Hallsville. When you reach I-70, continue straight across the highway where this road becomes Paris Road in Columbia. This is (just incidentally) the old stage road to Centralia. Continue south from I-70 on Paris Road .7 mile to College Avenue, then turn left. Drive south on College 3 blocks to University Avenue, and turn right. There is a parking garage on the right in 1/2 block. All spaces are reserved except there is metered parking all of the way at the top.

To reach Tour Stop 72:

Find your way back to Broadway and drive west. At the western edge of downtown you cross Providence Road. Keep a lookout for a cemetery on your left as you ascend the hill. The entrance to Tour Stop 72 is less than .2 mile west of Providence.

To reach Tour Stop 73:

Exit the cemetery, turn right on Broadway, then left on Providence Road. Providence Road intersects Interstate 70 1.2 miles north.

Once you turn on to Providence Road, you will be following the Lewis & Clark Trail until a point past Rocheport. The turns are all marked by Lewis & Clark Trail markers.

Enter I-70 westbound, and travel 10.9 miles west to Exit 115 (Route BB). Exit here and turn right. In about two miles you will arrive in the town of Rocheport. The next Stop is on the left, just after Clark Street.

The Society has one of the finest collection of George Bingham paintings in the country, including one of Bingham's renditions of Order No. 11 (he painted two). This iconic painting is the greatest work of art with a Civil War theme. It is also a political statement that contrasted Bingham's Unionist but Missouri Southern politics with those of the dreaded Kansan, Thomas Ewing. More on this theme will be found in Kansas City in Tour Loop Four.

Tour Stop 72

Historic COLUMBIA CEMETERY holds the graves of many of Columbia's famous figures, including James S. Rollins, the politician nearly caught in Centralia, James Waugh, Sheriff of Boone County who was in the coach with Rollins, and M. G. Singleton, who owned the land where Anderson and his men camped. In the south part of the cemetery is a plot containing the most African-American veterans' graves, we think, in the state. Also in the cemetery are the graves of Judge David Todd, uncle of Mary Lincoln, and the musician John William "Blind" Boone.

Tour Stop 73

The former ROCHEPORT BAPTIST CHURCH, built in 1860, is now the Rocheport Community Center. This is one of a dozen or so antebellum buildings remaining in Rocheport, which was sacked a few times during the war. This is one place to stop and learn the Civil War history of the town, but the whole town is a Civil War site.

Rocheport's Civil War history began just after the Civil War began. On June 17, 1861, Nathaniel Lyon brought a contingent of Union troops from St. Louis to this area by riverboat, having first taken control of Jefferson City. Lyon arrived here in the early morning hours in pursuit of a Missouri State Guard force that was assembling across the Missouri River, in Boonville. After tying up for a time, the transports ferried the troops across the river to a landing on the south side, and from there Lyon launched what would be the third land battle of the Civil War.

72 73

Before becoming a railroad town, Rocheport was an important river port servicing a wide swath of Boone and Howard Counties. It was well garrisoned by Union troops during most of the war, but in the summer of 1864 Rocheport came under the sway of Southern partisans. On July 18, Bloody Bill Anderson rode into town at the head of his small band. They managed to occupy the town for a week, then went raiding far into northeast Missouri. Anderson and his men returned to Rocheport, which he called his "capital" that summer, occupying it again from August 30 to September 7. He harassed river traffic on the Missouri River to such an extent that for a time traffic came to a halt.

We don't know if Anderson went back in Rocheport to launch the campaign that ended at Centralia, but it appears he was seven miles northeast of here on September 23, 1864, when the campaign got under way. There, at a place called Goslin's Lane, the guerrillas attacked a Union wagon train on its way to Rocheport with supplies and ammunition. In the evening of the same day, partisan bands assembled a few miles south of Fayette in neighboring Howard County.

On October 2, 1864, the federals burned Rocheport for reasons not known, but probably in retaliation for the Centralia raid. By some accounts, Anderson was in the woods nearby to witness the event, having returned here in the wake of Centralia to find a way across the river.

Our Tour Loop now turns north, but be mindful that Boonville and Tour Loop Three are very close by, via U.S. Highway 40. We will be following gravel roads for awhile as we move north on Loop Two. Description of the route north continues on page 101 of this Guide.

"I have killed Union soldiers until I have got sick of killing them."

Bill Anderson

THE RAWLINGS OF KENTUCKY

When you resume the Tour at Tour Stop 74 you will be at a place called Rawlings Lane, which was a farm road in 1864 that serviced property of one Commodore Perry Rawlings. Rawlings' grandfather Jonathan from Kentucky was an early settler of Howard County. Jonathan died here in 1823, the same year Commodore was born to a son of his first wife. James, a son of Jonathan's second wife, lived in Howard County as late as 1827, before moving to Galena, Illinois. James' oldest son, who was born in Galena in 1831, was John Aaron Rawlins. John Aaron Rawlins was the Chief of Staff to U.S. Grant during the Civil War. He died in September, 1869, while Secretary of War in Grant's cabinet. John's cousin, Commodore Rawlings, died in a freak hunting accident the following month on his farm near here.

The Gray Ghosts Trail™

The Gray Ghosts Trail is an initiative of Missouri's Civil War Heritage Foundation (with which the author is affiliated). The Trail highlights a number of battles and actions that occurred in central Missouri, which are described in some detail in Connecting Route C, at page 246 of this Guide. Also note the attractions in Fulton at page 251. Communities along and near Interstate 70 from Boonville east to Danville are combining efforts to bring special attention to heritage sites in the area, which is rich in Civil War history. Of particular interest are the traces of the old Boonslick Road, and a parallel road called the St. Charles Road, which were in use during the Civil War.

Additional information regarding attractions in Boone and Callaway Counties is available at these websites:

Columbia Convention & Visitors Bureau: www.visitcolumbiamo.com
Boone County Historical Society: www.boonehistory.org
Heart of Missouri (Fulton) CVB: www.heartofmotourism.org
Kingdom of Callaway Historical Society: www.kchsoc.org

Part III - Northbound

Tour Stop 74

This is the site of RAWLINGS LANE. You have traveled a section of road that was once the Fayette-Rocheport Road, which continued north from here to the town of Fayette. This point was then an intersection, where the Franklin-Rocheport Road dead-ended. The road to the left of you was that road. Opposite the end point of the Franklin-Rocheport Road, running east from here was a narrow lane that serviced the Rawling's property. This was Rawlings Lane.

Bloody Bill Anderson had been in and around Rocheport in July, 1864, as has been noted. At the end of August, after returning from a foray in the Kansas City area, he was roaming in southern Howard County when a Union cavalry unit left Boonville to give him chase. Perhaps 45 men of the 4th Missouri Militia Cavalry ventured out. They picked up Anderson's trail about a mile west of here on the Franklin-Rocheport Road. A local farmer warned Captain Joseph Parke, commanding the Union patrol, that it was Anderson and warned him not to tangle with the guerrilla force. Parke moved east after Anderson, nevertheless.

By this time it appears that Anderson had mastered the tactic of ambush, and he pulled one off here. With his entire force he rode up the hill that carried Rawlings Lane, leaving hoof prints of his horses to guide Parke into a trap. Most of his men took to the field to the north, then returned to this area and concealed themselves behind the small hill to your left. A few of the guerrillas were posted in the lane, over the crest of the hill to the east, and they would feign the role of rear guard, to gallop off to the east and bait Parke into commencing the chase.

Parke did exactly what was expected of him, and Anderson waited until the tail of Parke's column was fully within Rawlings Lane. The guerrillas poured over the hill from the north and attacked the federal detachment in flank. The resulting melee in the lane produced seven dead federals, and numerous wounded. The totals would have been higher but for the fact that a cavalry detachment out of Fayette came to Parke's rescue.

The Union dead were taken to Boonville and buried in the old City Cemetery, now Sunset Hills Cemetery. Parke, who apparently left his command when the fighting started, was dismissed from the service. Over the next several miles, you will follow the road used by Parke's men in a running fight during the retreat from Rawlings Lane.

To reach Tour Stop 74:

Go to the west end of 3rd Street in Rocheport, which is Central Street, and turn right. Drive north on this road, which becomes State Route 240, for one mile. Here you will turn left on U.S. Highway 40. Traveling west, drive .8 mile, taking the right turn-off for northbound Route 240. In about .6 mile, bear left at the "Y" that is here, and after driving southwest for about 1/4 mile turn right at the first road, a gravel road marked County Road 442. Drive west for 1/2 mile and stop at the first intersecting road.

To reach Tour Stop 75:

Take the left-hand route, which is County Road 442, for 3.8 miles. Turn right where this road ends, and drive north for about a half a mile. Take the next available left (at County Road 448), and then a quick right at County Road 455. Drive north on 455 for 1.4 miles and take in the view in the valley here where the road crosses a small stream. This is the likely place where Southern cavalry entered the Maxwell Road and began their assault on Fayette. This event is described at Tour Stop 78.

Continue north on County Road 455 for another .4 mile, to near the point where the County Road intersects paved Highway P. The road ends at granite monument that you can see from a distance as you ascend the hill here. Park at the end of the road near the monument.

This is the site of the SALT CREEK CHRISTIAN CHURCH. There is Civil War history in the church cemetery, which will be described. First, however, the backdrop for the "Fayette Fight," which occurred on September 24, 1864:

Much of what we know of the engagement at Fayette, and for that matter Rawlings Lane, comes from a small book published in 1913 called "The Babe of the Company," by Howard County's Hampton B. Watts. This work is a rather typical memoir, more of a reminiscence than a history. Watts lived nearly his entire long life in southern Howard County, though, and when he pinpoints the scenes of events his views are entitled to respect. However, what is recorded here is as much the product of the work of Howard County historian Bill Lay as it is of Hampton Watts.

Watts, known as "Hamp," was sixteen in 1864 when he joined Bill Anderson's gang. It's not clear that he was at Rawlings Lane, although he reported it in detail. But he was involved in the Fayette Fight, and one or the other of these actions was his first taste of combat.

Anderson had a band of about 80 men at this time, and on the night of September 23, 1864 he went into camp on the Bonne Femme Creek about two miles west of here. Camped in close proximity was another guerrilla force of about the same size, commanded by George Todd, along with a number of other guerrilla commands. On the morning of September 24, the entire force, in column of two's, took the road you have traveled and passed this point as it moved north on the Maxwell Road.

Their objective was the headquarters of the feared 9th Missouri Militia Cavalry, in Fayette. Just north of where you are on Highway P, where the Highway turns west, the Maxwell Road did (and still does) head straight to Fayette. This is the route used by Anderson's and Todd's men, but we detour west and stay on paved roads for now.

About the Salt Creek Church: The marker here was erected many decades ago by the Daughters of the American Revolution to mark the route (Route P) of the Boonslick Road. This intersection on the great western road was selected for the site of what is thought to be the oldest church in Howard County. The Salt Creek Church was founded in 1817 by Thomas Crawford McBride, a pioneer preacher for the Disciples of Christ and a first cousin of President Andrew Jackson.

The church is long gone, but its cemetery remains. Just to the northeast of the Boonslick Road monument is a tall stone with two names on it. What the stone says is set forth in the margin.

The Collins and Carter families had arrived here from western Missouri in the wake of Order No. 11, and the proximity in age of their teenaged sons, "Buck" Collins and Al Carter, suggests that the boys were best of friends. Their story comes to us from James Archibald Maxwell. Ten years old at the time, Maxwell was working a wheat field with his father, just on the left side of the road as you look south from this vantage point. We don't know if Buck and Al had formally joined the local Southern guerrillas. On September 12, 1864, the boys were south of here visiting their mothers when a lone rider in civilian clothes approached from the area of the cemetery. Collins and Carter decided to confront the rider, and rode up here. The rider was a scout for a detachment of federal cavalry that was coming on from the north, concealed by the hill upon which the cemetery sits.

The federals swept over the hill and chased the boys south, catching and killing Buck on the Maxwell Road a little south of here. They chased Al Carter into the property of Alfred Peeler, on the right side of the road to the south, and brought him to ground. Carter sported shoulder-length black hair, and the federals thought they had killed Bloody Bill Anderson. When they returned jubilantly to the Maxwell field with Al's scalp and announced their prize, Archie Maxwell's father said simply: "No, you got the Carter boy."

William W.
Son of T. and E. Collins
Died September 12, 1864
Aged 17 yrs., 11 mos., 16 days

Alfred H. Son of
J. H. and M. A. Carter
Died September 12, 1864
Aged 17 yrs., 11 mos., 17 days

Tour Stop 76

This Stop marks the QUANTRILL - ANDERSON COUNCIL SITE. The actual site, insofar as we can tell, is about 200 or 300 yards north on Route DD, but there is no place to pull over there.

Hamp Watts recalled that he and the rest of Anderson's men halted in the early morning of September 24, 1864, near the Cherry Grove School, and watched as "Bill Anderson, Quantrell [sic], Captains George Todd, Tom Todd and Dave Poole were seated on their horses, engaged in animated and heated argument."

The Missouri partisan rangers had spent the previous winter near Sherman, Texas, where they bivouacked among regular Confederate troops. Their behavior was appalling;

To reach Tour Stop 76:

Turn left on Highway P, and continue on P when it turns to the left. At a point 1.7 miles from the cemetery, Highway P intersects Route DD. Pull over to the right just before you reach the DD intersection. There is a paved area near a mailbox that will safely accommodate you.

General Henry McColluch at one point issued orders for Quantrill's arrest, on suspicion of murder of a Confederate officer. Anderson's small band, which had been quarreling with Quantrill's men, was sent out in pursuit of Quantrill. Both men returned to Missouri in the spring of 1864. Quantrill was mostly absent from combat that summer, and it is not clear how bad was the blood between him and Anderson. Quantrill's band dwindled to a handful of men.

Nevertheless, Quantrill appeared here south of Fayette and presumed to give advice to the likes of Anderson and Todd. The heated argument involved Anderson's plan to attack Fayette, and Quantrill's position that the plan was foolhardy. As mentioned in Centralia, we could overestimate the control that Anderson exercised over the other partisan bands, but here near the Cherry Grove School, Anderson's star ascended over that of the infamous Quantrill. This was a clear turning point in Missouri's Civil War. Quantrill, architect of the Lawrence massacre, was a brutal man who had, if not conscience, at least a regard for his reputation as a soldier. Anderson on the other hand was the proverbial rider on a pale horse and, in the words of the New Testament, the man who sat upon a horse near here "was Death, and Hell followed with him" (Rev. 6:7-8).

As regards Fayette, Quantrill was right.

Tour Stop 77

The obelisk is Fayette's CONFEDERATE MONUMENT. This is the burial place of 5 or 6 of the partisan cavalrymen who attacked Fayette on September 24, 1864. Their bodies were left on the field.

The Southerners' objective was a federal encampment north of town, situated on a ridge on or near the campus of Central Methodist University. The 9th Missouri Militia Cavalry had built a number of log barracks buildings, or "blockhouses" as the par-

To reach Tour Stop 77:

Turn right on Route DD, and drive north 6.2 miles to the intersection of State Highway 5, and turn right. In .2 mile, turn right on Park Street. This street jogs left after you have passed the grain silos, and then turn right on Watts Avenue. In about 1/4 mile this street intersects State Highway 240. Turn right on Highway 240 then quickly left on Main Street. In about .1 mile, near where two large trees hang over the road, stop and look for a prominent obelisk in the cemetery to your right.

The gravel road that extends south from the intersection of Highway 240 and Mains Street is the Maxwell Road that you left at the Salt Creek Church.

tisans called them, as winter quarters. The 9th Cavalry probably had no more than 50 men in Fayette this day. Ironically, much of the regiment was chasing the perpetrators of the attack at Goslin's Lane, which occurred the day before. Main Street is sunken here, and flanked by cemeteries, so it is a place particularly well suited for imagining the scene as Anderson and 250 men moved north on this very road. The men at the head of this column wore yankee blue, and were in the town before the alarm went out.

Anderson split his force as he approached the courthouse. Most of his riders moved along Linn Street, two blocks west, to attack the camp to the north. He detached some men to attempt to dislodge Union troops who had found protection in the brick courthouse. We're going to approach the scene of the battle in a clockwise direction, and then return to the Fayette square.

Tour Stop 78

This is the scene of the "FAYETTE FIGHT". The ridge that you see to the north is the likely site of the barracks of the 9th Cavalry - the "blockhouses" – which were the main object of Anderson's attack. This is a good place for a defensive work, particularly since the ridge is situated to protect Fayette from the north, overlooking the old road that is now Mulberry Street.

From your vantage point, look across the ravine to the north. Across this ravine Anderson's men made three futile charges. The attacks were disjointed. Not more than 75 men at a time charged across the ravine, although more than 200 were available to take part in the attack. Frank and Jesse James were among those who charged up this hill. Frank said later that this was "the worst scared I ever was during the war."

78

There were no more than a few dozen Union men holed up in the barracks, but their position was a strong one. The partisans lost 13 dead and 30 wounded; after the third charge, Anderson withdrew his band and trailed off to the north.

Alexander Franklin James
1843 – 1915

Jesse James' big brother Frank was born in 1843. Four years older than Jesse, Frank joined most of his neighbors in the service of the Missouri State Guard in 1861, and he was present at the battle of Wilson's Creek and siege of Lexington in August and September of that year. He left the army soon after Lexington, and soon after that began riding with William Quantrill.

Frank James served successively under partisan leaders Quantrill, Thornton and Anderson, and had a hand in many of the guerrilla skirmishes and actions that occurred in Missouri and Kansas in 1863 and 1864. He rode east with Quantrill in the Spring of 1865, and was with Quantrill on May 10, 1865 when the latter was shot and mortally wounded in Kentucky.

After the War, Frank was an active member of Jesse's gang at least until the Northfield, Minnesota raid in 1876. He was acquitted in two trials after he surrendered himself to authorities in 1882, following Jesse's death. He reached a certain level of respectability before passing away in 1915. His ashes were taken from the James Farm and buried outside of Kansas City when his wife Annie died in 1944.

To reach Tour Stop 78:

Go north on Main Street, two blocks past the courthouse to the point Main Street ends at the CMU campus. Turn left here (Elm Street) and drive a block west to Church Street. Turn right here and drive north about .3 mile, to a small road just after the complex of dormitories, which is called College Street. Turn right on College Street. Before you reach the bottom of the hill, park where you have a good view to the north.

To reach Tour Stop 79:

Turn right at the bottom of the hill, which is Corpew Street. Turn right again at the athletic complex, which is Mulberry Street. Now drive south along the campus until you have once again reached Elm Street. Turn right on Elm, then left on Main, and park in the courthouse square.

Tour Stop 79

This is the FAYETTE SQUARE. The magnificent courthouse here was built in 1887, replacing the Civil War era courthouse that burned in 1886. We direct your attention to the north side of the square, on East Davis Street in the area pictured below.

A man named Lewis Tomlin once owned a house and barbershop on this block. Tomlin was "a free person of color," having bought his freedom and that of his wife. We only know of one child of theirs, a girl named Marie Tomlin. Marie was a slave, owned by one Samuel Brown. She was the mother of two fatherless children when she met Jack Burton. Burton was raised a slave in the household of a near-neighbor of Brown's, Moses Burton. Jack and Marie married and had a child of their own. Then in 1853, perhaps as a result of some infraction or indiscretion, or perhaps because the lady of the house, Elizabeth Burton, died in February of that year, Jack was sold to a farmer in Saline County. His new home was 30 miles away, and his new owner refused to allow him to visit his family.

Jack Burton went on the lam. Much has been written about the events of the next several weeks, and some details of the story conflict from source to source, but it appears that Jack Burton visited his father-in-law's home on East Davis twice while he was on the run. The first time he was on his way to visit Marie. The second time was on September 28, 1853, just after he stabbed a man that day. The story of Jack Burton continues at Tour Stop 80.

Jack Burton, who would change his name to John Anderson, may have used the road that is State Route H when he fled the Tomlin house. The journey that Burton began here ended on the African continent, but before it ended it set off an international incident and changed the law of the British Commonwealth of Nations.

To reach Tour Stop 80:

Drive south on Main Street (the east side of the square) to State Highway 240, and turn left. Drive east 1/2 mile from this point, and turn left on State Highway 124. Then, turn left in .7 mile on Route H, heading north. In 6.2 miles, you will reach a point where Route H turns sharply left. There is a road, Route N, that continues straight from here to the old town of Burton. Turn into Route N, and get yourself turned around so that you can resume the trip on Route H northbound.

Tour Stop 80

The once thriving town of BURTON is ahead of you down in the next valley. The town was established after the Civil War when the now abandoned KATY Railroad came through that valley. There is nothing there to see, and we stop here only because the town was named for the family that owned Jack Burton. The Burton farm was, we think, about a mile south of here, and the Samuel Brown farm a mile and half south of Burton's. Moses Burton and his wife Elizabeth are buried in a cemetery 2 miles to the southeast.

Here we resume and conclude the story of Jack Burton, a/k/a John Anderson. We will use his alias from here on out.

The Anderson story is important for two reasons. The first is that Missouri tends to be left out of the story of the Underground Railroad. True, few people came to Missouri on their trek north, but many like Anderson started their journeys here. The second reason is that Anderson's story exploded on the international scene in December, 1860, precisely when the American secession crisis reached its peak, when South Carolina adopted articles of secession.

Anderson was roaming Howard County after he escaped his new master. Some say that he was searching out a man he thought would buy him so he could live closer to his family. On September 28, 1853, he walked into a tobacco field owned by Seneca Diggs, who was working the field with his 8 year old son and several of his own slaves. We think - we don't know - that the Diggs property was about a mile north of Fayette. By law and custom, white citizens of Missouri were obligated to confront and hold any African American found in the neighborhood without a pass, and Diggs did this. Anderson ran, Diggs and Diggs' slaves gave chase, and in the melee Anderson stabbed Diggs in the chest. Diggs died within a few weeks. Anderson escaped.

Jack Anderson

Anderson visited Tomlin in Fayette, then set out for Canada. He traveled alone, walking probably 100 miles or more through northeast Missouri slave territory, until he managed to cross the Mississippi. He found his way to Detroit, then went across the border to Windsor, Ontario.

Howard County did not forget John Anderson. Detectives nearly tricked him into re-entering the U.S. in 1854, but then he moved further inland, disappearing into one of Ontario's thriving colonies of escaped slaves. In 1860, though, Anderson revealed his deed to a friend, who later turned on him, and soon a fight for his extradition was underway. Missouri sent a delegation of witnesses to Canada, at Howard County's expense. Anderson lost round one when a court in Toronto refused a writ of habeas corpus, concluding that the allegations warranted Anderson's extradition on a charge of murder. This is what the treaty governing extradition required.

British anti-slavery interests then sought a writ of habeas corpus in the Court of Queen's Bench at Westminster Hall in London. The Court there decided that it had "concurrent jurisdiction" with the courts of Ontario - a novel opinion that must have surprised the whole of Canada - and issued its writ of habeas corpus requiring that John Anderson be delivered up in London. A legal crisis was averted when another Canadian court ordered Anderson released on a technicality. Then Parliament enacted the Habeas Corpus Act of 1862, barring recurrence of such interference with courts in the British possessions. John Anderson was free, and Canada itself was a little more free.

John Anderson did go to England, a guest of the British and Foreign Anti-Slavery Society, was feted in London and drew crowds all over the country. At the end of 1862, he boarded a ship, went to Liberia, and was not heard from again. Except, in 2008 his case in the Court of Queen's Bench was cited by the U. S. Supreme Court in its decision involving the Guantanamo prisoners.

North Missouri Railroad, 1863

Tour Stop 81

Once more you are on the NORTH MISSOURI RAILROAD. Near here, Bill Anderson's men crossed the tracks after they left Fayette on September 24, 1864, and after they menaced the county seat at Huntsville on September 25. The partisans camped the night of September 25 near the town of Middle Grove in Audrain County, about 8 miles due east of here. On the night of September 26, Anderson camped south of Centralia, which is about 20 miles southeast.

Huntsville was Bill Anderson's home town, where he was born in 1840. He had raided the town in July, 1864. This time he approached the town and demanded the surrender of the garrison there. The Union commander in Huntsville, Lt. Col. A. F. Denny, defiantly told Anderson to "bring it on." Mindful of the disaster at Fayette the day before, the partisan rangers departed in this direction instead. This place is the natural point for the partisans to have crossed the railroad, being equidistant from two garrisoned railroad towns in the area. The old town of Allen was north of present-day Moberly and is now incorporated in it (Moberly was established after the Civil War). Renick is about 3 miles south of here.

The next town south of Renick on the old railroad is Clark, Missouri. Near Clark, in 1893, Gen. Omar Bradley was born. He later lived in Moberly, where he graduated from Moberly High School, then worked in the railroad shops before entering West Point. The Bradley family was Southern, but Omar Bradley's maternal grandfather was a member of a Union militia regiment. He enrolled in Macon in 1862, a week after the Battle of Kirksville. These are the next stops on this Loop.

The North Missouri (by Bradley's time the Wabash Railroad) has profoundly influenced the military history of the United States ever since the day in July, 1861, that U. S. Grant arrived in Mexico, Missouri to guard it from marauding Southerners.

To reach Tour Stop 81:

Retrace your route to State Route H, and turn right (north). Drive north 8.5 miles, then bear right as this road becomes Route B in Randolph County. Route B continues north and east 1.6 miles to the outskirts of the town of Higbee. Turn left on Route A just north of Higbee. Drive north on A for 7.3 miles. Stop when you reach the railroad crossing that is just before Morley Street (Business route 63) south of Moberly.

General Omar Bradley

In 1866, Congress created the rank of "General of the Army of the United States" and Ulysses S. Grant was the first man appointed to this position. The rank carried four stars, as had Grant's Civil War rank of Lieutenant General. In 1944, Congress created a 5-star grade, it too denominated "General of the Army of the United States," and five men have held that rank. Omar Bradley received it in 1950, and he was the last of the five.

In 1859, a man named John Pershing was living in Warrenton, on the North Missouri Railroad, where he was employed as a track boss. That year he married a Warrenton girl, and they soon moved to Laclede, Missouri, where John became a shopkeeper. In June, 1864, when the Pershings' oldest son was not yet four years old, a band of Southern guerrillas led by Capt. Clif Holzclaw stormed the store in Laclede and held the family captive for a short time. The oldest son, John Joseph Pershing, went to college in Kirksville and became a school teacher. Then he entered West Point. In 1919, after commanding the American Expeditionary Force in France in World War I, Pershing was appointed General of the Armies of the United States, the equivalent of a 6-star general. He is the only man in U. S. Army history to achieve this rank in his lifetime. In 1976, as a token of respect Congress conferred the rank on George Washington.

Most assuredly, memories of what happened in places like Macon, Kirksville and Centralia were carried to the battlefields of 20th Century Europe.

General John Joseph Pershing

Tour Stop 82

To reach Tour Stop 82:

Drive north a 1/2 mile on Morley Street, and turn right (east) on State Route M. Go east for about a mile, then enter U. S. Highway 63 northbound. Drive straight north for 24 miles. Turn left on Main Street in Macon, which it the street just south of an overpass that crosses the railroad tracks. Go west on Main for 5 blocks, the stop near the intersection of Rollins Street.

MACON began its existence when the Hannibal & St. Joseph Railroad arrived here in 1858. At the time of the Civil War it was sometimes still called Hudson, then a nearby competing town that later became part of Macon. The North Missouri Railroad reached this point in February, 1859, just as the Hannibal & St. Joseph was completed across the state, and became the most important rail junction in Missouri. Sadly, the old North Missouri / Wabash line was abandoned in the 1980s. You can see evidence of the old junction in the immediate area of this Stop.

Union troops occupied Macon during the entire

Civil War, beginning on June 14, 1861 when the 1st Iowa Infantry arrived here. The 1st Iowa departed Keokuk by way of the river, debarked at Hannibal, and then were rushed here by rail. They built a substantial camp along the Hannibal & St. Joe, probably in the area just to the northeast of here. On June 18, the Iowans were ordered to Boonville (which Nathaniel Lyon had captured the day before). They boarded a train and moved south on the North Missouri to Renick. From there the regiment marched overland to Boonville. In July, the regiment marched to Springfield and in August took part in the Battle of Wilson's Creek.

1869 view of Macon

Macon was the second place where federal authorities meted out the ultimate punishment to Southern men who were enrolling in 1862 to fight for the Confederacy. This story is covered extensively in Kirksville and Palmyra, and touched upon in Mexico (Tour Stop 68). The Macon men were likely affiliated with Confederate Col. John Poindexter, who was himself captured in early September of 1862.

The date was September 25, 1862. The "enforcer" here was Col. Lewis Merrill, a career officer and West Point graduate who had raised his own regiment of cavalry in 1861, the "Merrill Horse," also known as the 2nd Missouri Cavalry. Merrill had rounded up a group of Southern sympathizers, 140 of them at least, and on September 24, had all of them but 10 transported to St. Louis prisons. The prisoners, while here, were confined to a hotel known as the "Harris House," about a block south at the corner of Rollins and Second Street. According to Merrill, the ten men who were not sent to St. Louis were two- or three-time parole violators. When the rest of the prisoners left for St. Louis, the ten were transferred to a freight car that sat on the railroad, where they spent their last night on earth.

Only one source describes the events that followed on September 26. It is a history of Missouri published in 1876. The men were marched on Merrill's orders to a place 1/2 mile south of town, described as a slightly declining prairie. An execution squad composed of men of the 23rd Missouri Infantry formed a square, separating into squads of six men each. Each of the condemned were marched in front of one of these squads, and the grisly task was performed in serial fashion. The killed prisoners were Frank E. Drake, A.C. Rowe, Elbert Hamilton, William Searcy, J. A. Wysong, J. H. Fox, Edward Riggs, David Bell, John Oldham and James H. Hall. *In Memoriam.*

Bvt. Gen. Lewis Merrill
1834 – 1896

Lewis Merrill was a native of Pennsylvania who attended West Point, graduating in 1855. His first service as a cavalry officer was as a lieutenant of the First U. S. Dragoons, Jefferson Barracks, Missouri. He served in the Second Dragoons in Kansas and on the frontier, and then with the outbreak of the Civil War he was commissioned Colonel of volunteers. In August, 1861 he raised a regiment of cavalry, the 2nd Missouri Cavalry. Most of the service of the 2nd Missouri was in North Missouri, but it also took an active part in the 1864 Price Expedition.

After the War, Merrill joined the U.S. Seventh Cavalry and was stationed on the western frontier, except for a stint in 1871-73 in So. Carolina where he fought the KKK. As a Major in the post- Civil War army, he was a subordinate of George Custer, but Merrill was on detached duty representing the Seventh Cavalry at the nation's Centennial celebration in Philadelphia in 1876. Missing Custer's stand at the Little Big Horn, Merrill died instead in 1896, and is interred in Arlington National Cemetery.

111

To reach Tour Stop 83:

From the point you stopped in Macon, drive north on Rollins Street, cross the tracks, then take your first right (Vine Street). Return to U. S. Highway 63, which is Missouri Avenue in Macon. Turn left (north) on Highway 63 and drive to Kirksville, which is about 34 miles to the north.

If you are approaching Kirksville from the south, stay on U. S. Highway 63 until you are past the most populated areas. This road is also Baltimore Street and State Highway 6. About .2 mile north of Illinois Street (State Highway 11), you will turn left on Cottonwood Street. Drive west for 7 or 8 blocks, and there is a city park on your left. Park anywhere near here. You will depart the area via Mulanix Street southbound. Mulanix forms the western border of the park.

If you arrive from the north on U. S. 63, look for Cottonwood Street on your right just after passing the Adair County Library. Follow the tour route from there.

Tour Stop 83 is Kirksville's MEMORIAL PARK. The park is on the site of the old Cumberland Academy, which served as a Union hospital after the August 6, 1862 Battle of Kirksville. This spot also marks the first position of the Union's battle line. The Battle of Kirksville was the climax of Porter's Raid.

Porter clashed with Union pursuers approximately 35 miles due east of Kirksville on August 5, 1862. He turned west towards Kirksville, where he arrived on the morning of August 6 with some 2800 troops, many now hardened veterans. Porter decided he would make his stand at Kirksville.

Union Colonel John McNeil had approximately 1000 troops with him, including elements of the Missouri State Militia, the Third Iowa Cavalry, and the "Merrill Horse." Unlike Porter, he had artillery. McNeil's force approached Kirksville from the east and northeast; McNeil's five guns were posted on these heights, facing the town.

Porter placed some of his troops in line of battle to the east of the town, and stationed more in the houses clustered around the county courthouse (on the site of the present courthouse). However, the bulk of his force formed at a fence rail west of town. Subsequently, a railroad, no longer used, bisected modern Kirksville from north to south The fence line ran from north to south at approximately the line of the future railroad, which you see when you visit Stop 85. Porter intended to draw McNeil into and past the town as his advance guard staged a retreat, and to meet and defeat him at the fence line.

McNeil designed a pincer movement, believing that the Confederates would do battle in the town. He arranged his forces in an "L" with its apex at the place you are standing. His lines extended west and south from this point.

When McNeil moved, both wings converged on the town and fought house to house. The Southern forces retreated as planned to the fence line, but McNeil's right wing, for the most part dismounted men of the Merrill Horse, effectively outflanked them. This, and the effectiveness of McNeil's artillery on raw troops, broke Porter's line and scattered his forces to the west.

About the Cumberland Academy: The school closed during the War, but in 1867 it was rented by Joseph Baldwin and became the site of his North Missouri Normal School. This institution has evolved over the years to become Truman State University, whose campus dominates the southern part of the city.

Tour Stop 84

This is the ADAIR COUNTY COURTHOUSE. The existing building was completed in 1899. The building that occupied the site in 1862 burned to the ground in 1865.

Kirksville's square was the scene of one of the most memorable incidents of the battle. Eight or ten troopers of the Merrill Horse, under the command of Lt. John Cowdrey, were ordered to reconnoiter the Confederate positions within the town. They dashed into the square (by some reports, driving through three of the streets that bordered it). Despite a hail of small arms fire from the Southern force occupying the town, Cowdrey returned to his lines, leaving two troopers mortally wounded, and three wounded less seriously.

Tour Stop 85

This is the KIRKSVILLE MASSACRE SITE. On August 7, 1862, on the order of Col. John McNeil, a firing squad executed fifteen Southern men his troops had captured at the Battle of Kirksville the day before. One more soldier was executed the following day, and we believe that occurred here as well. This was the first North-on-South atrocity during Missouri's Civil War, and had most of the hallmarks of the later events at Macon and Palmyra.

It is difficult at times to comprehend the rules of military conduct that prevailed in the nineteenth century. Before the last year of the Civil War, modern concepts for the treatment of prisoners of war were unknown. When the North and South began to experiment with the idea of incarcerating captured soldiers the results were famously disastrous. In the early years of the war, a "parole"

To reach Tour Stop 84:

Continue south on Mulinax Strieet for 4 blocks, to Harrison Street. Turn right here. Drive west 3 blocks, and park in the courthouse square.

To reach Tour Stop 85:

Drive straight ahead (west) on Harrison Street for one block, and turn left on Main Street. Go south on Main two blocks to McPherson Street, and turn right. Tour Stop 145 is a half block west. Stop where you have a view of the campus of A. T. Still University. Here you can detect the old line of the railroad, running north and south.

84

85

system allowed a captured combatant to return home if he swore an oath to await an exchange for a prisoner captured by the opposing side. If exchanged, he could return to active duty. This was a sort of free pass, but as the oath noted the penalty for violation was death.

Col. McNeil in his official report, stated matter-of-factly why he ended 16 lives:

"Finding that 15 of the persons captured had been prisoners before, and upon their own admissions had been discharged on their solemn oath and parole of honor not again to take arms against their country under penalty of death, I enforced the penalty of the bond by ordering them shot. Most of these guerrillas have certificates of parole from some provost-marshal or post commandant with them, for use at any time they may be out of camp. These paltering tokens of pocket loyalty were found on the persons of nearly all the men so executed."

Lt. Col. Frisby Henderson McCullough (sometimes spelled "Frisbie") was the most prominent of the Confederate soldiers captured at and after the Battle of Kirksville. He was the man executed on August 8, 1862.

McCullough became ill during the Kirksville fight, and after the battle he tried to get to his Marion County home on foot. Captured near Edina, Missouri, on August 7, he was transported back to Kirksville with the wagon train that was re-supplying McNeil. There is no evidence that McCullough was earlier paroled; unlike the recruits he and Porter were trying to bring south, McCullough had been south. He was, it appears, a regularly commissioned officer of the Missouri State Guard. He was executed wearing the uniform of a Confederate officer.

Joseph Mudd's report of McCullough's death came to him second-hand, but it is his account that survives.

"Upon the way to the place of his execution [McCullough] requested the privilege of giving the order to fire, which was granted to him. All being ready, he stood bravely up, and without a tremor in his manly frame or a quiver in his clarion voice, he called out, 'What I have done, I have done as a principle of right. Aim at the heart. Fire!'"

McCullough did not die cleanly, suffering only one wound at the hands of the firing squad. Before he was then shot to death, he reportedly said "I forgive you for this barbarous act."

Frisby Henderson McCollough

Part IV - Eastbound

Tour Stop 86

Tour Stop 86 is the TOWN OF EDINA, the county seat of Knox County. There is some Civil War history here, in addition to McCullough's capture. One year before Kirksville, Col. Martin Green of the Missouri State Guard drove Union home guards from Edina, then used the town as a staging area for his advance on Athens, Missouri. The Battle of Athens, the northernmost battle of the Civil War, was fought on August 5, 1861, and ended in defeat for the Missouri State Guard. Green returned to Edina following Athens.

We take the opportunity in Edina to introduce you to the Baker family, which in turn is your introduction to the happenings at Palmyra, 55 miles due southeast.

Knox County, Missouri, was formed in 1845 from what had been Lewis County. One of Edina's founders was Willis T. Baker, son of a prominent Lewis County pioneer, Judge John Baker. Willis Baker and wife Henrietta had 7 children, two of whom married daughters of William Smith. The Baker daughters-in-law had a brother named Hiram Smith.

Before 1862, Baker and his wife had left Edina and moved close to his father's original homestead in Lewis County. It was there that the Bakers' oldest son John became involved in an altercation with a unionist neighbor, which escalated to the point that the neighbor was shot dead. Willis Baker was the shooter. John Baker became a fugitive.

Tour Stop 87

Tour Stop 87 is the site of the BATTLE OF NEWARK, which occurred on August 1, 1862. You have returned to a time before the Battle of Kirksville. Let's step back a few days more, to the Battle of Moore's Mill.

On July 28, 1862, Porter was headed south with his recruits, hoping to end his occupation of North Missouri and get his recruits back to Arkansas. About 70 miles south of here, along present-day Interstate 70 near Fulton, Porter found his way blocked by converging Union cavalry. Against a superior force, Porter turned to give battle, and in the resulting Battle of Moore's Mill the Confederates were defeated. After this bloody encounter Porter moved north, now hoping to consolidate with a similar force of Confederate recruits assembled by Colonel John Poindexter in territory west of here.

To reach Tour Stop 86:

Turn around and head directly east on McPherson Street, which will in .7 miles intersect Baltimore Street, which is designated U.S. Highway 63. Turn right (south) on 63, and travel 1.8 miles to the intersection of Missouri Highway 6. Turn left.

You are now on the main road to Palmyra. The route tracks the original road that was used by Porter and his pursuers as they approached Kirksville, traveling in the opposite direction.

You will reach Edina on Highway 6 after you have traveled approximately 23 miles from the Highway 63 intersection. There is not a particular historic place to stop here, so pull into the gas station at the main intersection in town. This is where Highway 6 turns sharply to the right.

For Directions to Loop 87, see next page

87

To reach Tour Stop 87:

Drive east on Highway 6, out of the town of Edina, and continue on 6 for 9.3 miles to the center of the town of Knox City. Turn right on Highway E (Newark Street), and continue south on E for 11 miles, which brings you to the outskirts of the town of Newark (pronounced new ark). Turn left at Million Street, and drive east about a mile to Main Street. Turn left on Main, then drive two blocks south. Find a place to park near the gazebo on the town green, which is Tour Stop 6.

To reach Tour Stop 88:

Take Highway 156 east for 4.6 miles, then turn right (south) on Route D. In 4.0 miles, turn right into the gravel road at the Mt. Pleasant Baptist Church. Park near the church and walk to the cemetery in the rear. The next Tour Stop, pictured at left, is near the center of the cemetery.

Porter reached Newark in several days, capturing Paris in the process, and drawing more recruits to his banner as he covered 70 miles. By August 1, Porter reached the outskirts of Newark, which was garrisoned by a small detachment of perhaps 75 Union militia under the command of Capt. W. W. Lair, along with two hundred new recruits. Porter split his force, one part moving around town then attacking from the north. The balance of the Confederate force attacked up the hill that lies to the south of your location. Lair put up a good fight for a time from several of the brick buildings in town, but was forced to surrender. Porter then moved off in the direction of Kirksville. Within several days John McNeil's troops arrived, hunting Porter, and camped in Newark.

Tour Stop 88

This is the GRAVE OF HIRAM SMITH. His stone was erected by a politician by the name of G.W. Humphrey, who wrote this epitaph:

"This monument is dedicated to the memory of Hiram Smith, the hero that sleeps beneath the sod here who was shot at Palmyra Oct. 17, 1862 as a substitute for Wm. T. Humphrey my father."

This is a thread of the story of the Baker family of Edina.

Driven from Kirksville, Porter trailed off to the southwest, trying but failing to link up with John Poindexter. Presumably, Porter still intended to get his recruits south. Porter's plans were thwarted once again, as at Moore's Mill, and he dispersed his forces. It seemed Porter's mission had failed. Then, on September 12, 1862, he suddenly appeared at the western edge of Palmyra at the head of a column of 300 cavalry. He took Palmyra and set free political prisoners and parole violators detained in its jail. Within a short time after Porter departed, Union authorities had re-populated the Marion County jail. Three of the men arrested in Porter's wake were Willis Baker, Hiram Smith and William Humphrey. Baker, too old for military service, was presumably held in connection with the shooting in Lewis County. The alleged offenses of Smith and Humphrey are not known. Hiram Smith was 20 years old, and, it is said, a divinity student. Remember, Smith's brothers were married to Willis Baker's daughters.

Consult Tour Stop 55. William T. Humphrey was among the five Palmyra detainees, including Willis Baker, who were on schedule to be shot at the fairgrounds on October 17, 1862. Humphrey's wife, Mary, took his young daughter (from a prior marriage) to McNeil to plead for William's life, and McNeil relented. McNeil ordered his provost marshal, Col. William Strachan, to spare Humphrey's life. Strachan was not content to make an example with only nine lives, so just hours before the scheduled executions he decreed that a replacement for Humphrey was needed. This decision fell on poor Hiram Smith. We can speculate that his relationship to the Baker family was not a point considered in his favor.

Tour Stop 89

Tour Stop 89 is the GRAVE OF FRISBY McCULLOUGH. The McCullough homestead was close to this place, hence his body was brought here and buried at the Asbury Chapel after he was executed and interred for a time at Kirksville.

According to tradition, it was also near here, a few miles east on the banks of a stream called Troublesome Creek, that Porter's men murdered Andrew Allsman.

To reach Tour Stop 89:

Take the gravel road south, where it will reconnect with Route D. Turn right on D, drive about a quarter mile south, to the intersection of County Road 126. On your left there is a small country church known as the "Asbury Chapel." Pull into the parking area and walk around to the cemetery on the north side of the church. There is a stone shaped like an obelisk towards the far side, pictured at left. This is Tour Stop 89.

If you are approaching Palmyra from the west, you can continue the tour in Palmyra, starting at Tour Stop 55. To reach Tour 55 from your direction of travel, continue south on Route D for 11.7 miles to the town of Philadelphia, and there turn left on Missouri Highway 168. Drive east 13.2 miles to Main Street in Palmyra. Tour Stop 55 is just west of the town square, which is 5 blocks north on Main Street.

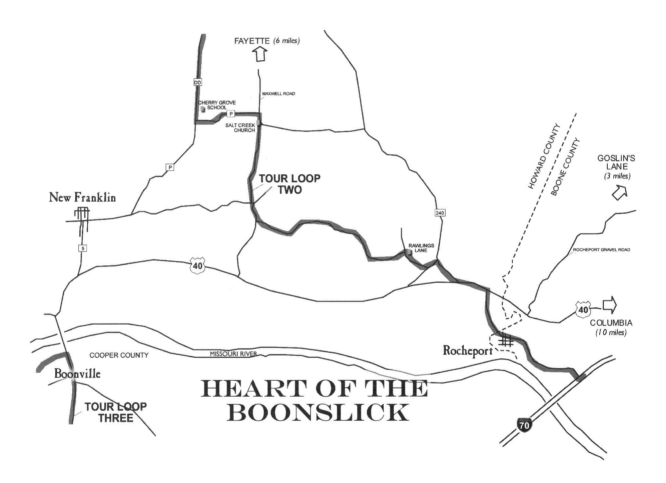

TOUR LOOP THREE

This Tour Loop covers a large part of Missouri's heartland, from the Missouri River in the north to the Osage River on the South. The principal campaign that is featured here is the cavalry raid that Confederate Colonel Joseph Orville Shelby conducted in October, 1863. This was, at the time, the longest cavalry campaign in United States military history. Part of Shelby's route was used in October, 1861, by Union forces commanded by Maj. Gen. John Charles Fremont. At that time, Fremont's was the largest infantry campaign in U.S. history. This loop, which is nearly all about cavalry, also features a significant part of the action during Price's 1864 Expedition. The Tour begins and ends in Boonville, on Interstate 70 west of Columbia.

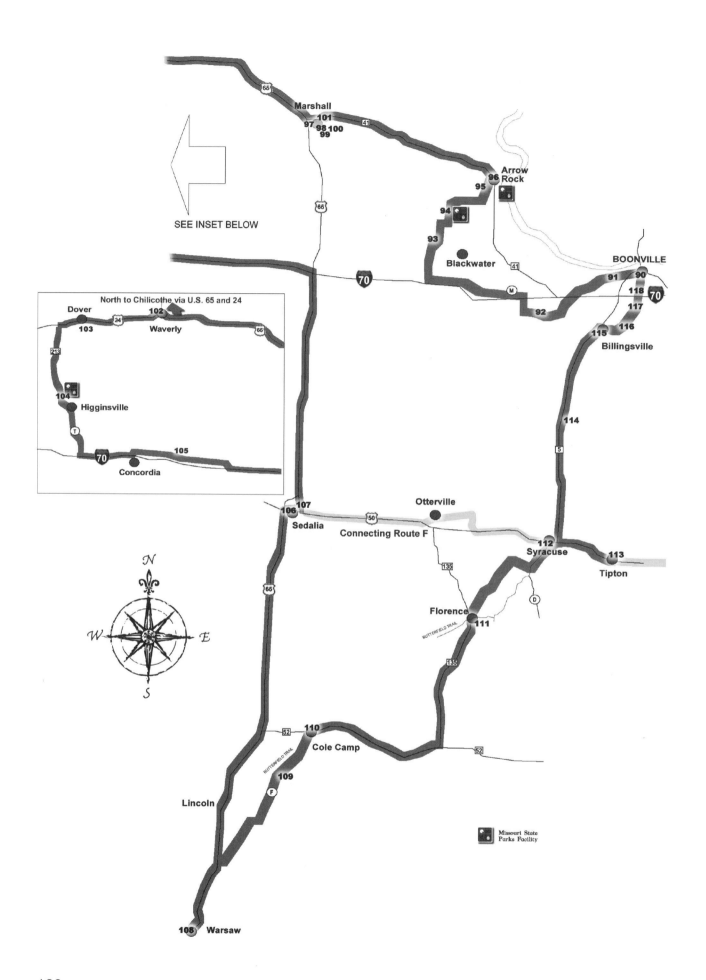

SEE INSET BELOW

Marshall
97 101
98 100
99

Arrow
Rock
96
95
94
93
Blackwater
BOONVILLE
91 90
118
41
92
117
115 116
Billingsville
M

North to Chilicothe via U.S. 65 and 24
Dover
102
103
Waverly
243
104
Higginsville
T
70
105
Concordia

114
5

107
106
Sedalia
Connecting Route F
Otterville
50
135
112
Syracuse
113
Tipton

65

N
W E
S

Florence
111
BUTTERFIELD TRAIL
D
135

52
110
Cole Camp
52
BUTTERFIELD TRAIL
109
F
Lincoln

Missouri State
Parks Facility

108 Warsaw

120

A TOUR OF SOUTH CENTRAL MISSOURI

A Knight to Remember

Prior to our Civil War, men who fought on horseback filled a particular role. To some extent, cavalry always had a role in reconnaissance, but primarily its function was to smash formations of infantry. As infantry armaments evolved, even up to the early nineteenth century, cavalry could trump infantry because the infantry could not reload their single-shot firearms in the face of a cavalry assault. Quite late in this evolution, as a result, cavalry still could and did go into a fight with sabers and lances, which were very effective once the infantry had discharged their weapons. Over the course of time, too, tacticians developed the concept of "light cavalry." These troops, as often as not, fought dismounted. Light cavalry moved combatants rapidly to the flanks or rear of an enemy force, where they could fight dismounted with single-shot firearms.

The advantages of cavalry, which existed at least up to the age of Napoleon, began to unravel with advancements in the range of firearms and artillery. The advantage shifted to the infantry. Cavalry's low point, perhaps, was signaled by the charge of the Light Brigade at Balaclava in 1854. Later, in our Civil War, the continued development of revolvers and breech-loading carbines enabled cavalry to fill a new role: A powerful offensive force that could operate independent of infantry.

The so-called cavalry raid may have had its genesis during our Civil War. Early examples of the cavalry raid - and Thompson's Big River raid highlighted in Tour Loop One is one of

Florence, Missouri

the first ever - were devised to cause the withdrawal of an opponent's massed infantry by destroying his lines of supply. These raids departed from the traditional role of cavalry, but only to a matter of degree. The distances involved were tremendously longer, but cavalry was still attacking the flanks and rear of infantry. One reason this happened was that new technologies of supply and communication - the railroads and the telegraph - allowed armies to move farther and faster than in the past. Ironically, in a way, these technologies left infantry more vulnerable to attack from the rear.

New cavalry tactics arrived in 1863. In July of that year Confederate legend John Hunt Morgan of Kentucky set out on a raid into Indiana and Ohio. In October, 1863, Joseph O. "JO" Shelby went on a raid into Missouri. By one of those coincidences that hardly seem possible, Shelby and John Hunt Morgan grew up together in Lexington, Kentucky. Their boyhood homes were doors away from each other on the west side of Lexington's Gratz Park. Morgan raised a lot of havoc in two states without facing much opposition, and was captured; Shelby went deep into a state where every county seat was an armed camp. He returned to his Arkansas base with his command intact.

In 1863, Shelby succeeded by moving at lightning speed and avoiding opposition rather than confronting it. Generations later, in a mechanized age, someone gave this a name. *blitzkrieg!*

Shelby's 1863 Raid

Shelby's Raid in 1863, a massive undertaking, touched upon many places mentioned in Tour Loop Five, to the southwest. However, the heart of the Raid, its climax, is the principal feature of the northbound route of this Tour Loop. You can track Shelby's route for 130 miles, all the way from Warsaw to Waverly. It is sobering, particularly for the dedicated traveler, to realize that this is less than one tenth of the distance covered by men on horseback in Shelby's Great Raid of 1863.

In 1863, two famous cavalry raids preceded Shelby's Raid. The first was Union Colonel Benjamin Grierson's raid behind Confederate lines, supporting Grant's move on Vicksburg. This operation, in April and May, covered nearly 600 miles in 16 days. Grierson found the safety of Union lines near Baton Rouge, and did not hazard a return trip. On July 1, 1863, John Hunt Morgan and his Kentucky Cavalry set off from his Tennessee base on a three week strike into Kentucky, Indiana and Ohio, his so-called Ohio Raid. Morgan covered about 800 miles, but he and most of his troopers were captured south of Youngstown, Ohio, on July 26, 1863.

When in September, 1863 Colonel JO

Shelby began planning his own raid, he must have been aware of Morgan's Ohio Raid, and its outcome. Shelby likely planned to outdo Morgan's feat. If he could take a force of cavalry back home to Missouri, to his hometown of Waverly, and return to Confederate lines in Arkansas, Shelby's raid would be the longest cavalry raid in the Civil War. In view of the short history of such operations, one should say it would be the longest in the annals of human warfare.

Shelby took 600 of the best men he could find, and struck north from Arkadelphia, Arkansas on September 22, 1863. He crossed the Arkansas River on September 27. On October 2, having traversed 250 miles, he entered southwest Missouri near the town of Pineville. He was joined by several small contingents of cavalry while in Arkansas, and then at Pineville by 400 troopers commanded by Col. John Coffee. His force was now 1,300 strong. His first target in Missouri was Neosho, site of a large union supply depot. On October 4, 1863 he captured the town, and a cache of supplies including 600 Sharps carbines. Shelby then went northeast, hitting small union garrisons at Bower's Mill, Greenfield, Stockton and Warsaw.

Shelby came north by way of the Butterfield Trail route, passing through Cole Camp and arriving at Syracuse on the Pacific Railroad on October 10, 1863. He sent detachments east to Tipton and west to Otterville. They destroyed 30 miles of track and the magnificent railroad bridge that spanned the Lamine River at Otterville. However, Union forces were rapidly zeroing in. The gathering forces on the Union side were led by Gen. Egbert B. Brown. Brown had perhaps 2,500 men under his command, mostly Missouri State Militia Cavalry.

Shelby fought a small engagement near Syracuse. The Confederate raiders then rode north and trotted unmolested into Boonville on October 11, 1863, presaging their entrance a year later during Price's Expedition. Pressed now from the south, Shelby left the friendly confines of Boonville the next day and moved west. Continuous skirmishing occurred on

Postwar View of Thespian Hall, Boonville

122

Born and raised in Kentucky, a Missourian by choice, Joseph Orville Shelby possessed the dashing charm of J.E.B. Stuart and the fighting instincts of N. B. Forrest. Before the Civil War, Shelby was a hemp planter and businessman in Waverly, Missouri, and by some accounts the richest man in Missouri. He had an active role in the Missouri-Kansas Border Wars of the 1850's, raising a troop of horsemen in Lafayette County and equipping them at his own expense. Joining the Missouri State Guard, he entered the War early and played an important role in the Battle of Carthage, July 5, 1861. His first assignment after joining the Confederate service was to organize and command the west's "Iron Brigade" of Southern cavalry.

In 1863, Shelby participated in all three of that year's great Missouri cavalry raids, including the greatest of all, which bears his name. The year 1863 also witnessed the Battle of Helena, Arkansas, where Shelby played a key role and suffered a severe wound. He nevertheless set out in October, 1863 on what would be the longest cavalry operation to that date in U. S. history, and perhaps for all time.

In 1864, Shelby commanded a division in Price's Expedition, and the rear-guard heroics of his command twice saved the Confederate invasion force, at Westport and at Mine Creek. Union Maj. General Alfred Pleasonton chased and fought Shelby in western Missouri during Price's Expedition. Pleasonton, who defeated J.E.B. Stuart at the Battle of Brandy Station in Virginia and commanded all Union cavalry at Gettysburg, called Shelby "the best cavalry general of the South."

The saying went that Missouri had five seasons, Spring, Summer, Fall, Winter and "Shelby's on a Raid."

Shelby spent his last years as U. S. Marshal for the Western District of Missouri, appointed by Republican President Grover Cleveland. He died in 1897, and is buried in Forest Hill Cemetery in Kansas City, on the hillside where he made his last stand during the Battle of Westport. To the present day, JO Shelby's funeral procession is the largest Kansas City has ever seen.

the 12th, as the contending forces moved northwest. Brown pushed part of his cavalry ahead of Shelby at the Saline County seat, Marshall, on October 13, and Shelby seemed to be trapped by the converging Union forces. Brown could bring at least 2,000 men to bear at Marshall, outnumbering Shelby at least 2-1. More importantly, Shelby had to divide his small force, leaving a detachment under Maj. David Shanks to protect his rear, while Shelby's main force had to cross a bramble-choked valley east of the town.

The Battle of Marshall ended when Shelby charged uphill and through the Union lines. His escape was miraculous. From Marshall, he headed north and then west, riding hard for Waverly. He made it, paid a visit to the family, and then headed south for Arkansas. Passing through Warrensburg, Lamar and Carthage, Shelby arrived back within Confederate lines on November 3, 1863. As a result of enlistments on the march, he had more men than he had started with, and also more guns, supplies and ammunition. The raid traversed at least 1,400 miles.

Fremont's Southwest Campaign

The secondary theme of this Loop takes us back to 1861. Sterling Price and his Missouri State Guard won notable battles during August and September, 1861, at Wilson's Creek and Lexington. John C. Fremont, the federal com-

mander in Missouri, was under a cloud that stemmed from these Union setbacks, from financial irregularities in his Department and from his failure thus far to take the field in pursuit of Price. Late in September, he moved an army out of St. Louis to Jefferson City. By the first week of October he had his troops in camp along the Pacific Railroad, at Tipton, Syracuse, and Sedalia. This was the "Grand Army of the West." With a strength of 35,000 or more men it was probably the largest army assembled in the field to this point in the War. It probably exceeded in size either of the armies that moved in the direction of Manassas, Virginia, in July, 1861. Fremont was poised to move a hundred miles south in pursuit of General Price. Positioned along the line of the railroad, his army would wait for the transportation and supplies it needed to launch an overland campaign toward Springfield.

The pressure on Fremont intensified. He began his campaign on October 13, sending Franz Sigel's Third Division from Sedalia toward Warsaw. On that day, Fremont was entertaining U. S. Secretary of War Simon Cameron in Tipton and Syracuse. Cameron had traveled from Washington to investigate affairs in the Department. On October 14 Fremont pushed off from Tipton, where he had made his headquarters. However, he left with only a fraction of his men. Then, the part of the Grand Army that did move spent 3 days to travel 45 miles to Warsaw, and 5 days building a bridge over the Osage River at that point.

Once south of the Osage, Fremont moved along the Butterfield Trail until he reached the town of Bolivar on October 24, 1861. He waited here for the rest of his infantry, and sent his cavalry ahead the remaining fifty miles to Springfield. The cavalry at Bolivar was the magnificently outfitted "Fremont Body-Guard", commanded by the Hungarian expatriate Maj. Charles Zagonyi. On October 25, Zagonyi, with the help of a cavalry detachment known as the Prairie Scouts, drove the State Guard out of Springfield. Unbeknownst to Fremont, President Lincoln issued an order on October 24, which would relieve him of command once he was found not in the presence of the enemy. Soon after Fremont entered Springfield on November 2, 1861, the order was delivered and Fremont departed the scene.

Gen. David Hunter succeeded Fremont in command of the Grand Army. With winter coming on Hunter had little choice but to withdraw from Springfield, which he did. The Southern army occupied Springfield until February, 1862, when another Union advance took the town for good.

Price's 1864 Expedition
Action in Central Missouri

Price's forces consolidated in Union, Franklin County, Missouri, after the debacle at Battle Knob. From Union, Price detached Marmaduke's Division to wreck the Pacific Railroad from Washington to Hermann, along State Route 100, while the rest of his army moved west, generally along the modern route of U. S. Highway 50. Price reached the outskirts of Jefferson City on October 6, camping south of town near Wardsville. Shelby's Division approached by a southern route, through Westphalia, and crossed the Osage River at Prince's Ford on the 6th. Shelby fought a small

PATHFINDER OF THE WEST

The life of the celebrated "Pathfinder of the West," John Charles Fremont, would fill a book and has. Son of a French Canadian, first Governor of California and first Republican candidate for President of the United States (in 1856), Fremont owed much of his success to his wife Jessie, the daughter of Missouri Sen. Thomas Hart Benton. He was extraordinarily famous already in 1856, having conducted several explorations to the West in search of a rail route that would put Missouri at the center of commerce with California. Jessie was a gifted writer who chronicled his journeys and became a one-woman marketing department.

The Fremonts were in Europe when the Civil War erupted. They returned somewhat leisurely to the United States and on July 25, 1861 Frémont officially took command of the Western Department of the U.S. Army, from headquarters in St. Louis. For the next few months he filled a role in the West that was for all intents and purposes the same role that George McClellan held in the East. By temperament, Fremont was the McClellan of the West, although it must be said that in 1861 Fremont accomplished far more in the field than did his east coast counterpart. He was not however fit for high command. He was relieved in early November and accepted a more modest command in West Virginia. Fremont would serve there until he resigned his commission in 1862, and he then left the army for good.

After the War, Fremont invested in the Southwest Branch Railroad in Missouri (predecessor to the Cotton Belt line) and began to build it west from its terminus at Rolla. The venture failed and all but bankrupted Fremont. In his later years, he returned to live in California, but while on a trip to New York died there of natural causes, in 1890. His beloved Jessie survived him, dying in Los Angeles in 1902.

The Butterfield Stage (Harpers Weekly)

engagement against elements of Missouri militia cavalry on the west bank of the river, which was unremarkable except that Shelby lost his favorite brigade commander, Col. David Shanks of Shelby's own Iron Brigade. Shanks was replaced by Gen. M. Jeff Thompson, recently exchanged after a stay at the Ft. Delaware military prison.

Price was so far staying ahead of his pursuers, but at the very least he had 4,000 men of Pleasonton's cavalry and 8,000 infantry from A.J. Smith's corps in hot pursuit. A force composed mostly of home grown Missouri troops, most of them cavalry and numbering perhaps 6,000, reached Jefferson City. They began entrenching furiously. On October 7, 1864, Price drove in the outer defenders at the Battle of Moreau Bottom, south of town, and some sharp skirmishing occurred at the fairgrounds, close to the campus of present-day Lincoln University. Then, Price simply withdrew.

We don't know why he abandoned his prime political objective without bringing on a general engagement, although arguably the memory of Pilot Knob gave him pause.

The Confederate host camped west of Jefferson City on the night of October 7, then moved westward, the divisions separating as before. Shelby moved southwest along the route of today's Highway C; his rear guard fought his pursuers at Russellville in western Cole County. Other units proceeded west out the old stage road, roughly U. S. Highway 50, and tore up the Pacific Railroad. The

Confederate army then moved northwest in the direction of Boonville. Price occupied Boonville on October 10, 1864 without a fight, but on the 11th and 12th he fought a considerable skirmish 3 miles south of town, at Petite Saline Creek. Price succeeded in keeping his Union pursuers at bay.

Price was able to rest and recoup in Boonville for at least two days, but was then forced to continue his move west. With his entire force he camped the night of October 13 near Nelson in Saline County, on the Blackwater River. Price sent Thompson and the Iron Brigade south, and they took Sedalia and 200 prisoners there. At the same time, he put columns in motion to the north and east, and on October 15 a federal garrison at Glasgow surrendered after a brief fight. Price captured a cache of arms, ammunition and supplies at Glasgow.

The wings of Price's force consolidated as they moved west through Marshall, and Waverly, along the old Santa Fe Road. Sporadic skirmishing occurred along this route, but it was not until October 19 that the opposing forces met in a general engagement. The battle occurred at Lexington, Missouri, near the scene of Price's 1861 triumph. Ominously, the Confederates were now facing additional Union troops from Kansas, coming east. Price drove the Union forces, under Gen. James G. Blunt, out of Lexington. Blunt moved back to the Little Blue River. The stage was set for Price's entry into Kansas City, and the climax of his grand expedition.

Part I - Westbound

Tour Stop 90

We begin at THESPIAN HALL, Boonville's most historic building. This is the oldest theater in continuous operation west of the Allegheny Mountains, and it has a splendid Civil War history.

We will not be covering all of the historic and tourist attractions in Boonville, but information is available at the visitors center a few blocks west of here, or at the museum on Morgan Street. In a field several miles east of Boonville, the third land battle of the Civil War was fought on June 17, 1861. That action ended at the old fairgrounds on Morgan Street. The Second Battle of Boonville was fought September 13, 1861, over the same fairgrounds, There African Americans might have first taken up arms in the Civil War.

During the Civil War, Thespian Hall was used as a hospital, a barracks and a morgue. When Sterling Price occupied Boonville for two days in 1864, he established his headquarters in this building. Here on October 11, and probably on these steps, Price met with Captain Bill Anderson. Tour Loop 2 passes by only a few miles to the north and deals with Anderson's operations in this part of the state; the near convergence of these routes is symbolic of the two wars, one conventional and one irregular, going in Missouri in 1864. Nothing is more symbolic of this dichotomy than the Price-Anderson meeting in Boonville.

Sterling Price, ex-governor of Missouri, Mexican War hero, slave-owner and one-time Unionist, was (to borrow a phrase) the very model of a Major-General. After three years of war, his honor was fully intact, although his reputation as a soldier carried less of a sheen. He was home in Missouri for the first time in three years, having been engaged in fighting a bitter, but nonetheless honorable, war in Mississippi and Arkansas. We have to imagine what went through Price's mind as Bill Anderson rode in from the north with a band of his chief lieutenants, human scalps dangling from their bridles. The scalps were tucked away at the suggestion of one of Price's aides. Then Anderson gave the General a pair of presentation pistols - stolen no doubt.

Price had summoned Anderson and the rest of the guerrilla chiefs to central Missouri to divert the attention of the federals. The guerrillas had been doing an effective job. Price, keeping his scruples to himself, sent Anderson east to wreck the railroad around Danville, Missouri, which Anderson did.

To reach Tour Stop 90:

To reach the starting point of this Tour Loop, exit I-70 at the Highway B Exit, No. 103, and drive north into town. Route B becomes Main Street. Continue north to Vine Street, and the first Stop is on your right here. This is a large brick building of grecian design.

To reach Tour Stop 91:

Drive north on Main Street 2 blocks to Spring Street. Turn left. In 3 blocks you will see, to the right, a spanish style building that is the old Katy Depot, and is now the trailhead for the Katy Trail State Park. This is not a Civil War site, but the Boonville visitors center is located here.

After you leave the visitors center, return to westbound Spring Street. Continue as this road becomes Santa Fe Road at the water tower. Drive a total of 1.3 miles since you left the visitors center, and pull over to the right shoulder where the Panhandle Eastern Pipeline facility is located.

To reach Tour Stop 92:

Continue west on Santa Fe Road, bearing left at a Y intersection once you have gone 1.5 miles. In about 5 miles from Stop 91 you will reach Exit 98 on I-70. Turn left in the direction of the Interstate, but continue south, passing over the highway on State Highway 135. Set your trip odometer as you cross the interstate. Go south 2.2 miles and turn right at Chouteau Springs Drive. The turnoff to Chouteau Springs Drive is somewhat hidden at a left-hand turn in Highway 135. Begin to watch for the turn after you head straight west at Martinsburg. Once on Chouteau Springs Drive, proceed west for 1.4 miles, and stop in the valley at the small bridge.

Tour Stop 91

This is the site of the LABBO HOUSE. During Shelby's raid in 1863, his men drove down this road, known then as the Georgetown Road, in the direction of Pilot Grove just as Union cavalry were entering Boonville. Two of Shelby's men stopped for breakfast here, and were shot dead on the porch when they dallied too long.

Tour Stop 92

In this valley was SULPHUR SPRINGS CAMP, where Price's Army camped the night of October 12, 1864 after it evacuated Boonville. In 1863, Shelby's cavalry also traveled the route you have just taken. On October 12 of that year, Shelby's rear guard skirmished with pursuing cavalry commanded by Lt. Col. Bazel Lazear, as they descended the hill from the east. Less than two months earlier, Lazear and his cavalry had chased Quantrill's command as it pushed on to Lawrence, Kansas, and ignominiously lost Quantrill's trail.

This valley, an interesting and historic place, was part of a grant in 1792 to Pierre Chouteau, son of one and half brother to another of the founders of St. Louis. In the last decades of the nineteenth century, the area became a grand resort built around the mineral springs that gave the valley its name. On a hot day, the odor of sulphur is still very much in evidence.

In 1863, while Lazear pressed Shelby's rear guard along this route, the bulk of Egbert Brown's troops trailed Shelby in a parallel column that took them several miles south of Chouteau Springs. Brown's route went through Ridge Prairie, and on to "Dick Marshall's", located just north of the modern town of Nelson.

Boonville Visitors Center

Tour Stop 93

Tour Stop 93 is DICK MARSHALL'S PLACE. We can't determine the exact location of the original Richard Marshall homestead, but by 1863 Marshall owned most of the property in your view. From Albemarle County, Virginia, he settled here in 1819. He was perhaps the first settler in Saline County. Known as Old Dick Marshall, he was in his 70s at the time of the Civil War.

As you came west from Chouteau Springs, you followed Shelby's 1863 route for part of the time, to where Route M crossed the Lamine River. Bazel Lazear continued his pursuit of Shelby's column up to this point. Somewhere near there, Shelby's rear guard ambushed Lazear as he forded the Lamine, effectively ending the pursuit from that quarter. Where you are now is the valley of the Blackwater River, which joined the Lamine at the Route M crossing. Shelby was north of the Blackwater, Gen. Brown to the south of it, and on the 12th of October the opposing Union and Confederate forces moved up the valley, skirmishing almost continuously.

Your approach to Nelson from the south, through the pretty valley on Bar Hollow Road, was the route of march of the main federal force pursuing Shelby in 1863. A detachment of the 7th Missouri Militia Cavalry commanded by future Missouri Governor Thomas Crittenden followed behind the main force. Crittenden's troopers had tangled with Shelby near Syracuse on October 10, 1863.

Here at Marshall's Place, the Blackwater is joined by Salt Fork Creek. Shelby and Brown moved northwest along Salt Fork and fought a major skirmish at Jonesborough, now the town of

To reach Tour Stop 93:

Drive west on Chouteau Springs Drive, bearing left at Short Drive, and continue west for a mile and a quarter until the road ends at Route M. Turn right (north) here and travel .7 mile to Interstate 70. Cross the highway and turn left on the north outer road (there is no entrance to I-70 here). This road designation changes from M, to K and finally to Z, but you want always to bear left and stay as close to the Interstate as you can, without entering it. At a point 6.8 miles west of the point you crossed Interstate 70, and where Route Z takes a left turn, you turn right on a gravel road called Salt Fork Road.

When this road ends in .8 mile, bear left and go west for .5 mile to Bar Hollow. Turn right here, and drive 1.7 miles north where you cross some railroad tracks and enter Main Street in the town of Nelson. Drive north on Main Street as far as it takes you, then right, then left, which puts you on Route H northbound. After proceeding .4 mile on this road, turn left on 152nd Road. Tour Stop 93 is a cemetery on the right, known as the Marshall Cemetery. Note, you will have to find a way to turn around as you leave. Do not back into Route H.

To reach Tour Stop 94:

Continue north on Route H for only about .1 mile, then turn right on Route AA. Drive north on AA for 3.1 miles to a road, on your right, that is the entrance to a cemetery that is Stop 94. The entrance is well marked as a State Historic Site.

Claiborne Fox Jackson
1806 - 1862

Claiborne Jackson was born in Kentucky. He joined his older brothers in Missouri in 1826, settling in the Howard County town of New Franklin. There, Jackson entered the mercantile trade. Blessed with a special acumen for financial matters, Jackson made a fortune in business, banking and land speculation. Later, he became active in politics, eventually becoming Missouri's Governor in 1861.

Jackson set a course early in his administration to bring Missouri into the Confederate fold. His decision to drill the state militia in St. Louis in May, 1861, was provocative. In the aftermath of the May 10, 1861 affair at Camp Jackson (named for him), pro-Union elements in St. Louis drove Jackson and the elected government from the state capital in Jefferson City. It is said that Jackson is the only Governor who has ever personally led troops of his or her state in battle, which he did at the Battle of Carthage, Missouri in 1861. Jackson headed a shadow government in Arkansas during 1861 and 1862. Wracked by stomach cancer, Jackson passed away near Little Rock early in December, 1862.

Napton, on the evening of October 12, 1863. They would next fight in Marshall on the 13th, also on the Salt Fork. Marshall is only 12 miles northwest of here.

In October 1864, Price was moving west on the same route taken by Shelby the previous year. Price detached part of his forces while he moved west from Chouteau Springs, sending some to Sedalia, and some to Glasgow. Price camped here at Marshall's plantation on the night of October 13, 1864, and then on the 14th moved on to Jonesborough and Marshall.

Tour Stop 94

This is the SAPPINGTON CEMETERY STATE HISTORIC SITE. You have been in Saline County since you descended the valley of Bar Hollow Road, and this part of Saline County is perhaps the most "Southern" part of Missouri. The graves at the Sappington Cemetery symbolize the demographics of this area, as do graves in the Sappington Negro Cemetery, which you passed just south of the turn-off to this place.

The most significant burial here is that of DR. JOHN SAPPINGTON. Sappington came in 1817 from Kentucky. He built a large plantation here and to the east in the direction of Arrow Rock. By the time of the Civil War, Dr. Sappington had died, but his extended family occupied much of the ground that you will travel once you leave here. Sappington had one son and four daughters. All four of his daughters married future Missouri governors. All of his daughters and their *two* husbands are buried in this cemetery. Miles Meredith Marmaduke, who served as Missouri's Governor in 1846, married Sappington's daughter Lavinia. Wartime Governor Claiborne Fox Jackson first married Jane Sappington, then Louisa, but each of them died in the early 1830s. When Jackson came to Sappington asking for the hand of his youngest daughter Eliza, it is said that the Doctor quipped: "You can have Eliza, but don't come back for the old lady. I want her for myself."

Jackson's grave is down and to the left of the cemetery entrance. He was the principal Southern protagonist in the drama that marked the opening days of the Civil War in Missouri. He was elected Governor in 1860 and unlike many of his slave-owning neighbors

94

he ardently took up the secessionist cause. He died in Arkansas in 1862, still technically Missouri's governor. He was re-interred here after the War, and his remains lie alongside Eliza's.

The son of Governor Miles Marmaduke was Confederate Cavalry General John Sappington Marmaduke. John, who was born near here on the Marmaduke plantation, was Missouri's Governor from 1884 to 1887; he died in office and is buried in Jefferson City.

When you arrive in Arrow Rock you will begin to discover the Santa Fe Trail. John Sappington's most important legacy arose from his proximity to this artery of western expansion. Sappington found an efficient way to extract quinine from the bark of the cinchona tree, and mass produce it in pill form. He sold millions of pills and saved many people who went west on the trails from the ravages of malarial fever.

Tour Stop 95

Here is the GEORGE MASON BROWN GRAVE. Known as Mason, the man buried here was a Captain in the Missouri State Guard who died, as the stone says, on September 13, 1861. This was the date of the Second Battle of Boonville. Mason was adjutant to his younger brother Col. William B. Brown. Allegedly, one of William Brown's slaves overheard Brown describing a plan to attack lightly manned Union entrenchments around Boonville. This man (name unfortunately not known) ran to Boonville to warn the garrison. Also, allegedly, this same man stood in the trenches and fired the shot that killed his erstwhile master, who was then leading a charge on the Union fortification. Mason took part in the charge, and he and his brother fell within yards of each other, each mortally wounded. William Brown is buried elsewhere, but his grave has not been located.

To reach Tour Stop 95:

Return to the point where you entered the cemetery from Route AA. Turn right. Route TT will be on your right just north of here. Turn right on TT and drive east for 3.9 miles to the west gate of the Arrow Rock Cemetery. Pull into the cemetery. The grave you have come to find is on your right about 4 or 5 rows from the entrance.

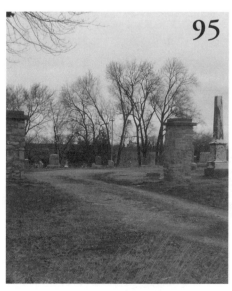

To reach Tour Stop 96:

Exit the cemetery and turn left. Drive east on TT for about 1/2 mile, and cross State Highway 41. This road becomes Main Street in Arrow Rock. Continue east on Main Street until you reach the commercial area near the Arrow Rock Tavern, and park anywhere in this area.

Tour Stop 96

The ARROW ROCK HISTORIC DISTRICT covers what is probably the most fascinating small town in Missouri. In August, 1821, the Kingdom of Spain signed a treaty that granted Mexico its independence, an act that had an almost immediate impact on central Missouri. Spain had forbidden trade between the United States and its colonial capital in Santa Fe; the new Mexican government sought such trade. On September 1, 1821, William Becknell set off from here with a few men and blazed the trail that would become the fabled Santa Fe Trail. Your route on the next trail segment follows Becknell's route - and Shelby's and Price's - until you turn south after reaching Dover, Missouri.

The official starting point of the Santa Fe Trail is across the Missouri River to the east, at a town called Franklin. The Boonslick Road terminated there. However, the trail had to cross the River. A ferry established at Arrow Rock soon made it the jumping off point for traders and settlers arriving by way of the River. In 1823, as a settlement began to take root here, George Caleb Bingham moved to Saline County with his widowed mother, and Missouri's greatest artist took his first steps into the world of art in this neighborhood. The most historic structure in Arrow Rock is the Bingham home, which he built with his own hands in 1827. As described in Tour Loop Four, Bingham's brush had a profound effect on Missouri's Civil War and its aftermath.

Price sent Gen. John B. Clark through Arrow Rock in 1864, and Shelby in 1863 sent a detachment here, but little is known about what happened in Arrow Rock as a result. A famous incident occurred on July 20, 1864, when guerrilla Tom Todd led a band of 100 into town. He surprised a small garrison of Union troops, supposedly in the process of shooting marbles on Main Street, and killed twenty-five with the loss of only one man.

96

Tour Stop 97

The SALINE COUNTY COURTHOUSE was constructed in 1882, the third courthouse on this site. In August, 1864, Confederates burned the Civil War-era courthouse to the ground. Two months later, Sterling Price's army came through here, but the reason for visiting Marshall is the battle fought by Shelby's men on October 13, 1863. We pick up the story where we left off at Tour Stop 93.

After skirmishing all day on October 12, Shelby's cavalry and Brown's force fought an inconclusive evening engagement at Napton, and then Brown went into camp there. Shelby proceeded up the Salt Fork and camped six miles southeast of Marshall. At 3:00 in the morning on the 13th, Brown sent Lt. Col. Lazear with 1,000 men west to block Shelby's westward line of march. Lazear reached Marshall before Shelby did, and posted his troopers in a north-south line several blocks east of here. Shelby, for his part, knew that 4,000 troops under Gen. Thomas Ewing were closing in from the west. Shelby thought he was facing Ewing.

To reach Tour Stop 97:

Return to the point where you entered Arrow Rock, and turn right on Missouri Highway 41. Drive west on 41 for 14.2 miles to Commercial Street outside of Marshall. Take the exit ramp to the right, then cross under Highway 41/240 as you head south. This road turns into Lafayette Avenue and then into Business Route 65. In about a mile since you exited 41, you will reach Arrow Street and the courthouse square. Tour Stop 97 is here.

97

To reach Tour Stop 98:

Circulate around the square to the northeast corner, which is North Street. Turn right. Drive east for 4 or 5 blocks until North Street ends at Brunswick Avenue. Stop near this intersection.

Tour Stop 98

Brunswick Avenue is THE UNION LINE. We think you are near the center of the line.

We've made some assumptions about the scene of the action here based on topography, the Official Records, and the work of Missouri State Historian Jim Denny. Tour Stop 100 is a marker erected by Missouri State Parks that provides an excellent overview of the battle, reflecting Denny's research.

The most relevant feature of the topography around Marshall is the deep ravines that run down to the Salt Fork from the town site, which sits atop the high prairie. At the time of the Civil War, the old Santa Fe Trail crossed the Salt Fork on a wagon bridge, then ascended a ridge between the two most northerly ravines. Eastwood Avenue, the historic road a block to the north, follows that ridge. Shelby moved his men into the ravines on either side of the road and launched a frontal assault on Lazear's line. The southernmost ravine is in front of you.

The tour route takes you south on Brunswick Avenue, and then east along the right flank of Lazear's line. Presumably, the Union line lay along the very edge of the ravine, along Brunswick, then curled east where a high point anchored the line on the south.

Tour Stop 99

MCGHEE'S POSITION was on a hill southeast of town, and this is probably the hill. Union Maj. J. H. McGhee led a battalion of the 1st Missouri State Militia Cavalry, which dismounted here.

To Reach Tour Stop 99:

Turn right on Brunswick Avenue, and then drive south for about .4 mile (6 blocks), to Yerby Street. Turn left. Drive east .5 mile and pull into the parking lot of the YMCA, where you have a view of the valley to the north.

The opening action of the Battle of Marshall was an attack on MdGee's position by a regiment of Shelby's cavalry, commanded by Col. J.C. Hooper. Hooper's Confederates, also fighting dismounted, tried to force their way up the hill but were repulsed.

Tour Stop 100

This is the BATTLE OF MARSHALL marker. You are positioned now to track Confederate movements as you drive back into Marshall.

Thinking he was trapped between the forces of Brown and Ewing, with Brown close on his heels, Shelby made a desperate decision to divide his force to protect his rear. Two hundred men under Maj. David Shanks dismounted and occupied the hill here, and on the south his line might have reached here. The Confederates partially destroyed the wagon bridge over the Salt Fork. The Union force approached from the east and tried to force a crossing of the damaged bridge, but Shanks' 200 held the position for two hours while the rest of the battle unfolded along Brunswick Avenue. While the fight at the bridge continued, Brown crossed many of his troopers by fording the Salt Fork north and south of Shanks' position, and ultimately enveloped Shelby's force.

Shanks was not facing the whole of Brown's force, but rather probably not more than 800 Union cavalry, supported by four guns that Brown placed in position across the river. Shank's command made a magnificent stand here, reminiscent of Lee's Georgians at Burnside's Bridge on Antietam Creek.

After leaving Shanks here, Shelby moved west along the ridge with the remainder of his men. On leaving here, you will exit the park on to Eastwood Avenue, and move west in Shelby's path in the direction of the next tour stop.

Shelby advanced to a point in the 700 block of Eastwood, and there unlimbered his guns. He faced a two-gun battery that Lazear had placed in the road near Brunswick Avenue. Lazear's gunners, however, only had grapeshot in their ammunition chests, and did not have the range to reach Shelby's line on the road. The Union guns moved forward 250 yards, to the area where Lincoln Avenue crosses Eastwood.

Shelby sent Hooper and Maj. George Gordon into the south ravine, to open the battle against McGhee's posi-

To reach Tour Stop 100:

Continue east on Yerby Street for .2 mile, and then go left where Yerby ends at the entrance to the Ridge Park Cemetery. Stay on this road for about one mile, always bearing left as you pass through Indian Foothills Park, until you reach a road on the right at the foot of a hill, just after you have crossed a creek. Take a right here, then a left, and head for the park pavilion that is up the hill in front of you. Tour Stop 100 is a marker that is on your right.

100

tion. The next attack came from the location of Shelby's guns on Eastwood Avenue, directly west into Lazear's battery. Three unsuccessful charges were made upon the Union guns, and then Lazear's guns were withdrawn when Confederate Col. John T. Coffee's men in the north ravine achieved a breakthrough at Stop 101.

The reports are not clear, but it appears that Shelby designed a rolling attack, from south to north, as he looked for a way out. He gradually changed his front so it stretched along Eastwood facing south, then mounted his men and went cross country in a northwest direction.

To reach Tour Stop 101:

Find your way back to the main park road, which you can reach by retracing your route, or by continuing north and looping back. Drive north to Eastwood Avenue, and turn left. You will drive west on Eastwood, past the sites of the Confederate and Union artillery posts, for a total of 1.1 miles, when you will arrive at Brunswick Avenue. This is a point just north of the point where you had turned south on your outbound trip. Turn right (north) on Brunswick and drive down into the valley. Stop just after you cross the old railroad right of way.

Tour Stop 101

Tour Stop 101 is the site of COFFEE'S ATTACK. The left flank of the Union line extended across the valley and probably on to the next ridge. The railroad was not here in 1863, but the long, gradual rise you see, extending into Marshall itself, was here. Topographically, this was the weak point in Lazear's line. This sector was defended by the Fifth Provisional Missouri Enrolled Militia, probably the least experienced unit under Lazear's command, and it was stretched very thin.

At or after the time Shelby was attacking the Union battery on Eastwood Avenue, Coffee's regiment moved forward from a position in the north ravine. His Confederate veterans brushed aside the Union militia - the Fifth regiment supposedly did not fire a shot before scrambling back in the direction of town. Shelby's Report claims that Coffee reached the town and raked the streets with cannon fire. Lazear reinforced his left flank. If the Confederates had reached the town it appears they withdrew during the final phase of the battle. In this final phase, cavalry arriving with Egbert Brown took position far on the Union left, to your right as you face north.

Shelby brought his men out of the south ravine and into line along Eastwood Avenue. Shanks withdrew west so his men could join this line. As Shelby prepared to move out to the northwest Union cavalry charged from the north. Shanks, along with the regiments of Hooper and Col. Dewitt Hunter, were cut off and fled to the east. They would not rejoin Shelby until Arkansas. Meanwhile, the rest of Shelby's men charged in column of twos up and out of the north ravine, and broke free. The scene of this improbable charge is, perhaps, the corner of Brunswick and Lacy Street, just up the hill to the north.

Tour Stop 102

To reach Tour Stop 102:

This is the WAVERLY METHODIST CHURCH. The core structure is the church that stood during the Civil War.

Shelby's column, in 1863, ranged far north of your route of travel, and arrived in Waverly about 3:00 a.m. on October 14. In 1864, Sterling Price probably used the route of U.S. Highway 65 - the Santa Fe Trail – and passed through Waverly on his way west.

Waverly was founded in the 1840s, and it is an odd thing that it was named for a Sir Walter Scott novel. Odd because a Kentucky hemp grower who moved here in 1858 would come to embody the Southern cult of chivalry.

Shelby was one of the men sent north in the summer of 1862 to recruit for the Confederate cause. In four days he raised a full regiment. His men, some of whom would follow Shelby all the way to Mexico City in 1865, were sworn into service on the steps of the Methodist Church. On September 9, 1862, this regiment joined two others south of Newtonia, Missouri, to form a brigade, Shelby took command of the brigade, dubbed the Iron Brigade.

Shelby's home, it is believed, was on the bluff near the very end of Jefferson Street. Kansas Redlegs burned the house down before Shelby paid his visit here in October, 1863. Shelby's huge rope factory filled much of the valley to the west. Making rope was what you could do if you had slaves and lots of hemp.

Drive north three blocks to E. Lacy Street. Turn left here. Go 3 blocks west, then north (right) on O'Dell Avenue. You will jog slightly to the left at Allen Street. If you are following the trail westward, then you must cross Commercial Drive, staying on O'Dell for another 1/3 mile to Highway 240/41. Be very careful when turning left on to the highway here.

If you are heading east, you can turn right on Commercial Drive at O'Dell to reach a ramp that will enter 240/41 eastbound.

To continue on the Tour Route, turn left on Highway 240/41, and drive west for 1.4 miles to U. S. Highway 65. Turn right. Drive 17 miles west from this point, then turn left to follow U.S. 24 into Waverly. The road jogs right, and then left, and in .9 miles turn right on Washington Street. Go north on Washington two blocks (noting the JO Shelby Park and statue as you go), and turn left on Kelling Avenue. Kelling ends in one block, and Tour Stop 102 is the church on your left.

102

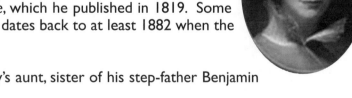

IVANHOE'S REBECCA

Enough of this knightly nonsense, you say. Well, author Washington Irving was a friend of Walter Scott. In 1817, Irving spent some time at Scott's estate in Scotland. Irving was also close friend to a prominent Jewish family in Philadelphia, and to a beautiful and accomplished woman of that family Her name was Rebecca Gratz. From Irving's description of her, Scott created the Jewish heroine of his novel _Ivanhoe_, which he published in 1819. Some say this is legend, but if it is, the legend dates back to at least 1882 when the New York Times made note of it.

The real Rebecca Gratz was JO Shelby's aunt, sister of his step-father Benjamin Gratz.

Return to U.S. Highway 24 by way of Jefferson Street, and turn right (west). You will reach the town of Dover in 9.5 miles. The next Tour Stop is in a cemetery that can be reached from S. Mill Street, which is the first cross street once you arrive in Dover, and is marked Route "F." Turn left on S. Mill Street, and drive south to the Dover Cemetery. The grave you seek is past the flagpole, nearly at the end of the cemetery. It lies in the Plattenberg family plot.

Tour Stop 103

The GRAVE OF JOHN NEWMAN EDWARDS is Tour Stop 103. It completes the story begun in Waverly. Edwards as a boy in Virginia apprenticed as a printer, and moved to Missouri in the mid-50s. During the War, he became Shelby's Adjutant, with the rank of Major, and was with Shelby in all of his engagements. Edwards' interest in writing came to the surface at this time, as if fell to him, in most instances, to write the battle reports for his taciturn chief. To quote from the Shelby/Edwards report of the Battle of Marshall, for instance:

"For two hours the fight raged evenly along the entire line, and the sun came out and looked down upon the dying and the dead, and the green fields of Missouri drank the blood of her best and bravest."

After the War, Edwards moved to Kansas City and founded the Kansas City Times. He remained a newspaperman for the rest of his life. An unapologetic Southerner, he also became the great chronicler of the Civil War in the West, through articles, editorials and books. Edwards' first two books featured the exploits of JO Shelby: *Shelby and His Men* (1867) and *Shelby's Expedition to Mexico* (1872). In his flowery prose he described Shelby: "There was much of Launcelot's love-passion about him, with all of Launcelot's chivalry and knightly bearing." Edwards wrote as though *he* was Sir Walter Scott, and the subjects of his work had been plucked from the "days of yore" and set down here on the Missouri prairie. But it was effective, and Shelby in his lifetime enjoyed a fame that eludes him now.

Edwards then turned to the tales of the Southern guerrillas. Supposedly, he wrote his next major work, *Noted Guerrillas, or the Warfare of the Border,* here in Dover where his father-in-law lived. Edwards applied the same romantic formula to this subject. Ultimately through his writings Edwards became a propagandist for the post-war cause of the James brothers. John Newman Edwards' enduring legacy is the legend of Jesse James. Edwards created it, and he turned Jesse into a western Robin Hood.

Part II - Southbound

Tour Stop 104

Missouri's CONFEDERATE MEMORIAL is operated by Missouri State Parks, and comprises the grounds of a home for aged Confederate veterans, and its chapel and cemetery. The home opened in 1891, and remained in continuous operation for 60 years, caring for veterans and their wives. It was closed shortly after the death of John T. Graves, "the last of Shelby's men." He died in 1950 at age 107.

The cemetery contains the graves of about 800 veterans, many of whom moved to Missouri after the Civil War. One grave holds *some* of the bones of William Clarke Quantrill, which were interred here in 1992. These bones were peddled years ago to the Kansas State Historical Society, which displayed them for decades in Topeka for the benefit of gawkers. Finally, twenty years ago, the Society was persuaded to part with them for a Christian burial.

Also in 1992, Quantrill's skull was buried alongside most of the rest of his remains in the family plot in Dover, Ohio. The skull was once the property of a fraternity in Ohio, which used it for thirty years as part of an initiation ritual. When the fraternity disbanded, the skull came to rest in the basement of the Dover Historical Society. All of Quantrill now lies in peace, some parts here, some in Ohio and, probably, a few fragments where he was first buried in Louisville, Kentucky.

Regardless of your persuasion, the Confederate Memorial and Cemetery is a "must see" for all Civil War travelers.

To reach Tour Stop 104:

Leave the Dover Cemetery and return to U.S. Highway 24. Turn left. Drive west for 1.7 miles to State Route 213, and turn left (south) here. In 6.4 miles you will arrive at an intersection of Routes 13 and 20, and here you take a sharp right, not on to Route 13, but rather into the grounds of the Confederate Memorial State Historic Site.

William Clarke Quantrill 1837 – 1865

The most famous Civil War guerrilla fighter was born in Dover, Ohio, in 1837. Well educated and the son of a schoolmaster, Quantrill took up teaching as a young man. He taught in Illinois and Ohio, then in 1857 he joined an expedition of Dover citizens who went to Kansas to stake land claims.

Quantrill was attracted to the pro-slavery movement in Kansas. When the Civil War broke out in 1861, Quantrill supposedly fought for the South at Wilson's Creek. The gruesome pinnacle of his career as a soldier came in August, 1863, when he led the raid on Lawrence, Kansas, that left 150 civilians dead in its wake. More of the Quantrill story appears in Tour Loop Four, at Stops 140 and 141.

Photo courtesy Missouri State Parks

To reach Tour Stop 105:

Exit the grounds where you had entered, then proceed south by turning left on Business Route 13, which is Main Street in Higginsville. Drive through Higginsville, 1.5 miles from the exit of the Memorial, then bear left. This street is still Main Street. In 4 blocks, turn left on 26th Street, which is County Route T.

You will drive 7 miles south on Route T, and there arrive at I-70. At about 4.5 miles after your turn on to 26th Street, north of the town of Aullville, you will be in the area of JO Shelby's post-War home, where Frank and Jesse James were occasionally entertained during their outlaw years. In any event, continue to I-70 and enter the highway eastbound. Exit I-70 at the next exit to the east, Exit 58 at Concordia, then turn left at the bottom of the ramp. Once past the large truck stop, turn right on the north outer road. Drive east for 2.5 miles and look for the entrance to a cemetery, in the distance on your left surrounded by white pickets. Turn here and drive up the lane to the cemetery.

ST. JOHN'S CEMETERY is the resting place of eight Union men who perished on October 10, 1864. A bronze marker tells part of the story, as do the German inscriptions on the grave stones that bear this date.

This is an introduction to the early German settlement of rural west-central Missouri, covered later in this Tour. In 1864, a large farming community inhabited this neighborhood. It was probably centered on the town of Emma, a mile and a half southeast of here. Concordia had not yet been laid out. Confederate guerrillas knew the community only as the "Dutch Settlement." It became a target during a guerrilla raid supporting Price's Expedition.

A hundred men under Capt. George Todd, and David Poole of Lafayette County, went on a raid through Cooper and Benton Counties, passing through or near Sedalia. As it approached Lafayette County, Todd's band came up the valley of Davis Creek. The local Home Guard was alerted to this movement, and managed to pull together 26 of its number who moved out to a point east of Emma to give battle. The Germans met the guerrilla force, probably, just south of the point where I-70 crosses Davis Creek, 2 1/2 miles east of here. After the engagement, one of the Union men purportedly escaped, but at least twenty-five lay dead on the field. There were no wounded.

Previously, Shelby fought a small engagement on October 14, 1863 as he crossed Davis Creek during his retreat from Marshall, but this occurred some distance west of here.

Tour Stop 106

This is the PACIFIC RAILROAD TERMINUS. Here in Sedalia, construction on the Pacific line halted for the duration during the Civil War years. The town was founded in January, 1861. Being the end of the line for the war years did not harm the commercial interests of this fledgling community.

Sedalia is now the home of the Missouri State Fair. Also the town is, proudly, the adopted home of musician Scott Joplin and the birthplace of ragtime music. Joplin was born in Texas in 1868, so his connection to Missouri's Civil War is quite attenuated. But the connection exists.

The founder of Sedalia was one George R. Smith, a native of Virginia and a Colonel in the Missouri Militia before the Civil War. During the War, he reached the rank of General in the Union army, in a staff position. Although once a slave owner, Smith became an ardent abolitionist before or during the War. When he died in 1879 he had a sizeable fortune, and his daughters used a part of it to establish Sedalia's George R. Smith College for Negroes. Joplin came to study classical composition at Smith College in 1896. Thus Missouri owes to Smith, and the defunct college that bore his name, the right to claim this musical genius as its own.

Sedalia's position at the end of the line brought commerce of a different type, when the Union Army established a military hospital here in the wake of Fremont's campaign in southwest Missouri. This intermediate facility cared for the sick and wounded pending transport via rail to the large hospitals in St. Louis. A momentous thing happened at the Sedalia military hospital when an Iowa woman named Annie Wittenmyer arrived in January, 1862 to visit her brother in the hospital.

Wittenmyer was appalled by the food served at the hospital. Her experience inspired her to develop a system of "Special Diet Kitchens," which by 1864 received the official sanction of the War Department. In addition to insuring that hospital patients got their fruits and vegetables, the system utilized dietary nurses and surgeons' orders to tailor diets to fit the condition and needs of individual patients. Annie Wittenmyer went on to do many things in her life, including a stint as the first national President of the Woman's Christian Temperance Union, but she is the mother of the field we know today as "dietary science." Dietary science traces its roots to Wittenmyer's long ago visit to Sedalia.

To reach Tour Stop 106:

After leaving the cemetery, turn left on the outer road and drive east 1.6 miles to the Emma exit on I-70 (Exit 62). Enter the interstate by the eastbound ramp, then drive east for 16 miles to U.S. Highway 65, and there turn south. Drive south another 16 miles to the first Sedalia exit, which is Route 765. This road becomes Ohio Avenue. Stay on Ohio Avenue for a little over a mile, until you cross the railroad tracks. Park anywhere in the area of the Amtrak station.

For a few days in November, 1861, William T. Sherman was in Sedalia as he took temporary command of three divisions. Two days into an inspection tour here, authorities in St. Louis sent him home to Ohio on an extended leave of absence. General Halleck noted in a communique to General George McClellan that Sherman was "entirely unfit for duty" due to his mental and physical condition. This was near the low point of Sherman's life and career. Crazy or not, he recovered his composure while on leave.

To reach Tour Stop 107:

Cross over to the north side of the tracks, then go right on Pettis Street, two blocks north. In about 3/4 mile, after this street becomes Saline Street, turn left on Veterans Memorial Drive and then drive north several blocks to the entrance to Crown Hill Cemetery. Drive straight ahead, one section past the first large monument that is on your left (Jaymes). At the next cross-road, turn right. You are heading for a large gray granite obelisk that marks the grave of George R. Smith, which should be in your sights by now.

Tour Stop 107

Stop 107 is CROWN HILL CEMETERY. You have come to see some grave stones, but also to see where Confederate cavalry consolidated before attacking Sedalia during Price's Expedition in 1864.

By October 15, 1864, Gen. Jeff Thompson had taken over command of a cavalry brigade in Shelby's division. Price dispatched Thompson to Sedalia. A small Union garrison defended the city (the Union cavalry had just passed through, moving westward in search of Price). Thompson's force numbered some 800 to 1000 troopers, and two or three pieces of artillery. He arrived here about 9:30 on the morning of October 15, after camping in the town of Longwood the night of the 14th. He positioned his artillery in the city cemetery. The city, and an earthwork on this side of it, are beyond the trees to the right of the communications tower you can see off to the southwest. This spot, where Union Generals Smith and Totten were eventually buried, is likely the location of the battery Thompson used to shell the town.

THE PATTONS AND THE TOTTENS

Missouri's James Totten was a native of Pennsylvania. He entered the U. S. Army in 1841 after graduating from West Point. For the next 142 years, there was a James Totten on active duty in the U. S. Army, until Colonel James Patton Totten retired in 1983. Great-great-grandson of the Civil War Totten, James Patton Totten took his middle name from his maternal grandfather, legendary World War II General George S. Patton, Jr. His father, Maj. General James W. Patton, married General Patton's daughter Ruth Ellen in 1940.

C.A.L Totten, son of Missouri's James Totten and grandfather of James W. Totten, graduated from West Point and served in the Army on the frontier. As a result of his 1880 book *Strategos: The American Game of War* (not to be confused with the board game Stratego), this Totten is considered by some to be the father of modern wargaming.

Thompson moved in on Sedalia from both east and west, and the Union garrison soon capitulated. Thompson's objectives were the railroad, and a herd of cattle that Gen. Price heard was in the neighborhood. Thompson tore up the railroad. No word on what happened to the beef.

The George R. Smith College

The grave of BVT. GEN. JAMES TOTTEN finds itself in a fitting place, as he was a regular army artilleryman. Totten died in 1871 while residing in retirement near Sedalia. He is most famous, probably, for his battery's action at Wilson's Creek in 1861. Totten's men nicknamed him "bottle-nose," apparently in acknowledgment of his fondness for strong drink. His habit if he had one seems not to have affected his performance in battle.

Leave the cemetery by way of the cross-road at the Jaymes monument. Go to that road but turn east towards the gated cemetery entrance. As you get close to the gate, on your left in section 6 is a monument with a tall shaft that has a draping and urn on its top. This is the grave of Confederate Maj. JAMES C. WOOD. Because he was a native Sedalian, Wood was the man who guided Thompson during his raid here in 1864. In 1863, as a Captain in Shelby's Iron Brigade, Wood destroyed the great railroad bridge at Otterville, about 12 miles east of here. Price's army destroyed it again in 1864.

To reach Tour Stop 108:

Exit the cemetery by turning right on Engineer Street. Drive south until you cross the railroad tracks, then proceed south another .7 miles to Broadway (U.S. 50). Turn right on Broadway, and go west for 2 miles to U.S. Highway 65. Turn left (south) on U.S. 65, then drive south for a total of 33 miles, to an interchange where U. S. 65 intersects with Missouri Highway 7. Exit and turn right on Highway 7, and proceed a short distance to Commercial Street, where you will turn left. Drive into Warsaw on Commercial Street. You will arrive at the courthouse square, and the street along the square on the north is Washington Street. Turn left at Washington, and Tour Stop 108 is one block east.

Tour Stop 108

The WARSAW CHRISTIAN CHURCH served as both a hospital and a stable during the Civil War. It is the town's most historic Civil War building. Warsaw, the seat of Benton County, has become a resort town. The Lake of the Ozarks reaches this far west, and fills the narrow valley of the Osage River. What has been good for Warsaw is not so good for us, though, because the military history here largely involves the river bank that is now under the lake.

This is the best place to start the loop tour if you arrive from the south or if you want to follow Shelby's Raid chronologically. A skirmish occurred here on October 7, 1863, when Shelby found a local militia force ready to contest his crossing of the Osage. He made short work of the militia, then entered the town and made off with a bounty of rations and supplies.

We have mentioned in the introduction Fremont's campaign in October, 1861, but now we need to fill in some more of the background.

Consider what was transpiring in the East during this time. After the Battle of Bull Run, Gen. George McClellan holed up in Washington for months; The Army of the Potomac fought only one battle of any note from July, 1861 until the spring of 1862, the Union disaster at Ball's Bluff, Virginia, on October 21, 1861. Meanwhile, Fremont was moving on Springfield, albeit slowly, with an army of some 38,000 men of all arms. This number exceeds the strength of either of the armies that fought at Bull Run. Fremont led the largest military force to march overland up to that point in the war.

108

On October 24, 1861, the last of Fremont's divisions arrived in Warsaw from the north. A 5500-man contingent commanded by Gen. Justus McKinstry, this division marched south on the route you will next travel, the Butterfield Route, from Syracuse on the Pacific Railroad. On the same day, Abraham Lincoln signed the order that would relieve Fremont of command. How all of this happened is covered at Tour Stop 112.

Part III - Northbound

Tour Stop 109

Tour Stop 109 is the UNION CEMETERY, also known as the Williams Cemetery. You will learn below about the Battle of Cole Camp, and reputably some of the battle casualties were buried here. However, there is reason enough to stop to visit the grave of Ezekiel Williams, a legend from an earlier time in the nineteenth century. Ezekiel's grave is just behind the church building.

Williams founded the town of Cole Camp in 1839, near the end of his eventful life. As a youngster in Kentucky, he served as a captain in a company of the Kentucky militia in which Thomas Lincoln, Abe's father, was a subordinate officer. In 1809 after he moved to Missouri he became one of a group of adventurers hired by William Clark to return Mandan Chief Big White to his village in present day North Dakota (Big White had accompanied Lewis & Clark on their return trip, and visited President Jefferson in Washington). Setting off from the Mandan village, Williams then spent the next several years exploring the Rocky Mountains, partly in an effort to establish a contact with the Spanish in Santa Fe. He is thought to have *discovered* Colorado. Upon his return to Missouri, he published a famous journal, fought in a Missouri battle of the War of 1812, at Cooper's Fort, and moved to Missouri's Boonslick. The land Williams acquired there was just opposite the Missouri River town of Arrow Rock. In 1821, the men who organized the first expedition down the Santa Fe Trail met at his house to plan the expedition. A young saddle maker from nearby Franklin, Missouri, by the name of Kit Carson, knew Williams. Williams' tales of his days as a mountain man inspired Carson to embark on a new career.

Ezekiel Williams died at Cole Camp in 1844.

While like much of the center of the state this area was originally settled by Southerners, a great influx of German immigrants occurred here beginning in the late 1830s. By the time of the Civil War, the population of the Cole Camp area had become predominately German. It is today one of few places you can find in Missouri where an authentic German culture has survived.

About the 1861 Battle of Cole Camp: Like German Americans in St. Louis, generally the rural Missouri Germans

To reach Tour Stop 109:

Retrace your route back to U.S. 65 via Commercial Street. Drive north, still on the route of your arrival, for 4.4 miles from the Highway 7 intersection. There is an unmarked road that enters from the right, just before Route T intersects from the left. Turn right on this unmarked road, then turn left when you reach a "T" just down the hill. This gravel road is a remnant of the famous Butterfield Trail, and if you're game you can drive a bit of it. Take the road to the left, and drive north .6 mile, where you jog east for .2 mile on a paved road. In .2 mile, take the first available left, on to another gravel road that is marked as the Butterfield Trail. Drive north on this road for 3.8 miles until it intersects with County Route H.

Turn right on H and then left in .3 mile (which is the first opportunity you have to turn left). You are again on the Butterfield Route, but from here to Cole Camp the route is paved. Drive 5.5 miles north after leaving Route H, and there you will come upon a white frame church that is on the right.

You can drive north on U.S. 65 to Route H from Warsaw, a distance of 10 miles, and pick up the paved portion of the trail 3.3 miles east of U.S. 65.

could be counted on to have pro-Union sentiments. Very early in the conflict, Germans in this area formed an organization called the "Benton County Home Guard," known also as the German Regiment. On June 18, 1861, these men would find themselves in the wrong place at the wrong time.

Having learned of Nathaniel Lyon's expedition to Jefferson City, the Benton County Home Guard mobilized and went into camp several miles southeast of Cole Camp. Meanwhile, pro-secessionists organized in Warsaw. They learned that the bulk of the State Guard fleeing Jefferson City and Boonville, along with the government-in-exile, were traveling down the Butterfield trail. The commander of the Warsaw force, Walter S. O'Kane, determined on his own initiative to attack the Germans at Cole Camp from the rear before they could block the State Guard's route of escape. O'Kane, with a force of several hundred, moved up the Butterfield trail on the afternoon of June 18, 1861. O'Kane attacked a Union encampment east of town about midnight on June 18, catching the German Regiment asleep. He delivered a severe blow to the Union men.

The history books tend to view the Civil War from the perspective of the conflict waged in the eastern United States. Many if not most visitors probably learned about the Civil War from this perspective. It may jolt them to know of the events unfolding in this small town in June, 1861. Up until the day before O'Kane set out from Warsaw, there had been four engagements in the Civil War, all in Virginia (and what is now West Virginia). The largest of these, at Big Bethel, occurred on June 10, 1861. It produced about 50 casualties. On June 17, 1861, Nathaniel Lyon force attacked the State Guard east of Boonville, Missouri, in a clash that produced more casualties than any engagement in the war to that date. Boonville set the stage for the Battle of Cole Camp, by forcing the State Guard to flee south. Cole Camp set the new record for casualties. It would hold it until July 5, when the State Guard, still moving south, confronted another group of German-Americans at Carthage, Missouri.

To reach Tour Stop 110:

Continue north on the Butterfield Trail (Route F) for 2.7 miles, to Maple Street, just past S. Boonville Street in the center of town. Turn left on Maple. Tour Stop 110 is on your left in about a block.

Tour Stop 110

This is THE COLE CAMP MUSEUM. It has a number of exhibits on the history of the town, and a very good exhibit on the Battle of Cole Camp, including a diorama of the battle site. The staff can direct you to a place east of town near where the battle occurred, and the marker installed there by Missouri State Parks.

We are now on the trail of JO Shelby, and his 1863 raid. Shelby's command left Warsaw on October 8, 1863, and rode up the Butterfield trail. Many of his men were wearing captured federal uniforms. When they arrived in Cole Camp they were welcomed by the population.   For two days they rested, and if Edwards' account can be trusted:

"Dan. Ingram reveled in the delicious cider; Peter Tron made love to innumerable moon-faced girls; Dave Shanks devoured their sour-crout and patted the matronly frows under their double chins; . . . "

Shelby had a man shot after he bragged to the supposed Union officer that he had just killed three secesh neighbors. Then, off he went, Boonville bound.

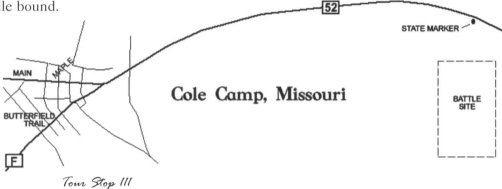

Tour Stop III

The town of FLORENCE was visited by Shelby as he made his way north. The Butterfield Trail headed east on the road in your front, then north to Syracuse by way of the next ridge. Our route will take you to the next Stop on a paved road. Contemporaneous reports indicate that Shelby went straight to Tipton after leaving here, although there are no roads to Tipton and probably were not then.

The night of October 14, 1863, the Confederate regiments detached from Shelby's main force at Marshall (Hunter's, Hooper's and Shanks') camped near Florence after engaging some federals in a sharp fight in town. Their escape from Marshall was as remarkable as Shelby's. Hunter came south along the border of Benton and Cooper Counties, and after leaving Florence on October 15, may have followed the route of Highway 135 south from this place.

To reach Tour Stop III:

Drive south on Maple to Main Street, and turn right. In two blocks, Main merges into State Route 52. From the point of the merge, drive east on Route 52 for 10 1/2 miles, and turn left on State Route 135. Go north on Route 135 for 11.4 to the town of Florence. Turn right on the main crossroad (Route JJ), and park here after you have made your turn.

To reach Tour Stop 112:

Drive east from Florence about 500 yards, where Route JJ turns sharply north. Stay on JJ for a total of 7.8 miles (since leaving Florence), until JJ ends at State Route D. Turn left, and drive north about 2 miles into the town of Syracuse, which is Tour Stop 112.

Tour Stop 112

Shelby's column reached SYRACUSE on October 10, 1863, after visiting Tipton. Shelby fought a small engagement 4 miles east of here, which you visit if you detour to Tour Stop 113.

Syracuse figured prominently in Fremont's 1861 Southwest Campaign, as the camp of McKinstry's division. Now a proverbial wide spot on the road, you have to imagine when Syracuse buzzed with activity. The date was October 13, 1861. McKinstry's 5500 men were camped in the fields surrounding the town, and a party of dignitaries rode over from Tipton to review the troops. They included the U. S. Secretary of War, Simon Cameron, and Lorenzo Thomas, Adjutant General of the Army. The official party had traveled by rail from Washington to see for themselves what Fremont was up to. Their concerns dated back to a series of events that had occurred beginning shortly after Fremont's arrival in St. Louis in July to take command of the Department of the West.

To begin with, Lyon lost the Battle of Wilson's Creek, and Fremont was accused of failing to supply and reinforce him. Then, Fremont awarded contracts to some California friends to construct fortifications protecting St. Louis, and he was accused of complicity in their profiteering. In mid September, 1861, Gen. Sterling Price and his State Guard attacked Lexington, Missouri and captured a Union detachment there. Fremont was accused of incompetence, and the "slows," in moving and equipping his army to attack Price. These were the ostensible reasons that Cameron and Thomas came to Syracuse.

There was more than a kernel of truth to the allegations of financial mismanagement in the Department, but strong evidence suggests that the political hatchet is what caused Fremont's downfall. John Charles Fremont had been the Republican candidate for

112

President in 1856, and he stood at the radical end of party politics. Central to Lincoln's strategy in 1861 was the principle that slavery must be *sustained* in the border states of Maryland, Kentucky and Missouri because any overt threat against the institution would drive them into the Confederacy. Lincoln had powerful allies in the Blair family, which not coincidentally had roots in all three of the border states.

On August 30, 1861, Fremont imposed martial law in St. Louis. Pursuant to authority he vested in himself he declared that slaves in the service of men supporting rebellion against the United States would be free. Fremont's edict upset Lincoln's delicate balancing act. Lincoln demanded that Fremont withdraw his order. He refused to do so, and Lincoln countermanded it. During this dispute in St. Louis, Fremont twice had Congressman Frank Blair arrested. While all of this was going on, however, Fremont used the power of his office to free some twenty slaves. Hiram Reed and Frank Lewis of St. Louis were the first men freed by this means, and whatever happened in Washington, Reed, Lewis and the others remained free and "forever discharged from the bonds of servitude." This was the first time the military authority of the United States was used for such a purpose.

Under pressure to take the field against Price's force in southwest Missouri, Fremont moved his army into position along the Pacific Railroad, but it was woefully equipped for the march. The Secretary of War found plenty of evidence in Tipton and Syracuse to bolster the call for Fremont's removal.

The case for and against Fremont was one of the factors that led to the formation of the Congressional "Joint Committee on the Conduct of the War." The case was argued in the halls of Congress in early 1862. Fremont was shuffled off to a command in West Virginia, where he distinguished himself only by military incompetence. Perhaps but for his subsequent military record he would be remembered now for gallant service in the cause for freedom.

Tour Stop 113

Tour Stop 113 is FREMONT'S HEADQUARTERS, the restored Maclay House. The building was constructed in 1858 to house the Rose Hill Seminary, a female academy, but abandoned at the beginning of the Civil War. Its 17 rooms provided suitable quarters for General Fremont and staff, which occupied it from October 9 to 14, 1861.

Another thing that happened in 1858 was the inauguration of the Butterfield Stage. In 1857, Congress determined to create an overland mail route to link the eastern United States to the new state of California. Like most policy questions at that time, the route became a controversy between North and South. The route would go south, through the desert southwest, and would start in St. Louis, but a compromise was worked out so another leg would start

To reach Tour Stop 113:

Take U. S. Highway 50 east for 5.4 miles to the town of Tipton. You will turn left on Route B when you arrive in town. This street jogs right, then left, and becomes Moreau Avenue. Take Moreau north for 6 or 7 blocks, then cross the Pacific Railroad tracks. In two blocks, turn left on Howard Street. The next Tour Stop is the large brick building at the northwest corner of Moreau and Howard.

in Memphis. The two legs joined at Fort Smith, Arkansas. The route from St. Louis extended via the Pacific Railroad to the western end of the line, at that time, Tipton. There, the mail was transferred from train to coach and the 2800 mile route to San Francisco commenced. The inaugural trip started out from Tipton on September 16, 1858.

The Butterfield Stage line was organized into a relay system, much like the later Pony Express. At its height, before operations halted in 1861, 139 relay stations and over 1500 horses and mules were employed in the venture. Fresh horsepower hitched up at each station stop (established about 17 miles apart) permitted the stage to average an incredible 120 miles per day.

You will now retrace your route back to Syracuse to begin the next segment of the tour. There is a roadside park to your left, a couple hundred yards west of the intersection of Moreau Street and Highway 50. A marker here tells the story of the Butterfield Stage.

About two miles west of Tipton, about where U. S. 50 straightens out a second time, there was an incident on October 10, 1863. It involved a locomotive that Union Lt. Col. Thomas T. Crittenden, Seventh Missouri State Militia Cavalry, had commandeered in Tipton. This was during Shelby's Raid in 1863. Crittenden, a Kentuckian who knew Shelby well before the war, intended to find out if the Confederates had destroyed the Lamine River bridge at Otterville. Part way to Syracuse, he ran into a small band of Shelby's men, and had the locomotive engineer reverse the engine and high-tail it back to Tipton in reverse. He collected what Union troops were still in Tipton, and they all took a fast train to Jefferson City.

Driving instructions resume where State Highway 5 intersects U. S. 50 east of Syracuse.

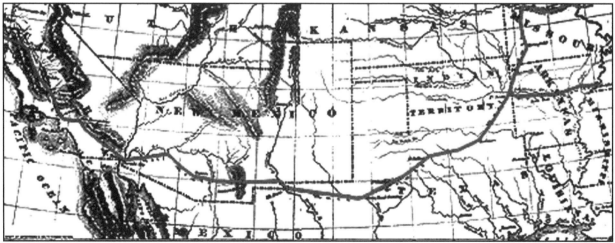

Route of the Butterfield Stage

Tour Stop 114

This is the RAVENSWOOD FARM. The house you see was built in 1880, and replaced a frame home that existed here during the Civil War. Nathaniel Leonard was born in Vermont in 1799. He came to Missouri in 1824 and settled here in Cooper County. More about the Leonard family, below, but first let's get re-oriented to the story of Shelby's Raid.

Information about Shelby's 1863 route is sparse, but we do have Shelby's report of an action on October 10, 1863: "Syracuse was also entered, stormed, and some prisoners taken, and by 4 o'clock I was off for Boonville." The 1883 History of Cooper and Howard Counties states that "On the night of the 10th [Shelby] camped near Bell Air, in a pasture belonging to Mr. Nathaniel Leonard." We think it clear that Shelby's main force took the route of Highway 5, and camped here the night after leaving Syracuse.

The Nathaniel Leonard who founded Ravenswood came from solid Yankee stock. His grandfather, an Episcopal minister in Connecticut, served as a chaplain to Gen. George Washington. Nathaniel's father and namesake, Capt. Nathaniel Leonard, was a military man who was in command of the garrison at Fort Niagara, New York, when the British captured the Fort on December 18, 1813. The lad Nathaniel was at home in the nearby village of Lewiston, New York, that night. Captain Leonard was home that night, as well. Not long thereafter, in 1819, one of Capt. Leonard's sons, Abiel, emigrated to Missouri and settled in Howard County. Nathaniel of Ravenswood followed him several years later, and soon began to assemble the property that became Ravenswood Farm. In its heyday after the Civil War, Ravenswood Farm would reach a size of 2200 acres, and was famous throughout the world for its herd of shorthorn cattle.

Despite their New England roots, the Leonards of Missouri were slaveholders. That's just a hint of the complex social culture that prevailed in rural Missouri in the years of the Civil War. However, the Leonards were staunch unionists. Nathaniel's son, a future proprietor of Ravenswood Farm, was Capt. Charles E. Leonard. In 1863, Charles led a detachment of Militia Cavalry that was chasing JO Shelby on his way north. In Boonville, Shelby would confront another Union force, led by Charles' cousin, Reeves Leonard of Howard County.

To reach Tour Stop 114:

From Syracuse, drive east on U. S. Highway 50, 1 mile to the intersection of State Route 5, and turn left. Drive north on State Route 5 for 10.4 miles to the entrance gate of the Ravenswood plantation. Pull into the gate when it is open; if it is not open carefully stop in the entrance, leaving yourself room to re-enter Hiway 5. The view of the highway is somewhat obscured from this position. Be careful.

114

To reach Tour Stop 115:

Drive north on Hiway 5 for 6.4 miles to an intersection, which is Old Highway 5. There is a sign on the road denoting the town of Billingsville, just short of this intersection. Turn right here, where there is a triangular patch of grass, and pause if you can before turning right in the direction of Billingsville. This is Tour Stop 115.

Tour Stop 115

This is BILLINGSVILLE, and the approximate site of the camp of Gen. Egbert B. Brown on the night of October 11, 1863. Brown was leading Union forces, about 1600 strong, in pursuit of Shelby, and many of them bivouacked here. Shelby's troops spent the night in Boonville.

The road that angles off to the northeast here is called Old Highway 5, but was once called the Bellair Road. In all likelihood, Shelby followed this road into Boonville on the morning of October 11, 1863, and Brown's troops followed him on the 12th. We will take a detour over to the Tipton High Road, though, and fast-forward to October, 1864. When you reach Tour Stop 119, you will be back on Shelby's 1863 route.

JO Shelby played a prominent role in Sterling Price's 1864 Expedition in Missouri. In this part of Missouri Price and Shelby followed Shelby's 1863 route nearly exactly. Shelby's Division might have followed routes several miles to the east of here, from the town of California to Boonville, but in any case Shelby, in the vanguard of Price's force, entered and occupied Boonville on the evening of October 10, 1864, one year (less a day) after he took Boonville during his 1863 raid.

The Tipton and Boonville Road, called the High Road, headed straight north from Tipton, parallel to the Bellair Road and about 4 miles east of it. On October 11, 1864, a Union cavalry force

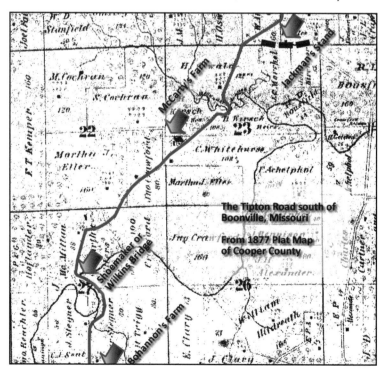

The Tipton Road south of Boonville, Missouri

From 1877 Plat Map of Cooper County

approached via the Tipton Road, and crossed the dominant stream in this area, the Petite Saline Creek. There ensued a two day battle known sometimes as the Battle of the Petite Saline, but also the Battle of the Tête Saline. This term was not, evidently, of French origin, but rather a slang term derived from the second syllable of the word petite, and pronounced the same way. The battle is described at Stops 116 and 117.

Tour Stop 116

Tour Stop 116 is the site of the PETITE SALINE BRIDGE on the Tipton High Road. Please do not enter the property on your right, but when the vegetation is low you can make out a stone bridge abutment on the near bank.

Union cavalry under the overall command of Brig. Gen. John Sanborn were trailing Price's army from the vicinity of California, Missouri. There are several accounts of the action here and at Stop 117. We draw our story mostly from the Report of Col. Sydney Jackman of Shelby's Division.

As the Confederates entered Boonville, Arkansas cavalry attached to the Division of Maj. Gen. James F. Fagan patrolled this sector. Shelby's Missourians were assigned to similar duty to the west, along the Georgetown Road (present day Highway 135). On October 11, 1864, elements of two of Sanborn's regiments crossed the bridge here and moved northeast along the road you are traveling. Somewhere in the next two miles they collided with Fagan's forces. These Union troops, mostly the 2nd Arkansas Cavalry commanded by Col. John E. Phelps of Springfield, twice attacked Fagan's entrenched forces, and twice were repulsed by Fagan's artillery.

Apprised of Sanborn's force, Shelby ordered Colonel Jackman to take his brigade from the Georgetown Road and reinforce Fagan. Jackman arrived two miles north of here at 5:30 on the afternoon of October 11, then assisted in driving Phelps' forces south and across the bridge in your front. Sanborn's troops camped in the bottoms across the way, 1/2 mile south at the Bohannon Farm. The Union cavalry maintained possession of the Petite Saline bridge that night. Meanwhile, part of Sanborn's force, under Cooper County's Col. Joseph Eppstein, was ordered from the Georgetown Road to this sector. We believe Eppstein, with about 400 troopers of the 5th Missouri Militia Cavalry, camped at Bohannon's the night of October 11.

To reach Tour Stop 116:

Turn right on the road (Fair Road) that heads south, and proceed south for about 1/8 mile to an angled turn. Bear left at this turn, and continue on Fair Road through the town of Billingsville for a total of 1.8 miles since you left Tour Stop 115. You will come to the bottom of a valley at approximately 1.6 miles, and the road turns to the left. As you start up the next hill, stop and park at the point the road is closest to the stream on your right.

To reach Tour Stop 117:

Continue your drive to the northeast. You are now on the Billingsville Road. Continue northeast on the Billingsville Road for 2.0 miles, pulling over as this road reaches high ground before it intersects with County Route B.

Tour Stop 117

You are at JACKMAN'S LAST POSITION during the Battle of the Tête Saline.

At dawn on the morning of October 12, 1864, Eppstein moved up the Tipton Road from Bohannon's and crossed the Petite Saline bridge. Dismounted, his troopers fought their way up the hill just north of the bridge and drove Col. C.H. Nichols' Confederate regiment back towards Boonville. Nichols - who would one day become the first mayor of Branson, Missouri - had camped the previous night on the hill, while Jackman with his other two regiments, Hunter's and Schnable's, bivouacked 3/4 mile to the northeast near the McCarty farm. Another fight occurred at the McCarty farm, where Eppstein dislodged Jackman's whole force by flanking it.

Jackman's troopers fought their way back to Tour Stop 117, arriving here about 10:00 a.m. on October 12, 1864. The Confederates brought their artillery into action here (either 2 or 4 guns depending upon whose report you believe), and formed a line behind a fence row. Eppstein brought up two pieces of artillery also, and for a while the contesting forces exchanged fire across the field to the south. Eppstein's attack was stymied, then broken up when Jackman ordered a counterattack. The Confederates chased Eppstein all of the way back to, and well past, the bridge on the Tête Saline. Evidently, the rest of Sanborn's division had by this time already withdrawn from camp at the Bohannon Farm and were in the process of retreating to California to regroup. The events here bought Price some time that he used over the next few days, as described at Tour Stops 91 and 93.

Alfred Pleasonton, Union Major General of cavalry, arrived in Jefferson City on October 7, 1864, just as the Confederates were leaving. Pleasonton pulled together the various federal cavalry units he found in that vicinity, about 4,000 of them, mostly Missouri State Militia Cavalry. As Pleasonton moved west, he added to his force until he had in his Second Division approximately 6,500 troopers. As discussed in Tour Loop Four, Pleasonton finally brought this formidable force to bear on Price on the outskirts of Kansas City, but the first significant clash of arms that involved Pleasonton's division occurred on the banks of the Tete Saline.

117

118

Tour Stop 118

Tour Stop 118 is a view of the BELLAIRE ROAD. This was the main road into Boonville from the direction of Springfield, and the point of entry when Shelby's men arrived in Boonville on October 11, 1863.

In 1864, during Price's Expedition, a company of Union cavalry dashed into the outskirts of Boonville and occupied several houses, until driven out by Confederate artillery. This incident on October 11, 1864 was part of the action involving Phelps' 2nd Arkansas, as described at Stop 116. As you exit this area by driving east on the intersecting road (Stanfield Road), turn left at Boonslick Drive and drive north to Logans Lake Road. The point where Stanfield meets Boonslick Drive was probably the deepest point of the Union advance on October 11.

To reach Tour Stop 118:

Continue northeast for about 1/4 mile. The Billingsville Road will intersect with Route B. Turn left on Route B and drive north 1.8 miles to Interstate 70. Continue across the interstate, then north approximately 1 mile to Logans Lake Road, and turn left. Drive west two blocks to a gravel road called Pink Elephant Road, and make a left here. Go south a couple hundred yards and park at the point where a road intersects from the left. You will use this road on the left to return to Route B.

THE BOONVILLE PORTRAIT

The photograph at right was snapped while Price's troops occupied Boonville in 1864. It is believed to be the only wartime photograph of General Joseph O. Shelby.

Noted Kansas City historian Howard Monnett wrote the landmark study of the Battle of Westport, *Action Before Westport, 1864.* In 1971, Monnett discovered an original print of this photo in an old building in Tombstone, Arizona. On the back was written a note signed "John Ringo," who claimed in the note that he rode with Shelby during the Civil War. All of this was noted by John H. Monnett (Howard's son, an author and noted historian of western history) in his foreword to the 1995 revised edition of *Action Before Westport.* The image was lost for decades until this discovery.

In the '90s PBS series The Civil War, filmmaker Ken Burns committed very few mistakes, but he identified this picture to be that of a Tennessee officer in Sam Watkins' chain of command.

This Tour Loop ends where Logans Lake Road intersects Route B. Turn left on Route B, Main Street, to visit Boonville. This is also the direction to travel if you are tracking Shelby's Raid from the south; The Loop begins at Thespian Hall, Tour Stop 90.

To exit the area, turn right on Route B and drive south to Interstate 70.

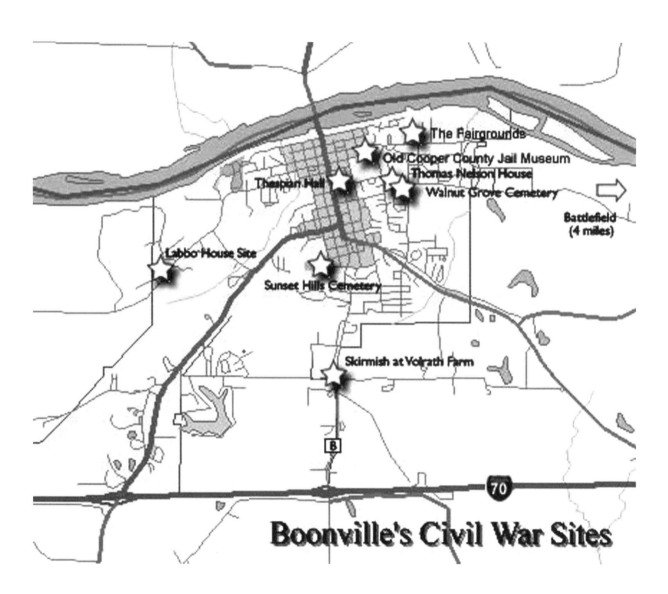

TOUR LOOP FOUR

As the Civil War began, what we know as Kansas City barely had any history at all. The great towns along the border then were Independence and Westport, which sprang up to outfit the freighters and the settlers who followed the Santa Fe, California and Oregon Trails in the 1830s and 40s. The Missouri side of the Missouri-Kansas border was overwhelmingly Southern in culture. Kansas, approached statehood in the 1850s with a strong influence from New England. Tour Loop Five starts and ends near the waterfront in old Kansas City, and explores an area of western Missouri that was among the most flammable when 1861 arrived, and that smoldered well into the 1880s. This is the land of Jesse James.

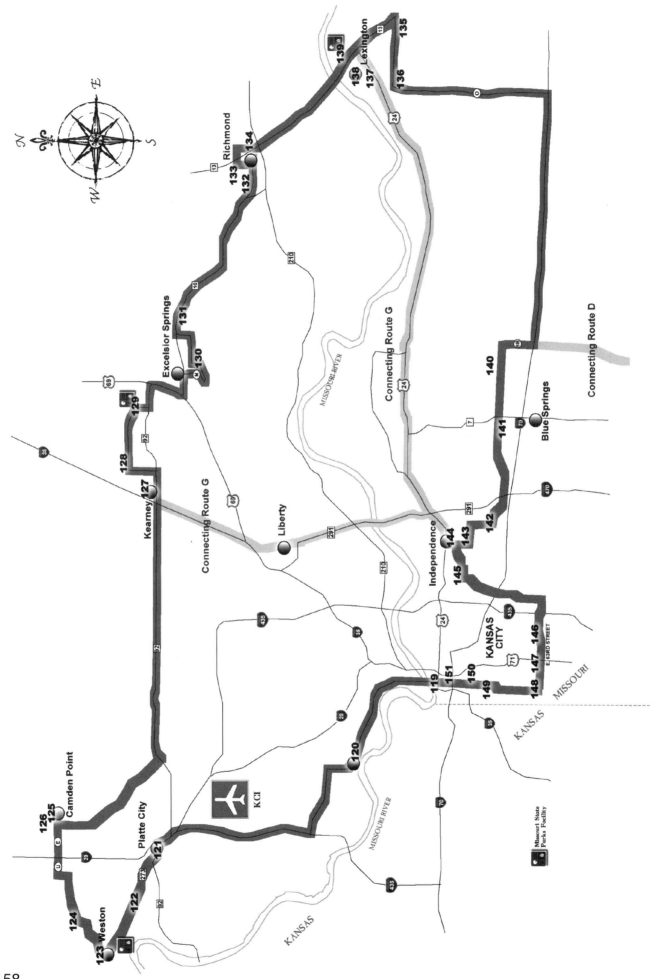

KCI

Connecting Route G

Connecting Route G

Connecting Route D

Richmond

Lexington

Excelsior Springs

Kearney

Camden Point

Platte City

Weston

Liberty

Independence

Blue Springs

KANSAS
CITY

E 63RD STREET

MISSOURI

KANSAS

KANSAS

MISSOURI RIVER

MISSOURI RIVER

Missouri State
Parks Facility

158

A TOUR OF THE REGION OF KANSAS CITY

Roots of Rebellion

This Guide began by describing the Boonslick Road, blazed by the sons of Daniel Boone. The westward progress of the Boone family did not halt in the center of Missouri. Rather, Boone's descendents continued west as centers of commerce moved west. Daniel Morgan Boone - who with his brother laid out the Boonslick Road - was one of the first white men to scout in the area of Kansas City. He moved there in the 1820s. Independence and Westport became boom towns. The trail-blazers settled down to farm and in some cases to make fortunes in the overland freight business. So it was with the Boone family.

Old Daniel Boone was born in Pennsylvania, but by his late teens he lived in North Carolina. Ever after that, the Boone family with all of its branches was a Southern family. Both Daniel and son Daniel Morgan Boone owned slaves, probably just a few at any one time. This is perhaps an inconvenient truth for people who rightly condemn the institution of slavery, but recognize

Machpelah Cemetery, Lexington

that our modern nation is defined by the experience of the advancing frontier, and by the courage and character of families like the Boones.

A family named Young followed the trail of the Boones, starting from North Carolina, then to Kentucky and finally coming to rest in Jackson County, Missouri. This family migrated about a generation after the Boones. The Youngs were not trailblazers, but they typified a Southern family adapting to life in the west in the years leading up to the Civil War. Solomon

Young arrived in Jackson County in 1841. He farmed and he grew a large family, which included a daughter Martha Ellen, born in 1852. Solomon Young and his wife Harriett owned a few slaves, as the Boones did. In the '50s Solomon stayed out of the troubles in Kansas, and he considered himself a Union man. Not all western Missouri slave owners stayed out of the Kansas troubles. Many dove into the fray. These are types of people who fueled a rebellion that rose in western Missouri in the 1860s.

Solomon Young's daughter Martha Ellen never forgot that in 1863 she, with her family, had to leave their home by the terms of Order No. 11. The Youngs were not loyal enough. She remembered the Kansas jayhawkers who pillaged the family home. And she would not let her son Harry forget these things. Martha Ellen Truman (née Young), lived until 1947. She once refused to sleep in the Lincoln Bedroom in her son's White House.

Harry S Truman was the first U. S. President to pick up the banner of racial equality. In 1946, he established a no-nonsense Presidential Committee on Civil Rights, and then he spoke publicly and forcefully for the use of federal power to guarantee equal rights. In 1948, perturbed by Congressional inaction on his agenda, Truman issued executive orders that integrated federal employment and the Armed Forces. Truman set out on this mission while some polls showed 80% of Americans against it. This is one legacy of Missouri's Southern culture.

Campaigns in this Tour

Price's Lexington Campaign

The Missouri State Guard achieved its most notable success in late September, 1861, during the interlude between the Battle of Wilson's Creek (August 10, 1861) and John C. Fremont's recapture of Springfield in late October. Fremont's administration in St. Louis was still reeling, from the loss at Wilson's Creek and from demands upon his Department emanating from southeast Missouri, when Maj, Gen. Sterling Price decided he would move to the Missouri River.

Price marched north from the direction of Springfield, pausing near Nevada to fight some Kansans under Kansas Senator Jim Lane. He moved in a northeasterly direction, and went into camp near Rose Hill in western Johnson County. Upon arrival in camp, though, Price learned that some federal cavalry were at Warrensburg. The MSG immediately broke camp and made a night march for Warrensburg, but there on September 11 Price found that the

federals had gone, retreating in the direction of Lexington. He moved his troops, perhaps 10,000 strong, north on the Lexington-Warrensburg Road and they arrived at Lexington on the 12th.

Lexington stood almost defenseless as Price moved north, but finally when his objective became clear Fremont dispatched a force from Jefferson City to occupy the town. This was the Chicago Irish Brigade, sometimes known as the "Irish Brigade of the West," commanded by Col. James A. Mulligan. Oddly, this was not a brigade at all, but rather a single regiment - the 23rd Illinois Infantry. It was composed almost entirely of Irish-American recruits from Chicago. Mulligan did not arrive in Lexington until September 9 or 10, and he pulled together a force that included the 13th Missouri Infantry, some militia and the cavalry from Warrensburg. He had about 2800 men in all. They dug in on the site of a Masonic college, on a hill east of town, and waited.

Price's army arrived and began to invest Mulligan's position on the evening of the 12th. A sharp fight occurred south of town on September 13, when Mulligan struck out in an effort to buy some time. The fight centered in

The Battle of Lexington (Harpers Weekly)

James Adelbert Mulligan was born in Utica, New York in 1830. Moving to Chicago with his Ireland-born parents at an early age, he became a lawyer there. Before the Civil War he served for a brief time as a clerk in the State Department in Washington. With war coming, he returned to Chicago and recruited a regiment composed almost entirely of Irish-Americans, the 23rd Illinois Volunteers.

In mid-July, 1861, following basic training, Mulligan and the 23rd Illinois moved to St. Louis. Soon they were ordered to Jefferson City, and were serving there when the call came to move to Lexington, Missouri. It had become clear that Sterling Price's State Guard was targeting that town. Mulligan had to surrender the place on September 20, 1861 after a week's siege, but by this time the Northern press had seized upon the plight of the Lexington defenders as the great news story of the day. When he did surrender, Mulligan allowed his troops to be paroled, but he would not accept a parole for himself, standing upon the principle that the Missouri State Guard had no authority to treat with an officer of the U.S. Army. Mulligan was released in late October, 1861. It is indicative of low morale in the North after Bull Run that Mulligan received a tumultuous hero's welcome upon returning to Chicago. He and his Irish brigade had at least stood their ground at Lexington.

From February to June, 1862, Mulligan served as commandant of Camp Douglas, the Chicago prison camp that later became a notorious killer of Confederates. While no unusual barbarity occurred during his short stint there, Mulligan got into some trouble for enrolling prisoners in the federal service, as well as for some financial irregularities.

Once returned to active service, Mulligan earned a reputation as a good field commander. He commanded the rear guard of a Union army in retreat at the Second Battle of Kernstown, Virginia, July 24, 1864. He was mortally wounded there, and later died in captivity. Mulligan became famous a second time in his brief military career for the last command he gave to his troops: "Lay me down and save the flag."

the city's historic cemetery south of town, and is known as the "Battle Over The Dead." Mulligan then retreated into his entrenchments and an extended siege began.

Gen. Price first managed to cut Mulligan off from any reinforcements seeking to arrive from North Missouri, and so could settle in, and wait for all his supplies and ammunition, before he went to the task of investing Mulligan's entrenchments. Price moved in on September 18, a day punctuated by a charge by the Irish Brigade, up and out of the trenches, in an effort to dislodge sharpshooters from the Anderson House near the battlefield. Then with all of Mulligan's men back in position on the college grounds, Price tightened the knot. There was little food, and the Union troops ran out of water on the 19th.

The battle and siege of Lexington is known as "The Battle of the Hemp Bales." The waterfront in Lexington was stocked with bales of hemp, ready for shipment down river. One of the officers of the Missouri State Guard - Gen. Thomas Harris gets the credit - suggested that

the bales be used as rolling breastworks. The bales were hauled up the bluff and soaked in water. The State Guard troops rolled them up towards the Union earthwork, constricting Mulligan's options and preparing for a final assault that was, in the end, unnecessary. On September 20, out of food and water, the Union defenders gave up. About 1,800 Union troops surrendered. Although the toll of dead and wounded, on both sides, was small, Lexington represented another in a series of devastating blows to federal fortunes. It brought an end to the first summer of the Civil War, a period that saw virtually no battle victories for the Union cause.

The Thornton-Thrailkill Raid

Northwest Missouri erupted in partisan warfare in July, 1864. What was happening in Northwest Missouri coincided with a brutal raid by Anderson in the north-central secton of the state. These events occurred a few months before Price's Expedition. Confederate authorities may have signaled the guerrillas in Missouri to prepare the way for an invasion. We know for sure is that Sterling Price knew of the activity in northwest Missouri as it was happening, and as he was promoting his plan to his superior officer in Arkansas.

The Thornton-Thrailkill Raid takes its name from two partisan leaders who played key roles in its execution. The first was John C. Calhoun Thornton of St. Joseph, and the second was John Thrailkill. Thrailkill was not in fact a guerrilla, at least not before July, 1864, but he was able to join the revolt in northwest Missouri after he managed to escape from the federal military prison in Alton, Illinois. Perhaps, Thornton and Trailkill each led all of the men part of the time, or some of the men all of the time, but there was

no chain of command in the sense those words are typically appied. A third man, Charles "Fletch" Taylor, was also involved in the raid, and in fact people in Clinton and Caldwell counties called it the "Thrailkill-Taylor Raid."

The raid began on July 7 in southern Platte County at a place called Parkville, when Taylor's men struck a hotel building that had been fortified to protect the town. The hotel was defended by so-called "Paw Paw militia," who also at that time occupied the County seat at Platte City. The action moved to Platte City on July 10, 1864, where the militia surrendered the town without a fight. Although the reader would think that the soldiers opposing the Missouri guerrillas would be Union troops, we hesitate to refer to the Paw Paw militia as such. The story of

this unusual militia organization is described in the first few Stops of this Tour.

Platte City, Missouri was a "rebel" town that was (and is) only a few miles from Fort Leavenworth, Kansas. The bold stroke engineered by Thornton and Thrailkill brought Union cavalry immediately into action, driving into the Missouri interior from the Missouri River port town of Weston. Men of the hated 15th Kansas and 2nd Colorado cavalries, both known for their jayhawking, gave chase, as did a detachment of the 9th Missouri State Militia Cavalry.

Battles occurred at Camden Point, Missouri on July 13, and at Fredericksburg on July 16 (near present-day Excelsior Springs). Then, a part of the Southern force went north to Mirabile and Kingston in Caldwell County, and to Plattsburg in Clinton County, and occupied these towns briefly on July 21. The raid petered out by the end of the month, but Thornton had brought a number of recruits into his fold, and they readied themselves for more action.

JESSE WOODSON JAMES

Jesse Woodson James was the second son of a prominent Baptist preacher who settled in Clay County, Missouri, north of Kansas City. Fifteen years old in 1863, James tried to join the Southern guerrillas who were active near his home. Too young they said. That year, 1863, he was home working the fields when local Union militia came to the family farm. They beat James and they hoisted his step-father by the neck a few times until he lost consciousness and maybe some of his mental capacity. The militia men were the James' neighbors. They were hunting the band that James wanted to join - the one big brother Frank James had already joined.

In 1864, Jesse James was old enough to join. Like most everything in his life, the date he went to war is subject to some question, but according to reliable sources he joined a guerrilla band on July 4, 1864. "Fletch" Taylor was recruiting in Clay County. James qualified for the job. Within a week, James had participated in an attack on federalized troops in Parkville, Missouri, and in the occupation of Platte City. He seems to have liked the camera, and vice versa, and he visited the photographer in Platte City on July 10, 1864. That visit produced the indelible image that appears on this page, documenting the very beginning of the public life of this memorable man. The camera captured the essence of the man and the times: Young and cocky, determined and dangerous.

James fought with Taylor during the Summer of 1864, and by the fall Taylor had combined his forces with those of Bill Anderson. Anderson took command; James became a student of this master of mayhem and murder. By the time he was seventeen, James had been wounded twice, the second time almost fatally. He surrendered to Union authorities in Lexington, Missouri, in May, 1865. By then, he had seen enough killing to last most men a lifetime.

Jesse James' career as most hunted and notorious outlaw in America began in 1866, and it lasted until his violent death in St. Joseph, Missouri, on April 3, 1882.

Price's 1864 Expedition
Action in Western Missouri

Price's movements in Central Missouri are described in the introduction to Tour Loop Three. We left him at Lexington, where a skirmish occurred on October 19, 1864.

Price moved west from Lexington on October 20, while Union Maj. Gen. James Blunt, who now commanded a cavalry division in the Union Army of the Border, was moving east from Kansas City. Blunt arrived on the banks of the Little Blue River, east of Independence and nearly within the limits of the modern Kansas City metropolis. Price reached the Little Blue on October 21, 1864, and a severe clash ensued there, followed by Blunt's retirement into Independence. The fighting continued east and northeast of Independence on the 21st. It was there that partisan chief George Todd was shot dead.

The fighting on October 20-21 did permit the Union Cavalry under Alfred Pleasonton, following from the east, to close the gap. In addition, regiments of Kansas militia were called up. These troops crossed into Missouri to bolster Blunt's defense.

The Big Blue River rises in Kansas, near Olathe, and it and its tributaries drain much of the area of Kansas City. Blunt attempted to hold the lower fords of the Big Blue, on the Westport road at Byram's Ford, and on the Hickman Mills road near where 85th Street now crosses the river. Maj. Gen. Samuel Curtis arrived to take overall command of the Union forces while Blunt was disposing his troops to hold the crossings of the Blue. This was on October 22, 1864.

With Shelby in the lead, the Confederate Iron Brigade easily outflanked the Union defenders at Byram's Ford. Jackman's Brigade, meanwhile, crossed the Big Blue to the south,

intent on reaching the Kansas border. A regiment of Kansas militia posted on the Hickman Mills Road put up a short but fierce fight in the area of Holmes Avenue and 78th Street. The Union forces then withdrew to Westport. The Confederates went into camp on the south side of Brush Creek - near where Country Club Plaza is now located. Price left a part of Marmaduke's command to the east to guard Byram's Ford, and Marmaduke's men formed Price's right flank. Pleasonton was on his way, and by now he was gaining steam.

Curtis assembled his army on the heights north of Brush Creek. At 4:00 a.m. on October 23, the federals moved into the valley and attempted to gain a foothold on the south side. Price counterattacked here, and the battle along Brush Creek raged for several hours. Meanwhile, at 8:00 a.m. Pleasonton's cavalry arrived at the Byram's Ford crossing. Marmaduke's Confederates contested the crossing and fought valiantly for three hours, before being forced back upon the plain south of Country Club Plaza, where Price's main body was still resisting Curtis' advance.

As a result of the action at Byram's Ford, Pleasonton's troopers had managed to flank Price. The Confederates began to withdraw, and escaped when Shelby's Division made a brilliant stand in the neighborhood of Troost Avenue and 70th Street.

What remained of Price's Expedition became a race down the Missouri-Kansas border, with Price trying to salvage his wagon train and the booty he gained during his operation, and the federals trying to bag Price's whole force. By this time, Price's force was seriously demoralized. The action in this quarter is described in connecting Route D. The narrative continues in the introduction to Tour Loop Five.

MAN UNDER THE BUS

Thomas Ewing, Jr. is to the Civil War in the West what William T. Sherman is to the war in the East. Both are damned and defiled for brutality exceeding the standards for humane warfare of the times. Ewing has been branded for what author Albert Castel calls "the most drastic and repressive military measure directed against civilians by the Union Army during the Civil War." This was Order No. 11, issued by Ewing on August 30, 1863.

Ewing and Sherman grew up in the same house in Lancaster, Ohio. Sherman was also a native of Lancaster. Sherman's father died in 1829, the same year that Thomas Ewing, Jr. was born. Ewing's father adopted Sherman, and ultimately Sherman married one of the Ewing girls. The two men, Sherman and Ewing, were for a time law partners in Kansas before the war. That is not to say that Ewing lived in the shadow of his older adopted brother. Ewing was successful in Kansas, and was the very first Chief Justice of the Kansas Supreme Court at the time Kansas achieved statehood in 1861.

Ewing recruited an infantry regiment in 1862, and entered the service as its colonel. He and his unit fought several battles in Arkansas, before Ewing was promoted to the rank of Brigadier General effective March, 1863. Thanks to political connections, he was the commander of the army's District of the Border when he issued his notorious order. Ewing had one opportunity to show his "grit" as a soldier during Price's Expedition in 1864, at Pilot Knob, and here he excelled. That story is at page 22 of Tour Loop One.

Ewing resigned his commission in April, 1865 and began practicing law in Washington, D.C. He represented three of the alleged Lincoln conspirators, including Dr. Samuel Mudd. As lawyers count victories, this engagement was a victory, since only one of his clients went to the gallows.

Ewing was practicing law in New York in 1896, when he stepped off a curb and was hit by a horse-drawn bus. His injuries proved fatal. He is buried in Yonkers, New York.

165

Roots of Rebellion

Part I - Northbound

Tour Stop 119

Tour Stop 119 is the ORDER NO. 11 MARKER. Placed by Missouri State Parks, the marker commemorates the site across the street. The Pacific House hotel was constructed in 1861. In 1863 this building was the headquarters of Gen. Thomas Ewing, Jr. who issued from here his notorious "Order No. 11." The marker contains an excellent description of the significance of this event, and provides a hint of George Caleb Bingham's relationship to this story. This is covered in the Tour Stops that precede this one as the Tour Loop closes in from the south (Tour Stops 150 and 151).

Few people realize that modern-day Kansas City holds a trove of Civil War treasures, largely because the Battle of Westport was fought right in the middle of its populated center. Near the end of this Tour several stops detail the action during this battle, the "Gettysburg of the West," fought on October 22-23, 1864. As a result, no major American city outside of Atlanta contains more battle-related resources within its corporate limits. As in Atlanta, unfortunately the march of progress has obliterated much of the evidence of the events that occurred here.

This Tour Loop is an extensive one, but if you want to stay close to the City find your way from here to Independence, pick up the Tour at Tour Stop 135 and then proceed in a clockwise direction. Alternatively, follow the route in reverse from this spot, and include the Battle of Westport driving tour in your itinerary. Brochures that provide directions for the battlefield tour are available at the Swope Interpretive Center in Swope Park, open Wednesdays through Saturdays during tourist season.

Still, the most significant Civil War theme you find in the Kansas City area is the guerrilla conflict that reached full flower in 1863. Tour Stop 119 marks both a beginning and an end. What ended was the gruesome month of August, 1863. A band of 300 men organized and led by William Clarke Quantrill completed a raid on Lawrence, Kansas on August 21, 1863. This horrible event - certainly the worst atrocity committed against civilians in the Civil War - produced an over-reaction. Ewing issued Order No.

To reach Tour Stop 119:

Find your way to the River Market area, north of I-70 as you enter the downtown part of the city from either east or west. The other major point of entry is from the north, via Interstates 29/35. If you arrive from this direction, go west at the first major interchange, following I-35 west In either case, exit at Exit 2D. You can follow the signs that direct Visitors to the Arabia Steamboat Museum, which is in the immediate area of Tour Stop 150. When you find yourself at the Museum (well worth a visit), go north to the next cross street, East 3rd Street, and turn left. Go west 3 blocks to Delaware Street, then turn left. In one block, you will see an old brick building on your left, and there is parking on your right where you can view our first Stop on this Tour.

11 on August 30. It compelled most of the residents of four Missouri border counties to leave their farms and homes. This huge swatch of territory was turned into a desert so that Quantrill's men could not find refuge among a Southern-leaning population. Peek ahead if you like, to Tour Stop 151, and you will see that Ewing had already employed this tactic on a small scale, with consequences that might have included the Lawrence Raid itself.

What began here in August, 1863, was a war without rules or bounds, which carried over to 1864 and set central Missouri ablaze.

Tour Stop 120

This is the site of THE PAW-PAW FORT. A paw paw is a wild bush that bears a fruit known as the "Missouri banana." When Lewis & Clark returned from the Pacific Coast, paw paws growing in the Missouri River bottoms in this part of Missouri fed a crew that was near the point of starvation.

The Union home guard in Platte County acquired the nickname "Paw-Paw Militia" from the legendary Missouri banana. Formed in 1863, these regiments of the Enrolled Missouri Militia had a peculiar history. Former Confederate soldiers and known Southern sympathizers made up the bulk of the Paw-Paw Militia. The Governor of Missouri instituted this social experiment. At the time he probably thought that the citizens of Platte County were more in need of protection from marauding Kansans than from Confederates or their allies in the bush.

In 1864, a substantial stone structure known as the Missouri Valley Hotel stood on this site. Parkville founder George S. Park built it in 1850. Later, the hotel became the first building of Park College, which was founded in 1876. The hotel was dismantled early in the 20th century to make more room for the railroad at the base of the bluff.

On July 7, 1864, a company of the 82nd Enrolled Missouri Militia - one of the Paw-Paw regiments - occupied the hotel when Confederate Col. John Thornton's men approached the town. With Thornton was a small partisan ranger band led by one of Quantrill's men, Charles "Fletch" Taylor. Sixteen year old Jesse James had joined Taylor's band a week earlier.

Reports vary. Union reports say that the Paw-Paws at Parkville surrendered the fort without a fight. Confederate accounts, notably John Newman Edwards' account, has Taylor's men (including the James brothers) storming the fort before the garrison surrendered. Here began the Thornton-Thrailkill Raid, and the killing season of 1864. Thornton left here, a number of Paw-Paws in tow, and moved to Platte City.

To reach Tour Stop 120:

Go south on Delaware Street to 5th Street. Turn left. Proceed east for six blocks until you pass under a highway overpass, then turn left (north) on Cherry Street. Cherry Streets runs north in parallel to the highway, which is State Highway 9, and in a few blocks this street turns into an exit ramp to northbound Highway 9. Take Highway 9 north. You will follow Highway 9 for about 7 miles, until you reach Parkville, Missouri.

As you near the Parkville business district, you will pass the main entrance to Park University, which is on the right of Highway 9. Take the next available left, about 200 yards west.

Tour Stop 121

The original part of the PLATTE COUNTY COURTHOUSE was built in 1866 to replace a courthouse burned by Union troops in 1861. The town was nearly destroyed at that time, and then in July, 1864, Platte City was burned again, this time in retaliation for Thornton's visit. Platte County is in a section of Missouri known as the "Platte Purchase." When the state was admitted to the Union in 1821 this area was reserved for Native Americans. But in 1836 the U. S. government acquired the area from several tribes for the price of $7,500, and opened it to white settlement. The Platte Purchase added six counties – an area almost as large as the states of Rhode Island and Delaware - in the extreme northwest of Missouri. A predominately Southern population settled here.

About 1861: Gen. David Hunter super-seded John Fremont on November 2, 1861, while Fremont's army occupied Springfield. David Hunter would become quite famous later in the war, in the eastern theater, where he command-ed the Army of the South from Hilton Head in South Carolina. He was known for his abolitionist views. As the new commander of Fremont's Army of the West, he did nothing except to order the withdrawal of the army, which was then dispersed. By mid-November, 1861, Hunter himself was commanding the Department of Kansas from a base at Fort Leavenworth. This Union stronghold is about 7 miles west of Platte City.

To reach Tour Stop 121:

Turn left on State Highway 9, which then turns north in a block. Go north on 9 a mile and a half to State Route 45 (Tom Watson Parkway) and turn left. In 4.6 miles enter Interstate 435 northbound. Inter-state 29 branches to the left in 8.3 miles. Proceed to Exit 19 on I-29, which is Main Street in Platte City.

After you cross the Interstate, you will go straight (west) on a small road that is Main Street for about 1.2 miles. The next Stop is here on your right in the center of town.

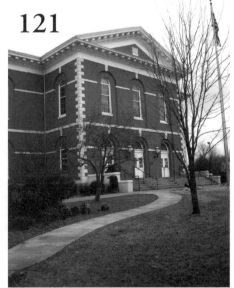

We are unsure what Platte Countian Silas "Si" Gordon was doing in November, 1861, except probably recruiting for the Missouri State Guard. He raised a small band in Platte County. He was accused of engineering the deadly collapse of a railroad bridge near St. Joseph in September, 1861, and he was high on Gen. Hunter's most wanted list. Gordon brought his men into Platte City in mid-November, and camped near here on the grounds of the former county courthouse. On December 1, Hunter issued an order from Leavenworth to the Platte City town fathers, to deliver up Gordon to him or he would burn the town. Gordon went elsewhere, and on December 16, 1861, a Union cavalry force entered town and made good on Hunter's threat.

As the Platte County courthouse burned, William Kuykendall stood bound on Main Street, along with two other Southern soldiers captured that day at the home of Kuykendall's mother, about a mile north of Platte City. Kuykendall's enlistment in the Missouri State Guard had expired, and he had come home to work through some details of his father's estate. Si Gordon had recruited his two companions, "Black" Triplett and Gabriel Close, who were preparing to move south to join Sterling Price's army. Unfortunately for Triplett and Close, there had been a skirmish with Gordon's recruits at the Bee Creek Bridge (Tour Stop 122) where two Union militiamen lost their lives. Probably to avenge their deaths, the federals put both Triplett and Close to death on December 17. Kuykendall's life would be spared because it was the loss of only two lives that had to be avenged.

William Kuykendall is the man who provides the connection between these happenings of 1861 and the Thornton-Thrailkill Raid of 1864. In 1864, Thornton left Parkville after occupying that place a couple of days, generally following the route that you have taken. He reached the outskirts of Platte City on July 10. Kuykendall, who it appears had spent the preceding two years at home, was with Thornton, serving as his adjutant. The commander of the Union force that occupied Platte City - more of the Paw-Paw militia - was absent when Thornton arrived, and the second-in-command, Maj. John Clark of the 82nd EMM, simply surrendered the town. Most of the Paw-Paws joined Thornton's small army.

Thornton moved out of Platte City on July 12, heading north to Camden Point. The federals moved back in on July 15, and burned Platte City a second time. Even churches went up in flames.

The Protect Missouri Flag

William L. Kuykendall
1835 - 1915

Descended from a Dutch family that setted in the Hudson valley in 1646, William Kuykendall was born in Clay County, Missouri and moved with his family to neighboring Platte County as a boy. He voluteered to serve in the Missouri State Guard in 1861, and fought at Carthage, Wilson's Creek and Lexington. Later, in 1861, while on a visit home near Patte City, he was captured and barely escapted execution by federal troops.

Kuykendall began recruiting for the Confederates in 1864. He was adjutant to John C. C. Thornton, with the rank of Major, during the Thornton-Trailkill Raid in Platte, Clay and Ray counties in July, 1864.

At the close of the Civil War, Kuykendall moved out west. In Deadwood, Dakota Territory in 1876, Kuykendall was elected by a Deadwood vigilance commiteee to be judge in an impromptu trial of a murder suspect. The suspect was Jack McCall and the victim was Wild Bill Hickok. The jury acquitted McCall, then a regularly constituted court convicted him.

Tour Stop 122

This is the site of the BEE CREEK BRIDGE, and the end of the story of Black Triplett and Gabe Close.

In late October, 1861, a small force of Union militia marched out of St. Joseph and occupied Platte City. Si Gordon had slipped out of town, and P. A. Josephs (commanding the Union militia) decided he had best return to base. On November 2, Josephs marched out of town on the Weston-Platte City turnpike, heading northwest in the direction of Weston and safety. Two miles out of town, at the bridge over Bee Creek, he found Gordon's recruits blocking his route. A minor skirmish followed; Josephs unlimbered an artillery piece, the Southerners ran out of ammunition, and the Union militia soon cleared the way and marched into Weston. Significant for our story, is that the fact two Union militiamen died of wounds suffered at Bee Creek.

On December 9, 1861, Col. W. James Morgan occupied Weston with his 18th Missouri Volunteer Regiment (Union). He issued from there a proclamation that amounted to a declaration of martial law in Platte County. He then marched on Platte City, and executed Hunter's order to burn it. Someone (one supposes Morgan) decided to exact an eye for an eye, and so on December 17, 1861 the federals marched Triplett and Close to the site of the skirmish at Bee Creek. They shot Black Triplett dead where he stood. Close ran, and managed to get across Bee Creek before a Union soldier met him on the other side and bayoneted him.

The chronicler of the history of Platte County, W. M. Paxton, provides the epilogue in his *Annals of Platte County, Missouri*: "Two days later I passed the scene of this tragedy, and saw the pool of Triplett's life-blood. Some one had, from his blood, written the letters 'U. S.' on the southwest corner of the bridge. This grim memento of the war was there for many years."

A week later, on Christmas Eve, Morgan wrote to the General commanding the Western Department of the Union Army, Maj. Gen. Henry W. Halleck, seeking guidance. Morgan had arrested two more men, this time for refusing to take the loyalty oath. and suggested that ". . .if I have them shot, and make an example I can have peace and the parties who take the oath will regard it in future." There is no record of Halleck's reply, but Morgan was relieved of his command in February, 1862.

Bitterness lingers in Platte County.

To reach Tour Stop 122:

Drive south on 2nd or 3rd Streets, to Branch Street, which is Missouri Highway 92. Turn right. Drive west on Highway 92 about a mile to the point that Highway 92 turns sharply left at an intersection. Do not turn left, but instead continue straight ahead on State Route 273. You will cross Bee Creek in about 2.8 miles. Pull over to the shoulder past the bridge, when you can safely do so.

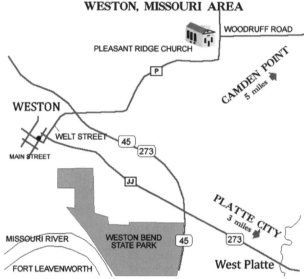

WESTON, MISSOURI AREA

To reach Tour Stop 123:

From Stop 122 at Bee Creek, continue west on Route 273, crossing State Highway 45 in about a mile and a half and continuing west on Route JJ. 2.2 miles to the west of the Highway 45 intersection, JJ (Walnut Street) reaches Main Street in Weston. Stop 122 is at 601 Main Street, which is a block south of Walnut.

Weston is easily accessible from Leavenworth, Kansas via highways 92 and 45, and from Atchison via Route 273 southbound.

Tour Stop 123 is the WESTON HISTORICAL MUSEUM, and your introduction to the history of this wonderful historic town. Weston was founded in 1837 in the wake of the Platte Purchase. Before the Civil War, the town exploded in commercial importance and population, so much so that it became the second largest river port in the state, after St. Louis. It was also an outfitting point for overland transportation to the west.

Ben Holladay, later known as the "stagecoach king" of the West, came here from Kentucky as a teenager in 1838, and got his start in business. He left a lasting legacy by founding a whiskey distillery, now known as the McCormick Distillery. It is the oldest one in the United States still operating at its original location.

The museum is open afternoons during the tourist season every day except Monday. It has a display of Civil War artifacts, and you can obtain information here about a walking tour of downtown Weston. Over 100 buildings in town pre-date the Civil War. They include the Mettier Building in the 500 block of Main Street, which served as a prison for Confederate captives, and the home of Mary Owens, about whom you will read at Tour Stop 124. Plan to stay in Weston long enough to tour the Weston Brewing Company on Welt Street, and visit the McCormick Distillery store on Main. Just a stone's throw from Kansas, this little town, seemingly transported here from old Kentucky, boasts a wealth of other cultural attractions.

123

Part II - Eastbound

Tour Stop 124

The PLEASANT RIDGE CEMETERY was established in 1848, several years after the Baptist Church that still stands at the corner of Highway P and Woodruff Road. Col. James H. Ford passed this way as he led his 2nd Colorado Cavalry and Jennison's 15th Kansas toward Camden Point on July 13, 1864.

The cemetery contains the grave of Jesse Vineyard, who died in December, 1862. He and his brothers were among the founders of the church. Jesse's wife Mary was buried by his side in 1877. A monument erected in recent years marks her grave, as Mary Owens Vineyard was "Lincoln's other Mary."

Jesse and Mary were Kentuckians. They were married there in 1841. Probably, however, Jesse had already joined the flood of settlers to the newly opened Platte territory. In 1837, Mary rejected a proposal of marriage made by Abraham Lincoln, who had met her when she visited her sister in New Salem, Illinois. Theirs was a peculiar courtship. The sister was the perpetrator. After Mary went back home to Kentucky, and Lincoln contemplated the memory of her first visit, the sister extracted from him a promise of marriage. Mary returned to New Salem for a second visit, and Lincoln showed his gawky side. In her memorable words, "Mr. Lincoln was deficient in those little links which make up the chain of a woman's happiness."

To reach Tour Stop 124:

Leave Weston driving northeast by way of Welt Street, which reaches a crossing of highway 45 and 273 north of town. Continue straight across the highway, on the road that is State Route P. Drive east and north on this road for a total of 2.6 miles to a red church that sits at an intersection. Slow as you pass the church. Your object consists of two graves and a memorial stone that sit near the southeast corner if the church (as pictured). Drive past the church, where you can park in a gravel lane that borders the church property on the north.

124

Tour Stop 125

You are at or near the site of the BATTLE OF CAMDEN POINT. It occurred during the Thornton-Thrailkill raid of 1864. Paxton's Annals of Platte County tells us that Col. J. C. C. Thornton and his recruits were camped north of town, on the road leading north, when the federals attacked. This is the road. There is little else in the record to go on. The best sources hold that the Union cavalry from Weston came up over this ridge to find Confederate skirmishers arrayed in the valley below.

The Union force included companies of the Second Colorado Cavalry. The Coloradans, formed in late 1863 as a cavalry unit by the consolidation of two infantry regiments, were just beginning to earn a reputation for jayhawking. Contingents of the 15th and 16th Kansas cavalries were also here, the former commanded by

To reach Tour Stop 125:

The road that intersects at Pleasant Ridge Church is Woodruff Road. You will drive east on Woodruff 3 miles to a T crossing at Rte. 371, and turn left. In about 1/2 mile, turn right on Route U. This road takes you east and crosses Interstate 29 in about a mile. Continue across the Interstate on the same road (now called Route E), for 2.5 miles to Route EE in Camden Point. Turn left on EE, and drive 1/2 mile to the highest point on this road. Pull over with a view of the valley to the north.

Charles "Doc" Jennison
1834-1884

Charles Jennison was a New York native, who resided in Wisconsin for a time before making his home in Kansas in 1857. He practiced medicine in Wisconsin, and also in Minnesota. In October, 1861, when the 7th Kansas Cavalry was mustered into service at Leavenworth, Jennison was appointed its Colonel. The regiment was soon dubbed "Jennison's Jayhawkers." Jennison led the 7th Cavalry during the first year of the war. The depredations of his troops have much to do with the modern connotation of the term "jayhawker." Jennison resigned in 1862 to return to civilian life, but he raised another regiment, the 15th Kansas Cavalry, in 1864. Ultimately, after the 15th fought during Price's Expedition and took to jayhawking also, Jennison was dismissed from the service. He died in 1884 at Leavenworth, of natural causes.

To reach Tour Stop 126:

Drive north on Route EE to the next cross road. Turn left. The next Tour Stop is on your left at the top of the next hill.

the most prolific jayhawker of all, Charles "Doc" Jennison. The 16th was formed in 1863 in the wake of the Lawrence raid, and Jennison came out of retirement to serve as its colonel.

The ladies of Camden Point had just presented a homemade flag to Colonel Thornton, known as the "Protect Missouri flag," and this presentation was the occasion for a picnic north of town. The seamstress of the flag was Eliza Kuykendall, wife of Thornton's adjutant. Colonel Ford sent out an advance detachment that engaged the Confederate pickets. Apparently soon after the skirmishes began a Colorado trooper captured Thornton's new battle flag. Years later, in 1905, the flag was returned to Kuykendall's possession, in a ceremony in Denver. By now a man of the Plains, Kuykendall returned the favor and donated the flag to the Colorado History Museum in Denver, where it remains today.

Ford brought some artillery into action, and soon after the fight at Camden Point became general, Thornton's men fled to the north and east. The federals then burned most of the town.

Tour Stop 126

The CONFEDERATE MONUMENT located at the Camden Point Baptist Church cemetery stands guard over the resting place of six Confederate soldiers who died in the battle of Camden Point. Placed here in 1871, this was the first monument dedicated to soldiers of the Confederacy erected west of the Mississippi River.

Jesse Woodson James fought at Camden Point, during his first month of service to the Southern cause. Our next stop is about 20 miles east, as the crow flies, and at the other end of a celebrated career.

A word about the next leg on your route. This is some history from a different era. You will turn left at the cross road just north

of the cemetery (Pleasant Hill Road), and after driving west .6 mile turn left on Interurban Road. This route takes you south for a distance of 8 miles along the right of way of the Kansas City, Clay County & St. Joseph Railway. This was an electrified trolley built in 1911 and operated until 1933. The old roadbed was paved some years ago, resulting in a marvelous drive in the country, reminiscent in a way of the Natchez Trace. Driving directions resume in the margin of this page.

Tour Stop 127

Tour Stop 127 is JESSE JAMES' GRAVE. Robert Ford shot Jesse James in 1882, in a house James rented in St. Joseph. He was first buried on the James family farm in Clay County, where his mother contended with souvenir hunters and potential grave robbers until she was quite elderly. In 1902, Jesse's remains were moved to the Mt. Olivet Cemetery in Kearney, where the James' family had acquired a plot. Following him in death, and to the family plot, were his devoted mother and wife (both named Zerelda), and his step-father, Reuben Samuel. Brother Frank, who died in 1915, is buried with his in-laws in Independence, Missouri (See Tour Stop 145).

Jesse James was twice buried in this grave, thanks to a part of the James legend that still grows over a hundred twenty years after his death. As in Elvis' case, some people have refused to believe that James was gone. A man named J. Frank Dalton who died in Granbury, Texas in 1951, claimed in his later years to be Jesse James. Texans went so far as to erect a monument over Dalton's grave, with Jesse James' name on it instead of Dalton's. Trading in battle-flags is one thing, but Missouri is not about to permit Texas or anyone else to steal Jesse James. In 1995, the grave in the Mount Olivet Cemetery was opened, After DNA tests, the experts concluded that Jesse James died in 1882 and was buried here in 1902.

Not to permit Texas to be outdone, in 2000 a judge in Granbury ordered the exhumation of Dalton's remains. But there was a mix-up in the cemetery records so they exhumed the wrong man. There has been no further effort to try that judge's patience. In 2003, the body of a man named Jeremiah James was dug up in Neodesha, Kansas, but he flunked his DNA test. Still another Texan, James Courtney (who died in the 1940s) has become a leading contender for the title of the real Jesse James.

Fun is fun, but if you come to see the grave please remember that you are in a cemetery, and that whatever you think of Jesse James, in this place he and his family deserve respect and solitude.

To reach Tour Stop 127:

After driving south on Interurban Road for about 8.8 miles, you will reach the intersection of State Highway 92. Turn left and drive east for 16.6 miles to Interstate 35. Continue east, crossing the interstate, for another 1/3 mile. Tour Stop 127 is in the cemetery on the hill on your right. The James' grave is near the center of the cemetery.

128

To reach Tour Stop 128:

Leave Mt. Olivet Cemetery and head east on Highway 92 (6th Street) for 1.4 miles to Jesse James Farm Road, and turn left. Drive north for 1.5 miles, then right. The well marked entrance to Stop 128 is on the north side of this road, about 4 miles in total from Interstate 35.

You have arrived at the JAMES FARM AND MUSEUM. This homestead was where Jesse James was born, son of Kentuckians Robert James and Zerelda Cole. Robert and his wife arrived in Clay County in 1842. Their first child, Alexander Franklin James – known as Frank – was born in January, 1843. The James' had four children, one of whom died in infancy. Their third child was Jesse Woodson James, who was born here in 1847.

Robert James was a Baptist preacher, in addition to being a farmer, and at an early age he was a prominent citizen of Clay County. When Jesse was almost two, Robert headed for the California gold fields. According to some sources, he hired on as the chaplain for a wagon train of gold-seekers; others suggest that he too went for the gold. He died of cholera soon after arriving there, just 32 years old. Zerelda married twice after Robert died, finally to Dr. Reuben Samuel who was the stepfather of the James children at the time of the Civil War. Zerelda lived until 1911, and is best known for her implacable defense of her "boys," and as protector of the sacred memory of Jesse.

The James Farm is on everyone's top ten list of Missouri tourism sites, and it may be the one that has been in operation the longest.

It became a destination for tourists soon after Jesse's death in 1882, when Zerelda made a decent living selling things she claimed belonged to Jesse. Frank James lived here in his last years (he died in 1915). He was as much an attraction as the house. Frank's widow Annie lived in the house until she died in 1944, and their son owned the property until he died in 1959. Clay County purchased the farm in 1978 from Jesse James' grandson. The James family maintained the house over all of those years as a sort of shrine, and it remains in much the same condition as it was when Frank James died. The museum houses many interesting personal artifacts.

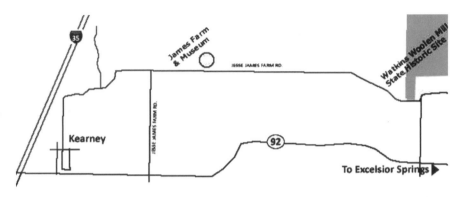

Go to the James Farm and take the tour. To people of Southern heritage, the house is indeed a shrine to the "Lost Cause," and the tour validates the Jesse James-as-victim element of the story. Even for the skeptical, there is no denying that the Jesse James story – not really a biography, but more an encyclopedia of all of the legends and myths of the post-Civil War west – has become a phenomenon like no other in American history. Like it or not, this is a story of Missouri that will endure for decades after all those now living are gone.

Tour Stop 129

WATKINS WOOLEN MILL STATE PARK preserves part of Waltus Watkins' Bethany Plantation, including a magnificent brick mill building that gives the state park its name. Watkins built a home here in 1854. Then, on the eve of the Civil War, he ventured into wool manufacturing. It is said that the mill opened for business on the day that Ft. Sumter was fired upon. Watkins managed to keep his business running during the Civil War, and the mill continued to operate until about 1900.

The mill building still has much of its steam-powered original equipment. The grounds include the restored Watkins home and a visitors center and museum. The mill is a national engineering landmark recognized by the American Society of Mechanical Engineers, and is also listed on the National Register of historic places.

To reach Tour Stop 129:

Exit the James Farm and turn left on 164th Street. Head east for exactly 3 miles, to the entrance of the State Historic Site, which you will find on your left.

129

To reach Tour Stop 130:

Leaving Watkins Mill, turn left on the road on which you arrived, and drive east and south about a mile until this road arrives once again at State Highway 92. Turn left on 92 and drive east until the highway intersects U.S. Highway 69 in 1.5 miles. Turn right on U.S. 69 then drive south for about 2 and 1.4 miles, to a road called Crown Hill Road. Turn left. In about 300 yards you will reach State Highway 10, here called Kearney Road. Turn left at Highway 10, and follow the road into Excelsior Springs.

Highway 10 snakes through Excelsior Springs. After you have crossed the creek in town, turn right on Route N (Marietta Street). Drive south on N for about two miles, to a road that intersects at a water tower. Take a left here, on Seybold Road. Continue east on Seybold for 1.3 miles until it dead-ends at Orrick Road. Turn left here and drive north .2 mile and pull into Raper Park on your left.

Tour Stop 130

Missouri's BATTLE OF FREDERICKSBURG began, as near as we can tell, east of the intersection of Seybold and Orrick roads. Thornton, Thrailkill and Taylor arrived at the old town of Fredericksburg on July 16th or 17th, 1864. They had some 300 men with them, mostly the men who had been at Camden Point a few days earlier.

Excelsior Springs was founded after the Civil War and after the railroads arrived. The attraction was (and is) the mineral springs that emerge into the East Fork of the Fishing River, just a mile to the northwest. By all means, visit Excelsior Springs while you are here. But Fredericksburg was the center of commerce in this area in 1864. All traces of the town have disappeared, and all we know is that it sat on a ridge on the old Liberty-Richmond Road. We have taken you out of your way so that you can drive a piece of the Liberty-Richmond Road, here called Seybold Road. This was a major artery that carried a scheduled stage all the way to St. Louis. Seybold Road is named for the old Seybold Tavern, which was located near the water tower at Route N. After the Civil War, John Wesley Ford acquired the tavern and surrounding land. He sold part of the property to his brother James T. Ford, and his boys Charles and Robert spent some of their early years there.

On July 17, 1864, the 2nd Colorado Cavalry was scouring Clay and Ray Counties in search of the Confederate force, and a detachment of 50 men of the 2nd Colorado on patrol came north on the Orrick road. The commander of the patrol spied some horsemen in blue coats, from a distance, and sent a detail forward to learn what men these were. The unknown bluecoats, posted at the intersection, were not Union men. They were the Confederate advance guard – Fletch Taylor's irregulars, the James brothers included. The fight started when the Union troopers got within 50 yards; they were driven back to the main force, which had dismounted down the hill to the east. Taylor's men charged. The Union cavalry resisted only briefly, leaving six troopers of the 2nd Colorado dead on the field.

130

Tour Stop 131

Tour Stop 131 is the PISGAH BAPTIST CHURCH CEMETERY. The church (now gone) was founded in 1849 by the Reverend Robert James, and so belongs on any driving tour that features events in the lives of the James brothers. There is more of a connection, though. In 2005, the Sons of Union Veterans, Camp 64, dedicated a marker to honor the six Coloradans who died at the Battle of Fredericksburg. Their bodies were brought here after the battle and buried in a mass grave, and it was not until recently that the location of the grave was discovered.

Tour Stop 132

The GRAVE OF ROBERT FORD is on this hillside overlooking the town of Richmond. The story of Robert Ford is a familiar one. It was featured in an under-promoted film in 2007, "The Assassination of Jesse James by the Coward Robert Ford" (Warner Bros.). Ford was murdered in Creede, Colorado in 1892, where he ran a successful gambling house. A strange coincidence (because Ford lived in Richmond) that 21st century tourists can include the grave of Jesse James' killer in this itinerary.

Ford was a very young man when he first aspired to join the James Gang, and he realized his dream in 1881. Some sources suggest that Bob Ford was involved in the Blue Cut train robbery on September 7, 1881 east of Kansas City. He was not there; his brother Charley (buried elsewhere in this cemetery) was. Blue Cut was the last of Jesse James' train robberies. In its aftermath the law closed in.

Tour Stop 134 below is the occasion to tell the story of the end of Jesse James. It came in St. Joseph on April 3, 1882, and marks the end of the turbulent time that was Missouri's Civil War. To put some perspective on the length of the reign of Missouri's most famous outlaw, Bob Ford was born in 1862 (contrary to the date on his tombstone), just before Jesse James left home to join Fletch Taylor's band.

To reach Tour Stop 131:

Drive north on Orrick Road for ½ mile, to the first available right turn (Fredericksburg Road). Turn right here and drive east for a mile to the next intersection. Turn left, and drive north for .7 mile, entering Highway 10 at this point by turning right. Drive east on Highway 10 .8 mile to the second road on your right, and turn right here (Pisgah Cemetery Road). The next stop is just a hundred yards are so down this road.

To reach Tour Stop 132:

Leaving the cemetery, drive north to Highway 10, turn right, and drive east for 9.6 miles to Business Route 10 near Richmond. Turn left here. Go east for 2.6 miles and enter the first cemetery on your left, which is called the Sunny Slope cemetery.

Tour Stop 133

Return to Business Route 10, turn left and drive into the center of town. Turn left on Thornton Street, just after the courthouse. Drive north on Thornton for ½ mile to Crispin Street (the cemetery and Anderson's grave is on your right as you approach Crispin). Turn right at Crispin Street and there is a parking lot just to your right.

Tour Stop 133 is BILL ANDERSON'S GRAVE. The end came for "Bloody Bill" in a small lane near Orrick, Missouri, 10 miles southwest of here. It was October 27, 1864, and Anderson was leading a band of guerrillas on a raid east, while Sterling Price was retreating from his defeat at Westport. Union Lt. Col. Samuel P. Cox with his 33rd Missouri Militia Cavalry got a tip that Anderson was camped near where Orrick now stands. He laid an ambush along a sunken road, and sent a detachment forward, guerrilla-style, to disrupt Anderson's camp. The ploy worked, and Anderson's men (Jesse James probably among them) mounted up and gave chase. Once caught in Cox' trap, most of Anderson's

men fell back, but Anderson charged headlong into and through the Union gauntlet, reins in his teeth, firing a revolver from each hand. He passed nearly through the lane but took two bullets to the head, falling from his horse face down in the dirt. He died instantly.

Cox' men found items on Anderson's person that definitely identified him, including an order Sterling Price handed him in Boonville two weeks earlier. Col. Cox had the body

MISTAKEN IDENTITY

Samuel P. Cox was a prominent citizen and merchant in Gallatin, Daviess County, Missouri. Cox had fought in the Mexican War, mostly to protect the Oregon Trail during the Sioux uprising in 1847. After that, he became a stage driver for Russell, Majors and Waddell. His reputation and experience were such that federal authorities in northwest Missouri called on him to take charge of tracking down Bill Anderson.

In 1869, Gallatin witnessed the first bank robbery in which Jesse James is positively identified as a participant. At the time, Samuel Cox was a director of the bank. James shot and killed a clerk who he believed was Cox, believing also that he had avenged the death of Anderson.

thrown in a wagon and transported to Richmond. Lurid stories tell of what happened in Richmond – Anderson's body decapitated and dragged through the streets, his head mounted on a pike. Probably not. The body was delivered to the local photographer who made two famous images. This may have started a grisly tradition that marked the deaths of infamous men up to John Dillinger's time. Then Anderson's body was brought here to the old city cemetery and buried, decently, it seems. Some militiamen stopped by that night to relieve themselves on the newly filled grave. Anderson's remains lay in an unmarked grave in this part of Pioneer Cemetery for more than a century. A simple stone, erected a few years ago, now marks the grave.

The old cemetery, now called Pioneer Cemetery, was once known as the Mormon Cemetery. This part of Missouri is prime territory for tourists who are on the trail of early Mormon settlement in the West. Before Nauvoo and Salt Lake City, the Church of the Latter-Day Saints had their headquarters in various places in western Missouri. Ultimately, in 1838 the Mormons were driven out the state, either because of religious discrimination, or competition for government lands, or both, and they removed to their new capital at Nauvoo, Illinois. Some of the early elders of the Church stayed behind in Ray County. The large granite monument in Pioneer Cemetery memorializes two men who are buried in Richmond, one in this cemetery and the other in the Richmond Cemetery. These men, Oliver Cowdery (buried here) and David Whitmer, were two of the three men who witnessed the revelation of the Book of Mormon to Joseph Smith, according to Church doctrine. This is a holy place for millions of people around the world, and the strangest juxtaposition of good and evil you may ever see in the space of a half acre.

Tour Stop 134

This is Richmond's ROBERTS PARK, and as close as we can get to the property once known as the Harbison Place. If the place was not here, it was very near here.

Bob and Charley Ford had a sister, in her early thirties, widowed with a young son. In December, 1881, Martha (Mattie) Ford Bolton was living in a house she rented from David Harbison.

The James gang was unraveling at this point. Many of Jesse's stalwart comrades from the years 1864-65 had drifted off, into obscurity or

To reach Tour Stop 134:

From the entrance to the parking area at the Pioneer Cemetery, turn right on Chrispin and drive east for .6 mile. You will carefully cross Missouri Highway 13 in the process. At Institute Street, turn right and then drive south for .5 mile to E. Main Street. Turn left. In a tenth of a mile, stop at the park.

Lt. Col. Thomas T. Crittenden
1832 – 1909

Missouri's twenty-fourth governor was born in Kentucky in 1832, nephew of famed Kentucky lawyer and politician John J. Crittenden. After studying law in the office of his uncle, Crittenden moved to Lexington, Missouri where he started a practice. When the Civil War began, he helped raise a regiment of cavalry known as the 7th Missouri State Militia Cavalry. Eventually he served as Lieutenant Colonel of that regiment.

After the war, Crittenden practiced law in Warrensburg, Missouri, in partnership with ex-Confederate General Frances Marion Cockrell. After his term as Governor, he practiced law in Kansas City, except for a period of years he resided in Mexico as United States consul general. He returned to Kansas City in 1897. Crittenden's son, Thomas, Jr., was the Mayor of Kansas City when his father passed away in that city in 1909. Crittenden is buried in Kansas City's Forest Hill Cemetery.

Crittenden was the losing lawyer in a 1870 civil trial in Warrensburg, known as the "Old Drum" case, a damage claim over the shooting of a dog. The winning lawyer, ex-Confederate congressman George Graham Vest, used his closing argument to coin the phrase "man's best friend".

respectability, and clearly the Ford brothers were no match for these veteran renegades. It seems even Frank James had abandoned Jesse's small group of supporters, and had given up his life of crime. This was, at least, the verdict of a jury handed down in circuit court in Daviess County, Missouri, in 1883. Frank James was on trial for a murder committed during a train robbery in Winston, Missouri in May, 1881. The prosecution sought to prove that Frank was riding with the James gang in 1881, as against his contention that he was living in the South as a peaceful citizen. Many of the witnesses for the prosecution were people implicated in Jesse James' death in 1882. What we know about the events of December 5, 1881 comes mostly from the testimony at the trial. This may have been Missouri's most sensational criminal trial during the nineteenth century.

Two of the James' old comrades were James "Dick" Liddil and Robert Woodson "Wood" Hite. Hite was a first cousin to the James boys. Liddil and Hite had both ridden with Quantrill during the War, and now both had an interest in Mattie Bolton. The Bolton house was a common rendezvous point for the outlaw crowd, and on December 5, 1881, Liddil and Hite were both there. So were Charley and Bob Ford. Liddil and Hite got into a violent argument, drew their weapons and wounded each other; then Bob Ford put a bullet into Hite's brain. The Fords buried Wood Hite in a shallow grave on the Harbison Place.

Bob Ford

The Governor of Missouri at this time was Thomas T. Crittenden. In the wake of the Winston robbery he proclaimed a reward of $5,000, each, for information leading to the apprehension of Jesse and Frank James. Now the Fords, and Dick Littil, had to answer to Jesse for the death of his cousin, and very soon thereafter Littil surrendered to the authorities. He cut a deal. Mattie Bolton paid a visit to Governor Crittenden to offer her brothers' assistance in bringing in Jesse James. For months, the Fords hid their connection to Wood Hite's demise while they became Jesse's closest confidants. On April 3, 1882, Bob Ford shot Jesse James in the back of his head, in a rented house in St. Joseph, while Jesse stood on a chair to straighten a picture on the wall. He and Charley pleaded guilty to the murder and were sentenced to hang, but on the same day Governor Crittenden issued them a pardon. Crittenden, a Union Colonel who had played a prominent role during Shelby's 1863 Raid, denied that he conspired with the Fords to assassinate James, but the fact is that the last symbol of Southern resistance in Missouri was no more.

Tour Stop 135

You have come out of your way to see THE SALT POND ROAD, once also known as the Sedalia Road and now called the Higginsville Road. This is a place to get your bearings before you enter Lexington. The three principal Civil War themes that Lexington offers its visitors are all represented here. The themes are discussed in chronological order.

The Missouri State Guard arrived on the outskirts of Lexington at approximately 3:00 p.m. on September 12, 1861. After leaving this place, you will pass State Route E, entering from the left. This was the old Warrensburg Road and Price's route of entry. Price moved up to the Salt Pond Road near where Hinklin Road intersects it, and then immediately moved in the direction of Lexington. According to the best available evidence, Price initially attacked along the Salt Pond Road about 3 miles to the west of here, and was thwarted when the federals burned a bridge. Price then moved back to a position along present Business Route 13 and attempted to flank Mulligan's troops on the west, resulting in the "fight in the lane" (probably near Tour Stop 136) and the "fight over the dead" at Tour Stop 137. At twilight on the 12th, Price broke off the action while his troops continued to come up. He camped at the old Lexington fairgrounds for 5 days while his supply wagons made the slow trip up from southwest Missouri.

You will visit the battlefield, at Tour Stop 139, where you will learn all of the details of the siege of Lexington, which began on September 18, 1861.

In October, 1864, as noted in the campaign summary, Price was moving west from Waverly when he arrived in Lexington on October 19. He came in three columns, with Shelby in the lead on the Salt Pond Road. Four miles out from Lexington, that is to say here, Shelby clashed with elements of James G. Blunt's

To reach Tour Stop 135:

Turn yourself around, then drive nearly back into Richmond on E. Main, ½ mile to Missouri Highway 13. Enter the highway by turning left, then drive a total of 13.3 miles to the south. You will pass Business Route 13 and U.S. Highway 24, both near Lexington, and emerge several miles to the southeast. Turn left at the road that is marked Burns School Road on the right, and stop at the intersection that is just north of Highway 13. This is the corner of the old Higginsville Road and the Lick Fork Road.

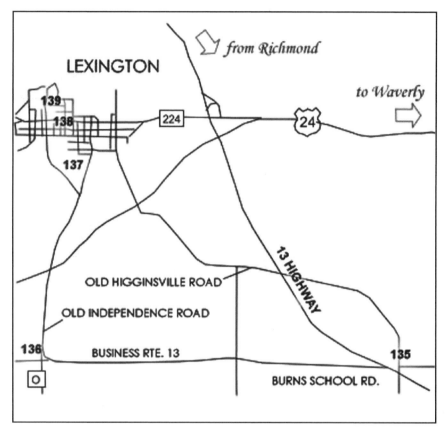

Division of the Union Army of the Border. Blunt had arrived from the south on October 18, in an effort to slow Price's advance. Blunt placed his force in position to retreat, as necessary, in the direction of Independence. Blunt sent two companies of the 15th Kansas Volunteer Cavalry to this point to picket the Salt Pond Road. These companies were the first to see action. The contending armies fought across the landscape that lies between here and Tour Stop 136, a cavalry action known as the Second Battle of Lexington.

Now we pick up the story of Jesse James. On May 15, 1865, near this place James' Civil War career came to an abrupt end, and the seeds of his legend were sown. The myth holds that Jesse was riding into Lexington to surrender himself, but a patrol of Union cavalry shot him through the chest and left him to die. True, a troop of Wisconsin cavalry did shoot Jesse in the lane south of Burns School. Jesse crawled into the bank of a stream to hide (which would have been Garrison Creek, a mile south of here), and then a local farmer took him in. The wound was grievous, but by May 21 he was able to travel. Someone drove him into Lexington and he took the oath of allegiance from a hospital bed.

John Newman Edwards, in *Noted Guerrillas*, told the story of the failed attempt at surrender. This tale in turn is the cornerstone of the "victim" scenario. James' subsequent life of crime resulted from a Union refusal to allow the Missouri partisan cavalry to "come in from the cold." A corollary of the story, also arising from the clash near Burns School, holds that James' wound required a lengthy convalescence that kept him out of action while some of the former guerrillas were renewing the violence that officially ended in 1865. More of this story at Tour Stop 138. At this point, suffice it to say that Edwards' surrender story is pure fiction.

The Confederate Memorial, which is Stop 104 on Tour Loop Three, is just 7 miles southeast of this intersection.

Part III - Westbound

Tour Stop 136

Tour Stop 136 is THE TRIGG-SHIELDS-DICKMEYER HOUSE, constructed in 1852. The house is located on the old Independence Road, which took a southern route from Lexington along present Highway 13, and continued further south (along State Route O) before turning west. If you have followed the Tour in sequence from Stop 134, and intend to continue to follow the stops to Kansas City, you will return to this point after visiting Lexington, and head south on Route O.

Some evidence, garnered from a 1903 pamphlet published by the Lexington Historical Society, suggests that Price's troops passed this way on September 12, 1861 when Price changed his point of attack from the Salt Pond Road to the Independence Road. Some skirmishing may have gone on here, as Price moved along a lane that fronted the home of State Guard General William Henry Shields – a lane that tracked the present course of Highway 13. The magnificent brick structure you passed on Bus. Rte. 13 is General Shield's home.

In 1864, Gen. Blunt knew he had only a temporary hold on Lexington. Although a large veteran army, consisting of Alfred Pleasanton's cavalry and the infantry Corps of Gen. A. J. Smith, were in pursuit of Price, Blunt lacked the manpower to do anything but try to slow the Confederate host. The notorious jayhawker, Col. Charles "Doc" Jennison, commanded the 15th Kansas Volunteer cavalry, which he had recruited in 1863. He occupied this house as headquarters the night of October 18, 1864. His troopers camped here as well as at the William Shields house, which is where Price made his headquarters the next night. By 1864, the Trigg family had left the Trigg-Shields-Dickmeyer house and gone to Texas. The house by this time was occupied by the family of Col. Thomas W. Shields. Thomas was William's son, and he commanded a part of Shelby's cavalry that was pounding down the road from the east.

A sergeant of the 15th Kansas memorialized the morning of October 19, 1864 in a letter home: " . . . we live on milk and honey this morning they is strewn all over camp and the best preserves that the rebbel General Shields house can furnish with silver spoons to eat them with." Sgt. James Abby was soon involved in a desperate rolling fight that began on the Salt Pond Road and ended near here.

To reach Tour Stop 136:

Return to Highway 13 and retrace your route for ¼ mile or so, turning left at Business Route 13. Drive straight west on Bus. Rte. 13 for 3.8 miles until there is a sharp turn to the right. Tour Stop 136 is the old mansion that is in the trees to the left just after this turn.

136

To reach Tour Stop 137:

Drive north on Bus. Rte. 13 for 1.6 miles to an intersection near the Dollar Store, which is 20th Street now and which used to be the old Independence Road. Continue north from this intersection for about a third of a mile to the next Stop, which is on your left here.

To reach Tour Stop 138:

Exit the cemetery and turn left on 20th Street. Drive north for 8 or 9 blocks to an intersection with a major street, that is not marked, but which sits just down a rise to the Wentworth Military Academy. Turn left here (which is Main Street, Rte. 224). Drive west for 7 blocks and make note of the corner of 13th and Main, but continue straight on Main Street, where Tour Stop 138 is a block and a half on your left.

Tour Stop 137

MACHPELAH CEMETERY, first used as a burial ground in 1839, is operated by the oldest Missouri corporation in continuous operation. Notable stops within the cemetery include a monument to Confederate soldiers and the graves of Pony Express founder William Waddell and his son-in-law, Confederate Colonel Alonzo Slayback. Slayback, an accomplished cavalry commander went to Mexico with JO Shelby after the war. Later, he became a prominent citizen and lawyer of St. Louis. Slayback's monument is pictured below left.

On September 12, 1861, Price moved north on the Independence Road, along your route of travel. In the old part of Machpelah Cemetery he confronted a force of Union infantry. Mulligan, still entrenching in Lexington, sent some companies of his Irish Brigade here to block Price's approach on the Independence Road. Price brought up Hiram Bledsoe's battery and shelled the Union position. The Union troops withdrew. Bledsoe's battery moved into position on the present grounds of the Wentworth Military Academy, a half mile due north of here and shelled Mulligan's position on College Hill At nightfall the battery along with the rest of Price's troops went into camp.

Tour Stop 138

The LAFAYETTE COUNTY COURTHOUSE, constructed in 1847. is the oldest courthouse in continuous use as such west of the Mississippi River. Even more distinctive is the cannonball that has remained lodged in the front left column of the courthouse since September, 1861. During the siege of Lexington, one of Price's cannoneers lobbed a shot from the other side of the Union entrenchments, and it plowed its way into this building.

On December 13, 1866, in the street in front of this place, a squad of militia troops, lying in wait on the courthouse steps, shot down Archie Clements. "Little Archie" - he was just over five feet tall - was Bill Anderson's favorite lieutenant in 1864. He took over Anderson's band after Bloody Bill's death in October that year. Clements was then 17 or 18 years old.

137

138

As in years past, after Anderson's death Clements' band and the other Southern partisan cavalry bands made their way to north Texas for the winter months. In April, 1865, perhaps later than usual, most trekked north again to the Missouri killing fields. It is said that they were en route home when they learned of Lee's surrender at Appomattox. David (or Davis) Pool took on the senior leadership role among the partisans who congregated in this part of the state. Most of these men stayed quiet when they arrived in Lafayette County. They were the odd men out. Government policy at this time encouraged Confederate troops in the field to give up the fight and return to their homes. The policy was working. But the status of the Confederate irregulars was not at all clear.

Two things of note happened in Missouri on May 7, 1865. First, a part of the partisan force heading north - the part that comprised the Anderson-Clements gang and included Jesse James - attacked the towns of Kingsville and Holden in Johnson County, about 30 miles south of Lexington. Kingsville was the home town of Archie Clements. The gang burned a number of buildings and killed a number of civilians. So, as it started out, the Spring of 1865 might have been like the Fall of 1864. In the second development on May 7, Union Maj. Gen. Grenville M. Dodge, commanding the military Department of the Missouri, let it be known to his field commanders that he would accept the surrender of the partisan cavalry. The timing of the offer was impeccable. While Dodge could not offer amnesty for civilian crimes, most of the Southern men who camped in and around Lafayette County had to stop and consider their options. With Pool in the lead, the moderate view prevailed. The symbolic end of the official Civil War in Missouri came on May 21, 1865, when Dave Pool rode into Lexington and surrendered 85 of his men. Later Pool persuaded 200 more men in the area to come in to Lexington to take their paroles.

Six days earlier, on May 15, 1865, when James was shot, the Union authorities had not yet undertaken any positive steps to arrange a surrender of the partisan cavalry. When they ran into the Union cavalry patrol on the Salt Pond Road, Jesse James, with Clements and Jim Anderson, were returning from a scouting mission, looking for a way to get their men north across the Missouri River. The raid on Kingsville and Holden was still fresh news, and these men were combatants, pure and simple.

The first peacetime daylight bank robbery in American history occurred in February, 1866, at Liberty, Clay County, Missouri. Clement is generally credited with engineering this event, and we also credit him with assembling the core members of the original James Gang. Although the bank building in Liberty, still standing, houses the "Jesse James Bank Museum," convincing

Col. Alonzo Slayback
1838 - 1882

Alonzo Slayback was born in Marion County, Missouri on the 4th of July, 1838. He attended the Masonic College in Lexington, Missouri, graduating in 1856. Consequently, he made his home in Lexington for a period of time before the Civil War, where he practiced law. In 1861, Slayback recruited a regiment of cavalry for the Missouri State Guard, and became its colonel. He later entered the Confederate service, serving as a staff officer to John Marmaduke Slayback was on detached service in Richmond for a time, and then returned to Missouri to recruit a battalion of cavalry, the "Slayback Lancers," which joined Shelby's division during Price's Expedition.

Slayback was with Shelby on his march to Mexico. After spending a year south of the border, Slayback returned to Missouri and settled in St. Louis. There, he eventually formed a law partnership with James O. Broadhead.

James Broadhead, who in 1878 became the first President of the American Bar Association, ran for Congress in 1882. St. Louis' fledgling St. Louis Post-Dispatch supported Broadhead's opponent. Slayback took offense at the Post-Dispatch's personal attacks on Broadhead, and confronted editor John Cockerill in his office. Cockerill shot Slayback to death; he was later acquitted of murder after a plea of self-defense. Many years later, a Post-Dispatch employee came forward to reveal that a pistol was planted on Slayback's body after he had been shot.

Archie Clements

proof that Jesse took part has never surfaced. The same is true for the second peacetime daylight bank robbery, in late October 1866 at the Alexander Mitchell and Company Bank here on Main Street in Lexington. Clements was only a suspect in those crimes, but on the first Tuesday of November, 1866, he provided the pretext for his extermination. This was the day of the first national election that followed the American Civil War. Clements with his band rode into Lexington, disrupted the local election and are believed to have intimidated enough voters to throw the balloting to the Democrats. The Radical Republican Governor raised a militia company and sent it to Lexington. Clements came to town on December 13, and the militia commander learned he was alone in the bar of the City Hotel. Two militiamen went to the bar to arrest him, resulting in a gunfight there and the wounding of Clements. He mounted his horse, then rode right into the trap the militia had laid here at the courthouse.

James' biographer T. J. Stiles calls Clements' death here "the most underrated moment in Jesse's life." It furnished another and potent reason for Jesse to go to war against the Republican establishment in Missouri. We think, too, that a fully recovered Jesse now took charge of the outlaw band that would bear his name.

To Reach Tour Stop 139:

Return to the corner of 13th Street and Main, and turn left. The road to the north is called John Shea Drive. Tour Stop 139 is ¼ mile to the north.

Tour Stop 139

This is the BATTLE OF LEXINGTON STATE HISTORIC SITE. The introduction to this Tour surveys the Lexington campaign, culminating in the siege of Lexington on September 18-20,

1861. The Visitor Center here has excellent exhibits and audio-visual programs, but you should spend time walking the battlefield. Plan to spend at least two hours here.

The Historic Site features the bullet-pocked home of Oliver Anderson, used as a Union hospital and fought over during a critical phase of the battle, together with substantial remnants of the Union entrenchments. This is just about the best battlefield park in Missouri.

Tour Stop 140

You have arrived at the KATE KING MONUMENT. It looks like a gravestone. Some say it marks the grave of the wife of William Clarke Quantrill. According to other sources, she is buried in the Maple Hill Cemetery in Kansas City, Kansas, near where she died a resident of an old folks home in 1930. Others say Kate King was not Quantrill's wife, but his mistress. The mystery of her burial and her marital status suits her, as hers was a life filled with mystery.

All we really know about Kate King is that she was the daughter of Robert and Malinda King and grew up on their homestead, about a mile and three quarters west of here. She met William Quantrill in 1861 or 1862 when he visited her parent's home. He was then camped in the neighborhood with the men who would form the nucleus of his famous band. When they met, Kate was 14 years old. They courted against the Kings' wishes whenever Quantrill returned to this area, which was often. If they married, and there is some evidence that they did, it was in August, 1863, just before Quantrill launched his deadly raid on Lawrence, Kansas.

Kate took the last name of Clarke, Quantrill's middle name, so that no one would associate her with him. She was with him through the winter of 1863-64, in Texas, and throughout the summer and fall of 1864 in Missouri. Quantrill did very little fighting in 1864, as has been noted elsewhere, while Bill Anderson and George Todd were taking charge. He and Kate and a small group of followers mostly camped out in central Missouri, in the Perche Hills of Howard and Boone Counties, north of the Missouri River. The others, tearing up central Missouri all the while, snickered about how Quantrill's "sand was gone" due to his liaison with Kate. In December, 1864, Quantrill headed off to the east - it is said he was going to Richmond to fight or surrender with Robert E. Lee. He sent Kate King to St. Louis, for her safety. Then in May, 1865, Quantrill was shot in a confrontation with Union irregulars at Samuels Depot, Kentucky. He lingered a few weeks, then died leaving Kate a widow at age 17.

The story goes that Quantrill converted to Catholicism on his deathbed, and he asked the priest who gave the last rites to send money to Kate in St. Louis (it is never explained how a man of his reputation was shot and captured by the federals but allowed to bequeath his life savings). Kate invested her inheritance in a St. Louis bawdy house.

To reach Tour Stop 140:

Make your way to Tour Stop 136, south of the City on Business Route 13. At the turn in the road, continue straight south on Route O and drive south for 10.3 miles, where O intersects Interstate 70. Enter the highway westbound. Go west 17 miles to Exit 24 in Grain Valley. Turn right after exiting, on Route BB, and drive north for 1.9 miles, then turn left on Pink Hill Road. Drive west on Pink Hill for 1.7 miles, to Slaughter Road, and turn north (right) here. You will drive about a half mile to the first road entering the modern cemetery here, but then drive all of the way around the newer cemetery until you find the historic Slaughter Cemetery as far as you can go north on this road.

A case entitled "State of Missouri v. Kate Clarke" reached the Missouri Supreme Court in 1873. The Court decided the important question of whether a St. Louis' ordinance that regulated the world's oldest profession superseded a state statute that outlawed it. The proprietress of the house in question was prosecuted under state law, and the Supreme Court solemnly decreed that sin could stay St. Louis. We don't know how many Kate Clarkes lived in St. Louis in 1873, but Quantrill's biographer William Elsey Connelley wrote in 1909 that Quantrill's Kate ". . . keeps a fancy house in St. Louis now, and is a noted woman there."

Tour Stop 141

To reach Tour Stop 141:

Find your way back to Pink Hill Road, and from the intersection of Pink Hill and Slaughter, drive west for 2.2 miles to Missouri Highway 7. Turn left here. In .3 mile you will come to NW Park Road, where there is a large wood sign directing you to the Burr Oak Woods Park. Turn right here and drive about .1 mile past the James Lewis Elementary School on NW Park Road. Tour Stop 141 is in a patch of trees near the parking lot on the west side of the school building.

Tour Stop 141 is the WALKER FARM SITE. A few tombstones in the family cemetery and a modern monument mark the site of the huge estate owned by Morgan Walker in 1860. This is one of the most historically important places in all of Missouri. It was the scene of the western equivalent of John Brown's Raid on Harpers Ferry, but turned upside-down.

William Clarke Quantrill, an Ohioan, became a Kansan. We are not compelled to defend him or condemn him. The challenge, for anyone who tackles the subject, is to explain him. The incident that occurred on December 10, 1860 at the Morgan Walker Farm provides some clues to his enigmatic character.

Quantrill was a native of a northern state, and a nondescript schoolteacher when he decided to move to Kansas. He arrived there in 1857. His background discloses no reason why he would side with the pro-slavery element in the Kansas strife, and during his first stay in Kansas he was at least undecided on the issue, judging by his letters home. He got into trouble during that first stay, and hired on as a drover to take some cattle to Salt Lake. He was gone for a year or two, including time spent in the Colorado gold fields living as a gambler. He returned to Kansas in early

1860, settling near Lawrence and returning to teaching. Quantrill was now a pro-slavery man. He kept his politics to himself for months, as he moved among the abolitionists in the most abolitionist of Kansas towns. Then he decided he would go over to the Missouri, pro-slavery side, and he would do it in a most unusual way.

Quantrill enlisted a number of abolitionist acquaintances - the record reflects a number anywhere from three to seven - and he chose Morgan Walker as the target for a raid. This was not an uncommon proposition in these years. High-minded Kansans would cross the border to liberate slaves. However, many if not most of the liberators were interested in liberating money, livestock, furniture and what-not, as well. This is what gave "jayhawking" a bad name. Quantrill and his crew, coming from Kansas, went into camp in the nearby woods on December 9, 1860. The next morning, Quantrill told his men that he would go to the Morgan Walker place to reconnoiter. Instead, he found the house of Morgan Walker's son Andrew. He laid out the whole scheme to Andrew Walker. Andrew organized the neighbors and they went to Morgan's house here and laid in wait. That night, Quantrill brought his raiding party up to the house and banged on the door, just after Morgan Walker returned home. The Kansans were admitted to the house, they discussed their intentions with Morgan, and as they prepared to leave to round up the slaves Morgan's neighbors and sons rose from hiding and let loose a barrage of shotgun blasts.

Edward Leslie, in *The Devil Knows How to Ride* (New York: DeCapo Press, 1998), tells the story best. He says only three Kansans accompanied Quantrill. One died on the porch of the house, and the two others fled, to be hunted down and killed the next day. Ironically, when a neighbor's slave found the two in the woods (one of them wounded), he reported their whereabouts instead of accepting an offer of freedom in exchange for help. Not ironic, really, because the most nefarious of the jayhawkers were known to take liberated slaves down south and sell them back into slavery.

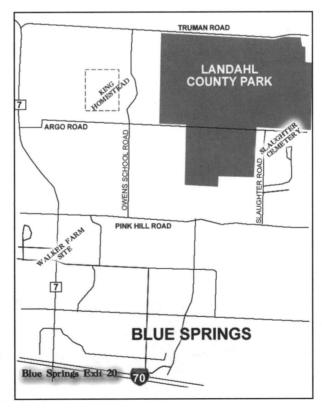

Quantrill did not gain the immediate stardom he anticipated for his grandiose plan, and indeed the sheriff of Jackson County had to place him in protective custody in Independence for a time. Most people found the story too hard to believe. But Andy Walker stood by him and helped turn local sentiment in Quantrill's favor.

Thanks to Leslie also for his description of Morgan Walker's daughter Anna, who had an affair with Quantrill early in the War: "Anna Walker had a good figure and a beautiful face, marred only by her nose, which was large and crooked." After Morgan Walker died, Anna took her proceeds from the sale of the farm and opened a bawdy house in Baxter Springs, Kansas.

To reach Tour Stop 142:

Return to the intersection of Highway 7 and Pink Hill Road, then turn left (west). The road designation changes to 39th Street, but you will stay on Pink Hill Road for 5.6 miles all together, until you reach Crackerneck Road, which is on your right just past the Target Store. Go north on Crackerneck for .6 miles, then turn right (the road you take is still called Crackerneck). In another .1 mile you turn left on E. 35th Street, and then almost immediately right again on Crackerneck. Within .2 miles you will cross a railroad. Take a look in each direction as you cross, then turn right just north of the tracks where there in parking in Van Hook Park.

Tour Stop 142

This is THE BLUE CUT. If you walk up the hill from the parking area, a vantage point along the tracks has a view to the west. This series of cuts through the hill is collectively known as the Blue Cut. Construction crews carved them out in the late 1870s as they brought the line of the Chicago & Alton Railroad into Kansas City. You crossed the Little Blue River to the east, and on the west is the Big Blue River; the high ground in between is the Blue Ridge. The railroad had to get up and out of the valley of the Little Blue. The steep grade in this section of the road set the stage for the events we describe, because a west-bound train had to huff and puff up the grade, slowing in the process.

On September 7, 1881, an express train from Chicago was ascending the grade when it confronted a pile of stones laid across the tracks in one of these cuts. The engineer brought the train to a halt. Masked men rifled the express car, and robbed the passengers. As was usually the case at that time, Frank and Jesse James were blamed for the robbery and no one ever establish definitively if they were responsible or not. However, it is generally acknowledged today that they were here. So, this was the last train robbery by the James Gang.

To reach Tour Stop 143:

Leave the park, turn right on Crackerneck Road, the drive west for .7 mile to Lees Summit Road. Turn right here and go 1.3 miles north to E. 23rd Street. After turning left here, drive west on 23rd for 1.2 miles to S. Noland Road. Turn right. In about a ½ mile you will see Tour Stop 143 on your right.

Tour Stop 143

This Stop is the WOODLAWN CEMETERY. Established as the Independence public burying grounds in 1845, the site known as Woodlawn Cemetery is hallowed ground for the families and descendants of the "Quantrillians." A number of the men who rode with Quantrill, including the Haller brothers and "Dick" Liddil lie at rest here. Liddil, you will recall from Tour Stop 134, was involved with the Ford brothers in the death of Wood Hite, and helped Missouri authorities bring Jesse James down. The most famous Missouri partisan cavalryman buried here is George Todd, whose biography appears at page 94.

The parents of First Lady Bess Truman are buried here, as is a great-uncle of Harry Truman, Col. James C. Chiles. Chiles distinguished himself in the Seminole War, and was on the Southern side during the Missouri-Kansas troubles.

Your next stop is the famous town square of Independence, and here we preview the First Battle of Independence (August 11, 1862). A number of Southern casualties of that battle were buried at Woodlawn after their bodies were taken from the field, most notably the Confederate commander, Col. John T. Hughes, and Colonels John R. Boyd and Christopher "Kit" Chiles, Jr. Kit Chiles, nephew of James C., was riding with Quantrill when he was killed at the Independence Square.

August, 1862, was a hot time in western Missouri. As described elsewhere in this Guide, the Confederate recruiters who flooded Missouri in 1862 were readying their new troops for the trip south into Confederate lines. Two of these recruiters were John T. Hughes - a schoolteacher who wrote a famous book about his experiences in the Mexican War - and Col. Upton Hayes. Hughes went into camp 5 miles south of Independence; the large Confederate flag he flew over the camp was visible from the Independence Square. A luckless Lt. Col. James T. Buel had 300 Union troops in Independence, and he simply ignored evidence that the Confederate forces were intending to attack him. Hughes called upon William Quantrill and Upton Hayes, camped with several hundred men near Blue Springs, and at dawn on

"The only thing new in the world is the history you don't know."

Harry S. Truman

The Truman Library, Independence

193

August 11, 1862 a combined Confederate force of perhaps 1000 men descended on Independence. See Stop 144.

An excellent brochure of Civil War sites in Independence, is accessible at http://www.indepmo.org /userdocs/tourism/CivilWar Brochure.pdf, or available at many of the various tourist attractions in town.

To reach Tour Stop 144:

Exit Woodlawn Cemetery on Noland Street, but drive straight across Noland. This street (Ruby Avenue) intersects in a block with S. Main Street. Turn right (north) on Main and proceed ½ mile north to the Independence Square.

Tour Stop 144

Stop 144 is the 1859 JAIL & MUSEUM. This is the main facility and museum of the Jackson County Historical Society. In August, 1862 it was occupied by some of James Buel's Union troops. Buel had his headquarters in a bank building that stood near the southwest corner of the square. Most of his troops were camped ½ mile to the southwest, in a field bordered by a stone wall, between Lexington and Walnut Streets.

Hays and Quantrill entered the square before Hughes (coming from the south) reached his objective, the Union camp on the southwest edge of town. Hays and Quantrill attacked the jail, the bank building and another brick building housing Union troops. Buel held out as long as he could. The first building to fall was the jail, which Quantrill captured. Meanwhile, Hughes overran the Union troops in camp while they were still sleeping. The surprised federals rallied behind the stone wall and inflicted a great deal of damage upon Hughes' command. Hughes died leading a flank attack at the wall. Not long thereafter, Buel ran up the white flag and surrendered the Independence garrison.

This old building was where Quantrill was held after the raid on the Morgan Walker Farm in 1860. Frank James was detained here in 1883 when he was implicated in the Blue Cut robbery. That charge was dropped.

Finally, according to legend, somewhere on or near the square there was a tavern that was, in 1862, the scene of a fight between a bartender and a customer that spilled into the street and threatened to create a general disturbance. A wagon driver taking an army supply train out of Fort Leavenworth happened to be in town that day. He fired his navy Colt revolver into the air and stared down the crowd gathering around the tavern. A woman who witnessed the event exclaimed "good for you wild Bill," which was strange because the man's name was James. The name stuck and the man was forever more known as Wild Bill Hickok.

Tour Stop 145

This is the Hill Cemetery, and the location of FRANK JAMES' GRAVE. A small modern stone marks his grave (his given name was Alexander Franklin James) and that of his wife, Annie Ralston James. A lot more history was made in this neighborhood, however, encompassed in your view of the park to the southwest.

We've mentioned that our Tour explores the roots of Missouri's guerrilla war. At this little-known spot you see the "bookends" of that war.

Frank James' ashes were buried here when wife Annie died He was the last man except Cole Younger to survive the famous outlaw gang. This property once belonged to Adam Hill, who established his home here in 1842. Then, like many Jackson County pioneers, Hill went into the freighting business on the Santa Fe Trail. His partner was Sam Ralston, whose home was east a few blocks on 20th Street. A year into their partnership Sam Ralston eloped to Kansas City with Adam Hill's daughter, Mary Catherine, and this union produced eight children including Ann.

In 1874, Annie Ralston ran off to Kansas City and married one of the most infamous men in America, at the height of his criminal career. The Pinkertons soon paid a visit to the Ralston house, but left the family in peace. Frank and Annie's marriage persevered, and as a result this plot was chosen for his final burial place. As the stone says, Annie lived well into the modern age.

The valley that runs through Hill Park was the scene of a Civil War skirmish known as the Battle of Rock Creek, on June 13, 1861. One of the Southern casualties of the battle may be buried here in the Hill Cemetery. In 1861, the recently organized Missouri State Guard, Eighth Division, established a camp on the west side of the creek in your front. A force of U.S. Cavalry from Fort Leavenworth attacked the camp from the west. It is not clear how many casualties ensued, but the State Guard's commander Edmund Holloway was killed and apparently so was Peter Land, the private believed to rest here alongside Frank James.

While the engagement at Rock Creek qualifies only as a skirmish, it was the first engagement west of the Mississippi River during our Civil War.

To reach Tour Stop 145:

Drive west on Lexington Avenue, which forms the southern border of the Independence Square, for 1.4 miles to Scott Avenue. Turn left on Scott, and drive south for .3 mile to East 20th Street, where you turn right. The next tour stop is .8 mile west on 20th Street, within a stone enclosure.

To reach Tour Stop 146:

Continue west on E. 20th Street for .2 mile, then turn left (south) on Maywood Avenue. Maywood merges with Westport Road in about 1/2 mile. Bear right on Westport Road and continue for .9 mile to Blue Ridge Boulevard. This road becomes the "Blue Ridge Cut Off" after .4 mile. Continue south. You will cross Interstate 70 near the stadium complex, then continue south for about 3 miles to the East 63rd Trafficway. Turn right here, and drive west for 2.2 miles. You will cross the Blue River and then some railroad tracks, and you need to turn right at this point, on Manchester Trafficway. There is a display just after you turn in here.

This marker commemorates the site of the BATTLE OF BYRAM'S FORD, which was actually two battles, on October 22-23, 1864. This site was for many years an industrial park, and some active businesses remain, but great progress has been made due to the private efforts of the Monnett Battle of Westport Fund to interpret the site and make it accessible to tourists. Byram's Ford marked the opening engagement of the Battle of Westport. The story is well described at the site, and you should spend some time here. Look in particular for the sign marking the road up from the ford, which is on the far east side of the area. As mentioned at Tour Stop 119, the battlefield now has an interpretive center, in Swope Park southwest of here. The driving directions take you past the center.

On October 22nd, Blunt's Kansans tried to hold this strategic crossing of the Big Blue, in one last effort to hold Price's army in check until Pleasonton's cavalry could catch it in a vise. But part of Shelby's Division crossed the ford and quickly disposed of Blunt's force, and then the 500 wagons of Price's supply train crossed here headed south to safety. At this point, the safety of the massive train was foremost in Gen. Price's mind. The great Expedition was reaching its climax.

The morning of October 23 saw the positions of the armies reversed, as Marmaduke's Division occupied the heights just to the west in anticipation of Pleasonton's arrival. A vicious battle ensued as Pleasonton's army, Col. John F. Phillips' regiment of Missouri Militia Cavalry in the lead, finally closed the gap. After several hours of fighting, Marmaduke withdrew and the flank of Price's north-facing line was broken.

TRAILS WEST

Independence was founded in 1827. Although steamboats had ascended the Missouri River as early as 1819, reliable passenger service did not reach western Missouri until many years later. The town's heyday arrived in the 1840s, when the Oregon and California trails were opened for passage of settlers to the west coast. By then, settlers could reach this point by way of the river. The road that crossed the Big Blue River at Byram's Ford was one of many roads that formed a network of routes that carried settlers west. Since departing Independence, you have closely tracked the route of the Westport Road and the Byram's Ford Road.

Tour Stop 147

This is the BOONE-HAYS CEMETERY. Here is additional background regarding the Confederate incursion into this part of Missouri in 1862. This is part of the story told in Tour Two.

The battles of 1861 and early 1862 for control of Missouri were fought for the Southern side largely by the Missouri State Guard, which was allied with the Confederacy. In early 1862, the men of the State Guard began to enroll in the Confederate service. The Confederate authorities changed Missouri's future in the conflict by deciding to send some newly minted and locally prominent Confederate officers back home to bring in recruits to fight for the Confederacy. This decision brought Joe Porter back to northeast Missouri. Dozens of other men, like Captain JO Shelby, did the same thing. In the area around Kansas City, the most prominent of these recruiters was Upton Hays.

The Hays family's roots in this area date to 1837, when Upton's father, Boone Hays, established a home on the high ground across 63rd Street to the south. Boone Hays followed his uncle Daniel Morgan Boone to Jackson County. Boone, whose grave is the most prominent at the Boone-Hays Cemetery, was the son of the Daniel Boone of Kentucky. Upton Hays was a great grandson of the explorer, through the marriage of Boone's daughter Susannah to William Hays, Boone Hays' father. By 1861, this part of Jackson County, pretty much as far as the eye can see in every direction, had become the property of the Boones and the Hays, and other Boone relatives such as the Muirs, the Berrys and the Scholls.

Fortunately, the letters of Upton's wife, Margaret Watts Hays, are accessible at www.wattshaysletters.com. They summarize the story of this prominent family, which pretty well summarizes the roots of Missouri's guerrilla conflict of the 1860s.

To reach Tour Stop 147:

Back to 63rd Street, go west .3 mile to Elmwood Avenue and turn left, entering Swope Park. Drive up the hill on Starlight Road and keep your eye out for a large prairie style building within the park that is off the road to the left. This is the Swope Interpretive Center, and visitors center for the Byram's Ford battlefield. Stop there if you can. Proceed west on Starlight then and exit the park at Swope Parkway. Turn right here and drive north a long block until you reach E 63rd Trafficway once again. Turn left here, and drive west 1.1 miles to Euclid Avenue. On your right here is a park sign noting the existence of the Daniel Morgan Boone Park. Turn right into the park.

Part IV - Northbound

To reach Tour Stop 148:

Resume your westward drive from the entrance to Boone Park, and drive west 1.4 miles to Wornall Road. Turn right. Tour Stop 148 is north three blocks on your right.

To reach Tour Stop 149:

Drive north on Wornall Road, which turns into Broadway a mile and a half north of the Wornall House. Continue north on Broadway for .7 mile, to W. 43rd Street, and there turn left. Take the first right, on to Bridger Road, and then in .2 mile turn right on Westport Road. It is best to park where you can find a place available. Tour Stop 149 is at the intersection of Westport Road and Pennsylvania Street, 2 blocks northeast of Bridger.

Tour Stop 148

Tour Stop 148 is the JOHN WORNALL HOUSE, is one of the few things that remain of the landscape here during the Battle of Westport. The house, built in 1858 and used as a hospital by both armies, houses a museum and is open to the public, except Mondays, from February to December.

Tour Stop 149

The Civil War marker here, BATTLE OF WESTPORT MARKER 1, was placed by the Civil War Roundtable of Kansas City. It commemorates a significant part of the 1864 Battle of Westport. Here was located the Harris House Hotel, which served as headquarters for Union commander Gen. Samuel Curtis.

The Battle of Westport is not within the scope of the theme of this tour, but this is a good place to stop, particularly if you are following this Tour in reverse order. The Westport area is packed full of history. The marker here introduces you to the Battle of Westport driving tour, a marvelous experience if you have time to drive the full tour. Finally, if you find a good vantage point, looking south, you will see that you are just uphill from Kansas City's Plaza, the great shopping place of the Midwest. From this vantage point, you see the hill beyond the Plaza, where the main action of the Battle of Westport took place, almost just the way General Curtis saw it from the roof of the Harris House.

A map of the driving tour of the Battle of Westport appears in this Guide at page 202.

Tour Stop 150

Kansas City's UNION CEMETERY has three important monuments and graves that we will visit on this tour; it is also Kansas City's most historic burial place. Take some time while you are here to see the graves of some of Kansas City's early settlers, including John McCoy and Alexander Majors.

At the entrance, stop at the Sexton's House (pictured below) and obtain a map of the cemetery. Drive to your right, on the road that is to the right, and then up that road. Do not turn at the first intersection, which permits you to make another right, but proceed straight ahead here. When you get nearly to the left-hand turn at the end of this road, look left and park your car. There is a flat stone under the large tree that marks the GRAVE OF JOSEPHINE ANDERSON. Josephine - Bloody Bill's sister - was killed in the collapse of the Union prison on Grand Avenue (Tour Stop 151) and was laid to rest here in August, 1863. Her gravesite was marked several years ago.

Make the turn to the left after you leave Josephine's grave, and drive north on this road for approximately 1/4 mile. The ornate stone shown in the photo above is the GEORGE CALEB BINGHAM GRAVE. Just to the right of this gravesite in the photo is a squat obelisk; the CONFEDERATE PRISONER'S MEMORIAL. The monument honors soldiers buried here who died while prisoners in Union custody.

To reach Tour Stop 150:

Continue in a northeast direction on Westport Road, until it ends at Main Street. Turn left. Drive north for 1.3 miles to the Warwick Trafficway, and turn right. The entrance to the cemetery you seek is right here, a block north.

150

To reach Tour Stop 151:

Exit the cemetery, go right on Warwick and then right again on E. 28th Street. This turns into Grand Boulevard. Drive in the direction of downtown for 1.3 miles, until you have passed over the depressed lanes of I-70, and then stop if you can in front of the Sprint Center.

George Caleb Bingham
1811 - 1879

Bingham's family arrived in Howard County, Missouri, in 1819, émigrés from Augusta County, Virginia. His father died while he was quite young; his widowed mother moved to Saline County and settled near Arrow Rock. Bingham had shown interest in art as a young child. By his early 20s he was able to make a living as an itinerant portrait painter. In the 1840s and 50s, he was painting scenes of boatmen on the Missouri River, as well as a series illustrating the rough and tumble of politics on the frontier. These paintings, including The County Election (1854), brought Bingham international fame after his work was rediscovered long after his death.

Bingham briefly served in a Union military unit at the outset of the Civil War. An occasional politician who was elected to the Missouri legislature for one term, Bingham was appointed Missouri Treasurer in 1862 and served in that post until 1865.

Bingham was the first man appointed professor of art at the University of Missouri, in 1877. He died two years later in Kansas City, and is buried in Union Cemetery.

Tour Stop 151

A futuristic monument to basketball squats on the site of the WOMEN'S JAIL DISASTER, August 13, 1863. This was a disaster, in the truest sense of the word, for a number of Southern women and their families; And, for federal authorities, it became a public relations disaster of the first magnitude. Some say - still say - that the disaster resulted from criminal acts in which federal authorities were complicit. Whatever your view, it can plausibly be said that no event in Missouri history had such far-reaching effects as this one.

Row-houses occupied this block of Grand Avenue in 1859, when the block extended over what is now the depressed highway lanes. The middle of the block facing Grand was about where the south end of the Sprint Center is now and there was a building in the middle of the block called the Thomas Building. George Caleb Bingham was the first tenant on the second and third floors. Here he had his art studio before the Civil War. Bingham's father-in-law owned the building. The upper stories had been vacated by 1863, and Gen. Ewing appropriated the floors for use as a detention facility. The federals arrested and detained a number of women - some were young girls - accused of aiding and abetting their guerrilla men folk. Of the nine female prisoners sent to the Thomas Building, three were the teenaged sisters of Bill Anderson.

The building collapsed on August 13, 1863, killing four of the inmates, one of whom was 15 year old Josephine Anderson. Another sister of Bill Anderson, Mary, was horribly injured.

People still debate the cause of the collapse. It has not been definitively established that the event precipitated the Lawrence

The Thomas Building, Kansas City

Raid. But we do know that Quantrill's partisan cavalry, then camped about 30 miles southeast of here, knew what happened before they launched the raid on Lawrence, and they launched it six days after the collapse. You will have to decide for yourself, but it seems most likely that Missouri's descent into years of brutal, vengeful warfare began right here.

The story would end here, but for the re-appearance of George Caleb Bingham. After the war, when his father-in-law had died, Bingham pressed a claim against the federal government on behalf of his father-in-law's estate, for the loss of the Thomas Building. He lost his claim. Bingham hated General Ewing for issuing Order No. 11. Bingham's hatred might be explained by his moral objection to Order No. 11, but it seems likely that he was also motivated at least in part by Ewing's role in the jail collapse, his property loss and the government's rejection of his claim. In any case, the events which unfolded following the awful occurrence here prompted Bingham to produce the most renowned work of art depicting a Civil War subject.

Martial Law, or Order No. 11 (Library of Congress)

To reach the beginning of Tour Loop Four (at Stop 119), drive north on Grand Boulevard a total of 12 or 13 blocks. You will pass under the Interstate before reaching E. 3rd Street. Turn left on E. 3rd, and drive west for 3 blocks to Delaware Street.

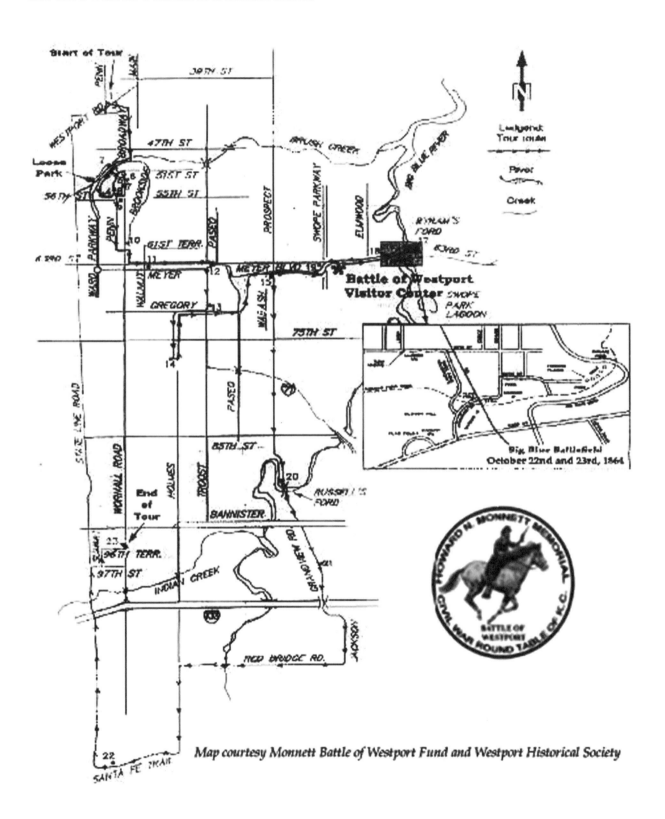

Map courtesy Monnett Battle of Westport Fund and Westport Historical Society

TOUR LOOP FIVE

Visitors from Kansas, Oklahoma and Arkansas take note: The part of Missouri with the richest Civil War battle history is the southwest corner of the state. The capital for Civil War tourism in southwest Missouri is the regional metropolis of Springfield, on Interstate 44 about 70 miles from the Kansas and Oklahoma border. South from Springfield runs the great highway of the Trans-Mississippi, the route of the Butterfield Trail, that still connects the only national Civil War Battlefields west of the Mississippi - Wilson's Creek near Springfield and Pea Ridge in Arkansas. The principal campaign featured in this Tour is the Pea Ridge Campaign, which is tracked for a distance of nearly 100 miles. Also featured is the Battle of Carthage, which was the first major land battle of the war.

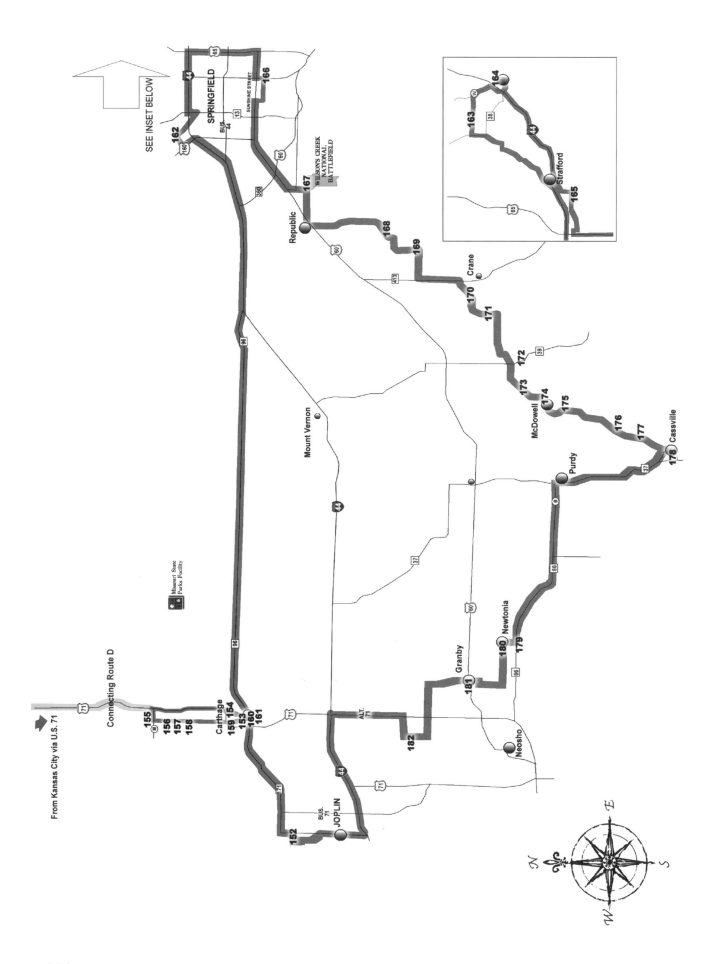

SEE INSET BELOW

SPRINGFIELD

WILSON'S CREEK NATIONAL BATTLEFIELD

Republic

Crane

Strafford

McDowell

Cassville

Purdy

Mount Vernon

Newtonia

Granby

Neosho

Missouri State Parks Facility

Carthage

JOPLIN

Connecting Route D

From Kansas City via U.S. 71

A TOUR OF SOUTHWEST MISSOURI

Ozarks Battlegrounds

A familiar Missouri lament is that Saint Louis would have out-paced Chicago to become the leading city in the Midwest, but for the Civil War and Lincoln's ascendancy. True, the Pacific Railroad out of St. Louis was stalled for a few years because of the war, but Chicago had insurmountable advantages. When the race to reach the West by rail got under way, the easy way through the Rocky Mountains lay far to the north, in Wyoming. Everything between Chicago and Wyoming is flat, so it just stands to reason. Human history is mainly a matter of geology. People take paths of least resistance.

The route south and west of St. Louis is not flat, except that a geologic accident left a long level-topped Ozarks ridge that extends for 100 miles from St. Louis to the city of Rolla in Phelps County. This terrain was quite suitable for roads of rail, and a railroad reached Rolla late in the 1850s, on the eve of the Civil War. Then progress stopped, even before hostilities began. The project had to wait until the engineers could get the rails down into, and then through,

Phelps County Courthouse, Rolla

the great valleys of the Gasconade River and its tributaries. The railroad builders paused, and meanwhile war intervened. Rolla, the end of the line, naturally became the great supply depot of the southwest. But because the Ozark Plateau was thrust up many ages ago, and because the rivers cut down into the land, west of Rolla people and supplies moved the old fashioned way. During the war, the long wagon haul from Rolla through the Gasconade country toward Springfield dictated many a troop movement and military strategy. The route was strategic

also because it carried the military telegraph from St. Louis to Fort Smith, Arkansas. The so-called "Wire Road" is the prime physical feature of this Loop.

Springfield lacked railroads in 1861, but it was a crossroads of considerable significance. One road was the Boonville Road that carried the Butterfield Trail from 1858 to 1861 (see Loop Three). The other major road was one from St. Louis that followed the ridge to Rolla, then snaked through the Gasconade valley and back up to the plateau near the town of Lebanon. This old road was originally known as the Kickapoo Trail, and later the Springfield Road. Many years later, in the age of automobiles, this route to Springfield through the Ozarks became the most beautiful stretch of fabled Route 66. The drive down Interstate 44, the modern equivalent, hardly does justice to the natural beauty, culture and history of the rugged Ozarks, which brims with streams and lakes, hardwood trees, hills, caves, gorges, glens and bluffs.

Much of the Civil War in the nation's southwest quadrant was fought on or over the roads that intersect at Springfield. This Loop, centered on Springfield, explores a region that abounds in attractions for Civil War tourists. If you arrive in the region from the east, stop in Rolla to get your bearings. In the Civil War, before the railroads and the superhighways, the likes of Captain Phil Sheridan, quartermaster, and James B."Wild Bill" Hickok and Buffalo Bill Cody, teamsters and wagon masters, traveled the road before you.

Campaigns in this Tour

The Wilson's Creek Campaign

The Wilson's Creek Campaign encompasses a series of movements by Union troops to southwest Missouri that followed Gen. Nathaniel Lyon's occupation of Boonville, Missouri on June 17, 1861. Lyon had moved aggressively on Jefferson City, driving the elected government from the capital city. Governor Claiborne Jackson was just organizing the Missouri State Guard. Jackson, other Missouri politicians and the would-be citizen-soldiers who favored the South's cause were all in desperate flight to the southwest. Lyon was determined to rid Missouri of the secessionist element, but the southwest would prove a tough nut to crack.

We date the beginning of this campaign within the Tour Loop area to June 23, 1861. On that day, Col. Franz Sigel with two German-American regiments arrived in the vicinity of Marshfield, Missouri. Lyon had designed a pincer operation in an effort to trap the State Guard before it reached Arkansas, and Sigel was moving down the Springfield Road with orders to block the escape if he could.

Sigel would take possession of Springfield on June 24. Meanwhile, Lyon in Boonville was delayed while he assembled the supplies and transportation he needed to commence a long overland march. He did not leave Boonville until July 3, 1861.

Sigel moved most of his command to Sarcoxie and Neosho, where he learned that regular Confederate forces and Arkansas state troops were entering Missouri to his south. Part of the drama that unfolded over the coming weeks revolved around the intentions of the new Confederate government for defense of the Trans-Mississippi West. The government appeared reluctant to reinforce Missouri state troops on Missouri soil. Sigel left 100 men in Neosho as his rear guard, and on July 4 marched north in search of a State Guard column moving south with Claiborne Jackson in command. Sigel must have thought that Lyon's force from Boonville was close on the heels of this column, and could smash it if Sigel could delay its progress, but Lyon was far away at this time.

Sigel marched to Carthage and then on the morning of July 5 moved into position several miles north of town. The State Guard probably outnumbered his command at least 3 to 1, but many of the MSG troops were unarmed. Nevertheless, the State Guard had in its ranks many accomplished soldiers with experience in the Mexican War and in the Kansas border conflict. They overwhelmed Sigel, but he managed to retreat to Carthage and then to Springfield, where he awaited Lyon's arrival.

Lyon's force arrived in Springfield on July 13, 1861 and went into camp west of town. The Union had about 6,000 troops in Springfield. They went about getting organized. The Missouri State Guard continued their movement to the south. They camped in the far southwest corner of the state to get equipped, trained and organized for offensive operations.

The MSG, commanded by Maj. Gen. Sterling Price, left their camp in the last week of

July, 1861, intent on attacking Lyon at Springfield. Confederate troops under Gen. Ben McCullough joined the march, which reached Keetsville on the Wire Road on July 28. The combined Southern force is estimated to have numbered 12,000. Some skirmishing occurred between August 2 and 4 as Price and McCullough neared Springfield. Then on August 6, 1861 the Southerners went into camp on the banks of Wilson's Creek, about 10 miles southwest of Springfield.

Lyon received orders suggesting he withdraw to the railhead at Rolla, but he decided he would strike a blow before he departed. He designed a dangerous plan of attack - another pincer movement with Sigel as the spoiler - and divided his small force. Lyon's attack came at 5 a.m. on the 10th of August, and completely surprised the slumbering Southerners. Sigel's men, who had taken a round-about route to reach the south end of the battlefield, held for a short time, but then fled back to Springfield. The Southerners composed themselves, and devoted full attention to Lyon and his 4,000 men holding a hill on the north, ever since known as Bloody Hill. The Union line broke after Lyon, at the climax of the battle, was shot fatally in the breast at the head of his troops.

Lyon's army evacuated Springfield on August 12, and marched overland to Rolla. Price's forces took possession of the town and held it until October 25.

WHEN THE WEST WAS WILD

James Butler Hickok was born in 1837 in a town now called Troy Grove, in north central Illinois. Hickok went to Kansas in 1856, where he was involved with James Lane's Free State Army during the Bleeding Kansas days. He probably served as a wagon driver, a skill he acquired as a teenager in Illinois. In July, 1861, while working in Nebraska for the Pony Express, he killed a man. Quickly acquitted, Hickok joined a Kansas infantry regiment in time to fight for the Union at Wilson's Creek on August 10, 1861. Hickok next went to work for the Army as a civilian wagon master. In the first winter of the War he and his brother Lorenzo worked out of Rolla, hauling supplies to Springfield. A younger friend from Pony Express days, William F. Cody, told in his autobiography of hauling freight with Hickok down the Wire Road. Cody also told fantastic stories of encounters the two had during the War, after Hickok had infiltrated the Confederate army. Solid evidence has Hickok gathering intelligence for the Union army in north Arkansas in 1864.

The Civil War in southwest Missouri came to an end precisely at the moment the great myth of the American West was born. As hostilities wound down, James Hickok was boarding in Springfield, his wartime base of operations. He hoped to win election to the office of sheriff. On July 21, 1865, after an altercation with an acquaintance named Davis Tutt, late of the Confederate service, Hickok strode into the Springfield Square. From across the square, Hickok put a pistol bullet in Tutt's heart. Tutt, allegedly, beat Hickok to "the draw," but Hickok's aim was true.

It was a petty dispute over a gambling debt, but this was the first quick-draw duel in recorded history. Shortly thereafter, a former Union Colonel returning to his pre-War career as journalist happened to arrive in Springfield. George Ward Nichols' experience here was the basis for a series of articles in Harpers New Monthly Magazine in early 1867. The Tutt duel, and stories of Hickok's supposed Civil War heroics, told by Hickok and swallowed whole by Nichols, filled the pages of this popular national publication. Wild Bill Hickok thus entered into the public consciousness, where he and his kind have held a perch ever since.

The Hickok-Tutt Duel, from a painting by Andy Thomas.

The Pea Ridge Campaign

The aftermath of the Wilson's Creek campaign is described in the Introduction of Tour Loop Three. Fremont's Fall 1861 campaign ended at Springfield, and is mentioned in one Stop in this Tour (162). The failure of Fremont's campaign left Price free to operate at will in the southwest over the winter and brought pressure for another Union campaign for Springfield. All over the North pressure for action intensified after President Lincoln issued his "General War Order No. 1" on January 27, 1862. Lincoln demanded that his commanders move against the Confederates on all fronts not later than Washington's birthday, February 22, 1862. Lincoln's order resulted from McClellan's inaction in the East, but McClellan characteristically ignored the order. Lincoln's commanders in the far West, though, got the message. For example, U. S. Grant took Fort Donelson in Tennessee on February 16, 1862. A new army and a new com-

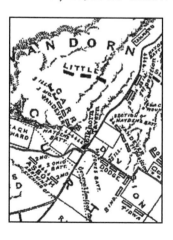

mander took over the war's westernmost theatre. The Army of the Southwest was organized late in 1861, and former Iowa Congressman Samuel R. Curtis was placed in command. Here was a man who was right for the job. Remnants of Fremont's army were huddled in Rolla, and along the Pacific Railroad in Otterville and Sedalia, staying close to lines of supply. Curtis joined the troops in Rolla on December 26, 1861, and took immediate measures to begin a campaign.

The federal campaign that ended in Pea Ridge, Arkansas, began from the town of Lebanon, Missouri in Laclede County on the Springfield Road. The troops from Sedalia and Otterville, and those from Rolla, marched to Lebanon late in January, 1862. Curtis established headquarters there, and 10,000 or 12,000 soldiers inundated the town. An obscure regular army captain, Philip H. Sheridan, became responsible for gathering grain and operating the mills that would fill the stomachs of the men in Lebanon. His ability to do so in the dead of a Missouri winter is perhaps a testament to his pugnacity, or perhaps we must credit the "generosity" of the local citizenry.

Curtis set off from Lebanon on February 10, 1862. He took his short-term objective, Springfield, within two days. General Price's State Guard precipitously retreated from Springfield, and then rushed headlong south on the old Wire Road bound for Arkansas. Elements of Curtis' army reached Bentonville, Arkansas by February 17, 1862, and federal cavalry raided Fayetteville on February 22. Curtis' army was well within Arkansas' borders.

A battalion of the 6th Texas Cavalry attacked federal cavalry holding the town of Keetsville (now Washburn), Missouri, on February 25, 1862. It was a minor affair, but the threat to his rear caused Curtis to pull his forces into a defen-

ENGINEERING A CAMPAIGN

Born in upstate New York in 1805, Samuel Ryan Curtis secured an appointment to West Point from Ohio and graduated with the class of 1831. He served briefly in the Army after graduation. Active in military affairs in Ohio, he became the Adjutant General of the Ohio militia. Then he commanded a regiment of Ohio troops in the Mexican War. Curtis was an engineer and a lawyer in Ohio. After the Mexican War, he moved his family to Keokuk, Iowa, where he continued to ply those professions.

In 1850, Curtis accepted the position of City Engineer of St. Louis. He served in this position until 1853. Among his other accomplishments there, he supervised the construction of St. Louis' first sewer system. In 1856, he returned to Keokuk and was elected mayor of that city, but almost simultaneously he received the nomination of the new Republican Party to serve as a U. S. Representative. He won election to this seat, and served in Congress until just after the outbreak of the Civil War. Curtis raised a regiment of volunteers, the 2nd Iowa Infantry, and he entered Army service as its colonel. He commanded this regiment for a brief period of time as it helped secure the Hannibal & St. Joseph Railroad, but then he returned to Congress in Washington. He receive a Brigadier's commission while Congress was in session in July, 1861, and at that point he resigned his seat and reported to General Fremont in St. Louis. Charged with establishing a camp of instruction in the city, Curtis' efforts produced the camp known as Benton Barracks, on the north side where Fairgrounds Park is now. He remained in charge in St. Louis when Fremont took the field in October.

Samuel Curtis is best remembered for leading an army into Arkansas early in 1862, resulting in a key victory of Union arms at Pea Ridge the first week of March. At the time, just a month before Shiloh, the Pea Ridge victory was overshadowed somewhat by Grant's mid-February win at Fort Donelson. Between March and July, 1862, Curtis marched his Army of the Southwest across the entire state of Arkansas, and captured Helena on the Mississippi. After the shock of Shiloh, and with McClellan's Peninsula campaign in the news, Curtis' march on Helena was hardly noticed.

Curtis eventually commanded the Department of Kansas. His troops were heavily engaged during Price's 1864 Expedition. It was Curtis, more than any other officer, who was responsible for the Union victory at the Battle of Westport.

General Curtis died in 1866, and he is buried in Keokuk.

sive position. The Union troops consolidated just south of the Missouri border along Little Sugar Creek and around a stage stop on the Wire Road called Elkhorn Tavern.

As he did before Wilson's Creek the previous August, General Price joined with General Ben McCullough and the regular Confederate troops that occupied northwest Arkansas. The combined force was soon able to mount an attack on Curtis' position. Price led the Missouri State Guard on a march around Curtis' right flank in the early morning hours of March 6, 1862, getting to Curtis' rear and attacking the Union position at Elkhorn Tavern from the north. Price's men nearly succeeded in routing the federals, but Curtis' army held its ground at the tavern. The Battle of Pea Ridge raged for two days, March 6-7, 1862, and finally the Confederates had to abandon the field. Two senior Confederate commanders, including the Texan, McCullough, died during the battle and the Southern troops retreated east in disarray. Confederate infantry never again entered Missouri in force.

The Prairie Grove Campaign

The Union Army of the Frontier was organized in October, 1862, and comprised of three divisions under the overall command of General John Schofield. Early in December, 1862, the 2nd and 3rd Divisions of the Army were settling into their winter quarters south of Springfield, Missouri. The 2nd Division, under Brig. Gen. James Totten, had encamped some 25 miles southwest of Springfield. The small Third Division, Brig. Gen. Francis Herron of Iowa commanding, was camped near the old battle-

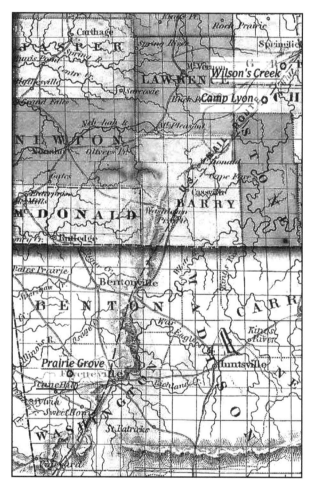

ground at Wilson's Creek, at a place called Camp Curtis. Because Totten was on leave in St. Louis, Herron was commanding both divisions, a total of about 6,000 men.

Brig. Gen. James Blunt of Kansas commanded the First Division of the Army of the Frontier, now deep in northwest Arkansas. On November 28, 1862, Blunt attacked a Confederate cavalry force at a place called Cane Hill. The opposing forces fought there for 9

hours, resulting in victory for the Confederates. After Cane Hill, Blunt realized his position was dangerously exposed. He sent a plea for reinforcements (by courier or telegraph depending on the account), which was received by General Herron at Camp Curtis on December 3, 1862. Herron's own division was on the road within three hours after he received this summons.

Trailed by the Second Division, the men of the Third Division marched an incredible 115 miles in the space of 3 1/2 days. Meanwhile, Confederate General Thomas Hindman, in command of the force that had engaged Blunt at Cane Hill, learned that Herron's divisions were on the way. He moved north to engage Herron's troops before they could join forces with Blunt. The Confederate army arrived on a hill at Prairie Grove, Arkansas; the vanguard of Herron's divisions arrived at the same place. Although half his men were still struggling or straggling along the Wire Road on this epic forced march, Herron succeeded in getting enough troops into action to engage Hindman's command and hold it until Blunt's Division moved north from Cane Hill and attacked. The brutal struggle at Prairie Grove ended in a draw, a tactical stalemate, but it enabled Union armies to stay and operate over the winter of 1862-83 deep in Arkansas. The Battle of Prairie Grove also set the stage for the next campaign featured in this Tour Loop.

Marmaduke's Springfield Raid

Missouri's John Sappington Marmaduke commanded the cavalry of Hindman's 1st Corps, Army of the Trans-Mississippi. In the wake of the battle at Prairie Grove, Hindman and his infantry were pushed south into the Arkansas River valley at Van Buren. Hindman now looked to Marmaduke's cavalry to relieve the pressure being exerted by the Union Army of the Frontier. Marmaduke targeted the Wire Road, which carried the supplies of the Army of the Frontier from the railhead in Rolla. Rolla is about 300 miles from Van Buren by this route.

Marmaduke moved north from the Arkansas River on December 31, 1862. His command, divided in two columns, entered Missouri on January 5, 1863. He had about 2,000 men. A third column, led by Col. Joseph Porter (of Porter's Raid fame), was detached from a Confederate army in east Arkansas. Porter's 800

LAST MAN STANDING

John Sappington Marmaduke's Southern pedigree was as grand as his name. Marmaduke was born in 1833 in Saline County, Missouri, second son of Virginia born Meredith Miles Marmaduke. His father was, in the 1840s, the eighth governor of Missouri. When Marmaduke was born, great-grandfather John Breathitt was the Governor of Kentucky. Marmaduke himself was Governor of Missouri in the 1880s, serving in that post with great distinction. He died in office in 1887.

Marmaduke graduated from West Point in 1857, and in 1861 he was a junior officer in the 2nd United States Cavalry. He cast his lot with the South. He was quickly appointed a Colonel in the Missouri State Guard - by his uncle, Governor Claiborne Jackson. Marmaduke commanded the State Guard in the first Civil War battle west of the Mississippi, at Boonville, Missouri. Marmaduke was wounded at Shiloh in April, 1862, after he enrolled in the Confederate service. At the end of 1862, he was appointed a Brigadier General. and then commanded a full division of cavalry in the Confederacy's Trans-Mississippi Department. His 1863 operations in Missouri are detailed in Tour Loops One and Five of this Guide. He also played a significant role in the July 4, 1863 Battle of Helena, Arkansas.

After Helena, Marmaduke criticized the battlefield conduct of his superior officer, General Lucius Walker. Walker was a nephew of former President James Polk. Walker challenged Marmaduke. Walker was the aggressor in this matter of honor, but Marmaduke was the winner. The duel, in September, 1863 outside of Little Rock, was the last one fought on Arkansas soil. Marmaduke was arrested, but charges were not pressed. Marmaduke commanded a Division in Price's 1864 Expedition to Missouri, but he was captured at the Battle of Mine Creek in Kansas, October 25, 1864. While a prisoner in 1865, he was promoted to Major General. Marmaduke was the last man promoted to that rank in the Confederate Army.

Brother Henry Hungerford Marmaduke was the last surviving member of the crew of the C.S.S. Virginia, until Henry passed away in 1924.

troopers were ordered to move toward the Wire Road and join Marmaduke's main columns at Hartville, Missouri on January 8. The Confederates intended to strike the Wire Road from Hartville, between Rolla and Springfield. Had the plan succeeded, and had Marmaduke stopped traffic on the Wire Road for even a few days, Shofield might well have withdrawn the forces that dangled out on the far end of the road. No doubt the Confederates hoped to compel the Army of the Frontier to settle into winter quarters in the vicinity of the Missouri border, not on the banks of the Arkansas.

While en route, Marmaduke learned that Springfield was lightly garrisoned, mostly by Missouri militia cavalry. He diverted the two columns under his immediate control toward Springfield. Marmaduke's cavalry reached the outskirts of Springfield around dawn on January 8. In numbers, the opposing forces were almost evenly matched, but the Union defenders of Springfield had the advantage of a series of

211

earthworks constructed for just this sort of emergency. Shelby's dismounted brigade launched an attack on the Union fortifications, just south of downtown Springfield. Col. Emmett MacDonald's battalion of cavalry joined in the assault. A fierce fight raged for most of the day. The Confederate were unable to dislodge the Union defenders, and finally went into camp south of town.

Marmaduke moved out the next morning (January 9), headed east on one of the roads to Rolla. He was in search of Porter's column. Consistent with the original plan Porter had reached Hartville, but a day late. All of the components of Marmaduke's invasion force finally connected on January 10, just east of the town of Marshfield. The Confederates fought a small cavalry battle at Hartville as they headed back to Arkansas.

Price's 1864 Expedition
Action in Southwest Missouri

Tour Loop Four ended in Kansas City, where the climactic battle of Price's Expedition occurred on October 23, 1864. The Confederate Army of Missouri retreated headlong down the Missouri-Kansas border. On October 25, Union cavalry caught up with the fleeing Confederates at Mine Creek, north of Fort Scott, Kansas. Here the greatest cavalry charge of the Civil War occurred. Price lost 1,000 men when 2,500 Union cavalrymen smashed into 6,500 Confederates caught straddling the creek. Shelby was not at Mine Creek, but as the survivors poured south his Division laid a defensive line at a place in Missouri called Charlot's Farm. Shelby delayed the Union advance there. Next, several miles southeast of Charlot's Farm, Price lost what was left of his wagon train, at a crossing of the Marmiton River between Fort Scott, Kansas and Nevada, Missouri.

Gen. James Blunt's Union cavalry division kept up the chase. Price's men, those that still formed part of an organized force, raced south through Carthage. JO Shelby's cavalry division turned to fight one last time, just south of the town of Newtonia in Newton County. Shelby dealt Blunt a blow sufficiently severe to persuade Blunt to break off the pursuit, and the Army of Missouri limped into Arkansas and Indian Territory. The second battle of Newtonia, on October 28, 1864, was the last Confederate victory west of the Mississippi, but Sterling Price's army had ceased to exist as a fighting force.

Part I - Northbound

Tour Stop 152

You are at the site of the RADER FARM. A dwelling here was owned by the Rev. Andrew Rader, a pioneer preacher of the Methodist Episcopal Church - South. Rader fought with the Missouri State Guard, and then transferred to the Confederate army and obtained an appointment as chaplain. He was in Arkansas in May, 1863. Rader's oldest child was Capt. William Rader, also in the Confederate service. William was riding with the command of Maj. Thomas R. Livingston, a native of Jasper County who had raised a cavalry unit called the 1st Missouri Cavalry Battalion. In these parts, however, Union sympathizers considered Livingston and his men to be "bushwhackers." In May, 1863, Livingston entered this area with his battalion and a detachment of Cherokee cavalry.

Major Livingston had a strong connection to mining, the primary industry in Jasper County. Before the Civil War, around the time of a major discovery in Granby, Missouri, lead and zinc were found lying near the surface in many places in Jasper County. One of the first lead smelters in the county was built and operated by Thomas Livingston at French Point, on Center Creek about 2 ½ miles north of here. Livingston happened to be camping in the area of French Point when he was attacked by Union cavalry on May 14, 1863. The Confederates were dispersed that day, but remained in the neighborhood.

Enter the First Kansas Colored Infantry. Since the first week of May, this unit had been stationed at Baxter Springs, Kansas, a dozen or so miles southwest of here. The men of the First Kansas were armed and trained under the authority of Kansas Senator James Lane, who began recruiting African-American soldiers in August, 1862. He did this despite contrary orders of the War Department. The First Kansas was one of several African-American regiments that traced their origin to a time before Lincoln's Emancipation Proclamation, which took effect on January 1, 1863. The First Kansas was the only one to engage in battle before that date. Several companies of this unit fought and defeated a superior force of Southern partisan cavalry at the Battle of Island Mound, in Bates County, Missouri, October 29, 1862. Island Mound was one of the signs of turbulent times that would change the character of the Civil War, although there the First Kansas fought only under the authority of the State of Kansas.

The Emancipation Proclamation represented the Lincoln Administration's change of heart regarding the enlistment of African Americans in the federal service, and it provided the

To reach Tour Stop 152:

Exit 6 on Interstate 44 is just inside the Missouri border in the southwest corner of the state. Go north from Exit 6 on Business Route 44 (Main Street in Joplin) for 4.2 miles, to West "E" Street. Turn left. This road turns to the north, and becomes Lone Elm Road, and also jogs left then right, but stay on the road for a total of 2.9 miles until you reach Fountain Road. Tour Stop 152 is at this intersection, and the site of interest is on the land to the north and east.

152

James H. Lane
1814 – 1866

The man who would be known as the "Grim Chieftan of Kansas" was born in Indiana, and rose to prominence there. He had a distinguished record as a Colonel in the Mexican War. He moved to Lawrence, Kansas Territory, in 1855, soon after (as a congressman from Indiana) he voted for the Kansas-Nebraska Act. He became a fierce "Free Soil" spokesman, and warrior, in the border wars with Missouri, and he became a Republican, as well. Lane was one of Kansas' first U. S. Senators when Kansas became a state in 1861.

Lane was in Washington when the Civil War broke out. A contingent of veterans of the Missouri-Kansan war was in Washington as well, and Lane organized them into a Company that defended the White House in the first days of the Lincoln Administration. Then he returned to Kansas. His actions as commander of "Lane's Brigade" in western Missouri brought him a great deal of criticism from South and North alike, most notably for the September, 1861 sack of Osceola, Missouri. His brigade was disbanded, and Lane returned for the most part to politics. In 1864, he took to the field again, as an aide to Gen. Samuel Curtis during Price's Expedition.

Lane shot himself in 1866. He is buried in Lawrence, Kansas.

legal basis for their enrollment. On January 13, 1863, while in camp at Fort Scott, Kansas, the men of the First Kansas officially became soldiers in the U. S. Army. At about the same time, African American regiments in South Carolina and Louisiana also received this distinction. Three engagements occurred before May, 1863 involving these other units. The Rader Farm was the site of the fourth such engagement of the Civil War.

In the Spring of 1863, Union authorities selected Baxter Springs (later the site of an infamous incident involving Quantrill's partisans) as a point of consolidation for various troops in the Union District of Kansas. The action at Rader Farm resulted from the need for subsistence for the troops assembled at Baxter Springs. A detachment of the First Kansas Colored Infantry, which had grown considerably since its baptism in October, 1862 and was near full strength, left Baxter Springs on the morning of May 18, 1863 to forage in Jasper County. The detachment consisted of 25 men of the First Kansas, and a smaller force drawn from a white artillery regiment. According to the best available evidence, their first stop was the Rader house. The federals were looting it when 200 men from Livingston's command came crashing in from the north. At least 15 men of the First Kansas died here, and two others were taken prisoner. Livingston also held three of the white artillerymen.

Col. James M. Williams, commanding the First Kansas Colored Infantry, arrived at the Rader Farm on the morning of May 19, 1863, with another 300 troops of the regiment. He found the regiment's dead still lying on the field, some in his words with "their brains beaten out." Williams detained a neighbor of the Raders living just to the north, and finding that the man had previously been paroled, had him shot. Inexplicably, Williams' men carried

153

"... I shall keep a like number of your men as prisoners ... and you can safely trust that I shall visit a retributive justice upon them for any injury done ..."

- J. M. Williams

the Union dead, and the dead neighbor, into the Rader house, then burned it to the ground. Williams' troops next moved north about a mile to the town of Sherwood, and wiped it off the map. The town site lay uninhabited until the recent development of a subdivision there.

On May 20, Major Livingston corresponded with Williams on the subject of an exchange of prisoners, but pointedly noted that the African American captives would not be exchanged. His position conformed to official Confederate policy, proclaimed by Jefferson Davis in December, 1862. The first test of this policy rested in the hands of Major Livingston. Williams responded the next day by threatening to retaliate in kind if Livingston's captives were harmed or killed. The story that survives, though not confirmed, is that Livingston executed one of his African American prisoners, Williams killed a Confederate in return, and Livingston's second prisoner was released. If the story is true, we can take grim satisfaction that one principle of racial equality – the value of a life – was first illustrated in the wake of the action at the Rader Farm.

On July 11, 1863, Tom Livingston was killed leading an attack on Stockton, Missouri, in Cedar County. One week after that, the 54th Massachusetts Infantry, an African-American unit, stormed Battery Wagner near Charleston, South Carolina.

Tour Stop 153

This is the CARTHAGE CIVIL WAR MUSEUM. The perfect place to get an overview of Carthage's Civil War history, and the battle of July 5, 1861. The Museum is also worth a visit just to see local artist Andy Thomas' heroic-size mural depicting the Battle as it raged in the courthouse square. The museum has a diorama depicting the battlefield that you are about to see, and a display devoted to Carthage native Belle Starr.

To reach Tour Stop 153:

Turn right on Fountain Road, and drive east for .9 mile to Main Street, Missouri Route 43, and turn left. In about a mile, at the Joplin Airport, turn right (east) on Missouri Highway 171. Drive east on this road, which will become Business Route 71, for 11.8 miles, to Garrison Avenue in Carthage. You will drive straight ahead for another four blocks to Grant Street. Turn right, and drive south one block. The next Stop is on your right before the square.

To reach Tour Stop 154:

Proceed north on Grant Street for another block, and turn left on Central Avenue. Go west on Central (which is the historic Route 66) for four blocks to N. Garrison Avenue, where you turn right. Drive north for approximately 1.2 miles, to the intersection of Highway "V", where you will see a brick home on your right, just after the intersection. Pull into the gravel drive for Tour Stop 154.

To reach Tour Stop 155:

Continue north on Garrison Avenue for about 1/2 mile, where a ramp lets you enter U. S. 71, northbound. Proceed north on 71 for 6.5 miles and turn left at Route M. Drive west 1.1 miles to the intersection of M and Civil War Avenue. Turn left and pull to the side of the road. Stop 155 is on the ridge behind you, to your north.

Tour Stop 154

Tour Stop 154 is the historic KENDRICK HOUSE. The house, built in 1849, is owned by Victorian Carthage, Inc., which has restored it to its Civil War-era condition and has opened it for tours and special events. Like many towns on Missouri's western border, Carthage was virtually destroyed during the Civil War - in this case, the greatest damage was done in 1863 by Southern partisans - so that few buildings remain from the pre-War period. The Kendrick House is one of the survivors. The house was not a factor in the 1861 battle, but did figure prominently in the other events and military activities that swirled around Carthage during the balance of the War.

Most notably, the Kendrick house served as headquarters for Confederate Colonel JO Shelby when his raiders visited a ravaged Carthage on their return trip, during the great raid of 1863. A skirmish, known as the Second Battle of Carthage, was fought between here and the town of Carthage on October 18, 1863. Previously, Carthage served as a major garrison point for Union troops, and the federals occupied the Kendrick House. The northern troops quartered their horses in the house, and hoof prints are very visible, still, on the parlor floor.

Tour Stop 155

Stop 155 is the STATE GUARD LINE OF BATTLE. A small memorial on the hillside includes a carved stone marker, replicated at some of the Tour Stops you will visit as you head south on Civil War Avenue.

You are near the line formed by the Missouri State Guard when it arrived from the north at about 8 a.m. on July 5, 1861, and stretched out along this slight ridge. Probably, the line of battle lay 1/2 mile to the north near the crest of this ridge, although the

OLD SACRAMENTO

During the Mexican War, the First Missouri Mounted Volunteers entered Mexico as part of what was known as the Doniphan Expedition. On February 28, 1847 the Missourians fought the Battle of Sacramento outside of the city of Chihuahua. Instrumental in the American victory, which opened the way to the occupation of Chihuahua, was a battery of artillery commanded by Capt. Richard Weightman. Doniphan's men captured at least two Mexican cannon at Sacramento, and brought them back to Missouri after the war. What is thought to be "Old Kickapoo" is in the Kansas State Historical Society Museum in Topeka, having been captured by the Kansans during Bleeding Kansas days.

A second captured cannon, "Old Sacramento," was in Lexington, Missouri when the Civil War began. Captain Hiram Bledsoe of the Missouri State Guard took possession of the piece, and after some refurbishment it became the centerpiece of his battery. Old Sacramento fought with Bledsoe on both sides of the Mississippi River, until it was, purportedly, melted down and recast in Alabama late in the war. Kansans claim to have "Old Sacramento" in the basement of a museum in Lawrence, Kansas. Not true.

State Guard infantry may have advanced to this point during the first phase of the battle.

Col. Richard Weightman of the State Guard, commanding a brigade, arrived here first. From his vantage point on this ridge he watched as Sigel's Union troops crossed the small stream ¾ of a mile in your front. Sigel placed 7 or 8 guns on the near side of this creek. Weightman had Hiram Bledsoe's battery of 3 guns, including "Old Sacramento." Soon, the rest of the State Guard's 4,000 troops came up, joining the line to the left of Weightman's position (your right). Weightman stationed Guibor's battery of four guns up the hill from you, giving the State Guard parity with Sigel's artillery. At about 11:00 a.m., the Civil War's first artillery duel commenced across this field.

Excellent cannonading on both sides took a toll during a 40 minute exchange, while State Guard cavalry probed both of Sigel's flanks. Sigel then commenced his first retrograde movement of the day.

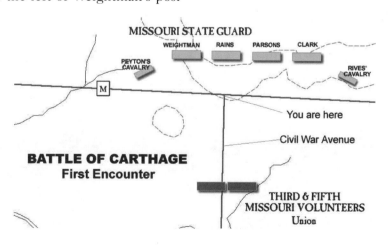

Part II - Eastbound

To reach Tour Stop 156:

Drive south on Civil War Avenue a distance of about .6 miles. Here on your right is a small driveway. Pull off the road at the entrance of this driveway, but please stay on public property. Tour Stop 156 is in this vicinity, on both sides of Civil War Avenue.

Tour Stop 156

This is the location of SIGEL'S FIRST LINE. Sigel took a very aggressive stance by advancing north of the small stream, then known as "Double Trouble Creek," which lies at the bottom of this valley to the south. He had two regiments of infantry, his own 3rd Regiment, Missouri Volunteers, and the 5th Regiment of Volunteers commanded by Col. Charles E. Salomon. These units had been depleted during the long march from Rolla, as companies were detached in order to garrison towns along the way. The 5th Regiment was deployed across the road at the center of Sigel's line, and the 3rd occupied positions on each flank. Sigel's artillery was in position on both sides of the road. He had left one of his field pieces at Tour Stop 157, to cover his retreat, and he had seven pieces here.

With the MSG cavalry threatening his flanks, Sigel moved back to a stronger position on Dry Fork.

To reach Tour Stop 157:

Continue south on Civil War Avenue. In about 1.2 miles you will cross a stream, which is the so-called Dry Fork of the North Spring River. Drive slowly up the hill towards the point where a farm house sits on your right, and look for a small monument. This is Tour Stop 157.

Tour Stop 157

On July 5, 1861, the BATTLE AT DRY FORK was fought over the ground you have just crossed. Dry Fork Creek was full to its banks and presented a considerable obstacle to the advancing infantry of the Missouri State Guard. The hardest fighting of the day occurred here.

As you face south, look to your left to the slightly elevated ground there. Sigel stationed the four gun battery of Capt. Christian Essig on this rise. Sigel put his other battery some distance to the west. The Harper's Weekly illustration on the facing page, sketched by a witness to the battle, presents the same view you have as you look north from Tour Stop 157, notwithstanding some exaggeration of distances and topography.

While Sigel was establishing his second line on this hill, the State Guard infantry was advancing in line of battle from its original position at Tour Stop 155. As the Southerners attempted to cross the swollen Dry Fork, they engaged Sigel's

troops. From this strong position, Sigel fended off the superior numbers of the State Guard for two hours.

During the next phase of his withdrawal, Sigel placed his supply wagons and artillery in the center, with infantry on all sides. This maneuver, called a hollow infantry square, has ancient roots but was purportedly employed for the only time in the Civil War at Carthage. As Sigel continued his withdrawal over the next two miles, the State Guard cavalry harassed Sigel's flanks and actually blocked his line of retreat, along Buck Branch, another small stream to the south.

Tour Stop 158

You have just crossed BUCK BRANCH. As noted above, Sigel pushed south from Dry Fork Creek. Here, he brushed aside the State Guard cavalry that had entered the bed of the creek. After clearing this opposition, Sigel fought a brief delaying action while he moved his artillery across Buck Branch. By this time, he was in full retreat.

The action at Buck Branch included a bayonet charge by Sigel's infantry, probably the first of the Civil War.

Tour Stop 159

This is the site of Sigel's ORNDUFF HILL LINE. The Union artillery halted here and took position to cover Sigel's crossing of the Spring River, which flows through the valley to the south.

The battlefield monuments are carved from the same material that now lies abandoned around you - "Carthage marble." Not marble, actually, but a fine limestone that provided the town of Carthage with its major claim to fame for about a century after the quarry first opened in the 1880s. Today, the man-made caverns that snake below Ornduff Hill are used for underground storage.

To reach Tour Stop 158:

Drive south on Civil War Avenue, this time for about 2.2 miles, to the next valley and bridge. Be careful to note any traffic in your rear, then slow down as you cross the bridge. You can get a brief glimpse of the creek this way, then proceed to a point when you can safely pull to the shoulder.

To reach Tour Stop 159:

Continuing your drive south on Civil War Avenue, cross under Highway 71 and proceed another mile. Here on your left you will pass some large stone blocks that surround an old quarry, and Tour Stop 159 is located just beyond the blocks. Turn left into a gravel drive, where you will see another stone monument like that at Stop 155.

To reach Tour Stop 160:

Drive south on in the direction of town, bearing right on Francis Street after you cross the river. In about .8 mile, you will reach Oak Street. Turn left, and drive east for 5 or 6 blocks until you reach Garrison Avenue. Jog right, then left, on to 4th Street, and then continue east for 3 blocks, where you will reach the courthouse square. Tour Stop 160 is on the northwest corner of the square.

Tour Stop 160

The BATTLE OF CARTHAGE MONUMENT was erected in 1999 by the Sons of Confederate Veterans. This stone contains a brief description of the events of July 5, 1861, and marks the place where the battle of Carthage reached its most critical stage. This is the scene depicted in the mural at the Carthage Civil War Museum on Grant Street. If you approached Carthage from the north, now is the time to visit the Museum near the northeast corner of the square. See Stop 153 in this Tour.

This is the highest point in Carthage, which is the reason it was selected for the courthouse site, and why Sigel attempted to make another stand here. The Union batteries were arrayed across the courthouse lawn, facing west, and it was here finally that the MSG infantry caught up with Sigel's force, at about 6:00 p.m.

When the State Guard surged into the square, a hotel and livery operation owned by John Shirley stood on the north side. His place extended from the center of the block to where the Carthage Water & Electric office is now.

To reach Tour Stop 161:

Traffic on the Carthage square rotates counterclockwise. Continue around the square to Grant Street at the southeast corner. Drive south on Grant for 3 to 4 blocks until you reach Chestnut Street. Turn Left. You will drive east for .7 miles, and then turn left just after crossing a set of railroad tracks.

Tour Stop 161

The BATTLE OF CARTHAGE STATE HISTORIC SITE, is located near a spring on Carthage's southeast perimeter. The railroad tracks you see generally follow the route of an old road from Sarcoxie, the route of Sigel's arrival and departure from the scene. Sigel camped here on the night of July 4, 1861 before he moved north in search of the State Guard. After he was driven from the square, he set up a final defensive position here, placing his artillery on the small bluff to the east. Sigel moved his troops southeast on the Sarcoxie Road, and some skirmishing occurred along this road as night fell. The MSG then abandoned the chase.

You are following River Street north as you move to the next tour segment. A detachment of MSG cavalry crossed the Spring River and approached the scene of the final action here along this route.

Tour Stop 162

This is the OLD MELVILLE ROAD. Two Union campaigns that targeted Springfield in 1861 touched down here.

Farm Road 127 is a remnant of the main road to Springfield from the northwest, and parts of the road are still called the Melville Road. Melville, now forgotten, was a town in Dade County located at or near modern-day Dadesville, Missouri.

From the Northern perspective, the prelude to the great Battle of Wilson's Creek was Gen. Nathaniel Lyon's attack at Boonville in mid-June, 1861. The Missouri State Guard troops he defeated at Boonville made their way southwest, pausing only briefly to defeat Sigel at Carthage. Lyon had some trouble securing transportation for the troops he assembled at Boonville. His march south in an effort to trap the Guard did not commence until July 3, 1861. He swung west from Boonville, to Clinton (where his force increased to 6,000 with the addition of some Kansas regiments), and then headed south through Osceola, Stockton and Melville.

As Lyon approached Springfield, it appears he left the bulk of his exhausted troops in camp several miles northwest of our Tour Stop, but we know that Lyon, with his escort and staff, passed this spot on July 13, 1861 as he rode into Springfield to meet Sigel. Lyon occupied the town for nearly a month, while the State Guard and its Confederate allies prepared for the movement that resulted in the Battle of Wilson's Creek.

This Tour Loop does not include a driving Tour of Springfield. Like most of Missouri's larger cities, Springfield has recognized its numerous Civil War resources. You can take an excellent driving tour of sites associated with the January, 1863 Battle of Springfield. If you are in this area to see Civil War history, be sure you visit all of the sites in this Civil War town. The best resource available is the History Museum of Springfield - Greene County, north of downtown at Boonville Street near the Chestnut Expressway.

One frequently neglected Springfield Civil War site, however, is the site of what is sometimes called the First Battle of Springfield. The battle occurred during John Charles Fremont's long nec-

To reach Tour Stop 162:

Drive north on River Street for .6 mile, and turn right on Route 96. Go east on 96 (which is the old Route 66) for about 37 miles, where you may enter Interstate 44 eastbound. From this point, drive east on I-44 for about 17 miles, to Exit 75. Turn left at the bottom of the ramp, and head north and west on U. S. Highway 160. In 1.1 miles, the first available right turn, turn right on Farm Road 106. In .6 mile, you will reach another road that enters from the left (Farm Road 125). Turn left here and drive north for .6 miles and pull over just before the intersection of Farm Road 127.

Belle Starr
1848 – 1889

The "bandit queen" was born Myra Maybelle Shirley on a farm near Carthage, Missouri. She moved to the city as a young child, when her father acquired a hotel on the town square. May, as she was then known, attended the finest schools in Carthage.

Reputedly, Belle was spying for the Confederacy while still a young teen, and the story goes that she was once captured and confined to the Ritchey Mansion in Newtonia (Stop 180). One of her brothers - she had five – was John "Bud" Shirley. Bud Shirley was a Confederate cavalry soldier who turned to guerrilla fighting; he was shot and killed by Union militia in Sarcoxie in 1864. That year, with Carthage devastated by the war, the Shirley family packed up and moved to Texas. Starr - a real name that she took from her third husband - made a name for herself in Texas, and in Indian Territory, mostly for petty banditry. She was shot to death in ambush near Eufaula, Oklahoma in 1889. Her lasting fame as an outlaw began at her death, when the National Police Gazette picked up her story.

glected campaign in October, 1861. This remote intersection, where Farm Road 125 crosses the old Melville Road, provides the setting for a description of the events leading up to the once-famous cavalry battle better known as Zagonyi's Charge.

On October 24, 1861, Fremont's large force consolidated on the Boonville-Springfield Road at and near a Butterfield relay station called Yost's (or Yoast's) Station, at the Polk-Hickory County line, 50 miles north of Springfield. Major Charles Zagonyi commanded Fremont's cavalry, which included a regiment known as "Fremont's Body-Guard." At Yost's, Zagonyi proposed to strike in advance of the infantry. During the evening of October 24 the Body-Guard set out for Springfield. Maj. Frank White's regiment of Prairie Scouts joined Zagonyi on the march. The Union force, perhaps 300 strong, would face 1200 or more Missouri State Guard troops who occupied Springfield.

Zagonyi's Charge

On the Boonville-Springfield Road (now approximately the route of State Highway 13), Zagonyi passed through Bolivar. While still eight miles north of Springfield, he captured some enemy pickets. One of them eluded capture, however, and because Zagonyi's advance was now known to Springfield's defenders, he left the main road. He came cross-country and passed this point on his way southwest. He took a round about route to reach the western approaches to the city. He then attacked a superior force of State Guard troops at a place now known as Zagonyi Park and defeated it in the first cavalry charge of the Civil War.

To continue to track Zagonyi's movement from north to south, drive to U. S. 160 via Farm Roads 125 and 106, then go south on 160 for a total of 3.9 miles to West Mt. Vernon Street. Turn left on Mt. Vernon and you will pass Zagonyi Park on your way into town. The driving instructions, however, take you in the opposite direction for now.

Tour Stop 163

You are near FORT SAND SPRING on the Wire Road. The road that enters from the south is part of an old trail that connected Lebanon to Springfield. This is not the original Wire Road, by most accounts, but evidently it took this name because a telephone line was strung along it early in the age of telephones. The original Wire Road, carrying the telegraph line in the years before and during the Civil War, was also called the Springfield Road. It ran 6 or 8 miles to the east, through Marshfield. Nevertheless, the road that brought you here was here during the Civil War and as often as not the troops and wagon trains that moved between Rolla and Springfield took this route. To protect the road, the federals built a fort, called Fort Sand Spring, some distance east of here.

The campaign that included the Battle of Springfield and culminated at Hartville is described in the campaign summary for this Tour Loop.

After the Battle of Springfield, Marmaduke's main force moved northeast on this other Wire Road. Shelby reported that his brigade camped at Fort Sand Spring on the night of January 9, 1863.

At the time, Marmaduke was trying to consolidate his forces; he was still waiting for his right wing, commanded by Col. Joe Porter, to join him. Marmaduke moved east and destroyed a federal fort in Marshfield, before joining up with Porter some distance east of Marshfield. The combined force, now intent on retreating to Arkansas, moved out on the route that is now Highway 38 east of Marshfield, and fought the Battle of Hartville on January 11, 1863.

The location of the Marshfield fort is unknown, but when you arrive there in a few minutes we turn our attention to the Pea Ridge Campaign. The next segment begins at Exit 100 on I-44, which is 7 miles southeast of you via Timber Ridge Road and Route W.

To reach Tour Stop 163:

Turn right on Farm Road 127, and drive southeast for 2.7 miles, bearing left as you go. This is the Old Melville Road, and it empties on to Kearney Street just a block west of State Rte. 13, known as the Kansas Expressway in Springfield. Go east to Route 13 then turn left (north). If you stay on our route, you will enter Interstate 44 at exit 77. Enter the interstate here, eastbound. Drive east 11.3 miles to Stafford, Exit 88, and turn left on Route 125 here.

Drive north on Route 125 for .6 mile, then turn right on Route DD. Stay on this road for 6 miles, where there is a right angle turn to the right. From here (You are on County Road J) you will drive .6 miles east to a marked road called "Old Wire Road." Turn left here. Stay on this road, northbound, for 1.8 miles where the road intersects Route E. Turn right and immediately jog left on State Highway 38. Drive north on Highway 38 for 1.4 miles to Timber Ridge Road, and turn right here. There is a granite monument on the southeast corner of this intersection, and this marks Tour Stop 163.

Part III - Westbound

To reach Tour Stop 164:

For westbound travelers, this segment starts at I-44 Exit 100, at Marshfield. After crossing or exiting the highway in the direction of town, take the first left you can take, on to the east outer road. This is called Banning Street. Stay on Banning for a total of 1.4 miles (Banning turns east after hugging the highway). Pull over at the 1.4 mile mark, after you have crossed Hubbell Drive, where there is a park on your left.

Tour Stop 164 is the site of the WHITLOCK MILL. It's not clear how long before the Civil War a grist mill existed at this site, but Marshfield was founded in 1856 and the mill was probably built about the same time. In 1861, a Springfield man, Thomas J. Whitlock, owned the mill. That winter after the Union army abandoned Springfield the Confederates took possession of Whitlock's Mill, grinding flour for Price's troops.

On February 9, 1862, Union general Samuel R. Curtis, in Lebanon, was preparing to march against Price's Confederate army. A force of federal cavalry commanded by Maj. Clark Wright descended on the Whitlock Mill and drove off the Confederate occupiers. Several were killed and wounded on the Confederate side in this, the first action of the Pea Ridge Campaign.

Incidentally, Whitlock had gone to California in 1850, and there discovered a vein of gold in an area near the Yosemite Valley that is still known as the Whitlock mining district. He sold out in 1852 and returned to Springfield before adding the Marshfield mill to his considerable Missouri holdings.

We return to I-44 by way of the courthouse square, where you can see a marker that describes the Civil War in Marshfield, and the World's only scale model of the Hubble Space Telescope. Astronomer Edwin Hubble, the father of the "big bang theory," was born in Marshfield in 1889.

HARTVILLE BATTLE

Hartville is the seat of Wright County, Missouri. It is east of Marshfield, about 25 miles, via Missouri Route 38. On January 10, 1863, a confederate force under Col. Joseph Porter camped near the town of High Prairie on Route 38 (then called Hazelwood). Marmaduke's cavalry joined Porter there, and on January 11 proceeded in the direction of Hartville. Although Porter had cleared the area the day before, a detachment of Union infantry and cavalry had arrived from the east and camped the night of January 10 west of Hartville. The two forces collided, and the outnumbered federals fought their way back to Hartville. The battle there lasted 4 or 5 hours. The Union men had to abandon the field, but punished the Confederates severely with cannon they posted on heights east of town.

Tour Stop 165

This house was CURTIS' HEADQUARTERS on the night of February 12, 1862, and near here occurred the first infantry engagement of the Pea Ridge Campaign. The house is the historic Danforth mansion, constructed by slave labor in 1839. Three of Curtis' divisions camped in this little valley - Pierson Creek - as they prepared to fight for control of Springfield.

Farm Road 212 is a remnant of the old Springfield Road. In the winter of 1839 the Springfield Road became a route of the Cherokees' Trail of Tears, called the Northern Route. The valley here was also a campsite for some of the unfortunate thousands of men, women and children who were forced to relocate to the new Native American lands in Oklahoma.

The advance element of Curtis' force, his cavalry, drove in some Confederate pickets along Farm Road 212 east of here, and suffered one casualty there. After the infantry went into camp, the Union advance skirmished with the Confederates again, two miles to the west. Some cannon fire soon drove the Confederates into Springfield. As night fell, Curtis' army bedded down in the expectation of a battle on the morning of February 13, but at the same time, Sterling Price, in Springfield, was putting his troops in motion to the south. There would be no battle of Springfield in 1862.

The next clash in the Pea Ridge campaign occurred on February 14, 1862, well to the south of Springfield, at Crane Creek.

To reach Tour Stop 165:

Go south one block from the square to Jackson Street, which is State Route 38, and turn right (west). Continue on 38 as it bears right about 3/4 mile from the square, and follow this road to its intersection with I-44, in another .7 mile. Enter I-44 westbound and drive about 12 miles west to the Stafford exit.

Exit I-44 at Strafford (Exit 88), southbound. State Route 125 turns east through the town and then turns south about 3/4 mile after the exit. Turn left on Route 125, and proceed south for .9 mile to Farm Road 212, where you turn right. In about .7 mile, Farm Road 212 descends into a valley, and then turns right at a "Y." Bear left at this intersection, on to Farm Road 213, and continue south for 1/3 mile until you emerge from the trees. Stop on the shoulder where you have a view of the large brick house that is on your left.

To reach Tour Stop 166:

Turn around and retrace your route back to Road 212 then continue straight at the "Y". The road will bend to the left. You are now on the Old Springfield Road, we think, and in just about 2 miles this road ends. Take a left here, in the face of a hill to the west that was probably the defensive position of Price's skirmishers. Turn right a short distance south of this intersection, staying on the paved road. This road ends in another two miles, at Le Compte Road. Turn right here and drive north .2 mile to Kearney Street and turn left. You will reach U. S. 65 in about 1/2 mile, and here enter the highway southbound.

Drive south 4 miles on U. S. 65, to the Sunshine Street exit, then turn right on Sunshine. Go west 2.1 miles to Glenstone Avenue, then left. Turn right on Seminole Street in a half mile, and the entrance to the cemetery that is the next Tour Stop is on your left

Tour Stop 166

The SPRINGFIELD NATIONAL CEMETERY was among the first established by Act of Congress just after the Civil War. Bodies of both Union and Confederate casualties of the Battle of Wilson's Creek were turning up in shallow graves throughout the area as the population returned to their homes, farms and civil life. Union dead were moved here starting in 1867. Then, Southern-leaning city fathers acquired a plot next door to the new federal cemetery, and the remains of sons of the South were exhumed and laid to rest. This happenstance produced something unique in the nation.

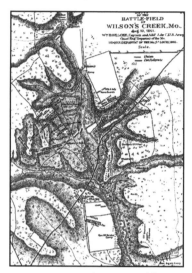

Although there are Confederate graves in many of our National Cemeteries, the Springfield National Cemetery is the only one that includes a Confederate cemetery within it. Drive to the south side of the grounds and you will realize the difference when you come upon the magnificent monument honoring Sterling Price that dominates the old Southern cemetery. In 1911, the Daughters of the Confederacy, which was then caring for the Southern graves, offered the grounds to the United States, and Congress passed legislation to accept this offer. The transfer of title was accompanied by a ceremonial breach of the stone wall that still separates the two halves. Other notable sites within the cemetery include the grave of MSG Col. Richard Weightman, the highest ranking Southern casualty at Wilson's Creek, who died leading his brigade, a monument dedicated to Nathaniel Lyon that once stood on the battlefield near his death site, and another monument to the Union defenders of Springfield during the battle of January 8, 1863. The cannon placed upright around the cemetery saw action in the Union works during the 1863 Battle of Springfield. The cemetery holds the graves of four Civil War recipients of the Medal of Honor, including Orion Howe, who earned his citation as a 14 year old drummer at Vicksburg.

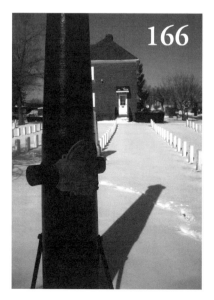

Tour Stop 167

WILSON'S CREEK NATIONAL BATTLEFIELD commemorates the battle of August 10, 1861, which Southerners call the Battle of Oak Hill. The battlefield park is everything you expect from a National Park Service facility of this kind, although it came into being by a different route than most. It was not until the 1950s that an effort got underway to acquire and preserve the ground of this critically important battle. As a result, you will not find monuments such as those placed by veteran groups in older battlefield parks, but you will see a landscape that nearly perfectly reflects rural Missouri in 1861.

The Southern forces comprised three elements. Ben McCulloch of Texas commanded regular Confederate units, mostly from Louisiana and Arkansas. The second element consisted of Missouri troops commanded by General Sterling Price. Thirdly, some Arkansas state troops fought here, at this early stage also not enrolled in the Confederate service. Lyon split his outnumbered force, sending Franz Sigel round-about from the east in an effort to block McCulloch's escape route. Lyon then attacked with his main force from the north and northwest, from Bloody Hill. A fierce battle - with a casualty rate that exceeded that at Bull Run in Virginia - raged for six hours as the Southern army slowly gained control.

The principal man-made feature on the battlefield, still evident, is the old Wire Road. You've had some introduction to this historic trace, also known as the Butterfield Trail or the Trail of Tears. In olden days, between here and northwest Arkansas only one road collected all of the traffic. The telegraph line that connected St. Louis and the federal outpost at Ft. Smith, Arkansas, gave the trace its "modern" name. What gave the road a reason to exist was the deep valley of the White River to the south. The White River valley today gives us Table Rock Lake and Lake Taneycomo and the miracle of Branson; 150 years ago travelers had to avoid that area. The Wire Road follows the high ground west of the White, and served as the gateway to northwest Arkansas and Indian Territory.

The stretch of this road from Wilson's Creek south to Fayetteville, Arkansas, has particular significance for Civil War travelers. Because of its strategic importance, the armies of the North and South tramped this route again and again. Many of the great battlefields of the Trans-Mississippi West – Wilson's Creek, Pea Ridge, Fayetteville, Prairie Grove and Cane Hill – lie on or near this road.

Our Tour takes you most of the way to Pea Ridge. Much of the original road that connected Wilson's Creek to Pea Ridge still exists. The road you're looking at here rises up the hill in front of Elkhorn Tavern on the field of Pea Ridge.

To reach Tour Stop 167:

Exit the cemetery and turn left on Seminole. Drive west for 1.5 miles to So. Campbell Street, and turn right here. Drive north 1/2 mile, past the Bass Pro complex, and turn left on Sunshine Street. Drive a total of 8.2 miles west on this road, which becomes U. S. Highway 60. Turn left on Route M, then right on Route ZZ. You will find signage along Highway 60 and for the rest of the route to Tour Stop 167.

Brig. Gen. Nathaniel Lyon
1818 - 1861

The first Union general officer killed in action in the Civil War was born in 1818 in Connecticut, to an old New England family. Lyon graduated from West Point in the class of 1841 and then fought in the war with Mexico. In California in 1850 after the gold rush, as a lieutenant Lyon commanded an expedition that produced what is known as the Clear Lake Massacre of Native Americans. In 1854, Lyon was transferred to Fort Riley, Kansas. He served in Kansas with the Second U. S. Infantry throughout the turbulent years of "Bleeding Kansas." Capt. Lyon was ordered to St. Louis in February, 1861. Upon his arrival in St. Louis, Lyon aligned himself with the pro-union interests of the powerful Blair family. Appointed Brigadier General of Volunteers, Lyon took charge of military preparations for the defense of St. Louis. After a confrontation with the largely pro-Southern Missouri Militia in St. Louis known as the Camp Jackson affair, Lyon planned and aggressively pursued a campaign into central and southwestern Missouri.

After he died at Wilson's Creek on August 10, 1861, Lyon's remains were transported by a special train through many of the major cities of the East, and laid to rest in Phoenixville, Connecticut.

Part IV - Southbound

To reach Tour Stop 168:

When you exit Wilson's Creek, cross the highway and proceed west on this road, which becomes Elm Street in Republic. From there, head south on State Route P for 5.8 miles until you reach the town of Clever. When this road (now Route K) turns left, continue straight ahead on Public Avenue. In two blocks, turn right on Inmon Street, which within a block or so changes it name to Old Wire Road. In 1.5 miles you will arrive at a small white frame building, on the right, which is built over a natural spring

Tour Stop 168

The spring house is built over Dug Spring, and you are near the scene of THE BATTLE OF DUG SPRING, August 2, 1861. The Wire Road angled southwest from Wilson's Creek, and except for this stretch has been pretty well obliterated over the years. The same is true for the next several miles of this tour.

Union General Nathaniel Lyon stayed in Springfield during the second half of July, 1861, but as August arrived he ventured out to scout the area. He put his infantry in motion down the Wire Road on August 1. After an exhausting march on the first day out, in 110 degree heat, they arrived at Dug Spring during the morning of August 2. As reported by New York Herald correspondent Thomas Knox, the spring was the scene of a near riot. There was a spring house on this site at that time, and it was lifted off its moorings and cast aside by a throng of Union troops after water. The infantry then went into bivouac.

While Lyon is moving southwest on the Wire Road, the Southern forces under Price and McCulloch reached a point about 8 miles southwest of here, on the banks of Crane Creek. They were feeling their way on the same road. From their base at Crane Creek they have sent out cavalry, under Gen. James S. Rains of the Missouri State Guard, to reconnoiter. Lyon has thrown out in his advance a battalion of the 1st U.S. Infantry (regulars) commanded by Capt. – later Maj. General – Frederick Steele, which deployed down the valley in front of you.

Late in the afternoon Lyon's camp was roused by the sound of gunfire down the valley. Rains, despite orders to avoid an engagement, was attacking Steele's force. Lyon dispatched federal cavalry and formed his main body of infantry in line of battle. Probably, Lyon anchored his line on the high ground

168

169

along Metzeltein Road (on both sides of the Wire Road as you look west).

After Steele withdrew, Rains continued his attack up the valley but ran into barrages from Lyon's artillery when approaching the Union line of infantry. Rains' horsemen, scattered and routed, raced the 8 miles back to Crane Creek. The affair became known in Southern circles as "Rains' scare." Days after the battle at Dug Spring, this road carried Price's 12,000 men northward to Wilson's Creek.

The next year, on February 14, 1862, half of Curtis' 12,000 man army marched down this stretch of road in search of Price. Franz Sigel, in command of the other half, was moving south on a route 5 miles to the west. Once again, at Sigel's urging, a pincer movement was under way. Sigel needed to beat Price to a crossroads at McDowell.

Tour Stop 169

This is McCULLAH'S HOLLOW, and you are at the point where the Wire Road crossed this valley. The road ascended the next line of hills, to the southwest, and passed through a small settlement called McCullah's Store, also known as Curran Post Office. The settlement was perhaps 3/4 a mile from here but is not accessible.

As Price and McCulloch advanced towards Springfield, Lyon was striking out from his Springfield base in the hope of confronting either Price or McCulloch before they combined forces. Lyon reached McCullah's Store on August 3, 1861 before he learned that Price and McCulloch had already combined and were camped at Crane Creek.

After driving off the advance elements of the Southern forces here in a small engagement, Lyon went into camp. He decided the following day to return to Springfield. The next time Lyon ventured out he collided with Price and McCulloch at Wilson's Creek.

To Reach Tour Stop 169:

Continue west on the Wire Road for .4 mile, and turn left on S. Metzeltein Road. Drive south for 1/2 mile to Spring Creek Road and turn right here. Proceed west, pausing as you cross the first bridge. The Wire Road used to run through here; It was later replaced by the tracks of the Missouri Pacific Railroad, which are now abandoned. This is the approximate area of the clash between Rains and Steele described above.

Take the first available left on Spring Creek Road, on to Pierce Road. Stay on this road south for 2.1 miles to Route M, and turn right here. Go west about .4 mile and pull over.

THE BROTHERS BLACK

The 37th Illinois Volunteer Infantry took part in Fremont's 1861 campaign, as well as the Pea Ridge and Prairie Grove campaigns. John Charles Black (at left) would ultimately be the 37th's colonel. His younger brother, Captain William Black (right), won the Congressional Medal of Honor for actions at Pea Ridge. John Charles received the MOH for gallantry at Prairie Grove. They were the first of five sets of brothers in American history to receive the nation's highest military honor.

To reach Tour Stop 170:

Drive west on Route M for 2.5 miles, and here you will turn left on State Highway 413; Go south for 2.5 miles where Route A intersects from the left. There is a sign here noting the existence of the Old Wire Road Conservation Area, which is your next stop. Turn right on this road, and drive down into a valley, about .8 miles, where you will see a Conservation Dept. parking area on your right. Pull in here.

From the parking area, look out over the valley of the CRANE CREEK CAMPGROUND. Moving north during the Wilson's Creek campaign, the bulk of the Price-McCulloch forces filed into camp here beginning on August 2, 1861, and filled this valley. This was to remain the Southern camp until August 5, while advance units were feeling out Lyon's federal forces several miles to the northeast.

Controversy exists about what happened in this valley during the morning of August 4, 1861. The Missouri troops at Crane Creek were organized under state authority, not subject to Confederate control.

McCulloch had shown extreme caution up to this point in the war in deploying enrolled or "regular" Confederate troops in "neutral" Missouri, and had clashed with Price before. At Crane Creek, McCulloch considered withdrawing his troops to Arkansas instead of pursuing Lyon. Price confronted McCulloch, at the latter's Crane Creek headquarters, on the morning of August 4. According to legend, handed down in the post-war writings of a Missourian, Price submitted himself and his Missouri State Guard to McCulloch's authority at Crane Creek in order to persuade McCulloch to continue the advance against Springfield. Probably, Price had agreed on July 30 to operate under McCulloch's command, but on August 4 Price threatened to break this agreement and attack on his own. Anyway, Price succeeded, and the combined forces moved together from here on August 5 or 6. They established their next camp on the banks of Wilson's Creek. The Southern commanders did not know on August 4 that Lyon was already withdrawing to Springfield.

Now we turn to the Pea Ridge Campaign.

A rear guard of Price's fleeing army camped in this valley on February 13-14, 1862. In pursuit, Union General Curtis sent a cavalry detachment ahead. This force, along with two mountain howitzers, took position on the heights behind you. The Union artillery lobbed shells from there into the Southern camp, beginning at dusk on February 14, causing a number of casualties. Curtis' cavalry then moved on the camp, capturing about 30, including an embarrassed Col. Thomas Freeman. At the time of the attack at Crane Creek, Curtis' army - two divisions that took this route - was camped near McCullah's Store. Here at Crane Creek, General Herron's

170

Third Division, Union Army of the Frontier, camped the night of December 3, 1862 as they were beginning their epic march. The men of the Third Division left camp at 6:00 a.m. on the 4th, marching west and south in the direction of Prairie Grove. Elements of the Second Division, including the 20th Iowa Infantry, arrived here just as Herron's troops were leaving.

Tour Stop 171

This is a nearly virgin WIRE ROAD SEGMENT. If you were to take the old road on the right you would travel about 3 1/2 miles before reaching the main tour route. We make note in the margin of the point where this road emerges on to the recommended route, which is Route TT. We do not recommend that you take the old road. Do not even consider it unless you are driving a four wheel drive vehicle with ample clearance. If you do go, 2 1/4 miles into the trek you will come upon a spring that emerges from a hillside on the left. Nearby are a monument and a wood sign erected by the landowner marking the location of Smith's Station on the Butterfield Stage. If you go, remember that this history-conscious family also prizes privacy and solitude.

If you start on this trail and decide you've made a mistake, the first available left turn will take you to Route TT.

Tour Stop 172

Stop 172 is near the BATTLE OF UPSHAW'S FARM. Here is a brief glimpse of Price's 1864 Expedition. A remnant of Price's army came through here on October 29, 1864, after the army broke up following the Battles of Westport and Mine Creek. Here, the Confederate force retreating toward Arkansas clashed with the Second Arkansas Cavalry – a Union outfit – and 50 Confederates were purportedly killed. Among the Confederates captured was Capt. Thomas Todd, a famed guerrilla who had joined Price's column during his raid.

To reach Tour Stop 171:

Drive west about 2.6 miles, to State Rte. JJ, and turn left. Go south for .7 mile to the first road that enters from your left. Park at this intersection with a view of the road to the west.

To reach Tour Stop 172:

Continue south on Rte. JJ for 1.5 miles, and turn right on State Route TT. Drive west 3.9 miles, then turn left on Farm Road 1200. In another 1/2 mile, go right on the first road you reach, and then west for 1.1 miles to State Highway 39. Where the road you are traveling angles to the southwest, you are again on the bed of the old Wire Road.

After you turned right on TT, at the point 2.8 miles west of your turn, the old Wire Road (Farm Road 1212) entered on your right.

Turn left (south) on Highway 39. Proceed south for about .4 miles; where Highway 39 turns to the left, continue straight on the smaller road. Pull over where this road bends to the left, in about 1/3 mile.

To reach Tour Stop 173:

Continue ahead on this road, bearing left when you complete the turn, and drive due east until you intersect with Highway 39. Turn left, and retrace your route back to the north, but only to State Route WW. Turn left. Go west for 1 mile, and turn right on the next road. As you drive west on this road, bear left and drive a total of .6 miles to the second road on the left, Camp Bliss Road. Turn left and drive south for a mile and a quarter. Look for a round pond on your right.

To reach Tour Stop 174:

Continue your journey south about 2.4 miles to the point where Camp Bliss Road ends. Turn right. Drive west .5 mile to an intersection with Route C in the small town of McDowell. Park at the intersection with a view of the road to the north.

Tour Stop 173

This is the site of Union CAMP BLISS. The pond is the Camp Bliss Spring, in Camp Bliss Hollow. Both are named for a federal base camp established here after the Pea Ridge campaign. It existed at least into the early part of 1863. Part of the 37th Illinois Infantry was stationed here in February, 1863. The men of the 37th Illinois, known as the Illinois Greyhounds, passed by this spot several times, when it marched with Curtis in February 1862 and with Herron in December of that year. This general area, and Cassville in particular, was home to the 37th Illinois for most of 1862. Then the regiment moved out of Camp Bliss to Vicksburg and beyond. This stretch of road is a section of the historic Wire Road.

Tour Stop 174

During the Pea Ridge Campaign, the valley to the south was the site of the SKIRMISH AT FLAT CREEK, February 15, 1862.

Recall that Franz Sigel had taken half of Curtis' army west, and intended to block Price's retreat by reaching McDowell before Price did. The road from the north, Route VV, comes from the town of Verona, 10 miles north. It was the route used by Sigel's two divisions. While Sigel probably moved too slowly, the divisions with Curtis on the Wire Road raced here on Price's heels. Curtis' divisions reached the point where Camp Bliss Road now ends just two days after Curtis entered Springfield.

As best we can tell, the Wire Road descended Camp Bliss Hollow and then headed straight south, crossing Flat Creek there. Across the way, at the base of the next bluff to the south, Price's Southerners threw up breastworks and showed signs of making a stand. Curtis paused, and placed the Third Iowa Battery on one of the hills that frame the mouth of Camp Bliss Hollow. It shelled the Southern position and a cavalry charge drove Price's men from the valley. Pursued and pursuers followed the Wire Road through the valley to the east, and emerged at Stop 175.

Some time after the Southerners fled, Sigel's 5,000 men came tramping down the road from Verona.

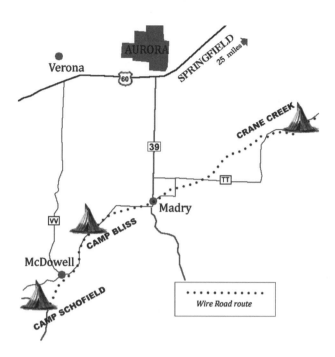

Tour Stop 175

Stop 175 is the site of CAMP SCHOFIELD, a substantial federal camp and recruiting station that occupied this area from June, 1862 until at least the summer of 1863. The place was also known as "Camp Three Widows," after a tavern operated by three women that was a favorite hang-out for the troops stationed at Camp Schofield. By the end of July, 1862 the Fourteenth Missouri Militia Cavalry completed its basic training here.

At least two of the regiments on Herron's classic march spent time at Camp Schofield. The 20th Iowa Infantry camped here the

To reach Tour Stop 175:

Turn left on Route C and drive 1.0 miles southwest, to a gravel road that sneaks up on the left. Turn left on this road (Farm Road 1142). Drive due south for .7 mile, where this road ends, and turn left (east). This road takes a very sharp turn to the right about 1/2 mile. Look to your right just after you turn, and stop in front of what appears to be the ruins of a house.

CHICKENS TO THE FRONT

The future chief engineer of the Union Pacific Railroad, Grenville Mellon Dodge, was colonel of the 4th Iowa Infantry when it accompanied Curtis' army on the march to Pea Ridge. In a memoir written fifty years later, he described the series of small engagements that occurred in this sector: " . . . my Regiment would go into line, strip themselves, and throw down the chickens, potatoes, apples, and other eatables they had foraged and taken during the day, and as they would go forward the troops in our rear would come up and gobble what they had dropped. About the third time the Regiment went into line I noticed the boys had left nothing but their knapsacks, and were holding on to their chickens and provisions."

To reach Tour Stop 176:

Continue south on this road, which becomes Route U, for 3 miles. Route U turns to the right part way to the next Tour Stop, but you need to bear left here. Slow at this intersection and set your odometer. You will go 2.3 miles south of U and then look to your right for a small grove of trees. Tour Stop 176 is in this grove.

To reach Tour Stop 177:

Continue driving south as the old road changes to State Route Y. The next Stop is 1.3 miles south of Crouch's Station, or 3.6 miles south of the intersection with Rte. U, where you set your odometer. The road turns to the right as you approach Stop 177, which is clearly visible in a small hill on the right.

To reach Tour Stop 178:

Continue south on Route Y for 3.4 miles, to Main Street in Cassville, which is Bus. Route 37. Turn left on Main, and drive south about .6 mile. The next Tour Stop, number 178, is on the courthouse lawn on your right.

night of December 4, 1862, its first night on the march. It and the 37th Illinois Infantry returned here from Prairie Grove in January, 1863, and wintered for a while.

Tour Stop 176

A rounded stone memorial within this grove of trees marks the location of CROUCH'S STATION on the Butterfield route. This was one of a series of identical markers placed in 1958 during the centennial of the Butterfield Stage. The centennial was celebrated with a fair amount of hoopla, in Missouri all the way to California. The 150th anniversary came and went in 2008 without much notice. Crouch's was the next stage stop south of Smith's Station.

Tour Stop 177

This Stop is ASH CAVE. The cave has no documented Civil War history, but in view of the extensive troop movements up and down the road at this point, doubtless the cave served as a shelter for soldiers of both sides many times during the war. You are stopping here because of the artifact that lies, or may lie, in the creek on your left, which is described on the facing page.

Tour Stop 178

You are at the site of the BARRY COUNTY COURTHOUSE. The present courthouse, built in the twentieth century, replaced the building commemorated here. On the courthouse lawn you will find a descriptive marker placed by the Missouri State Parks that describes the session of the secessionist legislature that convened nearby in October-November, 1861.

Cassville is the place where Price consolidated the State Guard troops under his command with the Confederate and Arkansas troops under McCulloch that had traveled up the Wire Road from Arkansas. Price reached Cassville from the west on July 28, 1861. His meeting with McCulloch occurred on July 29. They were joined here by the 7th Division of the Missouri State Guard, commanded by Gen. J. H. McBride of Houston, Missouri. The Southern force now numbered approximately 12,000. From Cassville Price and McCulloch launched the campaign that culminated at Wilson's Creek.

In 1862, Curtis' army came through Cassville on its way to Pea Ridge. From that time until the end of the War, Union troops occupied Cassville except for several months in the summer and fall of 1862. At that time, Confederate Colonel John Coffee's raid that ended in the Battle of Lone Jack precipitated a temporary Union withdrawal. A skirmish occurred in town on September 21, 1862, when a part of the new 1st Arkansas Cavalry (Union) came in from the south in an unsuccessful attempt to dislodge the Confederates. The federals reoccupied Cassville in mid-October, 1862. A large federal camp was established in the area of the city park, to the east of here along Flat Creek. Until recently breastworks were visible on the hill to the northwest where the water tower is located.

178

THE LOST CANNON OF WESTPORT

In southwest Missouri a story persists to this day that a 24-pound howitzer lies buried in Flat Creek near Ash Cave.

On October 22, 1864, the day before the Battle of Westport, Confederate forces successfully forced two crossings of the Big Blue River east of Kansas City; one at Byram's Ford and the other at Russell's Ford. The Russell's Ford crossing, made without opposition, put a portion of Shelby's Cavalry beyond the right flank of Kansas City's defenders. This force, under Col. Sydney Jackman, was ordered to make a "bee line" for Kansas. However, fortuitously the 2nd Kansas State Militia had been posted in Jackman's way. Attached to the 2nd Kansas was a battery known as the "Topeka Battery," which unlimbered its 24 pound brass howitzer on the road at a place called the Mockabee Farm, near 78th and Holmes Streets in modern-day Kansas City.

The Topeka Battery made a gallant stand, repeatedly discharging grape and canister into the face of Jackman's cavalry, and beating off 3 assaults. Finally, the gun and what was left of its crew were captured. The Topeka Battery suffered 8 killed in action, 4 wounded, and all the rest of its 80-man crew was captured. It is considered by many Kansans to be the gun that saved Kansas.

The howitzer is alleged to have been sunk here in Flat Creek during Price's retreat, to prevent its re-capture by pursuing federals. This is only one of a number of stories about the final resting place of the famous artillery piece, but the Flat Creek story rings true. This is largely because of a well publicized effort in 1910 to recover it from this spot, conducted under the auspices of the Kansas Soldier's Memorial Association. The leader of the expedition, one E. F. Heisler, used dynamite to dislodge logs that choked the stream where the gun was reportedly dumped. Heisler reported to newspapers that he did recover the cannon, but in fact he did not. Aside from being the Secretary of the Soldier's Memorial Association, Mr. Heisler was a newspaperman, too.

A second unsuccessful search of Flat Creek for the lost cannon occurred in the 1970s.

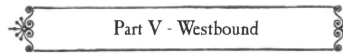

Part V - Westbound

To reach Tour Stop 179:

Tour Stop 179

Return by way of Main Street to Route Y but bear left there on Bus. Route 37. This road joins State Highway 37 in about 1.7 miles. Turn right on Highway 37 and drive north for 7.7 miles, to the town of Purdy, and turn left on Route B. Drive west on this road, which changes its designation to Route 97 and then Route 86, for 9 miles to the town of Fairview. Just after Fairview, bear right on State Highway 86 and proceed 6.1 miles to Stark City. Go straight as the highway approaches town, and drive into town. Go left on any of the north-south streets, to South Street then right. Your objective is the southwest corner of town, at the intersection of South Street and Wanda Street.

The SECOND BATTLE OF NEWTONIA was fought on and near this ground on October 28, 1864. Stark City was not here in 1864, but at this intersection Union cavalry chasing the Confederates after Westport formed its first line of battle, intending to inflict a death blow on Price's Army of Missouri. This was at the end of Price's 1864 Expedition. This would also be the last Confederate victory west of the Mississippi River.

Consult the campaign summary at page 212 of this Guide. Price had suffered devastating losses at Westport and then at Mine Creek, Kansas. He had opened some distance between himself and the pursuing federals, and his men went into camp a little south and east of here. Then Union Gen. James Blunt appeared, entering the area by way of the Granby Road over the slight ridge visible in the distance to the northwest. His two brigades of cavalry advanced to this point, and dismounted.

To meet this threat, just to the south and southeast of you, the Confederate Iron Brigade sallied out of their camp, along with two other brigades of Shelby's division. The Confederates also dismounted, and began to advance across a field, crossing two fence lines to reach this point. Blunt's men gave way, and Shelby pressed them towards the northwest, as Blunt's artillery placed an occasional shell into the Confederate ranks from a battery on the Granby Road, up on that ridge.

179

The battle reached its climax in a cornfield, .9 mile to the north on your right. Shelby pushed forward in a northwest direction; his right flank reached the cornfield, in position to flank Blunt's force. At this point, another Union cavalry brigade - Sanborn's - arrived on the scene from the north just in time. The tide turned and the federals pressed the Confederates back to this point, whence they retired into their camp. It is not recorded whether Price's army camped the night of October 28 there, as had been planned, but in any case the Union cavalry halted its pursuit. Price limped into Indian Territory, and returned to his Arkansas base without fighting again.

It is fitting that the Iron Brigade helped save the day here. A few miles south of here, in September, 1862, the new Confederate regiments of Shelby, Coffee and Hays had joined together to form the Iron Brigade. Surely the irony was not lost on the men of the brigade who made their last assault in Missouri on the Union line here.

Tour Stop 180

The RITCHEY MANSION was constructed in the 1840s by Matthew H. Ritchey, a prominent unionist in this area. It became the focal point of the First Battle of Newtonia, on September 30, 1862. The house is headquarters for the Newtonia Battlefields Protection Association, a grass-roots group that has labored for years to preserve the house and the lands around here that became the scene of two important battles of the Civil War. The house was often headquarters for Union and Confederate armies scouring this area, and was used as a hospital after the battles. A 2008 tornado seriously damaged the house, but the Association has conscientiously restored the house again.

The First Battle occurred on September 30, 1862 at a time when new Confederate recruits were pouring south, after the fights at Independence and Lone Jack. They camped in the Indian Creek valley, five miles south of here, at a place called Camp Coffee. This is where the Iron Brigade was born. Troops also came in from the Indian Territory and Texas to join the Missourians at Camp Coffee. Understand that you are now as close to Texas as you are to St. Louis.

The Confederates had designs on the lead mines in Granby, four miles away, which probably explains the rendezvous on Indian Creek. Matthew Ritchey had built a mill in Newtonia, across Mill Street and slightly west of his home. In the last days of September, 1862, the Confederates sent a detachment here to grind flour. The road that is now Mill Street was the main road between Neosho and Cassville. Ritchey had built a stone barn directly across the street, and stone walls lining both sides of the road. This was a good defensive position.

The Union had 4,000 men in the area - part of Brig. Gen. James Blunt's Army of the Frontier that would soon advance into Arkansas. Apprised of the Confederate presence, Blunt sent a column towards Newtonia. Advance elements of both armies clashed on September 29, north of here along the road from Sarcoxie. At 7:00 a.m. on September 30, Blunt's main force arrived on the Sarcoxie road, as did a contingent from the Confederate camp to the south, and the battle

To reach Tour Stop 180:

Drive north on Wanda Street for 1 mile, to State Highway 86. Cross the highway and go north one block to Mill Street. Turn right. Drive east on Mill Street for about a half mile, and Tour Stop 180 is well marked on your right.

180

Maj. Gen. James G. Blunt
1826 – 1881

Born in Maine in 1826, James Blunt was a sailor as a young man, and later a physician in Ohio. He moved to Kansas in 1856, settling in rural Anderson County. There he resumed his medical career. He became involved in politics as well, working on behalf of the Free Soil side in the Kansas debate.

Blunt entered the federal service in 1861 as Lieutenant Colonel of the Third Kansas Volunteer Infantry. In April, 1862 he received a commission as Brigadier General, commanding the District of Kansas. Although an amateur soldier and a "political" general, Blunt acquitted himself well as a field commander in many battles on the frontier, including the First and Second Battles of Newtonia, Missouri and Cane Hill and Prairie Grove in Arkansas. He commanded victorious Union forces at the largest battle fought in Oklahoma, at Honey Springs in 1863. He is remembered also for an ignominious affair at Baxter Springs, Kansas on October 6, 1863. Quantrill's guerrillas attacked a Union post there; Blunt happen to arrive while the attack was in progress. Blunt fled to Ft. Scott while many of the men of his staff and cavalry escort, and members of a regimental band, were slaughtered.

Blunt was promoted to Major General late in 1862. He is the only Kansan to achieve that rank in the Civil War. He died in 1881 and is buried in Leavenworth, Kansas.

began in earnest. Much of the fighting occurred to the north and northeast; a cemetery about a half mile north known as the Civil War Cemetery (because casualties are purportedly buried there) saw a good part of the action. You can visit the cemetery, where an Ohio battery was placed to shell the Confederate position. During the battle, the 1st Choctaw Regiment (Confederate) charged the 3rd Indian Home Guard Battalion (Union), probably near the north end of Main Street. This is thought to be the only time in the entire Civil War that Native American troops engaged directly in combat against each other.

The battle ebbed and flowed all around the town of Newtonia for most of the day. Ultimately the Union troops withdrew to the north, leaving the field in the possession of the Confederates.

A final note: In and around this area, Matthew Ritchey's son James recruited a company of Union soldiers for the 76th Enrolled Missouri Militia. One of the men who enrolled in the 76th was Pvt. H. W. McCurry, who entered service at Newtonia on December 30, 1862, presumably on the lawn of the Ritchey Mansion. Pvt. McCurry was President Barack Obama's great-great-great grandfather.

Part VI - Northbound

Tour Stop 181

The GRANBY MINES date from a discovery of a massive deposit of lead ore in 1850. The works here produced lead for the armies of the United States up until the Second World War.

Mining operations in Granby were suspended during the Civil War, but both Union and Confederate armies extracted and processed ore from time to time. The 22nd and 34th Texas cavalry regiments (Confederate) arrived here during the First Battle of Newtonia. They were joined several days later by the Confederate Indian Battalion. The Confederates went into camp a mile north on the banks of Shoal Creek, the scene of a skirmish on October 4, 1862. The Confederates were driven into Granby and beyond, in an action known as the Affair at Granby.

The Confederate victory at Newtonia had drawn a superior federal force into the area. The Confederates abandoned Newtonia the same day as the Granby Affair. Also on October 4, they left their camp on Indian Creek, headed south. The two armies contending in this area would next clash at Cane Hill, Arkansas, on November 28, 1862.

This Tour Loop is nearly complete, and now we return to the events of July, 1861. After you visit Tour Stop 182, if you intend to continue north, you will arrive in Carthage, where a battle was fought on July 5, 1861. Col. Franz Sigel was leading a small Union force from Springfield, with an eye to cutting off the Missouri State Guard as it fled south, as described in the campaign summary that introduces this Tour Loop. He brought one regiment down the road that is now U. S. Highway 60, through Granby to Neosho. Then he turned north, leaving only a company in Neosho to protect his rear against the regular Confederate forces under Confederate Gen. Ben McCulloch, threatening from his base in Arkansas.

McCulloch entered Neosho on July 5, and the small Union force there capitulated immediately. According to Goodspeed's History of Newton County, just then a wagon train with some of Sigel's supplies arrived in Granby via the Springfield-Mt. Vernon Road, and sent a courier to Neosho for instructions. The

To reach Tour Stop 181:

Drive west on Mill Street, then turn left on Route M, returning to the corner of State Highway 86 and Starling Road. Turn right on 86, and from this intersection drive west for 4.0 miles to Route B. Turn right (north) on Route B. Go north 2.0 miles and turn right on Old Cemetery Road in Granby. Take this road east for .4 mile to Main Street, and turn left. Drive north on Main for .9 mile to Valley Street (U. S. Highway 60), and cross Valley Street. Park in the area of the Granby Miner's Museum.

181

courier reported to a Confederate colonel, not realizing that Sigel had already gone. A contingent of Confederate cavalry soon arrived in Granby and captured Sigel's train.

To reach Tour Stop 182:

Continue north on Main Street, which becomes Route E. Continue north about 3 miles, and turn left on Foliage Road. Drive west on this road for 5.3 miles, crossing Highway 71 at the 3 mile point, and turn right on Carver Road. The next Stop is well marked, a mile and a quarter north, on your left.

Tour Stop 182

The GEORGE WASHINGTON CARVER NATIONAL MONUMENT was established by Act of Congress in 1943, the same year Missouri's great agricultural genius passed away. You would want to visit this site regardless of its connections to Missouri's Civil War, since you are in the neighborhood. There is a Civil War story here, though, and in fact two of them.

The proprietors of the farm that was once here were Moses and Susan Carver, German immigrants who moved to southwest Missouri in the late 1830s. The Carvers bought a young female slave by the name of Mary, who bore three children. The youngest child, George Washington, was born during the Civil War. Most accounts give his year of birth of 1864, but this date doesn't fit the chronology of Carver's early years. Other accounts put his birth date in July, 1861.

In 1864 a band of bushwhackers kidnapped Mary and her son from the Carver farm, and took them to Arkansas. Presumably, a market for slaves still existed in Arkansas. Presumably, too, Mary and her child were kidnapped in order to be sold down south. Whatever the case, Moses Carver agreed to give a horse to a man with Southern connections if he could find and return Mary and her son. The man found George somewhere down in Arkansas, but Mary had disappeared, probably dead. George came back to live on the Carver farm. It is said that he was always frail as a child as a result of his terrible ordeal at the hands of the slave-catchers. The Carvers raised him until he was eleven, and during his early childhood they excused him from most manual chores; he had time for his attention to be drawn to the nature that surrounded him. At age 11, he went to Neosho to attend school, and never returned except to visit.

We like the July, 1861 date for George Washington Carver's birth. Imagine that in the same month he was born a slave to a German-American family, 2,000 German-Americans passed by, or nearly by, his birthplace. On July 4, 1861, the day we celebrate our freedom, Sigel brought the elements of his army

182

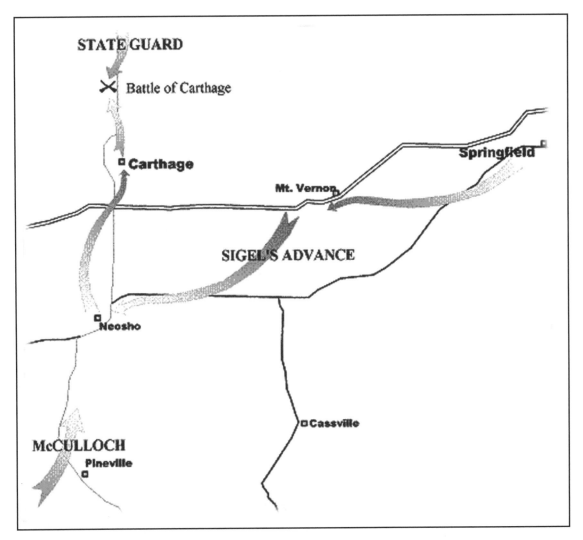

together at a place called Diamond Grove. The bulk of them came from Neosho to the south. Diamond Grove is named for a diamond-shaped grove of trees that was here on the prairie when the first settlers arrived. As a result, the town to the east named Diamond was built on a railroad and a main road developed there. But chances are Sigel's troops, marching from Neosho to Carthage, came up what is now Carver Road.

The frail boy raised here set out upon his life's path under circumstances so horrible we can scarcely imagine them. If ever a life was molded in the fire of adversity, his was. He survived the Civil War, and the overt hostility of a society wracked by racism. In a quiet and unassuming way he revolutionized the agricultural economy of the South.

The next time the kids ask why you are stopping at a Civil War site, tell them the story of George Washington Carver.

This Tour Loop ends at Exit 6 on Interstate 44, near Joplin. To reach the end of the Tour, drive north from Stop 182 to State Highway V, then right to U. S. Highway 71 (Alternate) in the town of Diamond. Turn left here, and drive north 6 miles to Exit 18 on I-44. Enter the interstate westbound, and drive west 12 miles to Exit 6. You may continue the tour from that point by following the directions to Trail Stop 152.

When you reach I-44, you can exit the area by heading east to Springfield, or if you continue north on U. S. 71 you will reconnect with Tour Loop Five in Carthage.

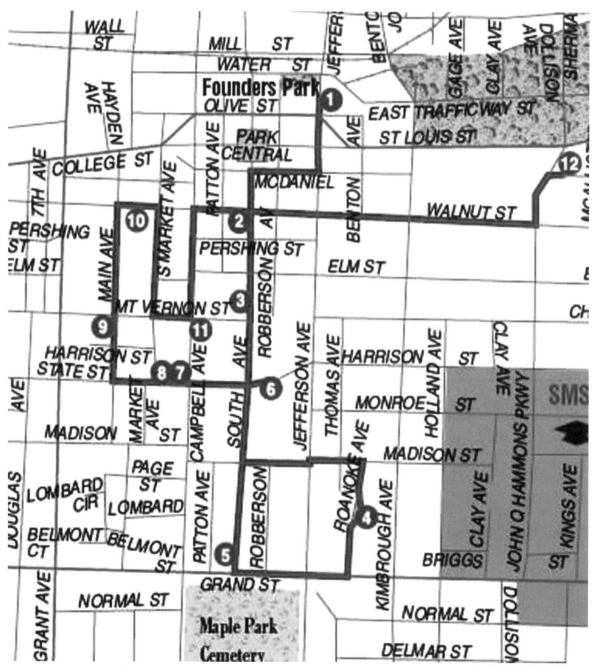

Driving trail for the Battle of Springfield

CONNECTING ROUTES

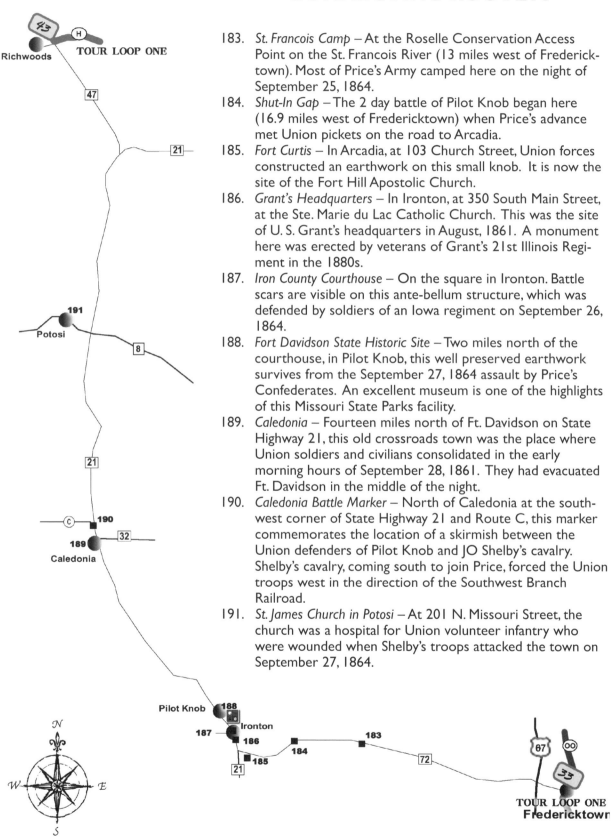

CONNECTING ROUTE A

183. *St. Francois Camp* – At the Roselle Conservation Access Point on the St. Francois River (13 miles west of Fredericktown). Most of Price's Army camped here on the night of September 25, 1864.

184. *Shut-In Gap* – The 2 day battle of Pilot Knob began here (16.9 miles west of Fredericktown) when Price's advance met Union pickets on the road to Arcadia.

185. *Fort Curtis* – In Arcadia, at 103 Church Street, Union forces constructed an earthwork on this small knob. It is now the site of the Fort Hill Apostolic Church.

186. *Grant's Headquarters* – In Ironton, at 350 South Main Street, at the Ste. Marie du Lac Catholic Church. This was the site of U. S. Grant's headquarters in August, 1861. A monument here was erected by veterans of Grant's 21st Illinois Regiment in the 1880s.

187. *Iron County Courthouse* – On the square in Ironton. Battle scars are visible on this ante-bellum structure, which was defended by soldiers of an Iowa regiment on September 26, 1864.

188. *Fort Davidson State Historic Site* – Two miles north of the courthouse, in Pilot Knob, this well preserved earthwork survives from the September 27, 1864 assault by Price's Confederates. An excellent museum is one of the highlights of this Missouri State Parks facility.

189. *Caledonia* – Fourteen miles north of Ft. Davidson on State Highway 21, this old crossroads town was the place where Union soldiers and civilians consolidated in the early morning hours of September 28, 1861. They had evacuated Ft. Davidson in the middle of the night.

190. *Caledonia Battle Marker* – North of Caledonia at the southwest corner of State Highway 21 and Route C, this marker commemorates the location of a skirmish between the Union defenders of Pilot Knob and JO Shelby's cavalry. Shelby's cavalry, coming south to join Price, forced the Union troops west in the direction of the Southwest Branch Railroad.

191. *St. James Church in Potosi* – At 201 N. Missouri Street, the church was a hospital for Union volunteer infantry who were wounded when Shelby's troops attacked the town on September 27, 1864.

CONNECTING ROUTE B

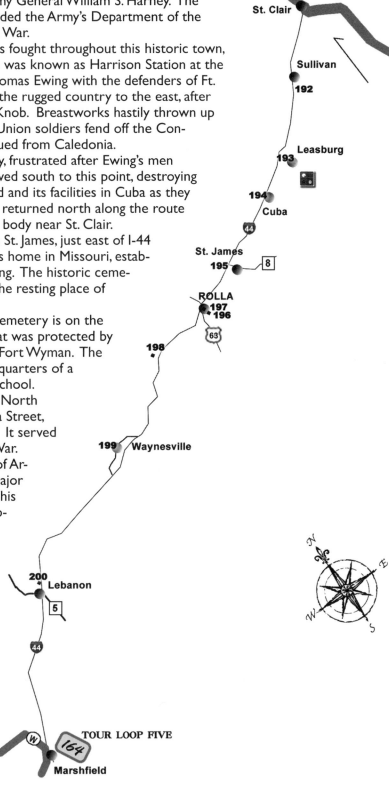

192. *General Harney Mansion* - At 332 South Mansion Street, south of downtown Sullivan (I-44 Exit 225), this massive limestone structure was the post-war home of Army General William S. Harney. The controversial Harney commanded the Army's Department of the West at the outset of the Civil War.

193. *Battle of Leasburg* - A battle was fought throughout this historic town, east of Exit 214 on I-44, which was known as Harrison Station at the time of the Civil War. Gen. Thomas Ewing with the defenders of Ft. Davidson emerged here from the rugged country to the east, after marching 60 miles from Pilot Knob. Breastworks hastily thrown up along the railroad helped the Union soldiers fend off the Confederate cavalry that had pursued from Caledonia.

194. *Burning of Cuba* - Price's cavalry, frustrated after Ewing's men were rescued at Leasburg, moved south to this point, destroying the Southwest Branch Railroad and its facilities in Cuba as they came. The Confederates then returned north along the route of I-44 and joined Price's main body near St. Clair.

195. *Veterans Home & Cemetery* - In St. James, just east of I-44 Exit 195, is the oldest veteran's home in Missouri, established in 1896 and still operating. The historic cemetery near the highway exit is the resting place of many Union veterans.

196. *Fort Wyman* - The Rolla City Cemetery is on the site of a large supply depot that was protected by a Union earthwork known as Fort Wyman. The site of the fort is about three quarters of a mile to the south, at Wyman School.

197. *Old Phelps County Courthouse* - North of the City Cemetery on Rolla Street, this building was built in 1860. It served as a hospital during the Civil War.

198. *Camp Totten* - Near the town of Arlington, this camp guarded a major ford of the Gasconade River. This site is now a commercial campground called the Arlington River Resort.

199. *The Old Stagecoach Stop* - The oldest building standing in Waynesville faces the Pulaski County square.

200. *Old Town Lebanon* - At the water tower on the north side of town, there is an area that has a street grid that does not match the newer town. This is the old trail town that Curtis used as his staging area to launch the Pea Ridge campaign.

CONNECTING ROUTE C

201. *Battle of Mt. Zion Church* - The site of a battle fought on December 28, 1861 is southeast from Hallsville, Boone County, 5 miles via Route OO. A Union force under General Benjamin Prentiss attacked a Confederate recruiting camp. The recruits were driven west along present-day Tim mons Road, to the point of the old church that stood near here. The church (at Mt. Zion Church Road and Flynn Road) was burned during the war and rebuilt later. Southern casualties are buried in the church cemetery.

202. *Old Auxvasse Cemetery* - Accessible by driving north on U. S. 54 from its junction with Interstate 70 (Exit 148), then east on County Roads 148 and 156, this old church was established on the Boonslick Road in 1828. The cemetery contains the grave of Virginia soldier Elijah Blankenship, one of few Confederates who crossed the stone wall during Pickett's Charge at Gettysburg and survived.

203. *Battle of Moore's Mill* - South of I-70 near Calwood, the site of this important 1862 battle can be reached by driving south from the Old Auxvasse Cemetery, or from Fulton via Route Z. Confederate Col. Joseph Porter's troops were defeated on the field that lies .5 mile south of the junction of routes Z and JJ. The battlefield is in pristine condition.

204. *Danville Female Academy* - Just off I-70 Exit 170, in 1864 this old frame building that was a chapel and dormitory for a women's' boarding school on this site (the center building in the period woodcut below). The building was spared by Anderson's men when they burned most of Danville on October 14, 1864.

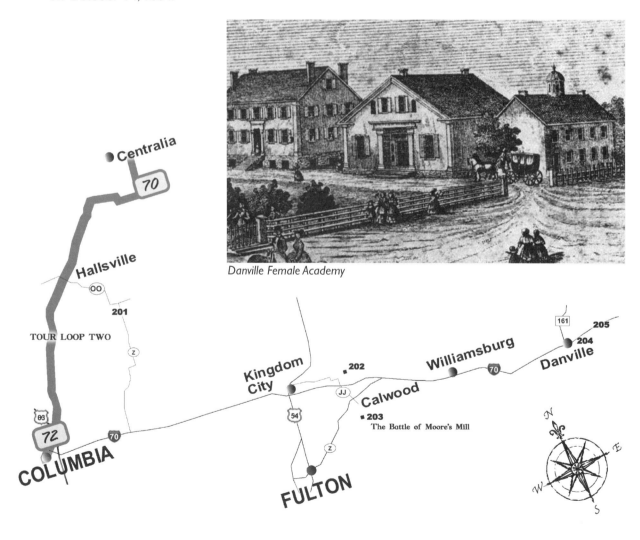

Danville Female Academy

205. *Sylvester Baker House* - .9 mile east of the Danville Female Academy on the outer road, this brick structure was the home of a Missouri legislator. During the Danville Raid, some of Anderson's men invaded the house, and they started a fire in the parlor. One of Anderson's men helped Mrs. Baker douse the flames; the evidence of the incident is still visible on the parlor floor.

206. *Battle of Hermann* - A series of small skirmishes occurred in this old Missouri River town on October 3, 1864, as Price's Confederates moved west along present-day Highway 100. Gen. John Marmaduke's division of Price's army was stymied briefly while the local German militia fired the town cannon in their direction. That cannon, ruptured in an accident after the war, sits on the grounds of the Gasconade County courthouse.

207. *Affair at Miller's Station* - During Price's 1864 Expediton, Marmaduke's cavalry moved west from Union, Missouri, largely unopposed. At Miller's Station on the Pacific Railroad, the Confederate cavalry captured a train full of supplies and uniforms. The train and the railroad facilities here were put to the torch. Miller's Station is now called New Haven.

Mt. Zion Church

CONNECTING ROUTE D

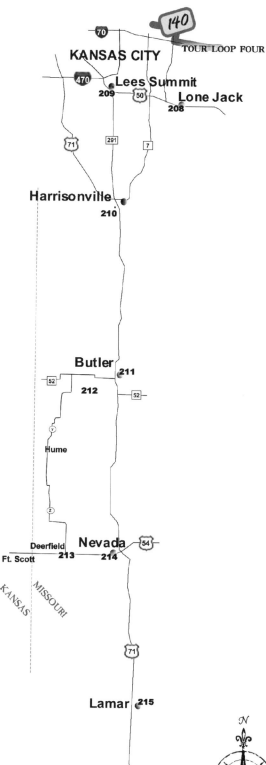

208. *Battle of Lone Jack* - A museum commemorates this August 15-16, 1862 battle on the eastern outskirts of Kansas City, on U. S. Highway 50. A graveyard containing dead from both sides is also maintained at the site.

209. *Lees Summit Historical Cemetery* - On 291 Highway at Langsford Road, just north of U. S. 50, this cemetery holds the remains of the most famous of the Younger brothers, Cole, Jim and Bob.

210. *The Burnt District Monument* - Near the new Cass County Justice Center, this monument takes the form of a solitary stone chimney. Cass County was one that suffered dreadfully by the enforcement of Order No. 11. This monument is a gripping reminder of those days.

211. *First Kansas Monument* - A bronze statue on the Bates County square depicts an African American soldier of the First Kansas Colored Regiment. The memorial was placed here in 2008 to commemorate the event at Stop 212.

212. *Island Mound Battle Site* - Missouri State Parks now owns 40 acres that encompasses the camp established by the First Kansas Colored. The undeveloped site is between Routes K and V on Marth Road. The first Civil War battle fought by African American troops occurred just to the south of the site.

213. *Battle of the Mules Marker* - A State Parks marker here, equidistant from Ft. Scott, Kansas and Nevada, Missouri, makes note of the 1861 "Battle of the Mules," fought south of here on Drywood Creek. Just to the north, in 1864, Sterling Price's Confederate army lost its wagon train trying to cross the Marmiton River.

214. *Bushwhacker Museum* - The city of Nevada is the county seat of Vernon County. The museum of the Vernon County Historical Society is housed in the public library at the northwest corner of the courthouse square, at 212 W. Walnut Street. A marker describing the Civil War in Vernon County is on the grounds of the Old Jail, a block north on Main Street.

215. *U.S.S. Benton Monument* - The town square in Lamar, Missouri, has a mounted cannon from the Mississippi ironclad *U.S.S. Benton*.

CONNECTING ROUTE E

216. *Grave of Thomas J. Higgins* - In St. Mary's Cemetery on the Palmyra Road (northwest of downtown Hannibal), lies the remains of this Union sergeant. Higgins was a color bearer during Grant's first assault on Vicksburg. He carried the flag all of the way into the Confederate works. In 1898 he received the Medal of Honor after his Confederate captors petitioned the government to award it.

217. *Hannibal Calaboose Site* - In literature (*The Adventures of Tom Sawyer*), this was the place where Muff Potter awaited trial. In 1862, in real life, this jail housed five of the Southern prisoners who would die at the Palmyra Massacre. There is a marker near the Hannibal waterfront that marks the site.

218. *Grave of Absalom Grimes* - The Barkley Cemetery is just north of New London, and near the center of the cemetery is the grave of "The Confederate Mail Runner." A boyhood friend of Sam Clemens, Grimes wrote a book about his many adventures in the Civil War.

219. *Ralls County Courthouse* - This is the place where Clemens' Ralls County Rangers were sworn into the service of the Missouri State Guard.

219. *Grave of Col. John Ralls* - In the Olivet Cemetery north of Center lies the Mexican War veteran whose fiery speech to the Ralls County Rangers is immortalized in Mark Twain's "The Private History of the Campaign that Failed." Ralls' country home, where the Rangers camped, was near by.

220. *Grave of John Wade* - On a very serious note, a stone in the Muldrow Cemetery marks the burial place of one of the ten men executed in Palmyra on October 18, 1862.

This route collects a number of sites that are associated with Samuel Clemens' brief military career. It also represents the quick route from Hannibal to westbound Interstate 70.

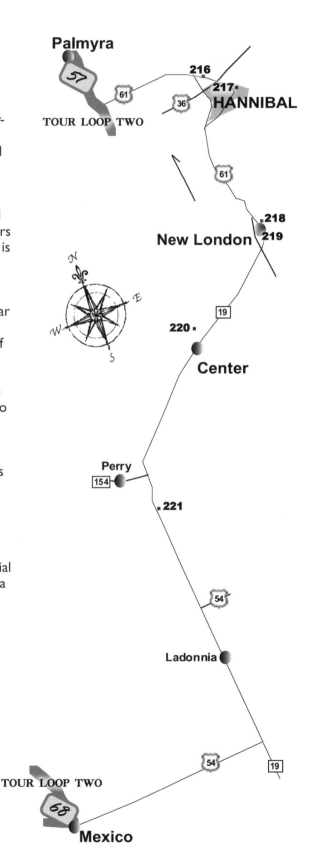

249

CONNECTING ROUTE F

222. *Grave of Sarah Amanda Wear* - The IOOF Cemetery is about a mile north of the Cooper County town of Otterville, via Boonville Street. The stone that faces you as you approach the cemetery honors the mother of Union Col. David Walker Wear and Union militia sergeant James Hutchinson Wear. Through James, her oldest, Sarah is the great-great-grandmother of President George H.W. Bush.

223. *The Otterville Trenches* - East of Otterville, one mile on Old Highway 50, there is a marker at a Department of Conservation access point on the Lamine River. This is the site of the Pacific Railroad bridge that was destroyed several times during the war. Opposite the Conservation area is a gravel road called Game Drive, which reaches U.S. 50 a short distance to the south. If you take this route, keep your eyes pealed as you look left (east), for a glimpse of magnificently preserved earthworks that Union soldiers dug to protect the bridge crossing. This is on private property.

224. *Missouri State Museum* - The Missouri Capitol building in Jefferson City houses one of the most interesting museums in the state. There are a number of permanent exhibits and artifacts associated with the Civil War, highlighted by a repository of over 125 Civil War regimental flags.

225. *Jefferson City National Cemetery* - Miller Street runs east and west, just north of the U.S. 50 expressway. The lower entrance to the national cemetery is on Miller Street, at Locust, about a mile east of the Capitol. This small facility was established in 1867 to re-bury the Union dead that had been interred all over the center of the state. The mass grave of most of the men killed in Centralia, and monument capping the grave, is a prominent feature in this place.

226. *The Soldiers' Memorial at Lincoln University* - South of the national cemetery on Chestnut Street is the campus of Missouri's Historic Black University. The main quadrangle of the campus, in the 600 block of Chestnut, features a monument dedicated to the soldiers of the 62nd and 65th regiments of the U.S. Colored Troops. The men of these regiments contributed a portion of their pay for the establishment of the Lincoln Institute, in 1867.

Jefferson City National Cemetery

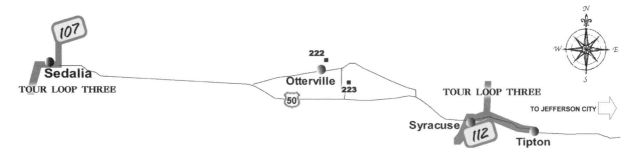

227. *High Tide Marker* - The residential area that is just east of the Lincoln University campus is marked by a circular street pattern that reflects the fact that a regional fairgrounds and race track occupied this ground at one time. At the point Fairmount Avenue intersects Moreau Drive there is a granite boulder that marks the farthest advance of Sterling Price's troops when they attacked the Missouri Capital on October 7, 1864.

228. *The John Hockaday House* - Located on a hill south of downtown Fulton, just off Bluff Street, this house was constructed by John A. Hockaday beginning in 1863. In 1872, while Hockaday was Missouri's Attorney General, former Confederate President Jefferson Davis was a guest in this house. Davis was on a speaking tour of the western United States, and spoke to a large crowd at Westminster College.

229. *Kingdom of Callaway Historical Museum* - At 513 Court Street in Fulton, this museum serves as a visitors center for Callaway County's most significant Civil War battle site, at Moore's Mill. There is a diorama of the 1862 battle (which occurred several miles northeast of Fulton). Callaway County is known as the "Kingdom" because in 1861 a Union militia officer signed a treaty that his troops would not enter the Southern-leaning county.

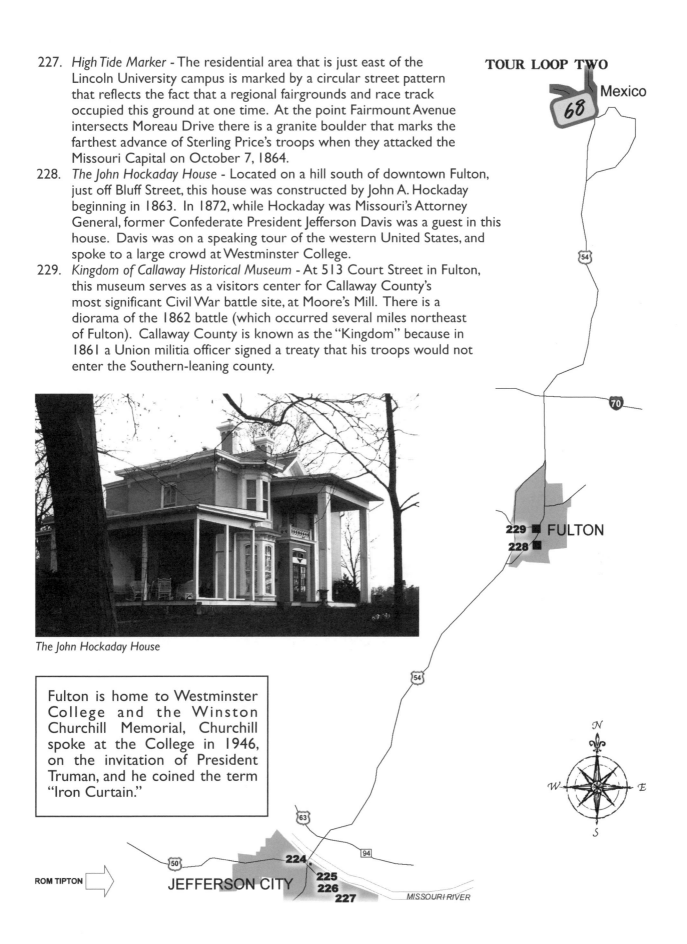

The John Hockaday House

Fulton is home to Westminster College and the Winston Churchill Memorial, Churchill spoke at the College in 1946, on the invitation of President Truman, and he coined the term "Iron Curtain."

CONNECTING ROUTE G

230. *Grave of Archie Clements* - Nine miles west of Lexington on U. S. 24 is the Waterloo Road, and 1/4 west of that is a small lane that leads to the Arnold Cemetery.

231. *Battle of the Little Blue* - U. S. Highway 50 crosses the Little Blue River 6.3 miles west of Buckner. To the south, and accessible by way of the first intersection west of the river, is a piece of the old Independence-Lexington Road. During Price's 1864 Expedition, Gen. Blunt's Kansas troops re-treated from Lexington on this road. Blunt left a small force to guard the wagon bridge that existed here, with instructions to burn the bridge and delay the Confederate advance. This Union force was belatedly reinforced, resulting in a sharp fight on October 21, 1864 that lasted several hours.

232. *Last Stand on Blue Mills Road* - Another 1/2 mile west of the intersection of U. S. 24 and the old road is the ridge where Blunt's men made a final stand before retreating to Independence. A walk in the New Salem Cemetery here offers a splendid panoramic view of the Little Blue Battlefield.

233. *Liberty Arsenal Site* - 6.1 miles north of the intersection of 291 Highway and U. S. 24 is an inter-section, which is Old 291 on your right. On the road to the left, inaccessible on the bluff, is the site of a federal arsenal that was attacked by Southern sympathizers on April 20, 1861. Although bloodless, this was the first incident of the Civil War that followed the firing on Fort Sumter in South Carolina.

234. *Battle of Blue Mills Landing* - East on Old 291 Highway, to the first road entering on the left (Liberty Landing Road), is a stretch of the historic road that connected the town of Liberty to the Missouri River. A battle was fought near here on September 17, 1861 when a small contingent of Union troops found several regiments of the Missouri State Guard blocking the route to the ferry landing at the River. The State Guard's victory kept reinforcements from northwest Missouri from reaching the beleaguered garrison at Lexington.

235. *Jesse James Bank Museum* - A public museum located on the square in Liberty, this is the site of America's first daylight bank robbery in peacetime, February 13, 1866.

236. *Jewell Hall at William Jewell College* - The main structure at this historic college in Liberty was constructed in 1850. It served as a hospital for Union troops wounded at the Battle of Blue Mills Landing.

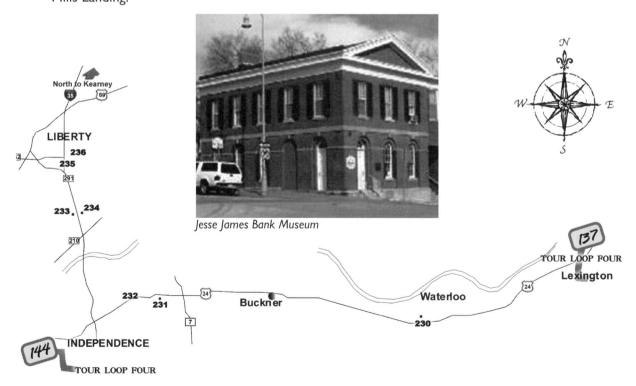

Jesse James Bank Museum

252

Acknowledgements

Except as noted below, the modern site photos that appear in this Guide are the property of the author.

Site photo 20 is courtesy of Missouri State Parks
Site photo 22 is courtesy of Lynn Bock, New Madrid, Missouri
Site photo 48 is courtesy of Ron Sansone, Pacific, Missouri
Site photo 90 is courtesy of Friends of Historic Boonville, Boonville, Missouri
Site photo 104 is courtesy of Missouri State Parks
Site photo 152 is courtesy of Carol Klinginsmith, Carthage, Missouri
Site photo 163 is courtesy of Sally McAlear, Springfield, Missouri
Site photos 169, 170 and 179 are courtesy of Ted Roller, Purdy, Missouri
Site photo 180 courtesy of Al and Marilyn of the Lucky Dog blog, http://luckydogwms.typepad.com

Site photos for sites 23 and 181 appear on the websites of The Sikeston Depot Museum (www.sikestondepot.org) and the Newton County Tourism Council (www.newtoncountymotourism.org), respectively. The author is grateful for the cooperation of these organizations.

Historic images, maps and photographs are in the public domain, except as noted below.

Page 3, image of Pvt. Reuben Bibb reproduced courtesy of Carol C. Schwartz, Lancaster, PA, who is the author of a biography of Reuben Bibb (*A Slave to Glory: Reuben and Ona's Story of Love*. Shippensburg, PA: Burd Street Press, 2002).
Page 21, Price engraving used with permission, State Historical Society of Missouri, Columbia.
Page 96, map courtesy of Bellefontaine Cemetery Association.
Page 122, historic photo of Thespian Hall is reproduced courtesy of Friends of Historic Boonville.
Page 176: James' farm photo reproduced courtesy of the James Farm & Museum, Kearney, MO.

The author wishes to specially acknowledge the Library of Congress' repository of Civil War images available at http://rs6.loc.gov/ammem/cwphtml/cwphome.html. The website of the U.S. Navy's Naval History & Heritage Command at http://www.history.navy.mil also deserves special recognition.

Dozens of people, too numerous to mention, have played a part in the production of this Guide. In every region of Missouri, custodians of our Civil War heritage willingly give of their time to share local experiences and stories. Special thanks to Ted Roller, Purdy, Missouri, and Tom Sweeney of Springfield, who introduced me to the Wire Road. Patrick Brophy of Nevada, Missouri and Arnold Schofield of the Mine Creek Battlefield, experts on Price's Expedition along the Missouri-Kansas Border. Paul Peterson, Army man and author, with whom I shared a fascinating afternoon in Kansas City, and the late Tim Cox, who shared his knowledge of the Little Blue Battlefield east of Kansas City. Andy and Dina Thomas, and Carol Klinginsmith, from Carthage. Retired Colonel Spike Speicher, and Lt. Col. Scott Porter, of Fort Leavenworth's Command and General Staff College, and noted Civil War authors. Colonel Ed Kennedy, Lt. Col. retired, who guided me through the chapel at Fort Leavenworth. In Southeast Missouri, Dr. Frank Nickell of the Center for Regional History at Southeast Missouri State University, and Larry Arnold of Dexter, the "architect" of the Confederate Memorial in Bloomfield. John Hollingsworth, Jefferson County, who showed me the Big River Bridge and astounds me whenever we meet. Bob Owens, who hosts my wife and I when we are in Cole Camp, which is often, and Roger Waters of Sedalia. Lorah Steiner, Columbia Convention and Visitors Bureau. Bill Lay of Howard County, and Ron Leake of Ralls and Craig Asbury of Monroe. John Robinson, formerly Director of the Missouri Division of Tourism, whose writings introduced me to the Brush Creek Church. Maryellen McVicker and Deborah Marshall of Boonville. Bill McClain of Montgomery County, and Peggy. Everyone involved in the Kingdom of Callaway Civil War Heritage group, including the late Mark Douglas. Very special mention to dear friends who have worked with Missouri's Civil War Heritage Foundation: Terry Ramsey of Nevada, Jim Robertson and Jack Chance of Columbia (who gave the world the Centralia battlefield), John Wilson of Camden County, Mike Duncan of Arrow Rock, and Colonel Spike of Kansas. Governor Roger Wilson whose interest sparked my imagination. Stuart Symington, "Tim," who has been my editor and teacher.

Selected Bibliography

Books:

Angus, Fern. *Down the Wire Road in the Missouri Ozarks*. Cassville, MO: Litho Printers, 1992.

Bartels, Carolyn. *The Civil War in Missouri: Day by Day, 1861 to 1865*. Shawnee Mission, KS: Two Trails, 1992.

Boernstein, Henry. *Memoirs of a Nobody*. Trans. Steven Rowan. St. Louis: Missouri Historical Society, 1997.

Breihan, Carl W. *Quantrill and his Civil War Guerrillas*. New York: Promontory, 1959.

Britton, Wiley. *Memoirs of the Rebellion on the Border, 1863*. Lincoln, NE: University of Nebraska Press, 1993.

Brooksher, William Riley. *Bloody Hill: The Civil War Battle of Wilson's Creek*. Virginia: Brassey's, 1995.

Castel, Albert, and Thomas Goodrich. *Bloody Bill Anderson: The Short, Savage Life of a Civil War Guerrilla*. Mechanicsburg, PA: Stackpole, 1998.

Castel, Albert. *General Sterling Price and the Civil War in the West*. 1968. Baton Rouge: Louisiana State University Press, 1996.

Castel, Albert. *William Clarke Quantrill: His Life and Times*. 1962. Norman, OK: University of Oklahoma Press, 1999.

Carter, Gari. *Troubled State: Civil War Journals of Franklin Archibald Dick*. Kirksville, MO: Truman State University Press, 2008.

Cottrell, Steve. *The Battle of Carthage and Carthage in the Civil War*. Carthage, MO: City of Carthage, 1990.

Coombe, Jack D. *Thunder Along the Mississippi: The River Battles that Split the Confederacy*. New York: Bantam, 1998.

Cozzens, Peter. *General John Pope: A Life for the Nation*. Urbana, IL: University of Illinois Press, 2000.

Daniel, Larry J., and Lynn N. Bock. *Island No. 10: Struggle for the Mississippi Valley*. Tuscaloosa, AL: University of Alabama Press, 1996.

Denny, James and John Bradbury. *The Civil War's First Blood: Missouri, 1854-1861*. Boonville, MO: Missouri Life, 2007.

Dodge, Grenville M. *The Battle of Atlanta and other Campaigns, Addresses, Etc*. Council Bluffs, IA: The Monarch Printing Company, 1911.

Dyer, Robert L. *Jesse James and the Civil War in Missouri*. Columbia, MO: University of Missouri Press, 1994.

Edwards, John N. *Shelby's Expedition to Mexico: An Unwritten Leaf of the War*. Fayetteville, AR: University of Arkansas Press, 2002.

Edwards, John Newman. *Shelby and his Men*. Waverly, MO: J.O. Shelby Memorial Fund, 1993.

Fellman, Michael. *Inside War: The Guerrilla Conflict in Missouri During the American Civil War*. New York: Oxford University Press, 1989.

Gardner, Michael R., *Harry Truman and Civil Rights: Moral Courage and Political Risks*. Carbondale: Southern Illinois University Press, 2002.

Gerteis, Louis S. *Civil War St. Louis*. Lawrence, KS: University Press of Kansas, 2001.

Gilmore, Donald L. *Civil War on the Missouri-Kansas Border*. Gretna, LA: Pelican Publishing, 2006.

Goman, Frederick W. *Up From Arkansas: Marmaduke's First Missouri Raid*. Springfield, MO: Wilson's Creek National Battlefield Foundation, 1999.

Gosnell, H. Allen. *The Story of River Gunboats in the Civil War*. Baton Rouge: Louisiana State University Press, 1949.

Grant, Ulysses S. *Personal Memoirs of Ulysses S. Grant*. New York: Literary Classics, 1990.

Hess, Earl J., Richard W. Hatcher III, William Garrett Piston, and William L. Shea. *Wilson's Creek, Pea Ridge and Prairie Grove*. Lincoln, NE: University of Nebraska Press, 2006.

Hinze, David C., and Karen Farnham. *The Battle of Carthage: Border War in Southwest Missouri, July 5, 1861*. Campbell, CA: Savas Publishing, 1997.

Hollingsworth, John Hampton. *The Battle of Blackwell*. Independence, MO: Two Trails, 2007.

Hughes, Nathaniel Cheairs, Jr. *The Battle of Belmont: Grant Strikes South*. Chapel Hill, NC: University of North Carolina Press, 1991.

Ingenthron, Elmo. *Border-Land Rebellion: A History of the Civil War on the Missouri – Arkansas Border*. Branson, MO: Ozarks Mountaineer, 1980.

Knight, Arthur Winfield. *The Secret Life of Jesse James*. Lenoir, NC: Burnhill Wolf, 1996.

Kollbaum, Marc E. *Gateway to the West: The History of Jefferson Barracks from 1826 – 1894*.

London, Charmian. *The Book of Jack London*. New York: The Century Company, 1921.

Leslie, Edward E. *The Devil Knows How to Ride: The True Story of William Clarke Quantrill and his Confederate Raiders*. New York: Da Capo, 1996.

McCullough, David, *Truman*. New York: Simon & Schuster, 1992.

McGuire, Randy R. *St. Louis Arsenal: Armory of the West*. Chicago: Arcadia Publishing, 2001.

Monaghan, Jay. *Civil War on the Western Border*, 1854-1865. Lincoln: University of Nebraska Press, 1955.

Mueller, Doris Land. *M. Jeff Thompson: Missouri's Swamp Fox of the Confederacy*. Columbia, MO: University of Missouri Press, 2007.

Nichols, Bruce. *Guerrilla Warfare in Civil War Missouri, 1862*. Jeffferson, NC: McFarland & Company, 2004.

Oates, Stephen B. *Confederate Calvary West of the River*. Austin: University of Texas Press, 1961.

O'Flaherty, Daniel. *General JO Shelby: Undefeated Rebel*. Chapel Hill, NC: University of North Carolina Press, 1954.

Parrish, William E., *A History of Missouri: 1860 to 1875*. Columbia: University of Missouri Press, 1973.

Perry, Mark. *Grant and Twain: The Story of a Friendship that Changed America*. New York: Random House, 2004.

Peterson, Cyrus A., and Joseph Mills Hanson. *Pilot Knob: The Thermopylae of the West*. 1914. Independence, MO: Two Trails, 2000.

Petersen, Paul R. *Quantrill of Missouri: The Making of a Guerrilla Warrior*. Nashville: Cumberland House, 2003.

Phillips, Christopher. *Missouri's Confederate: Claiborne Fox Jackson and the Creation of Southern Identity in the Border West*. Columbia, MO: University of Missouri Press, 2000.

Phillips, Christopher. Damned Yankee: *The Life of General Nathaniel Lyon*. Columbia, MO: University of Missouri Press, 1990.

Piston, William Garrett, and Richard W. Hatcher III. *The Second Battle of the Civil War and the Men Who Fought It: Wilson's Creek*. Chapel Hill, NC: University of North Carolina Press, 2000.

Rodemyre, Edgar T. *History of Centralia, Missouri*. Centralia, MO: Centralia Historical Society, 1936.

Rombauer, Robert Julius. *The Union Cause in St. Louis in 1861: An Historical Sketch of St. Louis*. Nixon-Jones Printing Co., 1909.

Rosa, Joseph G. *Wild Bill Hickok, Gunfighter: An Account of Hickok's Gunfights*. Norman: University of Oklahoma Press, 2001.

Ross, Kirby, ed. *The Autobiography of Samuel S. Hildebrand: The Renowned Missouri Bushwhacker*. Fayetteville, AR: University of Arkansas Press, 2005.

Schwartz, Carol C. *A Slave to Glory: Reuben and Ona's Story of Love*. Shippensburg, PA: Burd Street Press, 2002.

Schultz, Duane. *Quantrill's War: The Life and Times of William Clarke Quantrill*. New York: St. Martin's Griffin, 1996.

Scott, Mark E. *The Fifth Season: General "JO" Shelby, the Great Raid of 1863*. Independence, MO: Two Trails, 2001.

Sellmeyer, Deryl P. *JO Shelby's Iron Brigade*. Gretna, LA: Pelican Publishing, 2007.

Sheridan, Philip, *Personal Memoirs of General P. H. Sheridan, General United States Army* (Bantam Ed., 1991)(Paul Andrew Hutton, ed.).

Shirley, Glenn, *Belle Starr and Her Times: The Literature, the Facts, and the Legends*. Norman, University of Oklahoma Press, 1982.

Steele, Phillip W., and Steve Cottrell. *Civil War in the Ozarks*. Gretna, LA: Pelican Publishing, 1993.

Stiles, T.J. *Jesse James: Last Rebel of the Civil War*. New York: Random House, 2002.

Tucker, Phillip Thomas. *The Forgotten "Stonewall of the West" Major General John Stevens Bowen*. Macon, Georgia: Mercer University Press, 1997.

Winter, William C. *The Civil War in St. Louis, A Guided Tour*. St. Louis: Missouri Historical Soc. Press, 1994.

Willie, Franc B. Missouri 1861: *The Civil War Letters of Franc B. Wilkie, Newspaper Correspondent*. Edited by Michael E. Banasik. Iowa City, IA: Camp Pope Bookshop, 2002.

Wood, Larry. *The Civil War Story of Bloody Bill Anderson*. Austin: Eakin Press, 2003.

Wood, Larry E. *The Civil War on the Lower Kansas – Missouri Border*. Joplin, MO: Hickory Press, 2003.

Annual Register, or a View of the History and Politics of the Year 1861. London: Woodfall and Kinder, 1862 [editor unknown].

An Illustrated Historical Atlas Map of Jasper County, Missouri. Brink, McDonough and Company, 1876 [author unknown].

Articles, Newspapers and other Sources:

Barnes, Joseph W., "Bridging The Lower Falls". *Rochester History*. January 1974, Vol. XXXVI, No. 1.

Brown, Clark. *Franklin Co. Tribune, V.51, No.6, Fiftieth Anniversary Edition*. Newspaper article describing Murphy's company. 1915. 30 May 2010 <http://home.usmo.com/~momollus/FranCoCW/1MOInfRBA.htm>

Carle, Glenn L. "The First Kansas Colored". *American Heritage*. Feb./Mar. 1992.

Davis, Maj. Dale E. "Guerrilla Operations in the Civil War: Assessing Compound Warfare During Price's Raid". Diss. U. S. Army Command and General Staff College, Ft. Leavenworth 2004.

Dorsheimer, William. "Freemont's Hundred Days in Missouri," *Atlantic Monthly* (January 1862), 115-125

Frizzell Robert W. "Killed by Rebels: A Civil War Massacre and Its Aftermath". *Missouri Historical Review*. July 1977, Vol.: 71, No, 4.

Gallaher, Ruth A. "The Wittenmyer Diet Kitchens". *The Palimpsest* (Journal of the State Historical Society of Iowa) September 1931,Vol. XII, No. 9.

Geiger, Mark W. "Missouri's Hidden Civil War: Financial Conspiracy and the Decline of the Planter Elite, 1861-1865". Diss. University of Missouri-Columbia 2006.

Grover, George S. "The Shelby Raid, 1863". *Missouri Historical Review*. April, 1912, Vol. 6, No. 3.

Lay, William and Dyer, Robert. "Civil War Incidents in Howard County". *Boone's Lick Heritage*. March

1998,Volume 6, No.1. Reprinted at <http://www.rootsweb.ancestry.com /~mohoward/cwpart2.html>

Leslie, Edward E. "Quantrill's Bones". *American Heritage.* July/Aug. 1995.

Northway, Martin. "Missouri's Generals". *Rural Missouri.* July 2003.

Shoemaker, Floyd C. "The History of the Civil War in Northeast Missouri". *Missouri Historical Review.* April 1913, Vol. 7, No. 3.

Violette, E. M. "The Battle of Kirksville, August 6, 1862". *Missouri Historical Review* January, 1911, Vol. 5, No. 2.

"Annals of Iowa, The Army of the Southwest, and the First Campaign in Arkansas" (in two parts). 1866. Reprinted at <www.past2present.org>.

Excerpts of the 1884 history of Monroe County, Missouri. Web article. 29 May 2010 <
http://www.mogenweb.org/monroe/cohistcwacct.htm>

Letter from William Nevin to Cyrus A. Peterson, October, 1903. *Thomas Ewing Family Papers*, box 216 (Library of Congress).

"The Original of Rebecca of Ivanhoe". (August 27, 1882) *New York Times.*

Wisconsin Dept. of Veterans Affairs "Old Abe the War Eagle: Wisconsin's most famous Civil War veteran". Web article. 30 May 2010 <http://museum.dva.state.wi.us/ Edu_Old_Abe_Story.asp>

The author wishes to expresses his appreciation for the Cornell University *Making of America* website (http://digital.library.cornell.edu/m/moa), which contains the complete *The War of the Rebellion: A Compilation of the Official Records of the Union and Confederate Armies in the War of the Rebellion* (Washington, D.C.: Government Printing Office, 1880-1901. This work, also known as the "OR" or "Official Records" is a nearly inexhaustible supply of facts about the Civil War in Missouri, and elsewhere, and it is the primary source for all campaign-related information in this Guide. Special thanks also to the State of Missouri, Secretary of State and State Archives, which has placed rosters of Missouri Civil War troops online at www.sos.mo.gov/archives/soldiers.

Index of Places

Notes:

Notes:

Notes: